Gender and Sexuality in Latin America - Cases and Decisions

IUS GENTIUM

COMPARATIVE PERSPECTIVES ON LAW AND JUSTICE

VOLUME 24

For further volumes:
http://www.springer.com/series/7888

Cristina Motta • Macarena Sáez
Editors

Gender and Sexuality in Latin America - Cases and Decisions

Springer

Editors
Cristina Motta
Consultant on Sexual Rights
Buenos Aires, Argentina

Macarena Sáez
Washington College of Law
American University
Washington, DC, USA

Previously published by SIGLO DEL HOMBRE EDITORES, 2008, TITLE OF VOLUME I: LA MIRADA DE LOS JUECES: GENERO EN LA JURISPRUDENCIA LATINOAMERICANA; TITLE OF VOLUME II: LA MIRADA DE LOS JUECES: SEXUALIDADES DIVERSAS EN LA JURISPRUDENCIA LATINOAMERICANA

ISBN 978-94-007-6198-8 ISBN 978-94-007-6199-5 (eBook)
DOI 10.1007/978-94-007-6199-5
Springer Dordrecht Heidelberg New York London

Library of Congress Control Number: 2013937994

Printed on acid-free paper

Springer is part of Springer Science+Business Media (www.springer.com)

Foreword

Gender and Sexuality in Latin America: Cases and Decisions, edited by Cristina Motta and Macarena Sáez, is a long over-due book. It advances understanding of legal developments concerning women and LGBT persons in Latin America. For the first time, English speaking audiences will have access to commentary on decisions of national and international courts concerning rights of women and LGBT individuals in Latin America.

The cases and narratives presented in this volume expose the complexity of legal developments on gender and sexuality in Latin America. This book advances understanding of the rationales used in Latin American judgments concerning identity rights. It exposes the reasoning of judges that at the same time restrict and advance the exercise of rights by women and LGBT persons. It reveals a multifaceted legal reality where these individuals enjoy protections not yet achieved in other parts of the world, but, at the same time, shows how judicial reasoning has restricted their rights in much harsher ways than what is experienced in other regions.

The book explores the interplay between national and international law by analyzing decisions made by international bodies and courts such as the Inter-American Court of Human Rights. The Inter-American Court has been especially effective in strengthening the rights of women and LGBT individuals in the region with groundbreaking decisions that have recognized the right to be free from gender-based violence and the right to non-discrimination on the basis of sexual orientation.

This book is written by Latin American legal scholars with expertise on a broad range of legal issues: Citizenship by Cristina Motta, Family by Isabel Cristina Jaramillo, Health by Lidia Casas, Property by Helena Alviar, Violence by Julieta Lemaitre, Diverse Sexualities by Juan Marco Vaggione, and Violence based on Prejudice by Maria Mercedes Gomes. The chapters help to close the gap between the scholarship on gender and sexuality available in English and in Spanish. *Gender and Sexuality in Latin America: Cases and Decisions* will facilitate collaboration between scholars and activists from the global north and the global south who are interested in exploring the effectiveness of judicial reasoning in advancing the equality of all individuals, irrespective of their gender or sexual orientation.

Professor *Emerita*, Faculty of Law, University of Toronto — Rebecca Cook

Acknowledgements

Special thanks from the editors to:

Diana Hortsch, Director of the Law School Initiative for the Center for Reproductive Rights, who has been instrumental to complete this project. Without the support of Diana, and of the Center for Reproductive Rights, New York, this book would have not been possible.

Luisa Cabal, Vice President of Programs at the Center for Reproductive Rights for her vision and leadership within the ALAS Network.

Cora Sueldo for translating the book from Spanish and Michelle Mora for her valuable work reviewing and editing the translated work.

Juny Montoya for reviewing all chapters in their original versions and writing many of the questions that make this book a teaching tool for law schools.

The Ford Foundation, the International Programme on Reproductive and Sexual Health Law of the University of Toronto and American University Washington College of Law for supporting the work of the ALAS network and funding the original version of the book in Spanish.

All members of the ALAS Network who have contributed directly or indirectly to the work presented in this book. This is a collaborative work beyond the authors and editors.

Professor Tony Varona for his support and vision in pushing for this book to be available to an English speaking audience; Professors Ann Shalleck, Rebecca Cook, and Dean Claudio Grossman for supporting the work of the ALAS Network from its inception.

Neil Olivier, Diana Nijenhuijzen, and their colleagues from Springer for supporting this project and making it possible.

Juan Tokatlian, Alejandra Tokatlian, Gonzalo Flores, Alonso and Amanda Flores-Saez for their constant support. They make our projects possible, and our lives better.

Cristina Motta and Macarena Sáez

Biographies

Cristina Motta holds a degree in Political Science from the University of Paris II, an LLM from Harvard Law School and a *Licenciatura en Derecho* from the University of Los Andes in Colombia. She has been law professor at the University of los Andes in Bogotá and San Andrés in Buenos Aires. She is an independent consultant.

Macarena Sáez holds an LLM from Yale Law School and a *Licenciatura en Derecho* from the University of Chile Law School. She is a Fellow in International Legal Studies and the Faculty Director of the Impact Litigation Project at American University Washington College of Law where she teaches in the areas of Family Law and Comparative Law.

Isabel Cristina Jaramillo holds an SJD and an LLM from Harvard Law School. She obtained her *Licenciatura en Derecho* from the University of Los Andes Law School in Colombia. Currently, she is an Associate Professor at the University of Los Andes Law School where she teaches Family Law and focuses on Critical Legal Theory, the Evolution of Family, and Feminist Jurisprudence.

Lidia Casas holds a BA in Urban Development from Saskatchewan University in Canada, an LLM from the University of Toronto and a *Licenciatura en Derecho* from Diego Portales University Law School in Chile. She is a Law Professor at Diego Portales University Law School where she concentrates on Sexual and Reproductive Rights.

Helena Alviar is the Dean of the University of Los Andes Law School in Colombia. She holds an SJD and an LLM from Harvard Law School and a *Licenciatura en Derecho* from the University of Los Andes Law School in Colombia. Among other topics, Dean Alviar's research focuses on Law and Economics, Gender and the Law and Legal Theory.

Julieta Lemaitre holds a master's in Religion and Gender from New York University, an SJD from Harvard Law School and a *Licenciatura en Derecho* from the University of Los Andes Law School in Colombia. Currently, she is an Assistant Professor at the University of Los Andes Law School. Among other topics, Julieta's research focuses on Social Movements and the Law, Violence and Sociology of Law, Domestic Violence, and Sexual and Reproductive Rights.

Julieta Di Corleto holds an LLM from Harvard Law School and a *Licenciatura en Derecho* from the University of Buenos Aires in Argentina. In addition to her work in the Public Defender's Office in Argentina, Julieta teaches Law at the University of Buenos Aires Law School and the University of Palermo Law School.

Juan Marco Vaggione holds a master's and a doctorate degree in Sociology from the New School for Social Research in New York, and a *Licenciatura en Derecho* from the National University of Cordoba in Argentina. He currently teaches law at the National University of Cordoba. He specializes on Gender, Sexuality, and Secularism.

Maria Mercedes Gómez holds a master's in Gender Studies and Feminist Theory and a doctorate degree in Political Theory from the New School for Social Research in New York, and a *Licenciatura en Filosofia* from the Javeriana University in Colombia. She specializes in Philosophy and Criminal Law. Regional Program Coordinator for Latin America and the Caribbean Organization International Gay and Lesbian Human Rights Commission (IGLHRC), New York.

Contents

Chapter 1
Introduction

Cristina Motta and Macarena Sáez

Gender and Sexuality in Latin American: Cases and Decisions is designed to provide a valuable resource for law professors teaching in the areas of gender, sexuality, and the law, Latin American law, and comparative law.

The book was originally published in Spanish as the first casebook to cover gender and sexuality decisions in Latin America. With the generous support of the Center for Reproductive Rights in New York, a revised and abridged version of the book is now available in English.

The book analyses an array of decisions from Latin American judges in topics of great impact for women and LGBTI individuals. The decisions included in this volume may not show a particular regional or national trend, but were selected because of their argumentative quality, and their impact in a particular country. The main goal is to present issues faced by women and the LGBTI community in different areas of the law, and show how they have been addressed by courts in different countries. In some cases, statutory analysis is also included.

The book is based on two central ideas: On one hand, it presents a theoretical position that conceives the law as a complex social practice in which judges play active, autonomous and significant roles. On the other, it presents a critical legal analysis based on gender and sexuality perspectives on law.

C. Motta (✉)
Consultant on Sexual Rights, Medrano 1366, 1179 Buenos Aires, Argentina
e-mail: tokatlianes@gmail.com

M. Sáez
Washington College of Law, American University,
4801 Massachusetts Ave. N.W., Washington, DC 20016, USA
e-mail: msaez@wcl.american.edu

C. Motta and M. Sáez (eds.), *Gender and Sexuality in Latin America - Cases and Decisions*, Ius Gentium: Comparative Perspectives on Law and Justice 24,
DOI 10.1007/978-94-007-6199-5_1,

1.1

The first idea leads to enhancing the position of Latin American judges. Traditionally, they have occupied a subordinate position *vis à vis* political branches of government. A central idea in the separation of powers that guided the Roman-German tradition sought to ensure that the popular will would not be replaced by that of officials who did not represent it. This contributed to judges gradually acquiring an insipid image, not comparable to that of the other two branches of the State. Thus, during most part of the independent history of Latin America, the judicial function developed from the shadows.

In the last decades, however, judges have acquired an unprecedented pre-eminence. Driven among other things by "political institutions in the process of decomposition," as stated by Paul Ricoeur, judges perform a leading role in large parts of the Western world. High levels of political corruption have contributed to the discredit of legislative branches and of the political class in general. Judges, in some places, have become a new instance of legitimization of the state. This unprecedented role is also supported by the decisive alteration of traditional normative hierarchies produced by a growing weight of supranational norms within national states. The law, borrowing Dworkin's image, deposits Herculean demands on those who apply it. Thus, closely linked to morals and politics, and infallibly immersed in reality, the law will be applied correctly by judges who understand the theoretical and practical complexity of their mission.

In the case of individuals in disadvantaged groups like women and LGBTI, the transformation of the role of judges is promising. This is apparent in the selection of rulings offered in this book. The review of Latin American case law reveals two general trends among judges with regards to women and the LGBTI population: First, there are cases in which judges faced rules openly detrimental to the interests of women or sexual minorities. For example, there are some cases where gay and lesbian couples have challenged statutes restricting adoption to heterosexual married couples. In those cases, judges could have argued that given the clarity of the rule, and according to the role played by judges in the continental tradition, their hands were tied to a restrictive interpretation of family. Some judges, however, moved away from their traditional function and resorted to arguments with renewed interpretative power. This was the case of the Constitutional Court in Colombia when it ruled that in spite of a constitution that directly links family to marriage, and defines marriage as the union between a man and a woman, the correct normative interpretation of such concept ought to incorporate single women with children, cohabiting couples of gays, lesbians, and heterosexuals, and all those forms of family organization derived from constitutionally protected cultural or religious visions. Thus, in Latin America there are already examples of judges who are exercising their adjudicative function by privileging the application of principles over rules.

These cases, of course, coexist with decisions that show a moral position rejecting the inclusion of non-traditional families. Many times these rulings are supported by literal interpretations of black letter law. Others, represent narrow interpretations of principles that used correctly should have resulted in the protection of disadvantaged individuals. This is the case of a decision by the Supreme Court of Chile in 2004 that reprimanded the judges from a court of appeals that had affirmed a lower court decision granting custody of her three minor children to a mother who was living with her lesbian partner. The Supreme Court not only overruled the lower courts' decisions and granted custody of the children to the father, but went further to reproach the judges for not applying the best interest of the child principle, according to their own interpretation of it. To the Supreme Court, in this case the affirming judges had "omitted the preferential right of the minors to live and develop in the bosom of a normally structured family, appreciated in the social environment, in accordance with the traditional model proper to them."

1.2

The second basic idea behind this book is to analyze different decisions from the perspective of gender and sexuality studies of law. These theoretical positions, mostly developed in law schools of the United States, have had a strong impact on feminist activism and legal academia in Latin America. Each chapter of this book situates the discussion and analysis of cases within a feminist or critical perspective of the law. Although references to the work of American feminism and theoretical transplants are inevitable and many times beneficial, the book is still a work on Latin American law. The critical legal theories that have guided the analysis of the decisions selected for this book provide a framework for the construction of a modern adjudication narrative. One that exposes the damage derived from male and heterosexual domination. Thus, the book identifies itself with four fundamental notions of these critical perspectives: First, it accepts that sexual inequalities are grounded on the existence of dichotomist models which do not depend on biological sex but are the result of the social construction of the genders. Second, it admits that the values and attributions granted to each gender have triggered an unequal distribution of resources and power between men and women and between heterosexual and non-heterosexual individuals. Third, it recognizes that the law has been a privileged mechanism to preserve inequalities and that through legal constructions some sexual and gender identities have been endowed with legitimacy and legality and others have been denied such legitimacy and legal protection. Fourth, it considers that even though the law and legal institutions have been defined as neutral in terms of gender, they are actually a cultural and political construction that strengthens and naturalizes masculinity and heterosexuality.

These theoretical and critical references not only nurture a particular approach to the problems the book deals with, but they also guide the assessment of the decisions analyzed here. The influence of these perspectives in regional case law is evident. The wide acceptance of substantive equality as a goal, and the support of affirmative actions by some courts attest to this acceptance. More specifically, case law of the Colombian Constitutional Court offers abundant examples of the assimilation of these perspectives. The holding in which the Constitutional Court attributed monetary value to the domestic work of a "concubine," the one that prohibits the introduction in rape trials of evidence related to the sexual past of a victim of rape, or the one that reaffirms the constitutional support to mothers heads of household, are conclusive proof of this. At the same time, these judges face within their countries, and sometimes within their own courts, positions that reproduce the traditional model of adjudication. In this sense, the chapters on "Family" (Chap. 3) and "Health" (Chap. 4) offer a variety of illustrative examples.

1.3

The first part of the book focuses on regional case law affecting women. Six chapters deal with various rulings that have defined the scope and have marked the limits of Latin American women's rights. Each chapter presents a brief conceptual introduction and develops a series of topics arranged through specific problems which, in turn, are illustrated by a ruling, a statute, a report or a document. Once the ruling has been presented, each chapter provides issues for debate and questions aimed at ensuring the pedagogic use of the book.

The chapter on Citizenship (Chap. 2) offers an alternative and complementary analysis of the study of constitutional law. The chapter deals with the evolution of case law on citizenship from two different viewpoints: citizenship as an aspiration, in which the objectives of equality, reparation and emancipation of women through the law are studied and citizenship as belonging, in which the problems of identity and culture as new challenges to the traditional concept of citizenship are analyzed.

Regional case law shows a remarkable evolution. In terms of equality and reparation it is worth highlighting the adoption of substantive equality and the support of affirmative actions. With regards to emancipation, there is an evolution towards the support of horizontal effects of fundamental rights and courts are more willing to accept state intervention in private relations characterized by the defenselessness of one of its members. The chapter also discusses the conflicts that have their origin in the constitutional respect for cultural diversity and the challenges of massive migrations and globalization.

Overall, the chapter on Citizenship (Chap. 2) attests to the transformation of the role of judges and the use of critical perspectives of the law in the adjudicative processes.

The chapter on Family (Chap. 3) deals with problems derived from the institutionalization of the family in Latin America. It discusses various aspects related to the recognition of rights and the equality of women in the family showing a discouraging scenario for women. The chapter analyses the rights of concubines, as well as child custody and the treatment given to domestic and sexual violence within the family. The decisions covered by the book in this area show that there are some relationships deserving of state's protection and others that are left out as inexistent. For example, courts regularly deal with property division for cohabiting partners.

Some of these decisions present a conflict between different societal values. Should a court recognize cohabitation and distribute property when the woman claiming property rights has unknowingly cohabited with her own father? Courts tend to side with the protection of societal values grounded in moral or religious criteria to the detriment of protecting the weakest or innocent party to the conflict.

This chapter also explores the problem of equality already dealt with in the chapter on "Citizenship," (Chap. 2) but this time from the perspective of family law. Women's pre assigned roles are more apparent in the realm of the family. Judges tend to favor "motherhood" even to the detriment of women's autonomy. Thus, the chapter shows how maternity, in Latin America, is viewed as a privilege and not a right, among other things because mothers must assume the costs that fall upon those who do not actively participate in the labor market. To illustrate this statement the chapter examines the regional models that define child custody and it studies the cultural valuation of care work. In the case of child custody it concludes that case law tends to allocate child custody using arguments such as the moral quality of the mother; in the case of care work, it shows a mixed regional reality. In some cases unpaid domestic work is vindicated as economically valued, strengthening the idea that women are best fit to carry out care work. In other cases, domestic work is seen as an obligation of both spouses.

Finally, the chapter tackles the problem of violence in the family concluding that the norms on sexual violence and marital duties have been generally applied by judges but not without applying first traditional social norms that lead women to bear important doses of aggression before ending relationships, especially if children are involved. Family case law is still deeply anchored in the model of a family structure imposed by the Roman Catholic tradition, and several of these rulings are eloquent examples of the way in which the law has been a privileged method of conservation of the conditions and the consequences of inequality.

The chapter on Health (Chap. 4) deals with four major issues: reproductive autonomy, which is illustrated by the position of judges regarding forced sterilization and the role that religious or moral beliefs of health care providers play in the provision of reproductive services; abortion, which is studied on the basis of the judicial response to the conflict between confidentiality and the duty of doctors to report crimes, and the judges' responsibility in the profound legal insecurity in which non punishable abortions are carried out in the region; contraception is reviewed by analyzing the legal regulation of emergency contraception; last, the chapter analyzes the problems of reproductive health in teenagers, area in which the principle of the best interest of the child sometimes conflicts with teenagers' progressive autonomy and in others it is openly used to suppress such autonomy.

On these four subjects, the regional case law offers an uneven and imprecise picture. For judges, voluntary sterilization is a procedure inscribed within female autonomy; even though it is an option that social welfare systems may limit, the traditional requirements of judicial authorization to carry out the procedure have been mostly eliminated. Additionally, some decisions have limited conscientious objection of health care providers regarding these types of procedures to individual objectors, thus mandating institutions to provide the service by replacing the objector personnel.

Concerning abortion, until recently the Argentinean case was one of the most dramatic examples of lack of normative precision. Decisions that revolved around confidentiality, the obligation to denounce crimes, and the constitutional guarantee of non self-incrimination were inconsistently applied. In addition, this situation generated legal uncertainty in the face of a hypothetical duty of women to request legal authorization -or not- when they were about to practice a non-punishable abortion. Despite various legal decisions stating that in the case of non-punishable abortions such authorizations were unnecessary, doctors had insisted on requesting them. At least for the case of rape, this situation recently changed with the decision of the Supreme Court of Argentina allowing abortion in the case of rape without the need of a previous judicial authorization.

As it is evident, women's health, profoundly linked to reproduction, constitutes the space in which the female body is the center of ideological appropriation. Health is also the sphere in which the critique of the law from a gender perspective is most necessary.

The chapter on Property (Chap. 5) deals with a right that, in spite of being considered fundamental and of being guaranteed in all legal systems, is enjoyed by a very small number of women in the world. The cases analyzed in the book cover three thematic axes: the consequences of linking the female identity to maternity and access to property; the configuration of privileged access to property; and the tensions among marginalized groups. On the first point, it is stated that even though identifying women with care givers and men as breadwinners restricts the possibilities of the former of being owners, sometimes judges have valued reproductive work by giving it an economic value, allowing, therefore, access of women to property. The chapter analyzes how most legal systems in the region have repealed legal provisions that banned women from administering and owning property or businesses. On the second subject – the configuration of privileged access to property – the chapter presents the case of special treatment for reasons of population displacement derived from the Colombian armed conflict. It discusses, from the perspective of access to property and allocation of housing, the problem of women head of household also discussed in the chapters on "Citizenship" and "Family." Regarding the issue of marginalized groups, the chapter points out the difficulties faced by case law in establishing hierarchies among disadvantaged groups in matters such as the agrarian reform.

The chapter on Violence (Chap. 6) deals with three main themes: the paradoxes of criminalization, which questions the convenience of the use of criminal law and of the punitive power of the state to achieve women's emancipation. This subject is illustrated with the presentation of two regional pressing problems: femicide and rape as torture. On the first point, the book discusses the reports of the Inter American Commission on Human Rights and Amnesty International on the dramatic circumstances of violence against women in Ciudad Juárez. The second theme of the chapter is the evolution of international jurisprudence regarding states' responsibility derived from their inability to prevent rape as a general concern. Secondly, the chapter deals with the problems of criminal technique inherent in the definition of the crimes of violence against women. The chapter analyzes the use of force, the lack of consent, and the use of objective criteria to determine self-defense in cases of sexual violence. In general Latin American decisions have been slowly evolving to positive responses and a better understanding of violence against women.

The chapter on Violence (Chap. 6) also deals with restrictions to women's autonomy derived from the penalization of the conducts that victimize them. Two cases in which there is a conflict between autonomy and the interests of the State are considered. The first is the use of conciliation or mediation techniques in cases of family violence. The second deals with human trafficking and the difficulty of tackling the issue in a global context, in which the interest of protecting human rights, especially of women, coincide with the intention of developed countries of stopping illegal immigration.

Undoubtedly, in the subject of violence against women the claims of legal feminism, especially its radical version, have penetrated with great strength and have triggered greater consensus in the normative field than in other areas. Regional case law has appropriated a discourse of protection of women against the persistent violence that characterizes social and family relations in Latin America. The few exceptions to this rather generalized trend respond to the difficulties that senior judges have to face in order to consolidate their authority in the national sphere.

1.4

The second part of *Gender and Sexuality in Latin America: Cases and Decisions* covers case law related to LGBTI individuals. Chapters 7 and 8 deal with tensions between law and sexualities at two different levels: the sphere of family rights and the practices of violence based on prejudice. "Families beyond heteronormativity" analyzes how the family structure is gradually reconfigured on the basis of the existence of diverse sexualities. In their roles as same sex couples, as gay and lesbian parents, or as sons and daughters with different sexual orientations or gender identities, LGBTI individuals challenge different religious, moral, and legal conceptions of the family. The chapter focuses on the ways in which case law on sexuality not only widens the legal spaces for recognition of rights, moving the boundaries of the established family as a unique reality, but it also criticizes the characteristic heteronormativity of most legal rationales. In particular, case law is reviewed in three spheres of family rights: same-sex couples, the right to adoption, and child custody.

The chapter on "Prejudice-Based Violence" (Chap. 8), that closes this book, provides a theoretical framework of this particular type of violence. The chapter shows how violence against certain individuals that do not fit the heterosexual norm surpasses its individual dimension and acquires the quality of a message. After making a conceptual contribution on violence, sexual prejudice, heterosexuality as a rule, and the allocation of value to the difference, the chapter carefully examines the normative aspects of violence based on prejudice.

The legal issues that arise from violence based on prejudice are illustrated by analyzing three different problems: the invisibility of the homophobic motives behind violence, which many times don't make it into the official facts as constructed by the police and prosecutors; the risks of the double victimization; and the risks derived from the excessive emphasis on the difference or discretion in the application of the homosexual categories such as sexual orientation, gay or lesbian, among others. The chapter also deals with the concealment of extenuating factors such as ire and intense pain through the use of the so-called "passion crimes" category. The chapter ends with a reflection on the tensions between the private and the public spheres generated by expressions of non-normative sexual practices.

Gender and Sexuality in Latin America: Cases and Decisions is a joint effort to show not only obstacles to the full enjoyment of rights from all individuals in Latin America, regardless of their sex, sexual orientation, and gender identity. It is also, and for the most part, a tribute to good adjudication processes and legal decisions in Latin America. We hope that this book will contribute to a dialogue between Latin America and the Global South on issues that unfortunately affect human beings around the globe. We also hope that making these materials available in English will trigger more collaboration between law professors and students.

Chapter 2
Citizenship

Cristina Motta

The concept of citizenship, as constructed in modern times,[1] is characterized by an abundance of meanings because it is the center of important conflicting tensions on account of the transcendence of its scope.

The idea of citizenship refers, since ancient times, to the criteria of inclusion of an individual person in a political community. However, this concept has had two fundamental expansions: first, to incorporate the idea of equality in the distribution of rights, during political modernity, it will include defining who the citizen is, and ensuring that, when being one, the person will be treated in the same way as the rest of the citizenry. Since then, citizenship invokes both a legal-political status, which incorporates and excludes, and "a right to have rights"[2] that emancipates and includes subjects. Second, during the transition to the twentieth century, the concept of citizenship has expanded to incorporate the social and economic conditions that must exist in order for individuals to enjoy their rights. Since then, citizenship has been linked to equality of conditions.

The coexistence of these meanings – the legal belonging of a person to a given State, the ideal status in which the individuals attain entitlement to the rights and socio economic conditions for its exercise – turns the idea of citizenship into the

[1] The concept of modernity used in these interpretations is defined by Jürgen Habermas as the cultural, scientific, political, and economic model that surged in Europe at the start of the fifteenth century (though its existence was not self evident until the eighteenth century) and that in general terms, is defined as a rational process of secularization of the culture and of the development in societies characterized by capitalism and state bureaucracies. *See generally* Jürgen Habermas, *Le discours philosophique de la modernité*, Paris, Gaillimard, 1985, p. 2.

[2] These are the terms of Chief Justice Earl Warren of the US Supreme Court in *Perez v. Bronwell*, 356 U.S 44 (1958).

C. Motta (✉)
Consultant on Sexual Rights, Medrano 1366, 1179 Buenos Aires, Argentina
e-mail: tokatlianes@gmail.com

C. Motta and M. Sáez (eds.), *Gender and Sexuality in Latin America - Cases and Decisions*, Ius Gentium: Comparative Perspectives on Law and Justice 24,
DOI 10.1007/978-94-007-6199-5_2, © Springer Science+Business Media Dordrecht 2013

seat of important tensions of political thinking: the split between the human being as an individual and as a member of a political community; the universalism of fundamental rights and the peculiarity of communities; the abstract equality before the law and the concrete difference of the particular conditions of existence; membership and exclusion, among others.

The central quality of citizenship and the discussions that it summarizes allow us to affirm that a great part of the modern political experience can be synthesized in the fight for inclusion, within the idea of citizenship, of excluded subjects.[3] A remarkable part of this fight has been fought by the feminist thinking and action.

In order to study the rulings in which the regional justice constructs doctrines that are coherent with these theoretical and practical struggles, this chapter is divided into two sections: (1) citizenship as an aspiration, which will address the problems of equality, reparation and emancipation, and (2) citizenship as belonging, which will analyze the problems of identity and culture.

2.1 Citizenship as an Aspiration: Equality, Reparation, and Emancipation

The history of the feminist movement can be traced along the history of citizenship. The limited scope of liberal citizenship, in terms of the few subjects it included, was the fundamental impulse of the first feminist movement, which obtained its greatest triumph with the achievement of women's political citizenship and the right to vote.[4]

Without attempting to defy the liberal theory of society, feminism of equality or liberal feminism considered that the fundamental cause of women's disadvantages was reduced to the differences in legal treatment. These differences, they believed, meant that there would be less material resources available to them, led to their being judged by inappropriate standards, denied them equal opportunities and impeded that specific feminine damages be recognized if doing so could affect men. Since discrimination lay in the differential legal treatment, the efforts of the first relevant feminist action focused on achieving the effective realization of the liberal premise that states that all human beings must receive equal treatment before the law. This included fighting for the inclusion of women in the idea of citizenship,—limited to male, white subjects who own property—for wage equality and the prohibition of sexual discrimination in employment and the trades, and for

[3] Sandro Mezzardra, *Derecho de fuga*, Traficantes de Sueños, Madrid, 2005.

[4] Ecuador, in 1929 was the first Latin American country to pass the female suffrage. Brazil and Uruguay did it in 1932, Cuba in 1934, El Salvador in 1939, Dominican Republic in 1942 and Jamaica in 1944. Guatemala, Panama and Trinidad and Tobago in 1945; Argentina and Venezuela in 1947, Chile in 1948 and Costa Rica in 1949. Haiti in 1950, Antigua, Barbados, Dominica, Saint Kitts-Nevis, Santa Lucia, Granada and San Vicente in 1951. Bolivia in 1953, Belize, Colombia and México in 1954 (the latter did not provide for the right under the same terms given to men until 1958), Nicaragua and Peru in 1955, Honduras in 1957 and Paraguay in 1958.

the right of married women to own property. This feminist action, lasting the whole of the twentieth century, did not introduce a challenge to the prevailing model of citizenship but rather simply advocated for women's inclusion as beneficiaries of certain rights. Feminism of difference,[5] on the other hand, opposes this attempt at inclusion of women in the idea of citizenship comparable to that of males, and proposes that women's experiences, because they are women, be valued, and that maternity, care and the family provide orientation to the feminist political action. These proposals are based on the need for special legal treatment for aspects on which the differences are grounded.

The second period of the feminist thinking, termed the second wave, has its parallel narration in the history of social citizenship which expressed itself in overcoming the restrictive and exclusive civil and political citizenship and its limitation to formal equality and freedom with the incorporation of important social rights. From the feminist thinking point of view, this second movement is enriched with an important theoretical debate: the liberal social, socialist, and radical feminisms burst in as solid alternatives to the equality-difference dilemma. These ideas launch the first great challenge against the social liberal theory and its guiding idea of equality. Radical feminism understands that women's problems are not of inequality but of subordination. It considers that it is not about attacking isolated, easy to resolve deprivations of the law, but of fighting the patriarchal system conceived as a "system of structures and social practices in which men dominate, exploit and oppress women."[6] The idea of supremacy-domination is now opposed to the traditional duet of equality-difference.

Since male dominance is exercised through the control of women's bodies and sexuality, it is necessary to consider all aspects of social life, especially the private aspect, instead of focusing solely on the verifiable rights in the public space. In this sense, sexuality acquires exceptional preponderance. The chapter "Violence" (Chap. 6) of this book deal with these aspects in depth. Suffice it for the moment to highlight radical feminisms' idea of subordination, which, in terms of citizenship, means incorporating the personal in the political.

Within this general theoretical framework, there is an analysis of the jurisprudential development of the idea of citizenship for women in Latin America. The first stage, which occurred three decades later than in the United States,[7] brought about the expansion of civil and political citizenship. The second stage, which also happened three decades later, brought about the constitutional, penal, and labor reforms that promoted positive rights and were especially the expression of State censure to

[5] For the most in depth perspective on this subject, see Carol Gilligan, *In a Different Voice*, Harvard University Press, Cambridge, 1982.

[6] *See* Sylvia Walby, *Theorizing Patriarchy*, Blackwell, Cambridge, 1990.

[7] The United States approved women's right to vote 1920. "The right of citizens of the United States to vote shall not be denied or abridged by the United States or by any State on account of sex. Congress shall have power to enforce this article by appropriate legislation." U.S Const. amend, XIX.

violence and sexual dominance. The third is settled by the contemporary fights for cultural recognition and the economic distribution of a globalized space, and finds its expression in situations and judgments directed toward the protection of transnational rights.

The first judicial decisions described below tell of the way in which the region gradually constructed a theory of sexual equality. It will show the passage from a formal conception to a substantial idea of equality until reaching the constitutionalization of affirmative actions. The judgments presented here illustrate, as a public matter, the adoption of discrimination and violence in private spaces and relationships, and with it the adoption of the radical feminism perspective on behalf of the regional law.

2.1.1 Equality Before the Law

Legality, understood as the requirement to the law of obtaining its justification based on its formal characteristics, that is, the assemblage of general and abstract rules issued according to predictable procedures, is the idea that seems to govern Latin American jurisprudence regarding the issue of equality during most of the twentieth century. The differences between formal and material equality, however, burst into judicial rationales hand in hand with social citizenship and the model of the Welfare State. From the legal point of view, these changes became evident in the overcoming of formalism and in the rescue of the social facts and the social reality for judicial interpretation. The move from the exclusive use of logical and syllogistic methods to the understanding of law as a social practice, whose validity and efficacy incorporates the knowledge of the space in which it operates, is evident. It also verifies that the myth of the legislator's will as the only aspect guiding interpretation falls apart.

The judgments presented show these transformations and illustrate three legal problems related to the scope of the judicial interpretation of women's equality: the first is a historic document that expresses the way in which Argentina's legal culture of 1929 permitted the resolution of a typical case of equality before the law: the legal habilitation of women to occupy positions and perform functions that were forbidden to them. The second tackles the legal capacity of married women, and the third imports to the region the equality standard constructed by the Supreme Court of the United States for gender discrimination.

Supreme Court of Justice of the Argentine Nation
Ángela Camperchioli
November of 1921

Main Legal Issue:
Can an incapacity to perform a trade not expressly prohibited by law be applied by analogy to women?

Facts:
Mrs. Angela Camperchioli requests that oath be taken to her to enter the registry of public notaries. In spite of the fact that law number 1893 does not contemplate any inability of women to perform this office, the civil and commercial codes did establish women's inability to perform certain functions. The Court of appeal ruled that if the woman cannot be a witness in the signing of public instruments, much less can she perform as a notary.

Court Ruling:
The Court revokes the challenged ruling and prohibits the extended interpretation of restrictions to women's rights.

Extracts:
Supreme Court of Justice
[…] That the case of these proceedings considered thus, it is certainly appropriate to establish that, as recorded in the same judgment of the District Attorney through which the presented title is challenged […] there is no law or specific legal text that establishes the incapacity referred to herein, nor derived from the spirit of a law and from general principles of legislation and the law, a concept on which the challenged author has also based his declaration, which states such incapacity in spite of the affirmation that "no legal provision establishes literally that women are disqualified for the performance of the position of Notary Public."

That the precedents presented show that the denial to the requested registration is equivalent to the invalidity of the title and to the legal incapacity– of those who invoke it, since compliance or the consecration of a specific provision of the law does not matter, but what matters is the application by analogy or implication of principles or general provisions regarding incapacities and legal concepts of a different order, which although they may be similar to the limitation whose creation is sought, do not establish such limitation or govern the matter by explicit legal provision.

That under such circumstances, the capacity to perform the profession as notary that the appellant justifies through the presentation of unobjectionable title, granted by the authority instituted by law to such effect, cannot be invalidated until declared null, based on an alleged incapacity derived by induction from others that the common laws specifically enumerate, because if it were allowed to infer the legal capacities, even related to titles which accredit a capacity of the same order, the former would not constitute the exception but rather the general rule, and they would not be interpreted with a restrictive criterion but with the corresponding breadth of mind.

That as for the rest, without entering into an analysis of the legal status of women in our legislation, because that would imply exceeding our authority in the present debate, it is however pertinent to insist on that whatever restrictions are being imposed on her, none of these would authorize to impose others upon her through the extended interpretation of such restrictions, thus placing unjustified objections to the primary guarantees of the Constitution, which are equality before the law, the right to learn, to work, the right not to be deprived of that which is not prohibited by the law, with which a judicial ruling that annuls *de facto*, without explicit legal basis, a title of legitimately acquired professional qualifications, cannot be harmonized.

On these grounds [...] the challenged judgment is overturned [...]

Supreme Court of Justice of Panama
Action of unconstitutionality of article 26 of the Code of Commerce
February 8 of 1994

Main Legal Issue:
Does the norm that provides that for the validity of commercial acts carried out by married women the husband's later ratification is required, conflict with article 19 of the National Constitution?[8]

Facts:
A Panamanian woman files a complaint before the Supreme Court of Justice claiming the unconstitutionality of article 26 of the Code of Commerce which establishes that "... those who are legally of age may validly confirm obligations entered into through commercial transactions executed by them while they were underage. Likewise, the commercial acts executed by a woman with no explicit or tacit consent of the husband shall be valid, when they are later ratified by the latter."

Court Ruling:
The Court declares the challenged norm unconstitutional.

Extracts:
[...]
In the opinion of the Plenary the second paragraph of article 26 of the Commercial Code infringes upon article 20 of the Political Constitution which consecrates the principle of equality before the law. And this is so because the second paragraph of article 26 of the Commercial Code provides a distinct legal treatment for married women, by reason of their civil state, establishing that they cannot freely engage in commercial transactions since they need to be ratified by their husbands. This unequal treatment, this discrimination against married women, constitutes a violation of the constitutional principle of equality before the law enshrined in our Magna Carta in the following terms: Article 20: Panamanians and foreigners are equal before the Law [...]

Recently, the Supreme Court of Justice declared article 27 of the Commercial Code unconstitutional [...] In the part setting out the legal grounds of this judgment, the Plenary Chamber stated:

> In the article which unconstitutionality is claimed it is accepted that a married woman requires an authorization from her husband to perform commercial transactions, which must be revalidated, even if they were not authorized by the husband, if the woman obtains a declaration of nullity of the corresponding marriage. Therefore, it a detestable discrimination by reason of a person's 'civil status,' that is, of a woman, that conflicts with the content of article 20 of the Political Constitution in force, which consecrates the equality of all Panamanians before the law.

[8] "There will be no laws or personal privilege nor discrimination on account of race, birth, social class, sex, religion or political ideas."

In the present case, the discrimination arising from article 27 of the Commercial Code is derived from the distinction between married women and unmarried women, since the former are required, in order for their commercial transactions be valid, to have authorization from their husbands.

In the constitutional system in force, women have full equality at all times, whether they are married or not, which is why the possibility that consecrating the validity of acts executed by married women after the marriage be declared invalid must be eliminated.

Although the challenged article was conceived to protect women who acted without the husbands' authorization, it undoubtedly consecrates a discrimination, for no woman in full enjoyment of her civil rights must need authorization from the husband to perform commercial transactions, nor must the privilege established in favor of women who have been married before be explicitly consecrated, as is the case in article 27 of the Commercial Code. The explicit violence of norms as the one under analysis decreases the quality of life of a society that legitimately aspires to the prevalence of justice and equality inherent in peaceful cohabitation.

Every woman who is legally of age has full legal capacity to carry out commercial transactions, without the need for authorization from her husband to third parties, so it is unnecessary to consecrate the principle foreseen in article 27 of the Commercial Code. [...]

Therefore, we hold that the appellant is right as regards the claim of unconstitutionality referred to in the second paragraph of article 26 of the Commercial Code, because it violates article 20 of the Political Constitution.

Since the challenged norm must be declared unconstitutional by reason of the infringement upon the Constitution, the Plenary considers that to confront this precept with other constitutional norms is deemed unnecessary.

Supreme Court of Justice of the Argentine Nation
Cristina González de Delgado et al. v. Universidad Nacional de Córdoba
September 19 of 2000

Main Legal Issue:
What is the standard of equality applicable to discrimination based on gender?

Facts:
The parents of some pupils at a school dependent on the National University of Córdoba sought, by way of a writ of amparo, to have the Superior Council of the University prohibit the admission of women to the institution.

Court Ruling:
The Court of Appeals, by majority vote, rejected the action, and the Supreme Court of Justice formally declared the extraordinary appeal was appropriate and confirmed the challenged judgment.

Extracts:
[...]
In "United States v. Virginia" (ruling of June 26, 1996, published in 518 U.S. 515) the federal government filed a lawsuit against the state of Virginia and the Virginia Military

Institute. This prestigious school – famous for its methods and achievements – was the sole institution of higher learning in Virginia that provided education for only one sex: males. That policy of admission and the consequent impossibility of women to access the qualified education provided by the said school, led to the allegation of violation of the 14th amendment. The presentation before the Supreme Court was successful, and the Court considered that harm had been produced.

[…]

The court claimed that Parties who seek to defend gender-based government action that imposes categories, classifications or exclusions must demonstrate an "exceedingly persuasive justification (of such action)." Neither federal nor state government acts are compatible with the "*Equal Protection Clause*" when a law or official policy denies to women, simply because they are women, full citizenship stature, that is to say the opportunity –equal to that accorded to men– to participate and contribute to social development based on their individual talents and capacities. To defend gender-based classification or exclusion has the burden to prove that such action serves an important governmental objective and that the discriminatory means employed are substantially related with the achievement of those objectives. The justification has to be "genuine" and not rely on overbroad generalizations about the different talents, capacities or preferences of males and females. Inherent differences between men and women remain cause for celebration – the Court appreciates – but not for denigration of the members of either sex or for artificial constraints on an individual's opportunity.

[…]

The heightened review standard applied to sex-based classifications does not make sex a proscribed classification, but it does mean that categorization based on sex must not be used to create or perpetuate the legal, social and economic inferiority of women. In any case, sex-based classifications may be used to compensate women for particular economic disabilities they have historically suffered […]

[…]

In the US judgment a standard for scrutiny is proposed which, if not as strict as that used for classifications based on race or nationality, is extremely demanding (it is telling that the only judge who had a dissenting opinion found it undistinguishable from the "strict scrutiny" applied for these two last classifications: 518 U.S. 515, 596).

[…]

Even though the discussed US criteria (born in a normative framework as succinct as that of article 16 of our National Constitution) were applied as a hypothesis to the "Monserrat" case, the solution would be the same as that obtained in the light of the convention adopted by law 23179. Indeed, the plaintiffs have not shown (and much less, demonstrated), what would be the vital public interest that advises the exclusion of young girls from the benefits of the education provided by Monserrat, but rather that this vital public interest would consist in avoiding such exclusion, with involuntary speed, because it is based on a prejudice that, as such, does not deserve any justification […]

The facts put forward are evidence that Córdoba National University, by disposing that the registrations in the Montserrat National School be made with no gender distinction, has not only acted as the competent organ within the sphere of the powers vested on it, but furthermore, has removed a discriminatory barrier –which today seems morally and legally abominable– that impeded full participation of young women from Córdoba in the educational and cultural life of their province. The National University of Córdoba has also expressed its will to comply with the obligations of international conventions that require the country to integrate women in all aspects of social life and to remove discriminatory obstacles that might stand in their way.

[…]

That I cannot come to a close of these reflections without referring to the unrelenting efforts of the appellants to demonstrate that their claim is not discriminatory: "a circumstance which" they say "at this stage of the centuries all the undersigned find repugnant" […]. Such efforts seem vain to me. Their authors declaim their lack of discriminatory intention; but they remain petrified in that intention […] for, at the same time, through their stance they place obstacles to sex equality in all its creative and fair aspects, and not only do they omit to take into account that men's "being" is perhaps determined by women's "being," and vice versa (for which reason the exclusion of any of the two would be dangerous), but also (although the exclusion is not justified even then) that Argentina does not possess such a plethora of male talents at its disposal that it can afford to leave its female population without education, or half educated. The arguments utilized in the claim, both those relating to the incompetence of Córdoba University, and those of the conflicting constitutional values between the right of parents to choose their children's education and that of equality (they opt for privileging the former), cover up the real motive, truly discriminatory […] which could be expressed as follows: they say nothing against women; but they do not wish them to become integrated in a joint education with their male sons.

The plaintiffs' claim thus constitutes an offense to excluded women and, for the same reason, does not deserve judicial protection because it is incompatible with the need to lay the foundations of a democratic and intelligent society.

2.1.1.1 Matters for Debate

The three judgments show how the region's judges have gradually incorporated into the Latin American legal systems – chronologically and conceptually – women's equality. The subject of the first case, addressed since the first decades of the twentieth century, makes reference to the dismantling of the incapacity inherent in women; the second to the inability derived from marriage; and the third, concludes the process with the constitutional prohibition of gender-based discrimination. These cases also illustrate the significant changes in the way in which the judges construct their arguments, from the pure syllogistic operation, under the pretended neutrality of the legal action which gave rise to the 1929 ruling, to the evident incorporation of political, sociological and ethical arguments in the decisions.

In the first judgment, the general principles of the law, which included the prohibition to interpret the penalties, exemptions and legal bans in an analogical or extensive way, constitute the winning argument. In Argentina of 1929, to collect substantive arguments such as the attributes of citizenship, the rights to equality before the law and other principles which are today the fundamental pillars of modern States, was viewed as an excess. The decision is not in favor of equality, but is about the limits of the interpretation of the law.

It is important to reflect on the Argentine Congress' utilization of the male gender in the legal grammar as a basis for women's exclusion from performing certain functions. This problem was addressed in the Colombian Constitutional Court's contemporary case law that rules on the claim of unconstitutionality of article 33 of the Civil Code. […] In this respect, the Court states:

> […] by using generic expressions usually aimed at denoting only one sex – as is the case of the word "man" in its social use – but applied in a general sense, supposedly encompassing both sexes, in legally relevant definitions, we fall into what the doctrine has denominated "generic terms with a trap", that is, expressions that seem to include both sexes but are frequently excluding as regards women.[9]

In the third ruling, the judgment addresses a fundamental aspect in the constitutional conception of equality. It is the so-called equality test, in which the constitutional courts define the conditions in which an unequal treatment among human beings based on sex, race, national origin or other similar considerations is justifiable. The Argentine Supreme Court imports into this judgment the so-called "intermediate scrutiny" termed by the Supreme Court of the United States. The latter court adopted the term after an examination of intermediate rigor, comparing it with the strict scrutiny applied to discrimination based on race, and established the requirement that if there is to be sexual discrimination, it had to be substantially related with important government interest.

In the region, the Colombian Constitutional Court has established the equality test in the following terms:

> […] the difference in treatment based on any of the connotations laid out in the first paragraph of article 13 of the Constitution related to equality –sex, race, national or family origin, language, religion, political or philosophical views– is in principle prohibited, and will only be admissible if it meets certain conditions. To evaluate such conditions this prohibited criterion is qualified as suspicious, which imposes on the legal operator the application of a strict equality test, in order to determine:
>
> (i) Whether the act that promotes a different treatment has an end that is admissible by the Constitution and if it is a vital one;
> (ii) Whether the act is useful and indispensable to achieve the proposed end; and,
> (iii) Whether the act ensures proportionality between the benefit obtained and the negative impacts or harm it may cause on other legal rights, an exercise that will be treated next in this document.[10]

---

[9] Colombian Constitutional Court, ruling C-804 of 2006.

[10] Colombian Constitutional Court, Ruling C-355 de 2006.

2.1.2 Reparation

The social concept of citizenship demands not only the legal integration of excluded groups, but also the actual one. The recognition of rights that are inherent in social citizenship in Latin America has its more relevant constitutional manifestation in the efforts made by the region's judges, especially during the 1990s, to define a substantial concept of equality and incorporate extra legal arguments in the law's application, and thus defend a space of state action aimed at ensuring not only the formal but also the material effectiveness of rights.

Overcoming the inequalities and the discrimination against women thus implied going beyond the conquest of formal equality before the law and defending the constitutionality of norms that generate a discriminatory treatment in favor of women when doing so compensates for the tradition of exclusion. These decisions have generated vast case law that shelters the so-called affirmative actions. Affirmative action, or remedy discrimination, emerged in the United States constitutional debate on occasion of the Supreme Court's support of the University of California's special admissions program based on race in the 1970s.[11]

The extension of these actions to women implied accepting the constitutionality of regulations that discriminate in favor of them when with these they are compensated for their ancestral disadvantages. These decisions and policies have been, however, strongly criticized by feminist and non feminist authors. The former, consider that these types of programs can perpetuate women's inferiority, or demand that the precise meaning of compensation be defined, so as to not confuse it with the special treatment destined to pregnant women or the differences based on physical characteristics. The latter, consider that the damage implied in affirmative action in the modern concept of merit is unacceptable.

The cases put forth below illustrate the incorporation of this subject in the regional jurisprudence, and some of its inconveniences. The first ruling is a holding by the Constitutional Court of Colombia, which defines material equality and its difference with formal equality. The second lays out the doctrine of the Constitutional Court of Peru when it establishes the scope of affirmative actions, and the third accounts for the limits of these types of actions in the case of the quota laws when dealing with appointments by a selection process and merit.

Constitutional Court of Colombia
Ruling C-410 of 1994

Main Legal Issue:
What is the nature and scope of substantial equality?

[11] Regents of the University of California v. Bakke, 438 U.S. 265 (1978).

Facts:
The plaintiff claims the unconstitutionality of some articles of the law that creates a social security system claiming that it violates article 13 of the Constitution[12] when it establishes that to access the senior citizen pension and the enjoyment of a pension the requirements of age are different for both genders, favoring women, for whom the requirement involves a lower age.

Court Ruling:
The court rules against the plaintiff: it decides that all the articles under study are enforceable –clarifying that they are enforceable as related to the formulated claim. Its considerations refer, in the first place, to the difference between formal equality and substantial equality. It states that substantial equality has a remedial nature, aimed at defending persons and groups in conditions of inferiority.

Extracts:
[…]

Formal and substantial equality
The simplest approximation to the concept of equality is sufficient to point out that it does not respond to a univocal sense but rather admits multiple meanings which are applicable according to the peculiarities of each case. Through a historical perspective demonstrates the successive occurrence of two significant achievements: formal equality and substantial equality. The first category constitutes, in its beginnings, one of the most valued triumphs of the classic liberal state that reacted against the privileges belonging to the ancient regime, proclaiming the similar position of all before the law, so that the recipients are given identical treatment in the norms and in their implementation. Within this notion, the result is that citizens are the receivers of the same norms, without opportunity for exceptions for any person; because the law is universal, general, abstract and impersonal, "the same for all whether it protects or punishes," in the terms of article 6 of the French Declaration of 1789.

[…]

However, formal equality is not alien to the establishment of different treatments, it rests on relevant conditions that impose the need to distinguish situations that grant them different treatments, a hypothesis that expresses the known rule of justice which demands the treatment of equals with equality and of the unequal in an unequal way. It must be specified that initially, formal equality focused only on the effects of the law, regardless of the normative contents, a tendency that gradually

[12] Article 13 of the Colombian Constitution states "All persons are born free and equal before the law, they will receive the same protection and treatment from the authorities and will enjoy the same rights, freedoms and opportunities without any discrimination on account of sex, race, national origin or family, language, religion, political opinion or philosophy. The State will promote conditions so that equality is real and effective, and will adopt measures in favor of discriminated groups. The State will especially protect those persons who because of their economic, physical or mental condition find themselves in debilitated circumstances and will sanction abuse or harm against them"

gave way to an interpretation that, according to the postulates of the social state of the law, advocates for equality in the content of the law, incidentally permitting control over constitutionality aimed at examining the correspondence between the legislative activity and the Constitution, a superior reference that makes the law the appropriate normative means for the realization of the State's goals.

[…]

Substantial equality alludes to the commitment of removing the obstacles that in the economic and social levels construct effective *de facto* inequalities that oppose the effective enjoyment of rights. The underlying causes of these situations have to do, among other aspects, with scarcity, with unsatisfied needs of human beings, with historical phenomena of segregation and marginalization or with past injustices and the attempt to rectify them. Substantial equality reveals, therefore, a remedial, compensatory, emancipative, correcting character, defensive of persons and of groups situated in conditions of inferiority, through the promotion of positive actions of the public powers.

[…]

This confirmation that certain individuals and groups, in spite of being equal before the law are not really equal, exercises a remarkable influence on the same norm which, on occasions, abandons the traditional characteristics of generality, abstraction, universality and permanence, becoming specific, that is, directed at concrete sectors of the population, or temporal, inasmuch as its effects become exhausted in a given lapse of time; all with the aim of enhancing the social or economic conditions of its particular recipients.

[…]

However, whereas equality before the law is part of the assemblage of prerogatives recognized by the majority of democratic constitutional regimes, to whose legal organization it integrates, substantial equality, enshrined in the Superior Statute of some States, is perceived scarcely as an objective or end of the political system, which links the public powers to the transformation of the existing type of society into an ideal one, more conducive to the fulfillment of human aspirations in its multiple facets.

[…]

Even when formal equality between the sexes has been growingly incorporated into the Colombian legal system, substantial equality still constitutes a goal; the subsistence of social unequal realities attests to this. It is not about ignoring the progress that equality before the law represents; apart from the fact that its absence would be an enormous obstacle to the improvement of women's conditions, it is necessary to take into account that it leads the way to higher courses, because it permits to resort to the State organs in search of eliminating discrimination and legitimizes, in this way, the claim for effective opportunities to exercise rights and develop capacities without setbacks. It should not be forgotten that, in the framework of the idea of substantial equality, the exclusion of discrimination by reason of sex contained in article 13 of the Chart, is not limited to the mere prohibition but covers the constitutional purpose of ending the historical situation of inferiority suffered by the female population; that decision authorizes, within the principle of protection, to make positive decisions, aimed at correcting *de facto* inequalities, to compensate the relegation suffered and to promote real and effective equality at the economic and social levels. The protection measures, which imply special repeal of formal equality, demand the determination of those specially vulnerable ambits in which there is the need to operate; thus, together with the family and the State, the workplace is one of the spaces that offers most possibilities for discrimination on grounds of sex.

[…]

However, the matter that now occupies the attention of the Court, although it entails different treatments in effectively distinct situations, implies, on an additional level, the granting of legal relevance to the social differences of women to enhance their condition through the adoption of a compensatory measure of the difficulties they must face by virtue of their link to the labor market; this last aspect is situated within the perspective of substantial equality which, according to the postulates of the Social State based on the Rule of Law, is not limited to the mere function of guaranteeing or protecting, but advances toward a promotional function that is normally carried out through positive measures in favor of the discriminated or marginalized social groups. To proceed in a neutral way in the face of the social reality would entail ignoring the values, principles and ends consecrated by the Constitution, abandon the search for a fair society, respectful of human dignity, and empty the constitutional norms that prohibit discrimination against women and provide for their special protection of all content (arts. 43 and 53).

Supreme Court of Justice of Peru
Unconstitutionality of Law 28449

Main Legal Issue:
Is discrimination in favor of women if the aim is the search for material equality, constitutional?

Facts:
The appellant claims the unconstitutionality of law 28449 which applies new rules on pensions, changes the calculation basis of the new pensions discriminating between men and women and demands, for the pension for widowhood, that the men accredit incapacity for subsistence on their own means and demonstrate that they are not within a security system. This requirement is not extended to women.

Court Ruling:
The Court rejects the claim and confirms the constitutionality of the challenged norms for considering them examples of a legitimate affirmative action in favor of women.

Extracts:
[…]
The application of the right to equality does not exclude a differential treatment and such principle is not infringed upon if the difference is based on objective reasons.

[…]

To focus on the interpretation of the right to equality from a strictly liberal point of view would imply reducing the constitutional protection of the equality principle to a merely formal content, for which reason it is the duty of this Collegiate Court, of the public powers and the community in general, to endow the principle of equality enshrined in the Constitution with substance. In this sense, a positive link with the legislator to the fundamental rights must also be recognized, in such a way that the law should become the means of reversing the conditions of inequality or, which is the same, of reviving the conditions of equality of which the social reality could be dissociating itself, to the detriment of the constitutional aspirations.

[…]

The State has the obligation to adopt measures – usually legislative – with the aim of legally compensating economically, socially or culturally excluded groups; in this way, through such measures of "positive action" or of "inverse discrimination."

[…]

These measures are strictly aimed, through weighted provisions, at favoring the feminine collective, in the correct understanding that social reality still imposes the concession of greater support with the aim of ensuring them a life consistent with the principle of dignity.

[…]

The difference in treatment that the social security regimes have usually awarded to men and women should not be focused, *prima facie*, from the formal perspective of the right to equality before the law, that is, as the constitutional ban preventing that legislators introduce differences of treatment among persons who are in substantially similar situations without a reasonable or proportional basis, to the legal system.

On the contrary, the alluded differentiation must be approached under the material or substantial guideline that informs the right to equality, according to which there is an obligation of the State to adopt measures – normally legislative – with the aim of legally compensating economically, socially or culturally excluded groups; […]

[…]

The reasonability analysis of the implementation of rules for positive action is hindered when these are taken in favor of groups and not of individuals. However, a criterion of vital importance which facilitates the analysis is the presumption of social exclusion against certain groups, derived from the specific clauses of non discrimination provided for in paragraph 2 of article 2 of the Constitution. Thus, expressly, such mechanism, bans discrimination "[…] by reason of race, sex, language, opinion, economic condition," leaving an open clause in the hands of the legislator and the jurisdictional interpreter by adding "[…] or of any other kind."

Therefore,

"[…] the specific clauses of non discrimination mainly fulfill the function of protecting, by toughening the equality criteria, certain groups which, on account of their history of subjugation and the social underestimation to which they are subjected, do not belong to the dominating group which participates, debates and creates the legal norms." But another consequence derived from such clauses "[…] is materialized in the constitutional validation of the measures which are based on this feature to favor the socially damaged groups, that is to say, the affirmative actions, always within the limits of proportionality."

In this sense, there is a wide margin of presumption of constitutionality in the measures that favor the minority [...] or socially neglected groups, which could be considered to fall within these specific criteria. For example, women, certain religious, ethnic, foreign groups, and others of diverse natures.

[...]

Even though in recent years there has been an important degree of incorporation of women in social tasks in which they should never have been relegated (political participation, access to work positions, education opportunities, among many others), this task cannot be considered to have been consolidated in the Peruvian reality. A good part of our society still nurtures from patriarchal cultural patterns which relegate the female group to a secondary role, in spite of the fact that women's identical capacities with regard to the male group in all the ambits of life, whether it be in the political, the social or the economic sphere, is beyond discussion. The prejudices and idiosyncrasy [...] of a significant number of citizens (made up of both men and women) still maintain the gender problem in the country alive.

So, the Constitutional Court cannot consider measures that require some years less of age or of contributions to women, to access a pension of the social security regime, or those that establish a system of calculation relatively more favorable to women receiving pensions at the time of determining the total sum of their pension, unconstitutional. It is clear that such measures are strictly aimed, through weighted provisions, to favor the women's group, in the correct understanding that the social reality still imposes granting a greater support with the aim of ensuring them a life that is consistent with the principle of dignity.

And for this same reason, neither does the Constitutional Court consider unconstitutional that the legislator has not requested that the widow provide proof of the economic dependence in which she finds herself with regard to the deceased's pension. It is clear that the legislator has used this presumption as a point of departure based on the element from reality described above. Consequently, it is an authentic "affirmative action" in favor of women.

Inter-American Commission of Human Rights
Maria Merciadri de Morini
Argentina[13]

Facts:

[...]

The radical, petitioner alleged that by mutual agreement among its leaders, the Unión Civica radical political party of the Province of Córdoba had put together the list of six candidates that were running for the national deputy seats up for election on October 3, 1993. The list placed the names of two women in third and sixth place without taking into account that the party had five national deputy seats

[13] Report No. 103/01 case 11.307.

up for election. This was a violation of Law 24.012, called the Quota Act, enacted on November 6, 1991, which guarantees that at least thirty percent (30%) of the candidates on the political parties' slates for elective office are to be women, in numbers "proportional to the chances of being elected." Article 2 of Decree 378/93, which is the law's governing decree, stipulates that "the thirty percent quota that Law 24.012 sets for women, shall be regarded as a minimum. If application of the 30% formula results in fractions that are less than whole numbers, the minimum number shall be the number shown in the table attached as Appendix A, which is an integral part of this decree." The appendix in question states: "seats to be filled, five; minimum number: two." This provision is binding upon political parties when putting together their lists of candidates, and the consequence of failure to comply shall be denial of certification. The law also establishes the corollary right of citizens entitled to vote under the constitutional right of suffrage, to be able to vote for slates of candidates on which women are represented in accordance with the formula that the law stipulates.

The petitioner alleged that, as a citizen affiliated with that political party, she filed a complaint with the Board of Elections challenging the slate, which was rejected on the grounds that the "list of candidates was the product of a consensus built among all factions of the party, which agreed upon a single list." When she filed an appeal, the federal court denied her request and declared that she did not have legal standing to bring such action. The petitioner appealed that decision, but the Federal Elections Court also denied that she had legal standing to bring an action, on the grounds that she had no personal stake in the matter. The petitioner contends that the list drawn up by the Unión Cívica Radical party violates the right of the voter to equal opportunity, for men and women alike, to stand for elective office. She further argues that any citizen has the right to challenge the list, and need not be the party injured by his/her place on the list of candidates. The classic requisite that the plaintiff must have had a subjective right violated or his/her concrete interests disregarded is not the applicable paradigm, especially since the Argentine Supreme Court's ruling in Ekmekdjian v/Sofovich. She also cites Article 57 of the Political Parties Statute Nº 23.298, which gives members of political parties standing before the court "when the rights they are given in the Statute are denied and when the recourses within the party have been exhausted."

The petitioner filed an extraordinary appeal seeking reversal of the decision on grounds that it was unconstitutional, but the court refused to allow her appeal to go forward on the grounds that the election had been held on October 3, 1993, and that the matter had therefore become moot. Finally, she filed a complaint with the Supreme Court because of the lower court's refusal to allow her appeal to go forward. The Supreme Court, however, denied her appeal arguing that "the votes that the Unión Cívica Radical carried in the October 3, 1993 election entitled it to four seats in the Chamber of Deputies; this case was about who ended up in fifth place." The petitioner considers that the question was not "moot" because there is a very concrete "right of expectation" that has to be upheld were a vacancy to occur among those elected. As matters stand, if such a vacancy were to occur, it would be filled by a man–the one who is in fifth place—and not by a woman. It is for that reason that a woman should have been listed in fifth place and the man in sixth. Even had there been only four seats to be filled, two women should have been elected because one woman alone is equivalent to just 25% of the total, which is below the legally mandated quota.

Friendly Settlement Agreement:

[…]

3. The Argentine State recognizes that this decree serves to ensure women's concrete and effective participation in the lists of candidates for national elective office, thus reinforcing the rights upheld in law 24.012, as well as Article 37 of the Constitution, and in the counterpart provisions of the international human rights treaties to which Argentina is party.

4. Petitioner Dr. Maria Teresa Merciadri de Morini hereby undertakes to desist from the petition she filed with the Inter-American Commission on Human Rights, registered as case N° 11.307, as she recognizes that Decree N° 1246/00 adequately provides for the fundamental issues she raised in the complaint she filed with the Commission.

5. Both parties are grateful to the Inter-American Commission on Human Rights for its important contribution and ask that it give its approval to this friendly settlement and close case 11.307.

Constitutional Court of Colombia Ruling C-371 of 2000

Main Legal Issue:

Is the quota system at the decision-making levels of the public administration constitutional? Are quotas compatible with the merit system in force in the public administration? Are they applicable to the lists elaborated by political parties?

Facts:

The Secretary General of the Senate submits to the Constitutional Court a bill by which women's effective participation in decision-making levels of the public power is regulated, establishing a quota of 30% for these positions.

Court Ruling:

The Court defended most of the articles of the Law of Quotas, including the one that requests that women occupy a minimum of 30% of the directive positions in the executive branch, but excluded the positions of the administrative career and the judiciary, which are provided by the system of shortlists of three members or other lists, and elected offices. Finally, it also declared the article that establishes a quota in the candidatures of political parties unenforceable, since this would constitute a case of the State's interference in the internal organization of political parties, explicitly prohibited by the Political Chart.

Extracts:

[…]

It is frequently argued, by those who are contrary to affirmative actions like those consecrated in the regulatory bill under analysis, that an egalitarian system should guarantee that the conditions at the point of departure be equitable. In other words, if the State is to adopt affirmative measures in favor of certain groups to guarantee a real and effective equality of opportunity, these can only be aimed at removing obstacles in the conditions of departure but not in those of arrival.

It could then be stated, with regard to the matter under debate, that if the legislator wishes that women occupy positions in the highest decision-making levels, the important, and in principle the only permitted action, is to design and implement policies intended to stimulate access of women to superior education and remove the obstacles that interfere with this purpose. Once substantial equality is reached at the point of departure, each person's specific merits shall determine the quantitative composition at the point of arrival. Something similar to the Darwinian thesis of the survival of the fittest or the free play of the laws of the market in the economic field, that cannot and should not – from these perspectives – be corrected via artificial measures in order to avoid serious distortions in the field of nature or the sphere of society.

Such argument, irrespective of what may be thought about the ethical and political consequences of Darwinism and of economic liberalism, overlooks an inescapable fact, verifiable through empirical observation and corroborated by the statistics, namely: that the population qualified to perform offices of high political responsibilities is (and has been for a time now) equitably distributed between men and women, and that the scale is even more inclined in favor of the latter.

If in spite of the fact that today there is equality at the point of departure the situation at the point of arrival is still unequal, this is because it is not the merits, or not only the merits, that determine that the highest responsibilities of the State be in their majority in the hands of the men.

Aware of this situation, the members of the Constituent Assembly of 1991 established in the last paragraph of article 40: "The authorities shall guarantee the adequate and effective participation of women at the decision-making levels of the Public Administration," in evident harmony with paragraph 2 of article 13, that by providing that "The State shall promote the conditions for equality to be real and effective and shall adopt measures in favor of discriminated or marginalized groups," does not prejudge on the phase in which such discrimination takes place and consequently, legitimizes and, moreover, makes the action by the public authorities directed at correcting any inequity derived from discriminatory factors expressly prohibited in the same provision, mandatory.

Thus, if what is being sought is to guarantee real and effective equality of opportunity, it is necessary to remove obstacles both at the point of departure and at the point of arrival.

[…]

As already explained, the offices that are intended to be filled through the quota system are offices of free appointment and dismissal. Such jobs are "created in a specific way, according to the catalog of functions of the corresponding organism, to fulfill a directive, managerial, or leading or institutional guidance role, during the exercise of which fundamental policies or guidelines are adopted, or positions which imply the necessary confidence of who is in charge of such kinds of responsibilities."

When providing these positions, unlike those career positions, the nominator has freedom or discretion to designate the person he/she considers most fit. With regard to the President of the Republic, this faculty is expressly recognized in numerals 1 and 13 of article 189 of the Constitution.

Nevertheless, even though discretion of the nominator is implicit in the nature of such offices, it is clear that such discretion is not absolute, since it must necessarily be exercised in conformity with the constitutional and legal provisions. [...]

The same occurs, then, with quotas; although it is true that the provision constitutes a restriction to the sphere of the authority of free appointment and dismissal, this limitation is reasonable and is not of such nature that it may affect its essential nucleus. [...]

The career positions:

[...]

It is clear that to join, remain and be promoted in career positions, the essential criterion of selection is merit [...]

Since merit or the capacity of the applicants is the decisive factor in the selection process, criteria such as race, sex or political affiliation cannot have any incidence.

[...]

The exception contemplated in article 5 of the bill is, therefore, reasonable. The legislator could scarcely request that a percentage of the career positions be reserved to women, since irrespective of the candidates' sex, the one obtaining the best score should be selected.

The offices that are provided through the system of shortlists of three candidates or other lists:

[...]

the Court does not share the criterion of some of the participants, in the sense that women's inclusion in the three-member shortlists and other lists is a "simple salute to the flag." Even though this mechanism is not as efficacious as the quota system, since there is no guarantee that women will be elected, the international experience has shown that a measure such as the one under analysis, if it is accompanied by the serious support and commitment of the authorities, contributes to enhance women's participation in positions of power. In the case of Argentina and Paraguay, even though it should be warned that the legal obligation in those countries refers to the inclusion of women in the lists of candidates to occupy seats in the Senate and the Chamber of Deputies. [...]

[...]

the obligation of the nominator to choose women, until reaching a minimum percentage of representation of 30% [...] unlike the positions of "maximum decision-making level" and of "other decision-making levels," in the more reduced sphere of implementation. While the selection rule of article 4 is applied to a wide universe of offices, and to fulfill it the nominator can choose among multiple women those he considers most qualified, the jobs provided by the system of lists are only a few and necessarily one of the persons conforming the corresponding list must be chosen. Secondly, and here resides the fundamental difference, with the quota established in article 4 of the bill, the promotion of women as a group is sought, without sacrificing specific individual interests. Conversely, according to what is provided in the analyzed separate paragraph of article 6, it is to be expected that certain men, that is, those included in the list, despite being equally qualified to access the respective positions, will be automatically excluded, until such time as women are selected up to a minimum proportion of 30%. [...] it is clear to the Court that even though the analyzed measure pursues a constitutional objective and is adequate, unlike the one consecrated in article 4, it is neither necessary nor proportional *strictu sensu*, since it implies an excessive burden on some of the candidates, individually considered, who for the simple fact of belonging to the male gender are eliminated from the selection process. Such circumstance is undoubtedly discriminatory and therefore, contrary to the principle of equality. But in addition, what would be the sense of requesting that men and women be included in the lists, if the former cannot be taken into account? [...]

[...] Article 14 of the regulatory bill under study contains the following provision: "The Government must establish and promote mechanisms that motivate political parties to increase women's participation in the structure and development of their activities; among others, it shall see that those under its direction stimulate greater affiliation of women, their inclusion in a percentage of at least thirty per cent (30%) in the committees and directive organs of parties and movements. The presence of women in a percentage of no less than thirty percent (30%) in positions in which they have the chance of being elected in the lists of candidates to the different corporations and positions to be filled by popular election."

As correctly pointed out by the Court in ruling C-089 of 1994, "political parties arise as organizations whose mediation between the citizens and the political power contributes to consolidate democracy. They reflect political pluralism and through them, citizens' participation in the formation and expression of the popular will, with the aim of gaining access to power, to positions to be filled by popular elections and of influencing political decisions, is promoted and channeled." Women's participation in parties and especially as members of their directive organs or as candidates to positions to be filled by popular election, aim of article 14 of the bill, is a highly desirable objective in a democratic system in which the participation of all in making decisions which will affect them is sought to be guaranteed.

Nevertheless, such provision must necessarily be declared unenforceable, since ultimately, it constitutes a case of interference by the State in the internal organization of parties, which is prohibited by the Constitution. [...]

2.1.2.1 Matters for Debate

Progress

The holdings of the Colombian and the Peruvian courts evidence the constitutional adoption of the liberal egalitarian ideology that since the 1970s has gradually updated liberal thinking to take into account most of the critiques formulated by

Socialism. The constitutional adoption of material or substantive equality, as developed by the Colombian Court, not only expresses a major theoretical political leap, but also a theoretical-legal progress for the region. The judge, until a few decades ago confined to technicalities, acquires the unprecedented power of evaluating the facts and social reality. He must then resort to meta-legal concepts, since the logical and syllogistic methods are already ineffective. Indeed, to reveal the meaning of the principle of material equality requires evaluation and not simple application. This position is defended by the Colombian court when it affirms that substantial equality has a remedial, compensatory, corrective, and defensive character of persons and groups situated in conditions of inferiority. It is further reinforced by the Peruvian Court when it states that women remain relegated and subjected to a patriarchal cultural philosophy.

Quota Laws

One of the subjects of greater impact from affirmative action is that of quota laws.[14] In effect, toward the second half of the 1990s, the debate on these types of laws placed on the political agenda the political underrepresentation of women. Most of the legislations of the region have incorporated affirmative action[15] with varied results. In Argentina, for example, for the period 2005–2007, the Chamber of Deputies was composed of 35.8% women, a historical record since the enactment of the law. During the same time period, the Senate's percentage was 42.3%.[16] Unlike this successful case, women elected to the Chamber of Deputies in Brazil, for the period 2003–2007, reached only 8.19%.[17]

Quota laws face various types of inconveniences. In addition to the legal and constitutional obstacles shown in the Colombian Court's judgment, there are the practical obstacles derived from the disobedience of the adopted norms as evidenced in the Argentinean case. In the same way, the manner in which the lists are formed, or the election regime in force for the election of congress – be it in small or large districts, in a system of proportional representation of a majority regime, whether votes are for individuals or parties, etc. – deeply affects the results of political quotas. In general, women obtain better results in large proportional electoral systems.[18]

The two cases described above show an important problem: the defense of the degree of freedom granted to political parties in the elaboration of their lists. This

[14] For an in depth study on quota laws in the Andean regions, see Magdalena León, ed., *Nadando contra la corriente. Mujeres y cuotas políticas en los países andinos*, UNIFEM, Bogotá, 2005.

[15] Argentina (1991), Bolivia (1997), Brazil (1997), Mexico (1996), Panama (1997), Peru (1997) and Venezuela (1998).

[16] Jutta Marx, Jutta Borner and Mariana Caminotti, *Las legisladoras. Cupos de género y política en Argentina y Brasil*, Siglo XXI, Buenos Aires, 2007, pp. 85–87.

[17] *Id.*, p. 102.

[18] Mala Htun, "Democracia e inclusión política: la región andina en perspectiva comparada", en Magdalena León, *Nadando contra la corriente. Mujeres y cuotas políticas en los países andinos*, *op.cit.*, p. 55.

defense, which finds explicit support in the Colombian Constitutional Court when it declares that part of the law is unenforceable based on the defense of the autonomy of private associations, has also found an expression, implicitly, in the concrete practices of political parties of the region which, in spite of having quota laws that harbor the formation of egalitarian lists, have sought mechanisms to render them ineffective.

From a sociological perspective, this situation can be examined in the same way the scarce presence of women in political parties of Europe is explained. The deficient relationships between parties and women's movements, besides the characteristics of professionalization of politics and its autonomy in the face of other fields of social life, can help understand the impervious character of politics in the face of significant changes in women's role in the region.[19]

On the other hand, the success of quotas for women can be examined from various points of view. First, from the numerical perspective, starting from the number of women who were elected under the new norm. Second, from the concern for substantive representation of women's interests in the spheres of power. Many women activists, in fact, defended quotas because they considered that a greater female presence would improve the representation of gender matters and would increase the possibilities of carrying out policies directly related to women's interests. However, inclusion does not necessarily imply representation.[20] According to the experience of Latin American countries, there is a consensus that there will be success when the following conditions are met: first, quotas must be mandatory; second, they must specify rules regarding the position in the lists, for example, that women not be in last place; and third, that they be enforceable: political parties must be subject to the possibility of losing their seats in Congress in case of non compliance.[21]

2.1.3 Emancipation

As explained above, radical feminists do not believe in the idea that equality – formal or substantive – professed by liberalism, is suitable to resolve the problem of subordination. More than a fight for equality, it is about fighting against hierarchies. Radical feminism focuses on sexual and labor oppression, on economic dependence, deficient

[19] Catherine Achin y Sandrine Lévêque, *Femmes en politique*, La Découverte, Paris, 2006, p. 77.

[20] This distinction beings with a more complex conceptualization. According to Mala Htun, "This distinction corresponds to the two dimensions of the concept of representation described by Hanna Pitkin in her classical study *The Concept of Representation* (1967). On the one hand, representation can be understood as 'standing for', where presence is most important from a descriptive or symbolic sense. Legislators represent descriptively their constituents when they have similar physical features, share the same experiences, and serve as a symbol that evokes certain attitudes and emotions. On the other hand, representation is to act in favor of, or in Pitkins's terms, 'action for', that supposes that legislators must exercise their function of 'representation that actively promote the interests of the citizens that elected them'." Mala Htun, "Democracia e inclusión política: la región andina en perspectiva comparada," *op.cit.*, p. 33.

[21] Peter Smith, *Democracy in Latin America. Political Change in Comparative Perspective*, Oxford University Press, Oxford, 2005, p. 252.

access to education and all other aspects in which patriarchy is expressed. The major exponent of this perspective is Catharine MacKinnon, for whom:

> Sexuality is to feminism what work is to Marxism: that which is most one's own, yet most taken away. Marxist theory argues that society is fundamentally constructed of the relations people form as they do and make things needed to survive humanly. Work is the social process of shaping and transforming the material and social worlds, creating people as social beings as they create value. It is that activity by which people become who they are. Class is its structure, production its consequence, capital its congealed form, and control its issue.
>
> Implicit in feminist theory is a parallel argument: the molding, direction, and expression of sexuality organizes society into two sexes–women and men-which division underlies the totality of social relations. Sexuality is that social process which creates, organizes, expresses, and directs desire, creating the social beings we know as women and men, as their relations create society. As work is to Marxism, sexuality to feminism is socially constructed yet constructing, universal as activity yet historically specific, jointly comprised of matter and mind. As the organized expropriation of the work of some for the benefit of others defines a class-workers-the organized expropriation of the sexuality of some for the use of others defines the sex, woman. Heterosexuality is its structure, gender and family its congealed forms, sex roles its qualities generalized to social persona, reproduction a consequence, and control its issue.[22]

From the domination theory point of view, advances in the region in terms of overcoming patriarchal features have been expressed mostly in the field of criminal and labor law. Their manifestation in the regional legislation and jurisprudence are dealt with in the chapter "Violence" (Chap. 6). This section points out the advances of the constitutional doctrine in regards to the deregulation of private relationships of domination, an aspect on which female subordination has been based.

Indeed, the separation of the private and public spheres, and the remitting of women to the latter, has been a central issue in the feminist critique of liberalism. The consequences in terms of the lack of protection of the private sphere – the family – have been widely documented in the feminist theory.[23]

An essential problem of liberalism, according to feminism, is the defense of the principle of neutrality that led the State to abstain from intervening in spaces in which domination and violence are habitual. Especially in its radical aspect, feminism emphasizes that the concentration of power in private hands and the violence exercised in the intimate sphere are responsible for the impossibility to achieve a socially more egalitarian world.

State intervention to protect private relationships and the definition of the scope of autonomy in this space are, for this reason, a significant contribution to regional case law. The penal, labor, and civil norms eliminated acts and omissions which expressed gross patriarchal models; the integrity of the female body is today widely protected by law, and the home is no longer viewed as a sacred space, it is now

---

[22] Catharine A. MacKinnon, "Feminism, Marxism, Method, and the State: An Agenda for Theory", *Signs,* Vol. 7, No. 3, Spring, 1982, pp. 515–544.

[23] Martha Alberston Fineman and Roxanne Mykitiuk, eds., *The Public Nature of Private Violence*, Routledge, New York, 1994.

registered as a place in which, with fearful insistence, violence and coercion reign.[24] This aspect in particular is treated in the chapters "Violence" (Chap. 6) and "Family" (Chap. 3), and will not deal with it in detail at this point.

The following presents a judgment of a wider scope that focuses on the subordination of private contractual relationships and makes a pronouncement on the capacity of the liberal state to interfere in order to protect fundamental rights in these types of cases. The plaintiff meets the characteristics of individuals who suffer what has been termed "multiple forms of discrimination,"[25] that is, the characteristics that make her critically vulnerable: gender, race, and poverty.

Constitutional Court of Colombia
Ruling T-1042 of 2001

Main Legal Issue:
Is it an act of discrimination, contrary to the Constitution, to exclude someone from access to a good or service based exclusively on his/her social status? What is the difference between subordination and defenselessness? Is there constitutional protection of rights in private relations?

Facts:
Mrs. Calderón filed a writ of amparo against the general manager of the building in which she worked for infringing upon the fundamental rights to life, equality and free development of the personality. In the building, there was an elevator for the use of employees; these had to abstain from using the elevators exclusively for residents, visitors and tourists. When the employees' elevator malfunctioned, Mrs. Calderón was forced to take the stairs to reach the twenty-second floor apartment of Mr. Garcia Martinez, where she worked as a domestic service employee. The Second Penal Tribunal of the Municipality of Cartagena ordered that the defendant, within 48 hours after the notification of the decision, take the necessary measure so that in the future there is no discriminatory treatment to the plaintiff and she can use the elevator for residents and visitors when the employee elevator is out of service.

Court Ruling:
The Court holds that differentiation based exclusively on the condition of being employees or domestic services workers to prohibit the use of certain elevators of a co-ownership constitutes a discriminatory act based on the social status of a person; the fundamental rights to human dignity and to equality of these employees is infringed on.

---

[24] Nancy Fraser considers the nuclear family as "the site of egocentric, strategic, and instrumental calculation, as well as the site of usually exploitative exchanges of service, labor, cash and sex, not to mention, that is the frequent site of violence and coercion." Quoted in, Seyla Benhabib and Drucilla Cornell, ed. *"Introduction" to Feminism as Critic on the Politics of Gender*, Minneapolis, Minnesota University Press, 1987.

[25] Deborah King, "Multiple Jeopardy, Multiple Consciousness" en *Signs* 14 No. 1, 1998.

Extracts:

[...]

Regarding the difference between subordination and defenselessness, the Court has determined the scope of both institutions. While the relationship of subordinations is viewed as a normative situation, the relationship of defenselessness has factual nature. The Court has held:

> This Court understands that subordination refers to the existence of legal dependence, as occurs, for example, with workers in relation to their bosses, of with students before their teachers or before the directives of the institution to which they belong, whereas defenselessness, even though it refers to a relationship that also implies dependence of a person with respect to another, does not originate in the compulsory nature derived from a determined legal or social system but in situations of a factual nature by virtue of which the person affected in her/his right is defenseless, understood as the lack of the possibility of effective response in the face of a given violation or threat [...]

Fundamental rights between private individuals: the so-called horizontal effects of fundamental rights

[...]

The criterion par excellence that has prevailed in the constitutional doctrine and case law at the time of admitting the constitutional analysis of particular actions regarding their respect for the fundamental rights is the existence of a clear asymmetrical relation of power between private persons, a relation that from the start rules out, limits or eliminates a person's autonomy and justifies state intervention to avoid the debasement, the absolute instrumentalization, or the degradation of human beings. Thus, in the face of contractual, commercial relationships or relationship of an individual's full exercise of autonomy, the Court has held that, in principle, it is not pertinent to grant the constitutional protection of fundamental rights. Instead, in the case of private relationships, in which there are relationships of subordination or defenselessness – as is the case in labor, pension or medical matters, in matters of exercise of computer power, of co-ownership, of trade union sports or transport associations or religious associations, of family violence, or social supremacy – constitutional case law, following the parameters set by the Constitution itself, has intervened, in such situations, to safeguard the effectiveness of fundamental rights.

Inasmuch as, derived from his/her greater power, a private person has for example the capacity of imposing on another a set of rules, of making unilateral decisions which generate some consequences that have a deep impact on the passive recipient of the same, or of qualifying or defining another private individual's situation with the damaging or beneficial implications derived from it, it is not strictly possible to speak of horizontality in relations between private persons. Under these conditions of marked asymmetry of power, such a relationship resembles more those of a vertical type between the citizens and the State than those of the horizontal type that exist, for example, between two tradesmen.

[...]

Equality and non discrimination

[…]

In private relationships, the enforceability of the principle of equality has its limits in autonomy, pluralism and cultural diversity. Thus, the State could not impose respect of the right to equality to an association of persons who explicitly decides to exclude persons of another origin as potential members – society of nationals – or with certain characteristics – political, moral or religious beliefs. Schools exclusively for women, organizations only for members of a religious faith, or residential assemblages only for the elderly, would have as a constitutional basis the right to autonomy and the guarantee of pluralism. Now, what is valid for the relations of private self-determination par excellence, like the exercise of free association, is not valid for situations of subordination or defenselessness. In these situations, what was viewed as a legitimate differentiation within the individual or group preferences is now a potential discrimination or discriminatory act susceptible of constitutional control.

The Court, based on its case law, departs from the following concepts of discrimination and acts of discrimination:

> Discrimination, in its double meaning of act or result, implies a violation of the right to equality. Its constitutional prohibition is directed at impeding that the exercise of rights and freedoms of one or several persons be coerced, restricted or excluded, deny awarding access to a benefit, or a privilege to some, without an objective and reasonable justification.
>
> Discrimination is an arbitrary act aimed at damaging a person or group of persons based mainly on stereotypes and social prejudice, generally alien to the individual's will, such as sex, race, national or family origin, or for irrelevant reasons, such as language, religion or political or philosophical opinion, at making a person the receiver of a detriment or a benefit.
>
> […]
>
> The unequal and unjustified treatment that is usually present in the language of norms or in institutional or social practices, in a generalized way, to the point of being confused with institutionalism itself, or with the way of life of the community, being contrary to the constitutional values of human dignity and equality, constitute a discriminatory act, since it imposes a non legally or morally enforceable burden on a person.

We then have that for a discriminatory act to exist, in addition to an unequal treatment, it is also required that such treatment be unjustified, that is, lacking reasonability and causing a damage, be it because it generates harm, creates a burden, excludes someone from access to a good or service of common or public use, retains or withdraws a benefit. […]

2.1.3.1 Matters for Debate

The debate on the horizontal effects on human rights that the Colombian judgment provokes expresses one of the most relevant aspects of the contemporary State's and law's transformation. What is private? When must the State intervene in this space to make fundamental rights prevail? The Court's answer is twofold: labor relationships are private relationships where subordination reigns, which in turn is a normative matter. Defenselessness, however, has a factual nature. This differentiation, especially the affirmation on the factual nature of defenselessness, promises to endow judges with the tools to assess those situations in which women and sexual and racial minorities are defenseless due to the principle of State neutrality in private relationships still in force.

On the other hand, the case presented evokes one aspect that generates ample controversy in feminism and will be dealt with in Sect. 2.2: the multiple identities of women and the weight that forms of domination, not particularly of a sexual nature, have on their lives. Mrs. Calderon is not only a woman, she is also an indigenous person and a worker. Which is the most problematic dimension of her life circumstances? Her condition as a woman, as a domestic employee or as a member of a racial minority?

2.2 Citizenship as Belonging: Identity and Culture

The feminist movement, in the early twenty-first century, concentrates on the task of elaborating a theory capable of encompassing all women. The differences, no longer between women and men, but among women themselves, are the point of departure for a new group of ideas that react and reject the former feminism, liberal or radical, because they consider it essentialist, that is, because it projects on women and on men certain capacities or attributes that are historically and culturally acquired, and by doing so privileges the viewpoint of white, heterosexual and middle class women. This feminism is reproached for it having assumed the existence of the female experience irrespective of class, race or sexual orientation.[26] Women of traditional feminism, they state, are far from real women. By silencing the differences among women, the feminist movement has also allegedly hidden domination for reasons other than gender and the forms of subordination exerted upon, for example, poor, colored, foreign and lesbian women. Against generalization of experiences – for example, that of sexual subordination, – black feminism[27] states that rape is a much more complex experience for black women than for white women and that its occurrence depends more on color than on gender.

For postmodern feminism,[28] which raises a great part of these critiques, gender is socially constructed through social and political practices. Like the actor performing a role in a play whose script precedes and survives him, the subjects develop a gender role that is independent of their biological sex. The same happens with the rest of identities. Feminism assumes that collective identities are fictions and

---

[26] Peter Digeser, "Performativity Trouble: Postmodern Feminism and Essential Subjects", *Political Research Quarterly*, Vol. 47, No. 3, September, 1994.

[27] *See, e.g.*, Angela P. Harris, "Race and Essentialism in Feminist Legal Theory", *Stanford Law Review*, Vol. 42, 1990.

[28] Judith Butler, *Gender Trouble*, Routledge, New York, 1990.

believes that politicized terms of identity, such as "the women," are necessarily excluding and can only be constructed based on repression of difference.

For these reasons, it is now not about discovering what is the essence of the feminine and its difference with the masculine, but to reveal the way in which the different discourses construct an idea of the feminine and how they turn these differences based on sex into relevant differences and subordination mechanisms.[29] In this sense, the analysis of the law as a discourse that fixes identities, and in this case the feminine identity, is the subject of interest here.

On the other hand, this moment of feminist thinking coincides with the theories on citizenship described above, especially in their multicultural aspect. Multicultural citizenship pretends that the bond between the citizens and their communities not be neutral and that it account for the differences disregarded by the universal concept of citizenship. For its part, the branch of feminism that is akin to it, advocates for an idea of identity which, without falling again into the much criticized essentialism, permits women to identify themselves and constitute the differentiated citizenship.[30]

This section will focus on two subjects. It will approach the law as a discourse which fixes identities and the conflict derived from the confrontation between a universal conception of rights, and the constitutional adoption of cultural recognition.

2.2.1 *Identity*

From the point of view of identity, law, politics and its key categories, such as citizenship, have been denounced for their inability to conceive a subject not determined by gender. For this reason it has been considered crucial to analyze them as processes of production of fixed identities and not as the implementation of norms to already sexed subjects.[31]

In alluding to a characteristic field, from the point of view of penal law, feminism states that the law's action is multiple on identity and on women's role. According to Alessandro Baratta, it operates through the primary criminalization[32] when the acts women perform have a special relevance and cannot be controlled by the private patriarchy. The typical examples are abortion, infanticide and failure to provide child support. It also operates through negative selectivity, creating systems of immunity for men. Immunity operates in two ways: women are victims of a non-penalized violence or a penalized violence with reservations, – the cases of sexual

[29] Chantal Mouffe, "Feminism, Citizenship and Radical Feminist Politics" in, Judith Butler y Joan W. Scout, eds., *Feminist Theorize the Political*, Routledge, New York, 1992.

[30] Iris Marion Young, "Polity and Group Difference: A Critique of the Ideal of Universal Citizenship", *Ethics*, Vol. 99, January, 1980.

[31] Carol Smart, "The Woman of Legal Discourse", *Social Legal Studies*, Vol. 1, No. 1, pp. 29–44, March, 1992.

[32] Alessandro Baratta, "El paradigma del género, de la cuestión criminal a la cuestión humana", en Haydée Birgin, *El derecho en el género y el género* Biblos, Buenos Aires, 2000.

and physical violence, in particular between spouses – or the penalized forms of violence offend objective and abstract values but not concrete legal goods, such as the characterization still in force of crimes against sexual freedom, honor, or family order. Likewise, the law defines women in abstract terms when they are assimilated to minors or elderly persons, or imposes a model of behavior when only "honest women" are beneficiaries of certain prerogatives.

These subjects are dealt with mostly in the chapters on "Violence" (Chap. 6), "Health" (Chap. 4), and "Family" (Chap. 3) of this book. Below are two judgments that manifest the classifying capacity of the law in the definition of identities and roles.

Supreme Court of Justice of El Salvador
Unconstitutionality of article 196 of the Penal Code
September 10 of 1990

Main Legal Issue:
Does sanctioning, with lighter penalties, the rape of a woman prostitute infringe upon the constitutional principle of equality?

Facts:
A woman claimed the unconstitutionality of article 196 of the Penal Code that provides that within the "crimes against modesty and sexual freedom," what has been typified as "prostitute rape" states: "The rape performed against a woman who devotes herself to prostitution, shall be punished with imprisonment of three months to two years." She considers that the article infringes upon the principle of legal equality, the right to honor, personal intimacy and her own image, since the rape committed against a woman who practices prostitution receives a light punishment.

Court Ruling:
The Court rejects the claim and confirms the constitutionality of the challenged norm.

Extracts:
[…]
The fundamental right to honor has two basic aspects, which are: a subjective one, relating to the immanence or sameness that consists in the assessment that each person makes of him/herself or the moral quality that is committed to the fulfillment of duties; another, of an objective nature, which consists in the transcendence or formality composed of the recognition of our dignity made by others, which is reputation or fame that accompanies virtue.

[…]

When drafting the Code currently in force, the drafting commission based its work on article 271 of the bill of the 1967 Venezuelan Penal Code […] Such provision states: "Art. 271. Rape of prostitute. Whoever, through violence or intimidation, has forced a prostitute to have carnal access with him, shall be sentenced to prison for two or thirty months."

[…]

If it is not acceptable that article 196 of the Penal Code affects the principle of equality, much less can it be accepted, as claimed by the pleader, that prostitution constitutes a "profession" [...] Rather, the activity is considered a criminal offence in certain penal legislations, constituting the so called crimes related to prostitution.

[...]

In some legislations, according to the type of rape, a requirement for the passive subject has been added: that it be an honest woman, which adds a special connotation in order to consider that the crime has been committed [...] In effect, article 120 of the Argentinean Penal Code establishes: "A sentence of imprisonment of three to six years shall be imposed, when the victim is an honest woman over the age of twelve years and under the age of fifteen and not comprised in the circumstances of paragraphs 2 and 3 of the previous article."

[...] Here, the term "honesty," as expressed by Soler, is taken in a sense of sexual morality.

The criminal figure as described in Art. 196 of the Penal Code can, therefore, be considered a type of attenuated rape, taking into account the passive subject who does not fulfill the conditions of sexual morality required for the type of proper rape. Even though women who practice prostitution are not left without protection, their condition is taken into account to diminish the gravity of the criminal offense.

On the other hand, concerning the recipient of the prohibition contained in the noted provision, the active subject, no difference is made that could affect the principle of equality, since the noted valuation refers exclusively to the passive subject, on account of the activity dedicated to, which is a promiscuous sexual conduct and for a price.

[...]

Constitutional Court of Colombia
Ruling C-989 of 2006

Main Legal Issue:

Is the right to equality of a handicapped person infringed upon by a norm that privileges the dependence of a working mother over that of a working father?

Facts:

A claim is filed against the constitutionality of the expression "mother" included in a norm which creates the integral social security system and contains provisions on special and exempted pension regimes. The norm says: "[...] the working mother whose son suffers a physical or mental handicap, so qualified duly accredited and until such time remains in that condition and continues to depend on the mother, shall have the right to receive the special seniority pension at any age, provided she has entered the general pension system at least for the number of weeks required by the regime of medium premiums to access the seniority pension."

Court Ruling:

The Court holds the constitutionality of the article, with the understanding that the pension benefits provided for in the same article are extended to the father head of household of handicapped children who depend on him economically.

Extracts:

[…]

The measures that were […] adopted […] by the authorities based on the special constitutional support of which mothers heads of household are holders may also be extended to men who are in the situation, "but not because there is an alleged discrimination based on sex between both genders, but because the purpose sought by it is to make the principle of protection of children effective, in those cases in which these are under the 'exclusive' care of their father," in such a way that, if this protection is not extended to the father, certain rights of the children could be certainly be affected.

[…]

In other words, the affirmative actions established by the legislator in favor of mothers has its rationale in the special protection consistent with the constitutional mandate provided for in articles 44 and 47 of the Political Constitution, that advocates for the child's superior interest and the social rehabilitation and integration in the case of the physically, sensory or psychically handicapped, under any circumstance; it is for this reason that it cannot only protect the mother but this benefit should be extended to the father who demonstrates to be in the same factual situation.

[…]

In such a way that, by recognizing the pension benefit established in the challenged legal provision exclusively to mothers heads of household, there is a violation to the right to equality of the handicapped son who depends economically on his father head of household, for the simple fact of being the man and not the woman the one who responds economically for his maintenance, without taking into account the special condition of handicap he suffers, which is ultimately the cause for seeking his protection, so that not only he does not lack economic resources that would allow his adequate rehabilitation to social life, if this were possible, but also disregarding the fact that the father can take care of the handicapped son, providing him the necessary care and attention, without such circumstance being limited only to those cases in which the mother of the family has died.

[…] the Court shall declare the conditioned enforceability of the challenged term "mother," in the understanding that the pension benefit provided for in such article will be extended to the father head of household of handicapped children who depend on him economically, and it will be so noted in the operative part of this decision.

F. A. D. Protective Custody Moderation of its Own Authority Court of Penal Rights N° 8 Judicial Department of Lomas de Zamora, Argentina 2010

Main Legal Issue:

Does the norm that establishes house arrest only for mothers and not for fathers of children under the age of 5 infringe upon children's rights?

Facts:
A man accused of the crime of illegal possession of drugs for sale, requests the benefit of house arrest to take care of two minor sons under the age of 5 after the death of his concubine. However, the Code of Criminal Procedure reserves this benefit specifically for women with children under the age of 5, excluding any other type of family bonds and relationships.

Court Ruling:
The judge recognizes that the measure is reserved for mothers of children under the age of five. However, he states that the exercise of the shared paternal authority is attributed both to the father and to the mother, for which reason, given the family situation of the defendant after the death of his children's mother, and taking into account the fact that the defendant is the only one who is entitled to exercise paternal authority, he decides to grant the benefit to the father.

Extracts:
[…] Several works and reports of international organisms of human rights have published on the impact the incarceration of a mother has on her children and alert on the importance of considering such effects in legal processes: "when the children of incarcerated mothers and fathers are neither taken into account nor are children mentioned in the different stages of the criminal law process – from the arrest, going through the trial, and imprisonment […] the rights, needs and the boys or girls' best interest are being at best ignored, if not actively damaged…."

In the same sense, it has been also said that "States must seriously meditate on the cost implied in increasing the use of penalties of deprivation of freedom of women for non violent crimes, taking into account the very serious consequences that imprisonment of women have on the family and the importance of a good family relationship as a key factor in prevention of crime." For this reason, they must consider alternative sentences, with no deprivation of freedom, for offenders of non violent crimes. […] on the other hand, and before this time, the Civil Code established that: "The paternal authority is the assemblage of duties and rights which correspond to the parents regarding the persons and goods of their children, for their protection and integral formation" and "The minor children are under the authority and care of their parents. These have the obligation and the right to raise their children, feed them and educate them in a way consistent with their condition and wealth…" (article 265 C.C.).

Along these lines, it is clear that one of the most transcendent gender conquests of the 20th century has been the full exercise of shared paternal authority, since its exercise is attributed both to the father and to the mother in a joint way. […] However […] making special reference to the circumstances under which the defendant's family is found, as recorded in the present file, the characteristics of the death of the children's mother and concubine of the defendant and since the minors on account of their age have no independence regarding housing, labor and/or family, the limit specifically set to award an alternative and/or moderating measure "to the woman with children under the age of five" is directly opposed to the exercise of paternal authority […] to the Convention on the Rights of the Child and to the National Constitution itself, since the defendant […] is the only one entitled to exercise this right and duty regarding his two minor children.

2.2.1.1 Matters for Debate

Not only does the law establish identities, it also allocates roles. It seals the differences between sexes through language; the exceptions it contemplates for one of the two sexes or the different standards for the assessment of conducts are frequent examples of this. The first case reminds us that conceptualization of aggressions that affect the integrity and the autonomous exercise of sexuality of persons, such as crimes against honesty, were a constant theme in the region until the 1990s. The relationship between these acts and "sexual honesty" showed the protection of the penal system for those who were the owners, tutors of, or persons responsible for the women, consistent with a system enlarged by legal incapacities that excluded women's sexual autonomy and promoted their sexual modesty. Along these same lines, these norms incorporated the allocation of traditional roles and the separation between those who deserved State protection and those who did not. Privileges for "honest women," and aggravating circumstances for kidnapping of married women, among others, are eloquent examples of the law's capacity to define identities and generalize subjectivities.

The second and third cases, question the allocation of roles made by the legislators. For the legislators, the idea of care was exclusive of women, thus defining and reproducing identities. The suggestion is to break this classification and then incorporate men, but it does so taking into account the *de facto* situation: only those who perform the same role of care shall benefit. With this, it fulfills a prioritized conceptual function: the socially acquired separation of identity roles.

2.2.2 Culture

In November 2006, Pakistan adopted a law whereby women who were raped and who had the possibility of accompanying their claim with the testimony of five men could be acquitted from the crime of adultery after having suffered a rape. In Mexico, a claim lodged before the State Commission of Human Rights in 2004 narrates a brutal punishment on an indigenous woman of the *Otomí* community accused by members of her community of adultery. In Colombia, the Emberá-indigenous community imposed a sanction on a 14 year-old girl, consisting of keeping her left foot in a stock – an instrument made of two pieces of wood to restrain prisoners – for having maintained a romantic relationship with a policeman who did not belong to the community, and a series of claims opened the public debate on clitoris mutilation practiced on women of the same community.

These and many other similar narrations reveal the constitutional conflict of principles that the courts have had to deal with for the last two decades. A large part of multicultural societies, those in which multiple cultures cohabit and interact,[33] have recognized multicultural rights, especially the rights of self-government. However, this recognition has been questioned by those who, from the universal perspective of citizenship, and women's equality and dignity, consider certain cultural practices unacceptable.[34] In its strong version, multiculturalism[35] establishes that cultural groups must be guaranteed a series of rights that allow them to govern themselves in a broad manner according to their customs and beliefs. In its weak version, this broader view finds precise limits in the rights of the members considered individually. This is the argument that guides the critiques of some feminists.[36]

The judgments presented here describe the way in which the courts of Salta, Argentina and Pueblo Rico, Colombia dealt with the universal idea of rights and respect for cultural diversity.

Trial Court 2
Tartagal, Salta Argentina
December 15, 2006

Main Legal Issue:
What are the limits to legal autonomy of indigenous communities when their practices, constitutionally protected, violate fundamental rights?

Facts:
José Fabián Ruiz, a member of a Wichi community of Tartagal in the northern part of Salta, Argentina, is accused of having sexually abused a nine year old girl, the daughter of his concubine, belonging to the same ethnic group. As a result of that relationship the girl was impregnated and, at the moment of the girl's delivery, her mother reported the rape. The accused justified his action as being an ancestral custom in his community according to which a man living with a woman of the same ethnicity may have relations with her daughter, as well, if she is not his own offspring.

The case first came to the attention of the Judge of Targal Trial Court No. 2 who ordered the arrest of Ruiz for "aggravated sexual assault." Days after the accusation, the accuser and various members of the Wichi community requested that Ruiz be released, alleging that his conduct conformed to the norms of his cultural customs. The defense appealed the court's decision before Division III of Arraignment Court, who denied the petition and confirmed the decision to proceed against the accused.

---

[33] Amy Gutman, "The Challenge of Multiculturalism in Political Ethics", *Philosophy and Publics Affairs*, Vol. 22, No. 3, Summer, 1993.

[34] Susan Moller Okin, "Is Multiculturalism Bad for Women?" in, Joshua Cohen y Howard Matthew, *Is Multiculturalism Bad for Women*?, Princeton University Press, Princeton, 1999.

[35] *See* Ayelet Shachar, "On Citizenship and Multicultural Vulnerability", *Political Theory,* Vol. 28, No. 1, February, 2000.

[36] To explore an opposition to these arguments see, Letti Volpp, "Feminism versus Multiculturalism", *Columbia Law Review*, Vol. 101, No. 5, June, 2001.

The defense appealed this later decision before the Salta Court of Justice and this tribunal, by a three to one majority, decided to declare the legal actions taken as nullified and ordered that the accused be released.

Arguments by the Court are based on the fact that cultural autonomy of indigenous peoples is protected by the Constitution of the Argentine Nation. After this last decision described above, the Judge of Tartagal Formal Trial Court No. 2, in the decision that is transcribed here, resolved to proceed once more against Ruiz for the same crime. The defense appealed this decision twice more but on both occasions the proceedings in the superior court confirmed the judgment that is transcribed here.

Court Ruling:
Although the right to cultural identity is a form of human rights, it is indisputable that no practice, even if it should be based on ancestral customs or religious beliefs of a determined culture, can be acceptable if it places a person's dignity at risk. There exists no contradiction between recognizing the rights of minority groups to their cultural identity and criminalizing the conduct of a person, who is a member of that culture, against the physical, mental, and moral integrity of another person, most particularly if that person is under special protection, such as in the case of young girls and boys.

The judge based his decision on three principal arguments: First, he established that the consent and lack of physical violence do not prove the argument that the accused should be exonerated, because when dealing with a minor it is impossible to speak of consent freely given. In regard to the absence of physical aggression, the judge affirms that violence can be present in different forms and, in this case, it is evident that the minor reacted with reverential fear to the intimidating power of the authority who is charged with her custody, safekeeping, and education.

Second, the judge resolved the conflict between the indigenous community's autonomy and the right of the minor's physical, mental, and moral integrity, giving more weight to the greater interest of the child as was consecrated by the International Convention on the Rights of the Child, and negating the character of the right to community practices that place at risk the physical, psychological, emotional, and sexual integrity of any of its members.

Third, the judge affirms that Argentine indigenous communities are integrated into the majority culture, and for that reason cannot cite as proof of their argument that they are ignorant of the illicitness of their behavior.

Extracts:
[...]
And from all of this it becomes evident that when the action committed by the accused is analyzed, it falls within the category of a criminal offense, as long as the sexual abuse with carnal knowledge committed upon the minor is duly proven. [...]

It is for this reason that we declare that the accused, Fabian Ruiz, is the perpetrator who is materially responsible for the illicit action, and with the classification that is given, that he had knowledge that the minor was the daughter of his concubine,

Teodora Teherina, allows us to infer that there existed a disregard of consequences. That is to say, the primordial element to which the subjective legal entity is resigned, in other words the wanting dominated by the will of the objective legal entity, or in simpler terms, the will to act in reference to the result produced by the intentional action of imposing carnal knowledge on the victim, and being authorized to perform this action showed disregard. In dealing with the subjective aspects, the result is clear: that they cannot be seized or immediately grasped by the Judge, but instead, that they can and should be derived by means of conduct carried out by the active subject that forms part of the attribution.

The absence of vestiges of the physical violence turns out to be irrelevant, as well, because the rape also consists of moral violence, and, important to say, is performed with a degree of intimidation that is sufficient, and in this regard, in the matter of rape, the question that relates to force used and the victim's resistance is purely circumstantial. And in fact, depends on the assessment by the judicial system in light of the causes of the circumstances under which the menace might present itself: by means of words, power to intimidate, seduction, or, as in the case of the subject in question, that reverential fear and the authority that the accused had or has over the victim upon finding himself living with the mother of that minor in the same home and who had in his charge the custody, safety, and education of that same minor. For this reason, we declare that the absence of genital lesions do not rule out rape, nor does it rule out absence of violence, which is irrelevant, because of the fact that violence as we might express it may have been consummated using moral violence or sufficient intimidation.

We should also explain that the existence of consent on the victim's part can be associated with different consequences according to the different hypotheses contemplated in the criminal statutes. In this way, in cases where the victim should be younger than thirteen years old, as we are analyzing in these actions, sexual abuse always occurs whether or not the victim has given her consent. In effect, carnal knowledge of minors, whose age, even though it might be imprecise but was somewhere between nine and eleven years, in a manner that was repeated until pregnancy resulted, a method that supposedly was consented to by virtue of matrimonial relations that are accepted in certain indigenous communities, results in absolute violation of a person's physical, mental, and moral integrity and the dignity of the human being as described in article 5.11 of the Pact of San Jose, Costa Rica.

And these standards (in the pact) should not fail to be applied to the minor, Tejerina, because of the fact that both the victim and the victimizer belong to the Wichi ethnic group, because the Guarantees of Human Rights should be applied in all of the National and Provincial States in an egalitarian way to those who live there. This is stated not only in the National and Provincial Magna Carta in its Article 16, but also as it is based on the Law that considers that said consent in cases where it exists (as it has tried to be demonstrated here) is ineffective due to the lack of maturity that the victim would need in order to discern the significance and scope of the action. By virtue of the Law, whether or not the victim has given her consent, the conduct shall be contrary to the statute because what is being protected in this case is the victim's naivety, innocence, and her ineptitude, because she lacks the mental maturity required to understand the nature of the action; and therefore the subscriber duly accuses the perpetrator Jose Ruiz of the crime of Sexual Abuse with Carnal Knowledge with prejudice to the minor, Estela Tejerina.

Additionally, if it is shown by means of the medical reports concerning the victim that there had been no aggression or that there is no evidence of aggression against the minor, simply because this matter deals with a cultural concept belonging to that community, it does not imply that we should set aside the concept of Personal (physical, mental, and moral) Integrity of which Sexual Integrity is only one of the components.

Personal (physical, mental, and moral) Integrity also includes the right not to have to consent to agreements that are considered to be degrading, satisfying those standards, and includes the right to reject medical and biological objectives as a minimum concept of the most basic Human Rights. […]

We should not forget that the greater interest of the child is recognized in the International Convention on the Rights of the Child which refers to the problem about the relation of the child to culture and human rights, and that the interest of the child goes beyond any cultural standard that infringes on the minimum and elemental Rights of a minor, as it is established in its Preamble, in Article 8, point 1; Article 12, point 1; Article 15, point 2; Article 16, point 1; and cc. of the aforementioned Convention, which has constitutional roots in our Country in its Article 75 paragraph 22 with the Constitutional Reform of 1994. […]

As a separate matter it is sufficient to analyze the permanent or ongoing objections that are mentioned in this type of action by members of aboriginal communities, in which the objective is to include as acceptable certain illicit conduct for reasons that the aborigines have their own, diverse culture. The members reason that constitutional norms are rendered vulnerable by not respecting the prevailing norms and customs of the Wichi people, of which the accused is a member, insisting that the issue deals with a matrimonial union carried out with agreement of the parties and within the approved customs of his community and immersed in the usual social system of the Wichi people.

To that argument we should reply that any judicial analysis should take into consideration that the conduct carried out by the subject which is classified as a criminal offense does not hold up to the defense that maintains that it is a cultural practice of the Wichi community, of which the inchoate is a member. But the facts in this case before you very clearly reveal a tremendous cultural density and they create a particular line of thought, given that they entail the necessity of analyzing the tension that exists between the two viewpoints regarding indigenous communities or their members.

To think along this line requires a certain perspective: that without disregarding their fundamental rights, we should first consider the manner in which the terms have been established in various National Supreme Court decisions. In these decisions the Supreme Court expresses that the terms that are established in International treaties and particularly those dealing with Human Rights never involve the annulment of the principles, rights, and guarantees recognized in the dogmatic portions of the Magna Carta. And the guarantees in those should blend and reconcile with the doctrine of the Superior Tribunal according to which the interpretation of Constitutional norms should be carried out in a manner that is compatible with the requirements of a coherent union.

From this point of view, one cannot claim that there is inapplicability of National Criminal Law in regard to the indiscriminate exercise of rights derived from the condition of being indigenous and the fact of cultural identity, unless a status of absolute Constitutional Law were to confer upon those rights, a status which they do not possess.

And one can claim inapplicability even less when, as a consequence, a decision of this sort would entail the denial of other individual rights whose essence arises from the comprehensive interpretation of the norms that make up the constitutional framework that is applicable to this case.

It is worth mentioning [...] that the anthropology expert (that carried out) an analysis of the "privignatico" marriage, that is, a marriage in which a man marries the daughter of his wife's prior matrimony (in which the husband has relations with his wife and her daughter by a prior marriage), starts off from the possibility of a multiple or polygamous marriage in these societies. In fact, this kind of union is relatively common and, in every case, corresponds to rules of social organization that may be considered normal in this zone and in many parts of the world. [...]

[...]

Analyzing, here, the previously referred to anthropological studies that also are included in this case before you, it is emphasized, during the hearing of same, that the purpose of respecting the cultural identity of a group of human beings when it is expressed in behavior that is supported by their moral and social values, with their own procedures and, primarily when there is consensus with their own communities, is laudable; nevertheless, the sexual relation between an adult and a nine or eleven year old girl consummated in a Wichi community cannot be registered as a legal exemption that must be respected as belonging to another culture. [...]

We must ask ourselves, then, which is our real conviction in regards to the universality of those human rights that are established by international conventions, incorporated in our Constitution, and which should or should not be protected, because it is indisputable that the right to cultural identity is included as a component of human rights, and it is also indisputable that any practice founded on ancestral customs or religious beliefs that threatens a person's dignity cannot be considered to be a right. This was expressly affirmed by the 179 nations, among them Argentina, who signed the Beijing Declaration and Platform for Action in 1995 that was later ratified in New York in 2005.

The right of a community to a bilingual education forms a part of the right to a different cultural identity. It is not part of that right to violate the physical, psychological, emotional, and sexual integrity of one of its members, much less that of one of its minors. Thus, there is no contradiction between acknowledging the right to a different cultural identity and applying due punishment to one who, while being a member of that different culture, threatens the integrity and fundamental human right of another person. And this is particularly so if that person is in need of special protection, such as in the case of children, both girls and boys. Strangely, while the argument about cultural diversity has never been a valid argument when it comes to guaranteeing the other rights, the necessity of respecting "ancestral practices" or the "right to the habitual" is put forward when dealing with actions that harm the sexual integrity of girls.

To support the idea that a people's cultural identity should be respected does not imply a justification of the practices that are at odds with human rights, "equal and inalienable rights of all members of the human family," as is affirmed in the Universal Declaration of Human Rights of 1948. Within the notion of human dignity over centuries the culture of man's human rights has survived. Within the notion of human dignity over centuries there has survived the culture of man's human rights that teaches that aberrant practices (such as sexual abuse is) should be eradicated, regardless of how rooted they are in a particular culture. To protect human dignity the State is obligated to guarantee the rights of all people. It is truly inconceivable that "abuse with violence" "when there is no consent" of the victim should be distinguished from "abuse with violence" when, as is cited as a means of proof in this case, there was "consent" on the part of the child.

It must be added that there are two clarifications: by definition all abuse is violent; a sexual relationship between an adult and a child is – as stated in the Criminal Code – abuse, and when the perpetrator is related by family. It is "aggravated abuse by a related party." It involves an exercise of power by the stronger against the weaker, which is not always expressed as explicit violence. This is the case of the Wichi girl, of which it was said that there was no physical violence because it was a matter of "ancestral customs," in other words, these were habits that were accepted by the community. And in this manner, in those cases in which the victims are younger than 13, there is always sexual abuse involved, whether or not the victim may have give her consent. The reason for this, as we have stated on several opportunities in cases that are equal to this one, that the law consider that said consent in cases where it exists (as it has tried to be demonstrated here) is ineffective due to the fact that the victim lacked the maturity she would need in order to discern the significance and scope of the action.

By virtue of whether of not consent on the part of the victim exists, the behavior shall always be as described by law. Consent presupposes conscience, freedom, and understanding of the consequences of an action. It turns out to be attractive to some to allege that there was "lack of understanding" or "ignorance" on the part of the accused or say that he "is not conscious that his action is prohibited or illicit." We all know that in spite of the social and economic exclusion to which the aboriginal communities have historically been submitted, there has been effective integration in the majority of the directions of everyday life. In no other way could one explain that the aboriginal communities denounce any violation of their own human rights (an idea developed by western society in the 20th century), that they demand their rights of citizenship (a matter of contemporary debate), their right to ownership of the land, of running water, of decent living conditions, etc.

Colombia
Juzgado Promiscuo Municipal
Pueblo Rico, Risaralda
July 24, 2008

Main Legal Issue:

What are the limits to the autonomy of indigenous peoples? How can a change to their customs be promoted?

Facts:

The Emberá-Chamí community practices female genital mutilation. This consists of cutting and cauterizing the clitorises of newborn girls. This practice is customary for this community and appears to have two rationales: first, to prevent infidelity among adolescent girls and women, and to prevent, its practitioners believe, the clitoris from developing into a male organ for copulation if it is not removed promptly.

On January 10, 2008 the Civil and Criminal Judge of Pueblo Rico, Risaralda received a complaint of abuse of 16-day-old infants who had undergone genital ablation and were experiencing fever and vomiting from an acute infection. The petition sought the application of family violence laws to the case. Physicians and anthropologists became involved in the case and provided information about the origin and meaning of the custom and the health risks it presents.

Colombia is a multicultural society. The 1991 Constitution recognizes the autonomy of the nation's indigenous communities. Nevertheless, there is a broad consensus in the nation that any cultural practice that violates any of the four minimum fundamental rights (the right to life, right to physical integrity, right not to be enslaved and right to due process) must be changed, while respecting the indigenous communities' autonomy and providing support from the state institutions that are involved in these affairs.

Court Ruling:

The judge approaches the legal problem from three standpoints. First, he considers the conflict of rights in Colombia while acknowledging the autonomy of the indigenous peoples; second, he considers the problem of the absence of responsibility as an impediment to criminalizing a practice that is part of a culturally accepted custom; and third, he evaluates the results of the measures the State has taken to change this type of practice. Regarding the first point, the judge referred to the Colombian Constitutional Court's broad jurisprudence, which has clearly established the limits of the indigenous communities' autonomy but has indicated that changes to their customs must be brought about by consensus and with respect for their autonomy. With regard to the second point, the judge studies the way in which the practice would coordinate with the penal system of laws and concludes that, given the absence of individual responsibility, it is not possible to approach the practice within the frameworks of the penal procedure code or family violence laws. Detailed analysis of these aspects and a review of the extensive and varied body of reports provided by anthropologists and physicians lead the judge to conclude: first, that the custom of female genital mutilation clearly oversteps the limits of indigenous communities' autonomy and, therefore, it cannot be practiced.; second, that the practice cannot be criminalized because those who perform it do so without malicious intent; third, that although indigenous authorities have committed to eliminating the practice, they are not honoring these commitments and the measures to change the practice that the State has attempted to implement have not been effective thus far. Finally, he concludes that it is vital for the Colombian State to take clear and definitive measures to prohibit this practice.

Although Colombian criminal and family violence laws cannot be applied to cases of female genital mutilation that occur within indigenous communities, this does not mean that the only possible alternative is to rely on intercultural educational measures aimed at changing the custom. These are slow and inadequate. The State must adopt urgent measures to prohibit this practice, which violates the lives and personal integrity of girls and constitutes a violation of the national constitution and international humanitarian law.

Extracts:

[…]

3.1. The Autonomy of Indigenous Races Enshrined in the National Constitution.
In approaching the subject and arriving at the conclusion of the present verdict, we shall review article 246 of the Political Constitution and the Constitutional Court's pronouncements regarding said legislation. One of the legal problems that arises is what action the Colombian authorities should take with regard to a practice that is traditional within the EMBERÁ-CHAMÍ indigenous community in the Risaralda department, an action that was presented to this judicial office and initially considered an act of intra-family violence, and whether intervening in this practice for the purpose of eliminating it is a viable option given the ethnic autonomy recognized in the constitution.

Article 246 of the Political constitution states:

"The authorities of the indigenous peoples may exercise their jurisdictional functions within their territorial jurisdiction in accordance with their own laws and procedures, provided these are not contrary to the Constitution and the laws of the Republic. The law will establish the forms of coordination of this special jurisdiction with the national judicial system." […]

"The constitutional jurisprudence has established that there are four elements of indigenous jurisdiction: i) the possibility that the indigenous communities have their own legal authorities; ii) the power of these authorities to establish their own rules and procedures; iii) respect for the Constitution and the Law alongside the principle of maximum autonomy; and iv) the legislator's authority to specify the method by which indigenous jurisdiction is coordinated with the national legal system."

[…] 3.2. The Principle of Maximum Indigenous Autonomy and the Reiteration of this Principle in Different Contexts.
The body of past judicial arbitrations has also established that the principle that governs the exercise of indigenous jurisdiction is the principle of maximizing indigenous autonomy and minimizing restrictions on such autonomy, based on

the principle of respect for ethno-cultural diversity. In spite of this view, the jurisprudence has established certain limits on this jurisdiction [...]

[...] 3.3. Fundamental Constitutional Rights Constitute the Minimum Obligatory Principles of Coexistence for All Individuals.
Despite the fact that all citizens, including members of indigenous communities, are bound by the laws and the Constitution (Articles 4, 6, and 95 of the Political Constitution), it should be noted that the axiological system contained in the bill of right and responsibilities, particularly as it pertains to fundamental rights, constitutes an important limit on the principle of ethnic and cultural diversity and on the values held by the different indigenous communities inhabiting the nation, communities that, I mention as an aside, were represented at the National Constitutional Convention.

3.4. The Imperative Legal Norms (Pertaining To Public Order) of the Colombian Republic Take Precedence Over the Usages and Customs of Indigenous Communities Whenever These Norms Directly Protect a Constitutional Value that is Superior to the Principle of Ethnic and Cultural Diversity.
The interpretation of the law as a limit placed on the recognition of usages and customs is not that the legal norms simply cancel out these usages and customs. The regulatory nature of the Constitution makes it necessary to weigh the relative importance of various values protected by the constitution – diversity, pluralism – against those protected by the mandatory provisions of the law. There are intangible conditions of pluralism and ethnic and cultural diversity of indigenous communities that cannot be subject to legislation, as this would endanger their preservation and undermine their cultural wealth, which relies precisely on maintaining their cultural uniqueness. The special jurisdiction (Article 246 Political Constitution) and functions of self-government entrusted to the indigenous councils (Article 330 of the Constitution) must be exercised, therefore, in accordance with their usages and customs, but while respecting the pertinent mandatory laws that protect superior constitutional values.

3.5. An Indigenous Community's Usages And Customs Take Precedence Over Dispositive Provisions of the Law.
This rule is consistent with the principles of pluralism and diversity and does not imply to acceptance of customs *contra legem*, because it refers to dispositive provisions. The nature of civil laws, for example, grants a wide margin of autonomy regarding individual will, which, mutatis mutandis, serves as a basis for the precedence of certain usages and customs over norms that should only be applied in the absence of self-regulation by the indigenous communities.

The earlier position has been altered by Court jurisprudence. Indeed, verdict T-349 of 1996 established that, in the interest of maximizing indigenous autonomy, the limits on indigenous jurisdictional faculties are limited to an intangible core of rights, i.e., the right to life, the prohibition of slavery, the prohibition of torture, a minimum amount of respect for due process of law according to the respective indigenous community's world view, in penal matters, the legality of crimes and punishments. To prevent a situation from arising wherein any mandatory law could be invoked as a restriction on indigenous jurisdictional faculties, it was stated:

> The principle of maximization of autonomy becomes paramount in this regard, because it pertains to purely internal relationships, regulation of which is vital for the preservation of cultural identity and group cohesion. Limits on the ways in which internal control is exercised should, therefore, be the minimum acceptable ones, and should apply only to what is truly intolerable and constitutes a violation of the most sacred human rights.

[…]

Limits to indigenous jurisdictional faculties are confined to the core of intangible rights identified by the constitutional jurisprudence; these are: the right to life, the prohibition of slavery and torture, a minimum level of respect for the proceedings themselves in the context of the respective indigenous community's world view and, with regard to criminal matters, legality of the crimes and punishments. These limits, which are minimal as seen in evolution of the jurisprudence, are justified because they are "necessary to protect superior hierarchical interests and they are the least restrictive limits imaginable under the constitution."

[…]

4. Observed Legal Problems.

There are several legal problems related to this topic that must be resolved.

4.1. Does the FGM/A practiced by the Emberá-Chamí indigenous community in the department of Risaralda represent a danger to the lives and personal integrity of that community's women and girls, and can the practice therefore be considered intra-family violence?

4.2. Does FGM/A violate one or more of the four minimum fundamental rights established by the constitutional jurisprudence by limiting the indigenous autonomy recognized by article 246 of the Constitution?

4.3. If in fact this practice is found to violate the rights of indigenous women and girls, to constitute intra-family violence, and to violate the above-mentioned minimum fundamental rights, how should Colombian authorities address the problem?

[…]

The document provided by doctor Agustin Conde, a surgeon at the Universidad del Valle, specialist in gynecology-obstetrics and epidemiology and member of the International Federation of Obstetricians and Gynecologists – IFOG – clearly states that the practice of FGM/A carries risks of physical complications and intense pain, shock, hemorrhage, tetanus, septicemia, urine retention, ulceration of the genital region and lesions adjacent to the genital tissue. It also carries a high risk of future maternal morbidity, recurrent kidney and urinary tract infections, cysts, infertility and contributes to higher neonatal death rates in infants whose mothers have been subjected to the practice.

The extracts above allow us to state without a doubt that FGM/A is in fact a harmful practice that endangers, both in the present and in the future, the lives and personal integrity of women and girls in the Emberá-Chamí indigenous community in the department of Risaralda. Therefore, the practice could be said to constitute intra-family violence, given that it has also been established that this practice is carried out within families (refer to the information contained in the epidemiological files showing that the girls were taken to the hospital by their mothers).

[…]

4.2. Inapplicability to FGM/A of The Rules Regarding Protection From Intrafamily Violence And of the Penal Procedure.
Given that the practice of FGM/A is an existing custom of the Emberá-Chamí indigenous community in the department of Risaralda, and that it originated during the conquest and colonization, it cannot be seen as just an act performed by individual mothers and midwives in this community. Therefore, its treatment must not be governed by the regulations contained in Law 294 of 1996, the basis for article 42 of the Political Constitution and rules created to prevent, remedy and sanction intra-family violence. Nor is Colombian Criminal Legislation applicable, because it pertains to malicious or blameworthy behaviors that occur within the individual's environment and which are not present in these cases.

Article 33 of the Penal procedure code, paragraph 1, states:

"Article 33. Unimputability. A person who, while performing the customary and illegal action, is not capable of understanding its illegality or cannot be determined to possess such understanding due to psychological immaturity, a mental disorder, socio-cultural diversity or similar conditions, is unimputable."

This Article, among others that deal with security measures applicable to the individual who is declared unimputable for socio-cultural reasons, was contested before the Constitutional Court and court decision C-370-02 (…) declared it feasible under two conditions: i): that the unimputability does not derive from incapacity but rather from holding a different world view, and ii): that in cases of insurmountable errors whose prohibition stems from such cultural diversity, the person should be absolved and not declared unimputable, according to the stipulations of that court decision.

"The constitutionalization of a blameworthy criminal law gives rise to the following question: What should be done about behaviors that are as serious as crimes in that they affect essential legal rights and are traditional and are contrary to law, but are performed by persons who, due to certain conditions, could not act with guilt? This situation poses difficult questions for constitutional governments founded on the principle of human dignity, given that such persons cannot legitimately be criminally sanctioned for their conduct because they have not acted with guilt. But at the same time, society must take measures to prevent these behaviors that, although not performed with guilt, deeply affect essential legal rights, in that not only are they customary and are contrary to law but that, in addition, it is possible that the person could perform them again, in many cases, for the same reasons due to which he lacks the capacity to act with guilt."

"…In these events, the Penal Procedure Code does not establish punishments since doing so would violate the basic principle of a penal code based on guilt, but rather it provides for safety measures, whose purpose is not to sanction but to protect, heal, educate, and rehabilitate. And that is why the punitive statute does not demand that the responsible party's behavior be imputable, since this person lacks the capacity to act in a guilty manner."

"...And in a society based on law, founded on the principles of human dignity and on personal liberty and autonomy (P.P.C. Articles 1, 5, and 16) it is disproportionate for the legislator to choose the method that is most invasive of personal liberty, as would be criminal law, when other tools exist to protect the same legal rights and are les harmful to these principles. The criminal law system is a social legal system and so it is also limited by the principle of necessity, preferably being used as a last resort. Therefore, these unnecessary sanctions are found to be unconstitutional."

"...In such circumstances, to prevent persons whose world view differs from that of the majority from affecting fundamental rights considered important under national law, the state can, instead of imposing the majority's values through penalization, avail itself of other tools, such as intercultural dialogue, that allow for progressive respect and understanding between the different cultures that make up the Colombian nation (P.P.C. art. 70). In this case the criminal procedure itself, which eventually leads to declaration of innocence based on a culturally conditioned error or a declaration of unimputability, can lose its purely punitive connotation and become a privileged space for intercultural dialogue."

The same considerations can be applied to the law 294 of 1996, of which Articles 22, 23 and 24 describe conduct that is harmful to family harmony and unity and the respective sanctions to impose, whose applicability to Colombia's population is divided, given that paragraph 2, article 4 of law 294 states that in cases of intra-family violence in indigenous communities, the person with jurisdictional faculties to hear these cases is the respective indigenous authority, based on special jurisdiction provided by the Constitution in article 246.

Therefore it is not appropriate, as we have stated, to consider the practice of FGM/A as something that can be rectified or sanctioned under either of the two state legal systems, and so we must conclude that this practice constitutes neither criminal conduct nor intra-family violence. Rather, as we have explained, it is a practice that violates human rights and it must be handled in a different manner.

Now then, it is one thing for the penal code and law that protects against acts of intra-family violence not to be applicable to mothers and midwives because of the circumstance that have already been explained, and it is another thing to deduce, therefore, that the state authorities should confront FGM/A as described in the I.C.B.F. [Colombian Institute for Family Well-Being] information. The Interior, Justice, and Public Defense Ministries agree to "intercultural educational procedures to change the practice." As we shall discuss below, these are insufficient, ineffective, and slow in preventing risks to the lives and personal integrity of the girls of the Emberá-Chamí indigenous community as the practice continues. These agencies argue that ethnic autonomy must be respected; however, this constitutional value is inferior to the constitutional right to life and to other rights that outweigh the right to cultural diversity.

4.2.1. Limits on the Recognition of Indigenous Autonomy.
Having analyzed article 246 of the Political Constitution and the above-mentioned Constitutional Court verdicts that establish its scope and applicability, one can easily conclude, as in the previous point, that the practice of FGM/A exceeds the limits placed on indigenous jurisdictional function and on the autonomy of ethnic communities, since those limits include public security standards that protect more important constitutional values than that of ethnic and cultural diversity (Verdict 254 of 1994 M.P: Eduardo Cifuentes Muñoz).

The Court also indicated in that court decision that the greater the preservation of usages and customs, the more a community's autonomy should be recognized, which brings us to a subject related to the level of "contact" of the Emberá-Chamí indigenous community with the rest of Colombian society and specifically with the region's other inhabitants.

[...] We have before us a community that has shared with the descendants of Africans and those of Antioquians and Caucans, the territory that makes up the Risaralda department for more than 400 years in an intense cultural exchange, which was practically eliminated by the nearly complete Catholic religious indoctrination of the past 50 years. Therefore, this is a society that has had profound "contact" with our own, and although it has preserved its cultural identity and many of its usages and customs, it is incomprehensible that it has preserved such a barbaric usage or custom as FGM/A, which might be "justifiable or faintly admissible" in a society with a lesser degree of intercultural "contact or reconciliation" with the modern world, as can be said of some of the world's African or Middle Eastern societies.

[...]

The indigenous leaders did not allege at any time that the practice of FGM/A was a respectable or justifiable usage or custom in their community; on the contrary, they acknowledged that it was inadvisable, which begs the question whether this is in fact a practice that should be tolerated or permitted, or allowed to undergo a long-range transformation and not immediate prohibition.

The indigenous leaders appeared more worried about intervention in their own affairs and demanded that they themselves and the indigenous community be the ones who would resolve the matter. [...]

Given the fact that the indigenous leaders themselves tend, based on their "world view," not to defend the practice de la FGM/A as part of their cultural identify, it should be concluded that the practice is not one of the usages and customs that should be allowed by the Court when it states that greater preservation of usages y customs permits greater autonomy.

Now then, if, as we were concluding, the practice constitutes a failure to recognize one or several of the four above-mentioned minimum rights, we have a situation in which neither indigenous authorities nor the Emberá-Chamí community itself can rule on the matter alone, because as inhabitants of the Colombian Republic they must adhere to the Constitution and allow public order provisions that protect constitutional values superior to the principle of autonomy (which FGM/A fails to recognize) to supersede their other constitutional right to ethnic and cultural diversity.

[...]

Because the practice of FGM/A, as we have said, endangers the lives and personal integrity of indigenous girls and therefore constitutes a failure to recognize fundamental constitutional rights that take precedence over the constitutional right to ethnic diversity, consideration of the indigenous community's autonomy is not appropriate with regard to the topic. The practice of ablation violates human beings' most sacred rights, which consist of the right to life and other constitutional rights in coordination with those rights that are recognized by international treaties. [...]

4.3. Colombian State Authorities' Attitude, Including that of the Indigenous Authorities, Toward FGM/A

[...] It is clear that for the indigenous authorities and for representatives of the agencies entrusted with the protection of children's rights in Colombia (as they have explained to the Court) this agreement satisfies the expectations regarding women's and children's rights contemplated in the National Constitution and in International Treaties. This may not be true, given that the procedures established therein were not followed in the case of Marina Bateza, age 17, who was seen on December 7, 2007 and Angelica and Sorany Niaza Mejia both age 16, who were seen on December 14, 2007 at San Rafael de Pueblo Rico Hospital, Risaralda, more than a month after the agreement was signed (see the epidemiological reports on pages 3, 4 and 5). This failed to set off the procedures stipulated in the agreement, since on April 1, 2008, the date on which judges met with indigenous authorities in Pereira, Risaralda, which has been referred to elsewhere in this declaration, neither the indigenous authorities, nor the I.C.B.F., nor even the Public Advocacy Department, were aware of the case; they became aware of it only when the court notified them of these proceedings.

Based on the above, we can assert that the agreement provides no guarantee that the lives and physical integrity of the girls of the Emberá-Chamí community, in Risaralda, will be protected. Therefore, it is vital that we conclude that the Colombian state agencies that are parties to the agreement, including the indigenous authorities, are not adequately meeting their constitutional obligations to defend the lives, honor, and rights of those inhabiting the nation's territory.

And it bears repeating that while the intercultural education procedures aimed at transforming the practice are being initiated, many girls continue to suffer horrifying consequences and risk losing their lives as a result of this barbaric practice, which constitutes a violation of human rights.

The undersigned judicial operator finds it inconceivable that with regard to a practice considered by the agencies and persons linked to these proceedings as contrary to human rights, and following our conclusion, in this case, that the constitutional right to indigenous autonomy is outweighed by the constitutional rights to life and personal integrity, these agencies can attempt only to transform the practice when they should be agreeing to its immediate and urgent elimination. This is the only acceptable course of action in light of the international agreements on human rights.

A related topic is that once the practice has been completely prohibited, the indigenous authorities or the Colombian state does not resort in applying criminal sanctions against mothers or midwives within the community who fail to comply with the prohibition, due to what was explained earlier regarding the absence of individual criminal responsibility and because this matter involves a cultural usage or custom. At such a time when the practice is prohibited, only then it will be valid to address noncompliance with the prohibition by using educational procedures, intercultural dialogue and other procedures that, with great wisdom and competence, have been put forward by anthropologists, sociologists and social workers, whose studies are used to formulate policies aimed not at transforming the practice but at offering a socio-cultural perspective for working with those who fail to comply with the prohibition.

2.2.2.1 Matters for Debate

Feminism shares with multiculturalism certain essential features such as the critique of liberal individualism and the denouncement of the indifference of which women and the ethno-cultural minorities are the object on the part of a white and patriarchal hegemony. However, these cases illustrate the risks that multiculturalism may represent to women's rights, especially regarding the frequent conflicts between the commitments of gender equality and respect for the customs and practices of the ethno-cultural minority groups. The conflicts that arise from multiculturalism, from the constitutional and penal point of view, are very significant and are clearly laid out in the judgment and in the dissenting opinion of the Argentine case.

The Argentine ruling highlights the most relevant aspects of this discussion: the protection of the customs – sexual relationships with minors – based on the principle of autonomy of indigenous peoples, and the conflict generated by this protection in the face of international treaties signed and ratified by the Argentinean State. Likewise, as an argument to consider, it includes the immersion of the member of the minority culture in the majority society and, assessing the degree of this immersion, to be able to determine his responsibility for the violation or the ignorance of the norms that governs it. This subject makes reference to the possibility that this existence in two cultures offers him, to prioritize which shall govern his axiological referents.

The universal perspective of women's constitutional rights of their right to equality and dignity as expressed in the *United Nations Resolution on Harmful Traditional Practices Affecting the Health of Women and the Girl Child*,[37] the *Resolution on the Elimination of Crimes Against Women and Girls Committed in the Name of Honor*,[38] the *Plan of Action for the Elimination of Harmful Traditional Practices Affecting the Health of Women and Children of the Commission on Human Rights*,[39] or the

---

[37] Resolution 2005/28, http://www.un.org/womenwatch/daw/vaw/v-hrc.htm

[38] http://www.wunrn.com/reference/pdf/Crimes_of_Honor%20_resolution_english.pdf

[39] http://www.unhchr.ch/Huridocda/Huridoca.nsf/0811fcbd0b9f6bd58025667300306dea/d93233b755c3f6678025672b0050b116

Report of the Special Rapporteur on Violence Against Women, its Causes and Consequences, *Intersections Between Culture and Violence Against Women*[40] among others, demonstrates the existence of a consensus regarding the fact that harmful practices have become a recognized issue concerning the status and human rights of women and the girl child. The debate surrounding harmful practices has been intense since its inception in the framework of the United Nations in the 1950s.[41] Aspects such as the sovereignty of or the respect for cultural rights prevented the issue from being fully enforced in the human rights agenda until the mid-1970s. The adoption by the UN General Assembly of the Convention for the Elimination of All Forms of Discrimination Against Women (CEDAW) is considered a pivotal moment in the generation of consensus regarding the necessary elimination of harmful practices.

In order to clearly illustrate the behaviors that are part of the harmful practices, General Recommendation No. 19 of the CEDAW enumerated traditional practices by which women are regarded as subordinate to men or as having stereotyped roles that perpetuate widespread practices involving violence or coercion: family violence and abuse, forced marriage, dowry deaths, acid attacks and female circumcision.[42]

---

[40] http://www.unhcr.org/refworld/docid/461e2c602.html

[41] Harmful Traditional Practices Affecting the Health of Women and Children, UN Fact Sheet. http://www.unhchr.ch/html/menu6/2/fs23.htm

[42] CEDAW, General Recommendation No. 19, *see* http://www.un.org/womenwatch/daw/cedaw/recommendations/recomm.htm#recom19

Chapter 3
Family

The Nuclear Family as an Ideal

Isabel Cristina Jaramillo

The close relationship of family with the dominant discourses on sexuality, reproduction, production and violence has placed it in the center of multiple feminist debates. The object of criticism of twentieth century feminists has been the concept, dominant since the nineteenth century, of the nuclear family as a "natural order" that articulates a "natural" sexuality – the heterosexual and monogamous sexuality; a "natural" reproduction – the heterosexual reproduction and the mother in charge of upbringing –; a "natural" production – outside the home and in charge of the men; and a "natural" discipline – that of men over women and children and of women over children.

The family as a category of analysis may, in fact, include, and has included, groupings of different types; consequently, to state that it made its appearance in the nineteenth century may make no sense in many argumentative contexts. However, the ideas on family and practices that are dominant today do find their roots in particular debates begun in the nineteenth century, and which are still applicable.[1]

The ideal nuclear family, consolidated in the nineteenth century, emphasized four ideas. First, it emphasized that family should be the main place for the display of affection and the satisfaction of these types of needs. This implied, on the one hand, reinforcing the affective elements of matrimony, and on the other, centering affection as an ingredient of the relationship between parents and children.[2]

[1] *See* Lawrence Stone, *The Family, Sex, and Marriage in England, 1500–1850*, Harper, New York, 1979; Jacques Donzelot, *The Policing of Families*, Pantheon Books, New York, 1979; Philippe Ariès, *Centuries of Childhood*, Vintage Books, New York, 1962; Edward Shorter, *The Making of the Modern Family*, Basic Books, New York, 1977.

[2] *See* Edward Shorter, *The Making of the Modern Family*, *op.cit.*

I.C. Jaramillo (✉)
Associate Professor, Director of Research and Doctoral Studies, Facultad de Derecho, Universidad de los Andes, Bogotá
Correspondence: Cra. 1 Este No. 18ª 70, RGC 309, Bogotá, Colombia
e-mail: ijaramil@uniandes.edu.co

C. Motta and M. Sáez (eds.), *Gender and Sexuality in Latin America - Cases and Decisions*, Ius Gentium: Comparative Perspectives on Law and Justice 24,
DOI 10.1007/978-94-007-6199-5_3, © Springer Science+Business Media Dordrecht 2013

Secondly, it emphasized that women should assume the functions of housekeeping and raising children, given their special capabilities for doing so.[3] This role was reinforced in various ways: by highlighting the importance of breast feeding in children's nutrition and the creation of the affective bond between mother and child[4]; by stressing women's sensitivity and therefore, their unique ability to bestow on children the love needed for their development; and finally, by highlighting women's domestic skills and the intimate link between such skill and an appropriate development of children.

Thirdly, it emphasized that men should be in charge of both the economic and political production; they had to be the main actors in the workplace and in State affairs. This role was also justified on the basis of the presence of certain special qualities found in men.

Lastly and intimately related to all of the above, the family had to belong to the private space and consequently, its members had to solve their differences without state intervention.

3.1 Feminist Criticism of the Nuclear Family

Feminists have exposed and questioned the way in which the law has contributed to producing and sustaining the family as "natural order" from different viewpoints. It is useful to highlighting the viewpoints sustained by liberal feminists, cultural feminists, radical feminists, socialist feminists and critical feminists.

Liberal feminism states that regulation of the family restricts freedom, that it is discriminatory, and that this is detrimental to women. For this reason they have campaigned for both liberalization of divorce and formal equality in family law, between spouses, and between families established within the institution of matrimony or outside of such institution.[5]

Cultural feminism, for its part, questions the hierarchy in which family has been placed, as opposed to that of labor market and the State. Just as is the case with liberal feminism, it identifies inequality in the treatment of women, yet it does not allow for leveling the sexes using existing parameters, favoring instead the recognition of altruism, which lies at the root of the manner in which women build the family.[6] For cultural feminists, introducing the concept of women's "different

---

[3] *See* Susan Moller Okin, "Women and the Making of the Sentimental Family" in 11 *Philosophical and Public Affairs 1* (1982) and Ann Douglas, *The Feminization of American Culture*, Alfred A. Knopf, New York, 1977.

[4] *See* Edward Shorter, *op.cit.* and Jacques Donzelot, *op.cit.*

[5] *See Mujer, sexualidad y ley*, Divulgamos, Bogotá, 1988; Ligia Echeverri de Ferrufino, *La familia de hecho en Colombia*, Tercer Mundo, Bogotá, 1984; Marcela Huaita-Alegre, "Desigualdades de género en las consecuencias económico-financieras del divorcio", in Alda Facio y Lorena Fries, eds., *Género y derecho,* Ediciones LOM, Santiago, 1999, pp. 487–539; Marcela Huaita-Alegre, "Derechos de custodia, neutralidad de género, derechos humanos de la mujer e interés superior del niño o niña", in A. Facio y L. Fries, eds., *Género y derecho, op.cit.*, pp. 541–611.

[6] *See* Carol Gilligan, *In a Different Voice*, Harvard University Press, Cambridge, 1982.

voice" in the juridical language has been crucial, both in terms of considering this difference at the time of making decisions in concrete cases and of giving equal consideration to maternity as a life option.[7]

However, despite the fact that liberal feminism and cultural feminism have struggled to introduce reforms in the persistent concept of family, and the way in which the law influences its existence, neither of them has contested the idea of family as the best alternative for the organization of sexuality, reproduction, productivity, and violence. The lack of confrontation has been at the core of radical and socialist feminists' demands.

Radical feminists view the family as the mechanism that materializes the impositions of monogamy and heterosexuality, upon which the expropriation of women's sexuality[8] is based. They allege that the idea of family as a space of privacy, reinforced by law, has served to justify rape and to maintain women terrorized through violence or threat of violence by husbands and family members.[9] For some radical feminists, the law must change and move to intensify regulation of the male privilege to sexual access and to violence as ways of control. They propose, for example, to reverse the burden of proof between the parties and increase penalties in rape and domestic violence[10] cases. On the contrary, other radicals consider that male privileges should be rebutted though counter-cultural practices, such as "free love", *sorority* or solidarity among women, as well as physical training in order to be prepared to face possible aggressors.[11]

Socialist feminists, in turn, raise the idea that an effect on the traditional structure of family has been the expropriation of women's work, in the sense that they have been confined to the tasks aimed at ensuring subsistence of the family group, for which they receive no compensation.[12] They point out that this type of expropriation is the product of the capitalist system, which to a large extent is based on it, and that its main consequence is that the family, instead of being the privileged place of affection and altruism, has become contaminated by considerations of economic survival.[13] Among the bourgeois, they stress, economic considerations determine the marriage options and decisions on investment of time and money in the couple's children. Conversely, among proletarians, there is a problem in determining how to meet the affection demands in the midst of pressing economic obligations.[14]

---

[7] *See* Robin West, *The Difference in Women's Hedonic Lives: A Phenomenological Critique of Feminist Legal Theory*, 3 Wis. Women's L. J. 81 (1987); Carrie Menkel-Meadow, *Portia in a different voice: Speculations on a Woman's Lawyering Process*,1 Berkeley Women's L. J. 39 (1985).

[8] *See* Catherine MacKinnon, *Toward a Feminist Theory of the State*, Harvard University Press, Cambridge, 1991.

[9] *See* Mary Joe Frug, "A Postmodern Feminist Legal Manifiesto (An Unfinished Draft)", *105 Harv. L. Rev.* 1045, 1992.

[10] See chapter *Violence* in this book. See also, Duncan Kennedy, "Sexual Abuse, Sexy Dressing and the Eroticization of Domination" in *Sexy Dressing, etc.*, Harvard University Press, Cambridge, 1993.

[11] *See* Alice Echols, *Daring to Be Bad*, University of Minnesota Press, Minneapolis, 1989.

[12] Frederick Engels, *The Origin of the Family, Private Property and the State*, 1884.

[13] *See* Eli Zaretsky, *Capitalism, the Family and Personal Life,* Harper & Row, New York , 1976.

[14] August Bebel, *Women and Socialism.* Socialist Literature Co., New York, 1910.

Socialists support highly diverse strategies. For some, the solution to the problems mentioned above consists in making the bourgeois family model available to proletarians, which could be achieved through significant social services for workers' families. Others see it as necessary to socialize labors that are considered to be exclusively those of women, and in the domestic space. In this regard they have proposed the creation of community kitchens and day care centers, as well as of care centers for elderly and handicapped persons, among other projects.

The critical feminists, lastly, have expanded on a description of how the family ideology works, and of the relationship that develops between family and law, so as to reveal the limits of the debate, as it is happening today.

Instead of assuming that the ideas that serve to center the nuclear family are univocal, the critical feminists show that the family ideology is dominant, precisely due to its ambiguities and contradictions. In this sense, they point out that, just like "the family" has been defended because of its role in the satisfaction of needs for affection, it has also been criticized as being the zone in which the most destructive passions emerge. They add that while it has been posited that the State should not intervene in the family because the latter is private and its dynamics are resistant to legislative modeling, the State's intervention has been requested to protect the nuclear family from certain trends favoring its destruction. Though the State and the market have been glorified as spaces of personal satisfaction and development of the human being, the selfishness and aggressiveness that they imply have been rejected.[15]

Critical feminists assert that to assume that the family ideology is coherent and precise, strengthens the normative effect[16] of such ideology,[17] and is an impediment to imagining alternative ways of social organization.[18]

This chapter is divided into three topics, each of which corresponds to a way of understanding the incidence of family in women's oppression. Each topic will be presented according to the viewpoint of outlined theories and will then be discussed on the basis of questions arising from the other theories.

Equality within the family and inclusion of diverse families (1) discusses the recognition of rights of concubines, homosexual couples, and equality of women's rights in family law. Equality-based consideration of maternity as a life option (2) examines legislation in force in Latin America concerning child custody and valuing of domestic work. Finally, under male privileges within the family (3) the treatment of domestic and sexual violence within the context of family law is

[15] Frances Olsen, *The Family and the State: A Study on Ideology and Legal Reform*, 96 Harv. L. Rev. 1491 (1983).

[16] Janet Halley, "Recognition, Rights, Regulation, Normalization: Rhetorics of Justification in the Same-Sex Marriage debate" *in* Legal Recognition of Same-Sex Partnerships: A Survey of National European and International Law (Robert Wintemute and Mads Andenaes eds.), Hart Publishers, Oxford, 2001.

[17] Kerry Queen, *Mommy Dearest: The Focus on the Family in Legal Feminism*, 37 Harv. C. R.-C. L. L. Rev. 447 (2002).

[18] Frances Olsen, "The Family and the State: A Study on Ideology and Legal Reform", *op.cit.*

discussed. No subject specifically related with socialist feminism or critical feminism is included, but they provide foundation for many of the critiques included in the three other feminist viewpoints in the matters to be debated in each problem.

3.2 Equality of Rights Within the Family

Assuming that the law must recognize all human beings as equal, considering their equal endowment liberal feminists criticize the legislation that treats women unequally, and elaborate a narrative of progress in which women gradually obtain more equality as this unequal treatment is eliminated.[19]

In the case of Latin America, and particularly with regard to family, liberal feminists point out how the abolition of the marital power and of the marital privileges have paved the way toward women's equality. They claim, however, that the permanence of legal regulations that treat women in families differently is evidence that equality has not yet been realized.

Nineteenth century Latin American civil codes posit two institutions of colonial law: marital power and marital privilege. Marital power, or coverture, was the collection of powers the husband acquired, by virtue of marriage, over the person and the property of his wife. It included the power to decide on the post-marital residence, the exclusive faculty to discipline the children, to hold property in usufruct and to control women's sexuality.

The possibility of filing for divorce in case the wife did not follow the husband to a new place of residence, and of obtaining custody of the children as a consequence of the woman's breach of her duties as a mother and a spouse, made the first power effective. Some authors even admitted that the husband could resort to the police to make his wife return to the marital home.[20] The power to discipline the children translated into the possibility of requesting police intervention and into the father's ceasing to provide support in case of disobedience on the part of the children. Control over the wife's sexuality was insured by the capacity of the husband to persecute and kill the adulterous woman and in that of his taking possession of the wife's property in case of infidelity. On the other hand, the husband had the right to administer the entirety of the wife's and the community property, and to represent her judicially and extra judicially. The wife could only be authorized by her husband, or by a judge, to carry out certain transactions.[21]

---

[19] *See* Martha Minow, "Forming underneath everything that grows: toward a history of family law" in, *Wisconsin Law Review 819–894* (1985).

[20] For criticism of the this theory see Julien Bonnecase, *La Philosophie du Code Napoleon appliquée au Droit de Famille*, Paris, 1925, p. 18.

[21] *See* for a discussion on the martial authority, Sobre la potestad marital ver, por ejemplo, Eduardo Gutiérrez Piñeres, Curso De Derecho Civil Colombiano, op.cit., and Luis Claro y Solar, Explicaciones De Derecho Civil Chileno Y Comparado Imprenta Cervantes, Santiago de Chile, 1898, Vol. 1.

The marital privilege was generated by excluding those partners that did not comply with the required ritual actions, whether they be religious or secular, from the personal and property benefits of marriage, and as a result, their children were not considered to exist as such – with the exception of natural children, that is, children of parents who were single at the time of their conception, who could be voluntarily recognized by their parents. As a consequence of this, re-marrying when the first marriage had failed proved difficult.[22]

When marital power was eliminated in all Latin American countries, it was replaced by principles, later enshrined in law that women, just as men, are capable of representing themselves judicially and extra-judicially and that women have equal disciplinary powers over the their children.[23] Marital privileges, for their part, have decreased over the years: it is already accepted that co-habitation may have economic effects; it is possible for children born out of wedlock to obtain paternal recognition; children begotten and born within and outside of marriage have equal rights, and divorce regulations have become more flexible.

Liberal feminists interpret these changes as an achievement along the road to equality. Yet their arguments are still valid inasmuch as juridical systems still include regulations that entail the unequal treatment of women.

The arguments of liberal feminists on formal equality – or equality before the law – have been criticized both for their assumptions and for their consequences. That they ignore, according to their critics, the material and cultural conditions under which legal regulations function, taking for granted that objectivity or neutrality are achievable, instead of favoring "flesh and blood women," is damaging to their point. Three types of facts support this critique of liberal feminism: (1) since the nineteenth century, in spite of abolishing regulations which stated that wives were obligated to obey their husbands, rates of violence against women in "private" spaces have not decreased; (2) access of women to property has not improved significantly, in spite of the fact that they are no longer subject to marital power/coverture; and (3) the weakening of the marital privilege has not resulted in greater protection for children or the elderly, nor has it reduced women's vulnerability.

In the face of criticism, liberal feminism has reacted in two ways. With the aim of achieving equality of results and not simply of opportunities, some liberal feminists have incorporated the idea of disadvantageous or vulnerable groups to account for the material and cultural differences of women and to defend the distributive measures which accord them unequal treatment. Other liberal feminists have readily accepted the idea that results, once formal equality is realized, will be derived from women's options.[24]

---

[22] *See* Eduardo Gutiérrez Piñeres, *Curso de derecho civil colombiano, op.cit.*, and Luis Claro y Solar, *Explicaciones de derecho civil chileno y comparado, op.cit.*

[23] *See* Marcela Huaita-Alegre, "Desigualdades de género en las consecuencias económico-financieras del divorcio", en *Género y derecho, op.cit.*, y Magdalena León y Eugenia Rodríguez Sáenz, eds., *¿Ruptura de la inequidad? Propiedad y género en la América Latina del siglo XIX*, Siglo del Hombre Editores, Bogotá, 2005.

[24] *See* Catherine MacKinnon, *Not by Law Alone, in* FEMINISM UNMODIFIED, Harvard University Press, Cambridge, 1987; On Exceptionality, id.

Measures defended by liberal interventionists in family matters include special protection of maternity, special subsidies for women who are heads of household, child support regimes that compensate women's labor exclusion, and marriage property regimes in which the concept of community property prevails.

In spite of the fact that the defense of these measures is based on their temporal quality – they were conceived for implementation "while the field was made even" – they have been criticized for turning women into victims and vulnerable individuals, to the detriment of their own possibilities of emancipation,[25] and because their implementation implies dependence of women on the whim of bureaucratic agents.[26] They have also been criticized for introducing a contradictory characterization: as autonomous objects, on the one hand, and as vulnerable subjects, on the other. This is detrimental to women, as a standard opposite to that which is applicable as invoked upon them in each concrete case.[27]

This chapter includes two problems that illustrate both the potential and the gaps and contradictions in the arguments of liberal feminists: the balance between morality and equality, and discrimination of men when distributive measures of unequal treatment to women are adopted.

3.2.1 First Problem: Moral Imperatives as Limits to Equality

Jurisprudence of the Constitutional Court of Colombia shows how obvious the argument of equality of rights of men and women can be. In numerous rulings, the Court has established that the articles of the Civil Code of the nineteenth century that had not been reformed, and that provided unequal treatment to men and women, infringe on the equality clause contained in the Constitution.

However, rulings are still produced in which the argument of formal equality does not prevail. One of the features shared by these rulings is that the reason on which they are based, the pressing need to maintain the difference, is of a moral nature.

The distinction between law and morality is one which, unlike other political theories, is accepted by liberalism. In general, liberals claim that there are legal regulations governing behavior which, although legitimate and assumed as true regulations, are not juridical and therefore have no legally binding force: compliance with them cannot be guaranteed by an organized force. This recognition of morality, however, functions in conjunction with the imperative of reducing morality, as a basis of law, to the minimum possible level; the reason for this is the differences that exist between individuals regarding moral norms that are correct.

---

[25] *See* Wendy Brown, "Rights and Loses", in *States of Injury: Power and Freedom in Late Modernity*, Princeton University Press, 1995.

[26] *See* Nancy Fraser, *Justice Interruptus. Critical Reflections on the "Postsocialist" Condition,* Routledge, New York, 1997.

[27] Catherine MacKinnon, "Sex Equality: On Difference and Dominance" in, *Towards a Feminist Theory of the State*, Harvard University Press, Cambridge, 1989.

There is no solution to be found within liberalism for the matter of moral minimums. However, with an ongoing debate and multiple available answers, liberal feminists have posited that the problem may not be how much the morality minimum is, but the different morality standards that prevail according to sex and that are justified by arguments on gender, and the greater importance attributed to morality when dealing with sexuality and family.[28]

In the cases included in this section, claims for equality from women and non married couples have been rejected on the basis of the principle of good faith, the primacy of the heterosexual family and the prohibition of incest. Additionally, in some cases, children's rights have been invoked as a limit to the equality that was being claimed. The way in which the courts have constructed the juridical problem involved in the following case implies weighing equality and morality, since beyond the pertinent juridical norms, moral precepts have been invoked, and their normative value has not been questioned and for which no justification has been sought.

Supreme Court of Justice of the Argentine Republic
D. de P. V., A. v. O., C.
November 1, 1999

Main Legal Issue:

When the mother is prohibited from challenge the marital presumption of paternity of her son, is the right to equality under the Argentine Constitution and in the Convention on the Elimination of All Forms of Discrimination against Women infringed upon?

Facts:

Mrs. D. de P. V. filed before the judge an action challenging the marital presumption of paternity of her son. She was denied the appeal on the basis of lack of active legal standing of the mother in the procedure. She filed an extraordinary appeal requesting that the constitutionality of article 259 of the Civil Code, on which the judge's denial had been based, be reviewed.

Court Ruling:

Article 259 of the Civil Code, which attributes to the husband rather than the wife the right to challenge paternity, is not based on a privilege of males, but rather provides the husband with a legal method to destroy a legal presumption. Such a presumption does not function with regard to women, because their maternity becomes established by the proof of birth and the newborn's identity.

Extracts:

[...]

Not all different juridical treatments are indeed discriminatory as not every distinction of treatment can be considered offensive to human dignity. There are certain *de facto* inequalities that may be translated into justified inequalities of juridical treatment expressing a balanced relationship between objective differences and the

[28] *See A Vindication of the Rights of Woman with Strictures on Moral and Political Subjects*. Joseph Johnson, London, 1792.; John Stuart Mill, *On the Subjection of Women*, 1869.

aims of the norm (Inter-American Court of Human Rights, Advisory Opinion OC-4/84 of January 19, 1984).

[...]

The State has a reasonable margin of appreciation of the distinctions which, within the mentioned parameters, it may legitimately formulate based on common good. Along this line of thought, fatherhood and motherhood are not absolutely equal, and consequently, the legislator may contemplate reasonable differences. Article 259 of the Civil Code, which attributes to the husband and not to the wife the right to challenge paternity, is not based on a male privilege but rather provides to the husband the legal way to destroy a legal presumption – which does not fall, for obvious reasons, on women, since their maternity is established by the proof of birth and the identity of the newborn (article 242 of the Civil Code) – so that the subject on whom the presumption operates may have the possibility of showing that he is not the father of the wife's child, who was not born in compliance with the provisions of the law, thus exempting himself from the obligations of a paternity which is not his.

[...]

That the presumption of legitimate paternity, which is one of the fundamental pillars on which the right of filiation is founded, does not have as its basis the presumption of innocence enjoyed by the woman in her capacity as a married woman with regard to adultery, but the institutional value of the legitimate family and the positive aspect of providing immediate location to children born during marriage.

[...]

The expansion of the scope of legal standing to bring charges in the procedure challenging paternity which now also applies to the child, enshrined in the amended version of Law 23264, emerges from this tension between the imperative of ensuring access to knowledge of the biological link and that of maintaining tranquility and certainty in the family bonds, according to the consideration of the Nation's Legislative Power.

[...]

That a different composition of values in tension may eventually be enshrined by the Nation's Legislative Power while exercising its own jurisdictional authority, as has occurred, for example, in the legal systems currently in force in other countries that do not extend to the mother the capacity to initiate the legal action of challenging paternity—which would be absurd in the light of what has been stated in the precedent whereas clause 14—but rather, entitle her to a different legal action, provided certain requirements are met (art. 318 of the French code in force). In the light of *lege lata*, it is pertinent to conclude that article 259 of the Civil Code is consistent with the judgment of constitutional compatibility, since it does not transgress the fundamental rights invoked by the appellant, but captures a possible regulation of the values in tension, in accordance with the rights and guarantees of constitutional hierarchy.

[...]

That, on the other hand, according to the legislation currently in force in the Republic, denial of the mother's legal standing to file charges suit challenging paternity does not cause definitive effects on the challenged filiation, since such action remains open to the main party involved, who is precisely, in this case, the minor. Therefore, and in consideration of what has been said by the Public Defender and the Attorney General, the ruling of pages 292/294 is confirmed.

Supreme Court of Colombia
Martha Silvia Neira Torres v. Rigoberto Neira Reyes
December 19, 2005

Main Legal Issue:
Is the right to equality infringed upon when the bonds of parenthood between two related persons prevents them from getting married, and therefore the existence of community property is denied?

Facts:
MSN and RN co-habited for over two years. In the procedure aimed at claiming the declaration of the property society between permanent partners, the defendant presented proofs to demonstrate that he was the father of the plaintiff.

Court Ruling:
The Court considers that if there is a kinship relationship which the legal system considers incestuous, there exists no marriage union or community property between them.

Extracts:
[…]
It is a known fact that the reviewed Law 54 of 1990 dealt with regulating *de facto* marital unions and with establishing the property regime between partners arising from it; thus, in its first article, it defines *de facto* marital union, conceiving it as the cohabitation established by a heterosexual couple with characteristics of permanence and singularity, without the existence of a marriage bond between them.

[…]

the summarized legal disposition prescribes that a community property between two permanent partners is presumed to exist when two factual hypotheses are verified: the first – which in the opinion of the Court establishes a general rule – when between a man and a woman **with no legal impediments to marry**, there exists a *de facto* marital union for a term of at least two years; the second is aimed, in spite of its ambiguity, at establishing an exception to such rule, consisting in the assumption that notwithstanding the existence of the impediment concretely referred to herein, that is, the previous existence of a conjugal bond linking one or both partners with third persons, there is no reason for not presuming the existence of the mentioned community property, since such a community property would indeed exist if the previous marital society or societies had been dissolved at least a year in advance of the date in which the *de facto* marital union was initiated.

[…]

The Colombian legal system, in addition to prohibiting marriage between persons who are on the same line of ancestors, of descendents, or who are siblings (article 140 numeral 9 of the Civil Code), penalizes all carnal access or any sexual or carnal act with an ancestor, descendant, adopting or adopted person, or with a brother or sister, since such conducts have been considered punishable because they threaten the existence, conservation and development of the family, a basic institution of our system whose protection is proclaimed in the Political Constitution in its articles 5, 15 and 42.

[…]

if between members of a couple there is a kinship relationship that the legal system considers incestuous, no marital union of any of the types described in Law 54 of 1990 shall exist between them, least of all that of community property. Of course, if that which the rest of the legal system strongly represses were blindly protected by the mentioned law, it would constitute an inconceivable paradox.

[…]

It cannot be stated […] that if as mandated in numeral 4 of article 1820 of the Civil Code, the incestuous marriage generates community property, nothing would prevent the marital relation between persons linked by any of the degrees of kindred that typify the offense of incest from generating in turn community property, inasmuch as marriage, unlike marital union, – and here lies the inappropriateness of its assimilation – constitutes a singular juridical act whose effects operate as long as it is not declared null by a judicial decision, which as a general rule is not retrospective in the light of the provisions of article 148 *Ibidem*, a phenomenon which, by straining the subject matter, may not happen in a *de facto* situation such as extra marriage relationships, for which reason the legislator, anticipating this situation, sought to impede from the start the occurrence of effects to unions affected by this impediment.

[…]

From all that has been posited on this issue, it may be inferred that in this lawsuit the pretenses of the plaintiff are bound to be rejected, since between the parties there is the impediment of kindred (father-daughter) which, as mentioned before, not only impedes the formation of the claimed community property but also, and more conclusive, that it hinders, at its root, the birth of the marriage union defined in the first article of the mentioned law. Consequently, the first instance ruling should be confirmed.

3.2.1.1 Matters for Debate

The Right to Challenge Paternity

With the exception of Colombia, which recently amended its legislation,[29] Latin American law regulates the challenging of marital paternity quite strictly and establishes limits to the challenging of extramarital paternity. As indicated in the Argentine ruling, such limits may be justified by the superior interest of the minor

[29] *See* Ley 1060 de 2006, Colombia.

to obtain certainty on his/her filiation, and by conserving of the principle according to which no one can be compelled to confess guilt. This principle would impede the wife from confessing her adultery in order to establish her child's filiation. At the same time, however, to exclude women from intervention in the determination of children's filiation threatens the principle of equality and limits the chances of determining the true filiation.

The Regulatory Effect of the Recognition of Rights to *de facto* Couples

The last case included in this section is exceptional: it excludes a type of *de facto* family from the protection normally conferred upon families by the legal system. This case allows us to observe how the law reacts to a conflict of values: on the one hand, the judges decide to support lack of good faith, and allow the offending co-habitant to benefit from his/her dishonest behavior. In the Colombian case, the woman had lived as the partner of her cohabitant without knowing that she was his daughter; she found out when he presented the evidence during the judicial proceeding with the purpose of eluding his economic responsibilities derived from co-habitation. On the other hand, because incest is a concept that is repugnant to the law, the justices dismissed the woman's request, who had cohabited in good faith with the man who turned out to be her father.

In this decision, and in the legislation that supports it, there is an underlying tendency to reinforce the family as part of the natural order. It would be pertinent to ask oneself once again what the value is of insisting on including *de facto* families. The trend to include more couples as family has been criticized from two viewpoints: in the framework of policies of structural adjustment and the rise of family priority in the satisfaction of needs; this trend seems to favor a greater concentration of resources rather than their re-distribution. It has been pointed out, for example, that homosexual couples benefitting from an extension of the scope of the notion of family would be those having greater economic resources.

On the other hand, the inclusion of more couples seems to close the spaces of resistance to State regulation of sexuality, since it eliminates the possibilities of allowing "free love" to thrive. Even more so, one could think that this regulation once more favors marriage – there are more elements that are negotiable between spouses in marriage than there are in *de facto* union in the form in which they have been regulated by Latin American legislators and interpreted by the judges.

3.2.2 Second Problem: Equality as a Means to Not Discriminate Men

Another group of noteworthy and problematic cases is the one that uses the liberal feminism argument of equality to defend men from exclusions introduced in order to take care of special needs of women.

The argument of special norms for special needs is not foreign to liberal feminism, although some would prefer to call it "interventionist liberal feminism." Liberal interventionists, in favor of a special treatment, contend that guaranteeing equality before the law does not guarantee equality in practice, since women, as disadvantaged players, do not enter into the spaces previously forbidden to them with the same skills or resources. Special treatment would also be justified when a certain group of women, due to a combination of various oppression factors, appears as particularly vulnerable.

In the case presented below, certain special measures for women were justified because of the special vulnerability of the favored groups: women who are heads of household. The argument of equality for men in the face of measures of differential treatment for women denies precisely the assumptions on which the requirement to include this differential treatment is based. The argument that there are men in equal circumstances as the women in favor of whom the measure is established is not true: from a social point of view, men have had historic advantages that have been perpetuated in gender discourses.

Constitutional Court of Colombia
Ruling 1039 of 2003

Main Legal Issue:
Does a norm that grants special labor protection to "mothers" discriminate against men?

Facts:
Two citizens challenged the unconstitutionality of article 12 of Law 790 of 2002, which impedes, as part of the implementation of the Program for Renovation of Public Administration, the removal from the aforementioned Program of mothers who are heads of household with no economic alternative.

Court Ruling:
The Court declares the expression "the mothers" contained in article 12 of Law 790 of 2002 constitutional, but establishes that the special protection provided for in the norm may be extended to fathers in the same situation, to protect the predominance of children's rights and those of the family group to which they belong.

Extracts:
[…]
For the defendants, the expression "the mothers" contained in article 12 of Law 790 of 2002 infringes upon […] the right to equality, the family, equality of rights and opportunity for men and women and, especially, children's right, inasmuch as the norm excludes men from the benefits of the protection foreseen in the law, in spite of the fact that the situation which originates it, namely to be head of household, can be equally applied to men.

[…]

The expression "the mothers" […] far from setting a preference in relation to any other person, consecrates labor stability for the most vulnerable sector of the

Colombian population, since on account of the circumstances of the country's current situation, low participation of women in the workforce is an increasingly serious problem.

The Constitution itself, in the pursuit of real and effective equality, has enshrined the special support of the State to women who are heads of household, and while implementing this support, the Program of Renovation of the Public Administration seeks to avoid that mothers who are heads of household with no economic alternative be withdrawn from the service.

The aforementioned means that the general rule will be the permanence of women who are heads of household in their jobs, as a consequence of the obligation of the State enshrined in article 43 of the Constitution, without this being interpreted as an infringement upon the right to equality, for just as the Court explained in a recent pronouncement, men and women must be treated in an equal way, that is, without discrimination, but taking into account that since women have traditionally been the object of sexual discrimination, they are the holders of specific legislative measures contemplated only in their favor and not in that of men [...]. However, regardless of the protection bestowed on women who are heads of household, it must be understood that what the legislator seeks to protect is the family group that depends on her, especially the children.

[...] Within this context, it must also be understood that it makes no difference whether one spouse or the other assumes the condition of head of household, inasmuch as the subjects of protection are the minors, whose rights have pre-eminence over the rest, as established in article 44 of the Constitution.

That is to say, according to what has been set forth above, women are not protected in situations such as the one being analyzed by the Court in this case merely for being women, nor men for being men, but one or the other insofar as they act as heads of household, on account of the constitutional protection to which the family is entitled (article 5 of the Constitution), and especially children, as provided for, we reiterate, in article 44 of the Constitution, for they, on account of their condition, must be especially protected in all that relates to their fundamental rights.

3.2.2.1 Matters for Debate

The ruling reveals how the argument of equality may hide the material reasons that justify an unequal treatment. In the case of protection of women who are heads of household, the special treatment has been justified mainly because of their enormous vulnerability. The Court's ruling does not consider the fact that "fathers who are heads of household" are not equally vulnerable, since the job markets favor them with better salaries and more opportunities; additionally, the market offers them more chances of finding a new partner – in this aspect women are also at a disadvantage.

However, one might wonder if the type of welfare that the challenged regulation advocated, the same that cited the family as natural order, was indeed an action without costs. The emphasis on the need that mothers personally care for their children, for example, seems to reinforce the idea that the best way to raise children is through personal and individualized contact. On the other hand, the emphasis on the idea that the fathers, or mothers, who are heads of household should be those to guarantee the economic survival of the children, reinforces the role of the family at the time of guaranteeing the wellbeing of individuals, with the consequences this may have on redistribution of income.

3.3 Maternity and Care

As opposed to liberal feminists, cultural feminists do not believe that women should seek formal equality with men. They claim that women live their lives and make decisions on the basis of considerations and values different from those of men. However, the problem of this lifestyle lies in that it does not receive the same recognition as that of men.

With regard to the family, cultural feminists have emphasized the need to recognize maternity as a life option and to stress the feminine values of altruism and solidarity evidenced in the relationship of women with their children. In Robin West's words:

> Our potential for material connection engenders pleasures and pains, values and dangers, and attractions and fears, which are entirely different from those which follow, for men, from the necessity of separation. Indeed, it is the rediscovery of the multitude of implications from this material difference between men and women which has enlivened (and divided) both cultural and radical feminism in this decade (and it is those discoveries which have distinguished both radical and cultural feminism from liberal feminism).[30]

For cultural feminists, existing juridical systems punish maternity: they impose high costs on women who opt for it, and they do not recognize the values of altruism and solidarity, but rather individualism and competition.[31]

The recognition demanded by cultural feminists concerning the way in which women view life includes, for example, requirements related to maternity leaves of two years or more,[32] the privileges of mothers regarding custody of children,[33] and the introduction of the "feminine perspective" in the analysis of cases.[34]

Latin American juridical systems are far from materializing this recognition. In all countries maternity is a privilege, but in no case a right; that is, women can be mothers, but they must assume all the costs imposed by the juridical system even if

---

[30] Robin West, "Jurisprudence and Gender" in, *55 University of Chicago Law Review 1* (1988).

[31] Robin West, "Jurisprudence and Gender", *op.cit.*

[32] Jude Cassidy, "The Nature of a Child's Ties" in Jude Cassidy and Phillip R. Shaver, eds., *Handbook of Attachment,* The Guilford Press, New York, 1999, pp. 3–20. See also, Arnlaug Leira, "Caring as Social Right: Cash for Child Care and Daddy Leave" in *5 Social Politics* 362 (1998) and Barbara B. Bergmann, "Subsidizing Child Care by Mothers at Home," *Working Paper Series*, September 1999, Foundation for Child Development.

[33] Martha Albertson Fineman, *The Neutered Mother, the Sexual Family and Other Twentieth Century Tragedies*, Routledge, New York, 1995.

[34] Robin West, *Caring for Justice*, New York University Press, New York, 1997.

they do not actively participate in the labor market.[35] These costs include, particularly, child care. Its cost implies that women either cease to participate in the labor market or pay for the service at a lower cost than the mother's earned income from the workplace. No costs are covered by maternity leave, which last only between three and four months, and which barely recognizes the medical handicap that ensues after giving birth.[36] On the other hand, the values of altruism and solidarity, and the contextual gazes, have little importance in Latin American juridical systems. In the cases involving legal and physical custody of children, for example, procedures are, to a large extent, blind to contextual specificities, and so are the substantial answers that the juridical system authorizes the judge to offer.

Cultural feminism, just like liberal feminism, has been strongly questioned. In the first place, it is criticized inasmuch as it intends to claim as inherent in women values that women have had to assume in a context of oppression.[37] Secondly, the values that cultural feminists claim as intrinsic to women are not different from that which has been claimed as pertaining to the culture of native Africans, of indigenous peoples and of the poor.[38] It is noted that with their support of maternity as a way of personal fulfillment of women, cultural feminists have come very close to validating maternity as a natural event and family as a natural order.[39] Finally, cultural feminism has received criticism because, in practice, its radicalization has led to the defense of segregationist projects which have failed.[40]

In relation to this subject, the most important cases are those associated with child custody and with women's work in their homes. These cases reveal two nuclear problems: assessment of maternity, on the one hand, and cultural assessment of the work of caring the other.

3.3.1 Assessment of Maternity

From cultural feminism's point of view, maternity is a unique experience for women, and should be considered as such by law. In their opinion, maternity gives women a privileged perspective on the needs of their children and an unparalleled ability to satisfy these needs. In contrast, men, on account of their materiality and socialization,

[35] *See* W. N. Hohfeld, *Conceptos jurídicos fundamentales*, Centro Editor de Latinoamérica, Buenos Aires, 1968.

[36] *See* Luisa Cabal, Mónica Roa and Julieta Lemaitre, eds., *Cuerpo y derecho*, Temis, Bogotá, 2001.

[37] Catharine MacKinnon, "Difference and Dominance: On Sex Discrimination", *op.cit.*, and Catharine MacKinnon, *Toward a Feminist Theory of the State*, *op.cit.*

[38] *See* Ann Fury, "Ideological Myths in Women's Liberation", *Everywoman*, December 1970.

[39] *See* Catharine MacKinnon, *Difference and Dominance: On Sex Discrimination, op.cit.*, and *Toward a Feminist Theory of the State, op.cit.*

[40] *See* Alice Echols, *Daring to Be Bad*, *op.cit.*, and Janet Halley, *Split Decisions: How and Why to Take a Break from Feminism*, Princeton University Press, Princeton, 2006.

do not have this ability to connect with or care for the weaker: men conceive their relations as relations between equals; they must be governed by rights that ensure cohabitation.[41]

Cultural feminists claim that mothers should be privileged when legal and physical child custody are in dispute, but that they also be protected from eventual impoverishment resulting from having children under their care.[42] In this respect they defend the elimination of the general standards on the "child's best interest." They argue that, on the one hand, the standards open the way to the prejudice of judges on how mothers should ideally behave[43] and, on the other hand, force women to accept negotiations that affect their economic interests and those of their children (the indetermination of the standard represents a risk they are not willing to assume).[44]

Instead, cultural feminists choose the standard of the primary caretaker: this principle recognizes the connection between the minor whose custody is disputed and the adult who has taken care of the child in the past.[45] Although the standard does not determine that custody be awarded to the mother – who is generally the primary caretaker –, it offers a better guarantee for the continuity of the relationship between mother and child. This standard, implemented in to law by two states in the United States of America, however, far from satisfies the recognition of maternity claimed by cultural feminists and the connection of mothers with their children in custody cases. The text of the statute(s) contain(s) a clause which generates criticism specifically on the presence of an exclusion criterion: that the mother is "inadequate", for this has been interpreted to the detriment of women who work some hours outside their homes, awarding custody to men who work even more hours in the labor market.[46]

The preference of cultural feminists for the primary caretaker standard has received criticism because it reinforces the conditions that lead to the impoverishment of women and for being insufficient in deciding most cases in which custody is disputed. Indeed, some feminists point out that defending the primary caretaker standard as something that favors women reinforces the traditional ideas of maternity

---

[41] Robin West, *Jurisprudence and Gender, op.cit.*

[42] *See* Nancy D. Polikoff, "Why Mothers are Losing: A Brief Analysis of Criteria Used in Chile Custody Determinations", *7 Women's Rights Reporter* 235, 1982, p. 236, Martha Albertson Fineman, *The Neutered Mother, the Sexual Family and Other Twentieth Century Tragedies, op.cit.*; Robert Mnookin and Eleanor Maccoby, "Facing the Dilemmas of Child Custody", *10 Virginia Journal of Social Policy and Law* 54, 2002, and Joan Williams, "Do Women Need Special Treatment? Do Feminists Need Equality?", 9 *Journal of Contemporary Legal Problems* 279, 1998, Joan Williams, "Is Coverture Dead?", 82 *Georgetown Law Journal* 2227, 1994.

[43] *See* Nancy Polikoff, "Why Mothers are Losing: A Brief Analysis of Criteria Used in Chile Custody Determinations", *op.cit.*; Frances Olsen, "The Politics of Family Law", 2 *Law and Inequality* 1, 1984; Laura Sack, "Women and Children First: A feminist Analysis of the Primary Caretaker Standard in Child Custody Cases", 4 *Yale Journal of Law and Feminism* 291, 1991–1992.

[44] Robert Mnookin y Eleanor Maccoby, "Facing the Dilemmas of Child Custody", *op.cit.*

[45] *Ibíd.*

[46] *Ibíd.*

and alienates men even more from their children. This results in maternity becoming a burden for women and that the economic costs derived therefrom end up being assumed mainly by women.

The primary caretaker standard is not useful when there are two or more persons that have been equally involved in the care of a minor whose custody is disputed. In these cases, necessarily, an expert is finally summoned to determine who the minor is most affectionately bonded to, with the negative consequences this may entail, or other parameters which reinforce traditional notions of maternity and paternity and are detrimental to women are applied.

In Latin America there are three currently prevailing models on custody and personal care of children. The first model is the one of the minor's best interest or the child's wellbeing; the second is the one of the mother's preference, except when there is a justified cause that warrants that the father be the one who gains custody[47]; and the last model is one of assignment of custody taking into account age, sex and proven cause for divorce.[48]

In spite of the different models, decisions on legal and physical child custody pose similar problems. In this chapter, cases of conflicts between biological fathers and mothers and between foster fathers and biological mothers are included. These cases evidence, in general, the importance of "moral" qualifications of the mother and the opinion of the children when determining to whom it is pertinent to award custody. They reveal the low assessment of the bond that is established between mothers and children and of the values of altruism and solidarity that informs them.

Constitutional Court of Bolivia
Miriam Rosa Villagómez Michel v. Ricardo Alarcón Pozo
February 21, 2006

Main Legal Issue:
Is the right to cultural differences of women infringed upon when custody of her minor girl is taken away from a woman for having re-married and the opinion of the minor involved is not taken into account?

Facts:
The appellant lost custody of her daughters by virtue of the appeal filed by her ex-husband. She claims, in a constitutional *amparo* appeal, that the decision was based on an improper assessment of evidence based on gender prejudice, and that due process was infringed because the opinion of the minor involved not taken under consideration.

Court Ruling:
The Constitutional Court decided that the mother could only file the appeal on her minor daughter's behalf; that the file for *amparo* could not be used to determine whether an inadequate assessment of proof had taken place during the legal process

---

[47] Article 225 Civil Code of Chile.

[48] Article 444 Civil Procedural Code of Colombia.

with the consequent violation of the minor daughter's right to due process for not having taken into account her opinion in the procedure that led to assigning custody to the father.

Extracts:

[...]

From which it is the case in order to sustain the complainant's pretense, regarding the content and grounds of the challenged decision, this Court would have to review and analyze the elements of proof and the criteria assumed by the challenged vocals at the time of issuing the Court Decision A-014/2005, of January 10, and carry out a new assessment of the same, inasmuch as the appellant claims that the challenged authorities based their decision on false and groundless conclusions and statements, as well as on a gender prejudice and devaluated stereotypes of women on account of the condition of divorced woman of the appellant, ignoring that the Constitutional Court cannot issue judgments on matters which are of the exclusive competence of the ordinary and administrative judges and courts established by the juridical system, least of all attribute itself the faculty of reviewing the assessment of proof that these authorities may have made, inasmuch as the ambit of protection of constitutional rights is only opened when the infringement of rights and guarantees is evident, which may occur, among other situations, when the proof presented has been ignored by the judge or when the assessment that has been made is arbitrary and unreasonable, which in this case does not occur, nor has it been shown by the appellant, a circumstance which renders it impossible for this Court to analyze the content and the grounds of the challenged Resolution.

[...]

Article 12 of the Convention of the Rights of the Child, ratified by Bolivia by Law 1152 of May 14, 1990, points out that: "1. States Parties shall assure to the child who is capable of forming his or her own views the right to express those views freely in all matters affecting the child, the views of the child being given due weight in accordance with the age and maturity of the child. 2. For this purpose, the child shall in particular be provided the opportunity to be heard in any judicial and administrative proceedings affecting them, either directly, or through a representative or an appropriate body, in a manner consistent with the procedural rules of national law."

[...]

Impose the obligation on authorities for them to ensure a proceeding within which the minor's situation is defined, that they stimulate and allow minors to express their opinions in all matters relevant to them, which does not imply, needless to say, that children should be asked to give their opinion when they do not wish to do so or show no interest in doing so.

[...]

That the decision of the Court of Appeals was adopted without previously hearing the opinion of the minor Daniela Fernanda Montalvo Villagómez —descendent of the appellant—, ignoring the norm contained in article 103 of the CNNA (*Código del niño, niña y adolescente* – Code of the Boy, Girl and Teenager), an omission on the part of the appealed that effectively infringes on the right of minors to freedom of expression and opinion, a circumstance that determines the propriety of the present appeal in relation to that particular matter.

Constitutional Court of Guatemala
Ángel Uriel Peña López v. The First Judge of First Instance of the Family Branch of the department of Alta Verapaz
May 11, 1999

Main Legal Issue:
Are the rights of the biological mother infringed upon when she is denied custody of some of her children, taken care of by another couple exclusively for several years and who show signs of having entered into deep psychological crises when faced with the perspective of living with her?

Facts:
The plaintiff, the biological mother of two minors, gave them away to a couple in exchange for a monthly stipend. After several years without visiting them, she requested that legal and physical custody of her children be awarded back to her. After an initial conciliation, in which she agreed a visitation regime with the non-biological parents in charge of caring for the children, she decided to initiate a new procedure to obtain custody and care. The judicial decision by which the rights of the biological mother were protected was challenged to protect the rights of the children, who were deeply affected by the changes.

Court Ruling:
The Court protected the minors' rights and ordered that they be left under the care of the couple they considered their foster parents while the necessary measures were taken to guarantee an adequate decision concerning their case.

Extracts:
[…] The regulations of the Convention [on the rights of the child] weigh up options and provide guidelines to find a balanced solution in cases like this one, in particular to satisfy especially the minors' best interest. It sets out an obligation to consider and implement special measures, independently of the parents […] among others, their permanence for a reasonable time in child care facilities […] specialized care for the psychological recovery and consequent preparation of the minors to become integrated, in due time, into the natural home […] to request the cooperation of the biological parents and temporary guardians to ensure the development of personal relations between those and the minors […] to obtain the posterior opinion of the latter, when deemed convenient […] and of assistance to parents and guardians […] necessary for the former to responsibly assume paternity […] and guardians adapt to the future circumstance of the physical decrease of their home members, paying due attention to their opinion […] Such measures, since they are consistent with the national legislation on protection of the family, are comprised within the faculties of the Judge, as provided by […] the Law of Family Courts and […] the Code of Minors. In accordance with and based on what has been stated, this Court understands

that not having exhausted the due procedure prior to making the ruling, the challenged judge infringed upon the rights of the minors requesting *amparo*; had the *amparo* been granted in the first instance, the operative part of the judgment under analysis must be confirmed, adding the way in which it is laid down in the judgment, as concerns its effects.

3.3.1.1 Matters for Debate

Maternity as a Natural Quality

Irrespective of the reasons brought forth by the justices, it is pertinent to ask oneself whether it is in women's best interest to emphasize the special relationship of women with maternity and their natural capacity for being mothers. As has been noted by the liberal feminist the impact of vindicating maternity as equivalent to femininity implies that the options of those who wish to be mothers and of those who do not are significantly removed. The liberals claim that more would be achieved if child-raising were universalized as part of that which in contemporary societies means being a man and being a woman.[49]

Alternatively, to defend maternity as an essential element of femininity is to ignore the different forms in which women have been mothers in the course of history, such as, for example the fact that some women assault and abandon their children.[50] To turn maternity into something essential, then, would have the negative effect of condemning women to being mothers, and at the same time condemning children to being placed under the care of persons who may not be the fittest to be in charge of them.

The Indetermination of the Cultural Parameter

Those cases in which two women enter into a dispute claiming their right to be the mother of the same minor reveal up to what point claiming maternity as an essential quality of every woman is insufficient when resolving who should prevail in this role. The cases propose different answers. The parameter according to which maternity is an essential quality of women does not mention the specific weight that should be attributed to the relationship that a woman may have built with a particular child when faced with the fact that another woman has given birth to that child.

---

[49] Nancy Fraser, *Iustitia Interrupta, op.cit.*

[50] Nancy Sheperd Hughes, "M(Other) Love", in *Death Without Weeping*, University of California Press, Berkeley, 1991.

3.3.2 The Cultural Assessment of Care Work

Another claim that may be associated to cultural feminism is that of equal assessment of women's work at home, a labor that is linked to the survival of family members. For cultural feminists it is fundamental that the contributions of women in this field be recognized, and that in addition, they be given the same importance that is given to people in trades within the labor market.

Using this viewpoint as a point of departure, cultural feminists defend equal social pay for care-related work women perform. This implies that the possibility of mothers to opt to personally care for their children to be socially guaranteed. The reasons for this concert the fact that the care that each mother gives to her children is different from that which other persons can give them[51]; and that because for women this is a privileged form of obtaining personal satisfaction.[52]

This implies that jobs analogous to care-giving, that women carry out in exchange for a salary – nursing work, pre-school and junior school teaching, care of handicapped or elderly persons, services of cleaning and cooking, among others – be considered equal to those linked to male values of competition and requiring equal qualifications – transport, security, work in manufacturing, work in construction, among others.

In this respect, cultural feminists support both the figure of community property for couples, as opposed to the one of separate property systems with compensation through payments for child support[53] and maternity leaves of three or more years and equal pay in the care-related workplace.

Traditionally, Latin American law has considered that care work carried out by women is valued and supported by the existence of community property or joint property. This is reflected by commentaries contained in jurisprudence and in the ruling included below. To illustrate two types of objections to these interpretations of care work or of domestic work, two additional texts are incorporated: the justification of a bill presented in the Colombian Congress, and a ruling of the Constitutional Court of Guatemala.

[51] Linda McClain, "Care as a Public Value: Linking Responsibility, Resources, and Republicanism", *76 Chicago-Kent Law Review* 1673, 2001.

[52] Dorothy E. Roberts, "Spiritual and Menial Housework", *9 Yale Journal of Law and Feminism* 51, 1997, and Mona Harrington, *Care and Equality*, Alfred A. Knoff, New York, 1999.

[53] *See* Janet M. Riley, "Women and the Law of Community Property", 69 *American Society of International Law Proceedings* 25, 1975; Deborah L. Rhode y Martha Minow, "Reforming the Questions, Questioning the Reforms: Feminist Perspectives on Divorce Law", in Stephen D. Sugarman y Herma Hill Kay, eds., *Divorce Reform at the Crossroads*, Yale University Press, New Haven, 1990, and Joan Williams, "Is Coverture Dead", *op.cit.* See also, Reva Siegel, "Home as Work: The First Woman's Rights Claims Concerning Wives' Household Labor", 103 *Yale Law Journal* 1073, 1994.

Constitutional Court of Guatemala
María Eugenia Morales Acuña de Sierra v. the State of Guatemala
June 24, 1993

Main Legal Issue:

Is the right of recognition of the cultural difference of women infringed upon when it is established that their main right and obligation as a spouse is to care for the children and carry out domestic tasks?

Facts:

The complainant requests that the norms of the Civil Code of Guatemala that establish different rights and obligations for wives and husbands concerning care of children and maintenance of the household be declared unconstitutional.

Court Ruling:

The Court concludes that the challenged legal regulations are constitutional by considering that instead of being discriminatory they are protectionist, and that the unconstitutionality of norms aimed at the protection of children cannot be ruled.

Extracts:

[...]

The complainant states that article 110 is unconstitutional as it stipulates [that] "The husband must offer protection and assistance to his wife and is obligated to provide her with all the necessaries for the maintenance of the home in accordance with his economic possibilities. The woman has especially the right and the obligation of taking care of their children during childhood and of directing the domestic tasks".

She claims that this provision infringes upon the principle of equality contained in article 4 of the Constitution. Here the principle of legality valid – both for the husband and the wife – is once more applicable [...] each one of them is a part of an institutional unity termed marriage, in which both have rights and obligations derived from such institution, among them, the obligation they have of maintaining the home which, according to this legal provision, lies with the husband, but is not exclusively his because pursuant to article 128, it also falls on the wife, which is a way of ensuring the protection of the children. In this case the woman's right is that of requesting the husband to take care of the home's maintenance, and the protection that he owes her is no longer in her capacity as a woman but on account of the existence of a constituted home, as well as her role as a spouse and a mother, since both exist as such, husband and wife, which is a basic special capacity in family organization, protected by the Constitution as specified in article 47. Therefore, none of the two spouses may withdraw from their obligations once the marriage is contracted and the home is constituted. Mutual help and the value on which marriage rests are oriented to raising the children, which is dealt with in articles 78 and 79 of the Civil Code and in the provisions related to planned parenthood. For this reason, if the law had not contained the provision of article 110 on the husband's obligation to protect and assist the wife, she would have been left unprotected in her role as a mother. [...] The regulation sets a prerogative, is not discriminatory but rather protectionist; a norm aimed at the protection of children cannot be declared unconstitutional.

[...] Article 113 of the Civil Code reads: "A woman can have an employment, exercise a profession, industry, craft or trade, when by doing so she is not damaging the interest and care of the children or the rest of home tasks". The complainant challenges the phrase "when by doing so she is not damaging the interest and care of the children or the rest of home tasks". When analyzing the quoted article, it may be noted that it does not contain any clause prohibiting women to enter an employment; quite on the contrary, it is a positive precept that enables women to perform the activities listed in it; however, no right can have an absolute nature, but it must be subject to certain limitations. In this particular case, the right contained in the quoted article must be exercised in harmony with the aims inherent in marriage. Indeed, marriage is a social institution that recognizes rights and imposes obligations, among these, those of educating and feeding the children contained in article 78 of the Civil Code, in accordance with article 47 of the Constitution, which organizes the family on the legal basis of marriage and planned parenthood, and article 52 of the Constitution determines that maternity is protected by the State, which is responsible, in a special way, for guaranteeing strict compliance with the rights and obligations derived from it. In this sense, both the husband and the wife have unavoidable obligations concerning the minor children they may beget, because it is not only a matter of breeding offspring, but also of being responsible in taking care of the children. These types of obligations do not imply that paying attention to minor children overrules the right to work. Both aspects may be developed simultaneously and, in real life, almost in all homes or in most of them, women perform tasks in the different fields of social activity, as workers in factories, secretaries, as general staff or chiefs in offices of the public or private sector, in the different professions, as teachers, in the judiciary, in State executive positions, in the field of politics and in others. In any case, it is up to each wife to deal with her work activities and take care of her responsibilities as a mother imposed upon her by marriage.

[...] Article 114 of the Civil Code is also challenged; it reads as follows: "The husband may oppose that a woman engage in activities outside the home, if he provides for the maintenance of the home and his opposition is based on sufficiently justified motives. The judge shall summarily resolve what is pertinent".

In this regard, it may be noted that the challenged regulation is closely linked to article 113 of the Civil Code, previously considered. Indeed, article 113 – in harmony with the ends inherent in marriage and with the rights and obligations derived form maternity, as has already been said – lays out the obligation that when a woman has an employment, exercises a profession, industry, craft or trade, by doing so she shall not damage the interest and care of the children or the rest of home tasks; article 114, on the other hand, grants the husband legal standing to oppose the wife's involvement in activities outside the home, if he provides what is necessary to maintain the home and his opposition has justified motives, in which case it is up to the competent judge to resolve the matter without further legal enquiry. When confronting both articles, the following becomes evident: women's activities outside the home, which the husband can oppose – in conformity with article 114 of the Civil Code – are those referred to entering an employment, exercising a profession, industry, craft or trade, provided for in article 113 of the same Code; the only person with legal standing awarded by article 114 to claim the said opposition is the husband, if and when the following two conditions are met: that he provides all that is necessary for the maintenance of the home and that he has justified motives for the opposition; this justification must obviously refer to the case in which the activities outside the home to be carried out by the woman, allegedly damage the interest and care of the children and other home tasks which, according to the law, it is incumbent upon the woman as a wife and mother to perform; besides, the husband's mere opposition is not sufficient, but the agreement of the spouses in conformity with article 109 of the same Code is also needed and only in case of disagreement can the decision be submitted to a competent judge; in this respect, it should be noted that the judge is not a stranger, since the jurisdictional activity exists precisely to resolve conflicts and, in this case, to limit any eventual arbitrariness on the part of the husband and to determine whether the motives presented by him refer to the protection of the children and to compliance with obligations legally attributed to the wife and mother; that is, in conformity with the purposes inherent in marriage reflected in article 78 of the same Code, in conformity with article 47 of the Constitution—and with obligations derived from maternity; strict compliance with these obligations are guaranteed in article 52 of the Constitution. Consequently, article 114 of the Civil Code is not unconstitutional.

Senate of the Republic of Colombia
Bill 02 of 2005
By which article 154 of the Colombian Civil Code is amended
("No more female slavery in the home")

The Congress of Colombia
DECREES:
Article 1. Article 154 of the Civil Code will now read: "Article 154. *The following are grounds for divorce:*

1. Extramarital sexual relationships of one of the spouses, except in those cases in which the plaintiff has consented, facilitated or pardoned such behavior.
2. The grave and unjustified non-compliance by one of the spouses of the duties imposed upon them by the law as such and as parents.
3. Outrageous behavior, cruel treatment and offenses against property.
4. The habitual drunkenness of one of the spouses.
5. The habitual abuse of hallucinogenic substances or drugs, except when prescribed by a doctor.
6. Any illness or serious and incurable abnormality, physical or psychological, of one of the spouses, which places the mental or physical health of the other spouse at risk and renders the continuity of the marriage community impossible.
7. Any conduct of one of the spouses tending to corrupt or pervert the other, a descendant, or other persons who are under their care and cohabit under the same roof.
8. Physical separation, legal or *de facto*, which has lasted longer than two years.
9. Consent of both spouses manifested before a competent judge and recognized by the same through a ruling.
10. Inequality in sharing domestic responsibilities, care of ancestors and descendants or of any other dependent persons under their care.

Article 2. This law shall enter into force from the date of its publication and it repeals all those that oppose it".

Carlos Moreno de Caro
Senator of the Republic

EXPLANATORY PREAMBLE

A crucial assumption, used in Colombia and in the rest of the Latin American countries, is that a woman's dignity cannot be preserved unless the woman is, in each *significant* aspect, exactly equal to the man. Any recognized difference between man and woman may be utilized as an excuse to treat women in an unequal way.

Discrimination between the two will inevitably lead to forms of *unfair* discrimination – to treat a woman as inferior to man in her value as a person or capabilities and therefore not worthy of the same prerogatives and privileges that man has. What is to be feared is that women be restricted to caring for the home and the children as the only sphere in which she can fulfill her true vocation, especially if the main differences between sexes include the close relationship of women with pregnancy and upbringing of the children.

[…] Working women have faced the systematic cuts of labor rights for several decades, job loss, lower salaries than those perceived by men and tasks mostly relegated to an extension of domestic tasks, in addition to family tasks and responsibilities, violence within the family, abandonment by the partner and maintenance of children; these issues have gradually been taken care of by the drive of women and the State, but even today, in the 21st century, social behavior codes looks at women's work out of the corner of the eye and represses them to family tasks and especially domestic work, where the partner is a DON [a high-placed or noble individual].

Since the mid-19th century, the presence of women in the workplace has been significant. Most activities were an extension of the tasks that women traditionally carried out in their homes, but the fact of working and receiving some money placed them in a different situation. Many of them had to move continuously in the city, breaking the domestic seclusion to which women of middle and low sectors were subjected, to be heads of their households.

The wage-earning woman

Equality between men and women in the workplace is still far from being achieved. However, the number of persons of the female gender with employment increases day by day. Not only does the amount of jobs change, but also their characteristics do as well. However, the proportion of women who hold high positions is considerably lower than deserved on account of their level of proficiency.

Women started to work as a result of economic need; women of the lowest economic levels, married or single, worked outside their homes. Women's salaries tend to be lower. Besides, working women had and still have to carry out their home tasks at the same time as those of their workplace. The increase of women's presence in university is a phenomenon that dates back to the 70s [...] worldwide.

A factor that affects the possibility of holding positions of leadership in enterprises is that women leave and re-join the workforce when they get married or have children, since this kind of work does not permit such leaves.

Another factor is that many times women do not receive the necessary motivation to show their capabilities, since they are subjected to carrying out tasks considered of little importance within the firm. In addition to receiving an economic remuneration they must also receive an emotional one.

Women who do not work for wages often feel frustrated in their personal fulfillment and excluded from modern life. Those who work are harassed by the idea (sometimes promoted by the family and social environment) of being bad mothers or bad wives, and even by the idea that a woman must of necessity be a mother. A woman who has achieved the balance between her maternal longings and her fulfillment as an individual shall establish a more beneficial relationship with her affections.

Discrimination of women

Discrimination within organizations is evidenced in different ways. The most common one occurs at the time of assigning tasks. It falls to women to perform administrative tasks, or she may find work as a receptionist or a secretary, whereas executive management posts are reserved for the males.

Women who reach one of these positions, in general, achieve this only after having worked for long periods of time within the institution, having developed a career within it. In this way they can demonstrate their capabilities and be taken into account. The problem arises when a woman wishes to apply for a high position and she has not belonged to that enterprise: she will most probably not be selected, no matter what her academic merits or her expertise may be.

In other cases employers have no doubts about women's capabilities but they prefer not to hire them because of the potential costs of a possible pregnancy. In yet other cases, discrimination is related with cases of women who are married or have children, supposedly because of the fear that these women may have higher absenteeism than men, since they have to take care of their families. However, statistics show that female workers who hold positions of responsibility, even if they have children, are not absent from their jobs more often than men.

In the past few centuries, incredible progress has occurred with respect to the position of women in the workplace. More and more women are now acceding to posts which were traditionally considered exclusive of men. Expectations they hold of themselves contribute to [the fact that they] propose [to accomplish] higher goals.

However, women are not yet being heard; this is evidenced, for example, by the fact that Latin American women decide to congregate in women's meetings to obtain support from others who understand their situation in society. Besides, it is still difficult for women to have access to high positions. Entrepreneurs refuse to hire women to perform traditionally masculine tasks. Equal qualifications have less value in the hands of a woman than in the hands of a man, and even if they are admitted, promotion is much harder for women than for men.

In order to be promoted, women have to accumulate greater merits. The role of women as autonomous and responsible individuals, capable of combining their role as mothers and as workers, is not recognized. This is a step that must be taken by society. Adaptation to this double role may be facilitated by the creation of high-quality, safe public services which ensure care of children while the mother remains away from her home performing her work.

Women must stop being viewed as housewives. To this end, women must continue to excel professionally and personally. The government, in turn, should do something more than just promoting women's work with words.

Women account for 50.55% of the population, i.e., close to 23,275,014 in 2005; in Colombia over 80% of women who work receive less than two minimum wages, since payment for extra hours, Sundays and public holidays was eliminated and/or reduced. As a result of the provisions of Law 789, in our country there are now more women who are heads of household, i.e., 90% of working women who invest their salaries in family needs. Thirty-five percent are affiliated with social security, and over 50% of persons in a situation of forced relocation are women and girls.

The role of the traditional woman

The role of women is predetermined [by the way] in which they must […] behave in the home and in society. They must be good housewives and support their husbands. In urban areas the role of women is gradually changing, but the stereotypical role still has a strong presence. This presence still manipulates most women in urban and rural areas into maintaining the traditional role. The three ways in which women must be are behavior in the face of society, care of the children and support to husbands.

[…] For example, […] many women still think that it is not good to go out to parties alone. There are certain norms that must be obeyed if you are a woman. One of the reasons why women are subjected to numerous rules to act in society is, at least partly, religion. In Mexico, the influence of religion is significant. Many rules concerning men and women are issued in churches, but they appear to be more unbalanced in the case of women. For example, women need to wait until marriage to have sexual intercourse, but men are allowed to exploit women sexually. At the same time, children learn these norms from their mothers.

In addition, husbands demand a great deal of attention from women. A good wife takes care of her husband with great affection. She cooks, cleans his clothes, pampers him, and so on. She lives with the idea of making him happy according to the role of the traditional woman, and what happens with the modern working woman?

We can see that women in the home and in society must follow certain norms. Women are always under surveillance by all. The world expects them to behave in […] a good way [during] the whole time. More women have become independent from society, though.

Conclusion

The Political Constitution of Colombia [...] enshrines special guarantees and rights of women and historically discriminated groups.

Within the international framework, the Convention on the Elimination of All Forms of Discrimination against Women, CEDAW, the Inter-American Convention on the Prevention, Punishment and Eradication of Violence against Women – Convention of Belém do Pará –, the Beijing Declaration and Platform for Action and the Vienna Declaration and Platform of Action have become the main references for the OAG (Observatory on Gender Matters).

Based on social equity, the gender approach is incorporated, inasmuch as it has its foundations on the construction of relations of equity between women and men, in the recognition of equality of rights and in respect for gender diversity.

Equity is another fundamental concept in the objective of the present law, since based on this principle there exists an unequal treatment in favor of women who are in a situation or position of exclusion and equal treatment for those who are under conditions of equality. In the understanding that "the principle of equality is translated into the right to non-granting of exceptions or privileges which 'exempt' some individuals from what is conceded to others in identical circumstances".

The Law of Equality of Opportunity for Women, Law 823 of 2003, constitutes an institutional framework to guarantee equity and equality of opportunities for women in the public and private ambits.

Equity between women and men is thus defined as an unavoidable dimension of human development and as a strategic objective for a sustainable development, centered on the persons. The principles that rule the policy are: equity, equality, participation and respect for women's rights.

Respect for women is the objective of the present law, respect in the home from the spouse or partner, by sharing domestic tasks and child upbringing, since double-shift employment for women is partly doing away with Colombian homes.

Lack of support from the spouse, stress and daily fatigue make women from different social levels avoid participation in marital relations in couples with children.

In Spain, for example, 40% of female workers carry out the home tasks unaided, and invest five times more time than the men in cleaning, cooking, ironing and caring for the children.

To reach a balance between family and domestic tasks is one of the most important issues in modern human relationships. Respect for the biological characteristics and the fight against "machismo" underlie the aim of the amendment of the Civil Code, since in this way a group of women and men shall become aware of their sex in the family and of the commitment they have assumed concerning their children, by creating as a cause for divorce the unequal participation in these tasks, from that point expanding these causes beyond those of non compliance with the obligation to cohabitate, help each other and maintain mutual fidelity.

3.3.2.1 Matters for Debate

First Matter for Debate: The Myth of Domesticity

The documents dealing with the subject of care work, or domestic work, included here, present different perspectives on how to treat this matter: the first strengthens the idea of women as the best fit to perform care work, and consequently advocates for regulations which reflect this social preference; while the legislation proposes that domestic work or care work be considered an obligation of both spouses and be treated as such in the regulation of divorce. These proposals, however, are based on the assumption that certain tasks, necessarily or ideally, should be performed by some family member without receiving any pay. In the early twentieth century, Charlotte Perkins Gilman termed this assumption "the myth of domesticity"[54]; she defined it as such because it is based on ideas not grounded on reality: that all human beings, and particularly women, can adequately perform, as well as enjoy domestic tasks; that it is more efficient that each domestic unit take care of all the tasks; and that all human beings, particularly women, are equally qualified to care for and educate children. The author proposes that these tasks receive the same treatment as others, subject to work specialization, according to preferences and attitudes, and to training requirements comparable to those of other jobs.

The Trap of the Marital Society

As mentioned previously, the idea that the marital society compensates care work is quite generalized in Latin America. Not only is it unfair that those who devote themselves to care work do not receive economic recognition, but in addition the marital society has turned into a perverse incentive to maintain the traditional division of work between the sexes and the distribution of resources among classes within society. The marital society functions as a mechanism to maintain the division of sexes at work, because it represents precisely a form of compensation for those devoted to care work. By relying on this compensation, women have an incentive, or at least a certainty concerning their economic future, when they decide not to participate in the work market.

Additionally, the belief that care work is compensated by the existence of the marital society reproduces an existing class bias: the marital society can only compensate something if the couple has indeed managed to accumulate assets that may be distributed. If the couple only has the man's salary for its economic subsistence, women obtain nothing at the time of dissolving the society, since future salaries are not a part of the marriage society.

[54] Charlotte Perkins Gilman, *The Home, Its Work and Influence*, AltaMira Press, Walnut Creek, 2002, pp. 36–61.

3.4 Sexual and Non Sexual Violence Within the Family

Radical feminists claim the regime that permits the expropriation of feminine sexuality[55] adopts its form in the family, and that one of the ways in which it persists is through women's discipline, exercised through what is termed domestic violence.[56] In their opinion, the family is aimed at trivializing and rendering invisible the mechanisms of oppression of women.

In this sense, radical feminists aim mainly at eradicating the "residual tolerance"[57] of current societies in the face of sexual violence in the streets, homes and the workplace, and in the face of domestic violence. They claim that, in order to protect other social interests such as the "intimacy" of the home, family harmony or comradeship in the workplace, women have had to tolerate unacceptable levels of violence. These interests have been protected, in their opinion, by detracting from women's credibility and trivializing their experiences of "harm,"[58] and by requesting evidence of moral certifications which are not requested to men in the same situation.[59]

With regard to sexual violence, radical feminists have promoted the creation of doctrines on sexual violence between spouses, between acquaintances, and on sexual harassment.[60] They have also fought to generate legislation that seeks compensation for victims of pornography and that avoids circulation of pornographic materials particularly damaging to women.[61]

In the matter of domestic violence, they have generated a doctrine on battered woman's syndrome; promoted the massive creation of homes for women and their children, victims of violence,[62] and encouraged the adoption of legislation on mandatory police intervention, even if intervention is against the victim's will.[63]

---

[55] Catharine MacKinnon, "Feminismo, marxismo, método y Estado: una agenda para la teoría" en Mauricio García Villegas, Isabel C. Jaramillo Sierray E. Restrepo Saldarriaga, eds., *Crítica Jurídica*, op.cit.

[56] Catharine MacKinnon, *Towards a Feminist Theory of the State, op.cit.*

[57] Mary Joe Frug, "A Postmodern Feminist Legal Manifiesto", *op.cit.*

[58] Duncan Kennedy, "Sexy Dressing, Sexual Abuse and the Eroticization of Domination", *op.cit.*

[59] Catharine MacKinnon, *Towards a Feminist Theory of the State, op.cit.*, and Alice Echols, Daring to be Bad, *op.cit.*

[60] One of the most important works on this matter is Susan Estrich, *Real Rape*, Harvard University Press, Cambridge, 1987.

[61] Sexual harassment as sexual discrimination is an idea developed by Catharine MacKinnon in *Sexual Harassment of Working Women: A Case of Sex Discrimination*, Yale University Press, New Haven, 1979. An extraordinary compendium of articles produced on the twentieth anniversary of this book is, Catharine MacKinnon y Reva Siegel, eds., *Directions in Sexual Harassment Law*, Yale University Press, New Haven, 2004.

[62] On the damages caused by pornography *See* Catharine MacKinnon, "Not a Moral Issue." *Yale Law and Policy Review* 321 (1984). See also, Drucilla Cornell, ed., *Feminism and Pornography*, Oxford University Press, Oxford, 2000.

[63] *See* Elizabeth Schneider, "Particularity and Generality: Challenges of Feminist Theory and Practice in Work on Woman-Abuse", *67 New York University Law Review* 520, 1992 and "Theory and Experience in Constructing the Relationship Between Lawyer and Client: Representing Women who Have Been Abused", *64 Tennessee Law Review* 1019, 1997.

Legislative changes put forth by radicals have been questioned for various reasons. First, it has been noted that the emphasis on women's victimization places their empowerment in a second place. Critics state that this has an allegedly negative effect on women in two senses: on the one hand, it dissuades many women victims of sexual or domestic violence from seeking help, since this would imply admitting themselves as the victims they do not wish to be. On the other hand, it implies that women who are victims must assume that such victimization marks their lives in such a way that the fight to overcome the trauma caused by violence will take a very long time.[64] Finally, the idea of "victim," associated to the battered woman syndrome, is criticized for having been used against women in custody disputes filed by State agencies or by their children's father.[65]

Secondly, it is pointed out that the legislative changes have not been accompanied by regulatory changes within the bureaucracies.[66] Some criticism places special emphasis on the fact that mandatory intervention of police is not accompanied by social services that allow women to demonstrate the need for an intense protection and to obtain the necessary resources to protect their lives and the lives of their children in the face of future attacks by their husbands or permanent partners.[67]

Thirdly, they claim that the emphasis on dominance as a characteristic of sexuality has resulted in leaving women with few spaces to envision their own pleasure in sexuality.[68] Finally, some critics note that radical feminists have not dealt with the costs of their interventions on black and poor men. Generally, this group has a higher rates of incarceration and is against whom the laws supported by the radicals have been enforced with greater rigor, even when they are not the main perpetrators; Radicals have also neglected the costs for persons of diverse sexual orientation, who are the target of the repressive State apparatus as refers to matters of sexuality.[69]

Since colonial times, in Latin American law, domestic violence is a ground for divorce.[70] Sexual violence, in contrast, has not even been imagined as a possibility

64 Martha Mahoney, "Legal Images of Battered Women: Redefining the Issue of Separation", *90 Michigan Law Review* 1, 1991.

65 Kathryn Abrams, "Sex Wars Redux: Agency and Coercion in Feminist Legal Theory", *95 Columbia Law Review* 304, 1995, and Janet Halley, *Split Decisions: How and Why to Take a Break from Feminism, op.cit.*

66 *See* Mary E. Becker, "Domestic Violence, Child Abuse, and the Law: Double Binds Facing Mothers in Abusive Families: Social Support Systems, Custody Outcomes and Liability for Acts of Others", *2 University of Chicago Law School Roundtable* 13, 1995.

67 Deborah Epstein, "Effective Intervention in Domestic Violence Cases: Rethinking the Roles of Prosecutors, Judges and the Court System", *11 Yale Journal of Law and Feminism* 3, 1999, and Margret E. Bell y Lisa A. Goodman, "Supporting Battered Women Involved in the Court System", *7 Violence Against Women* 1377, 2001.

68 Jill Davies, Eleanor Lyon y Diane Monti-Catania, *Safety Planning with Battered Women*, Sage Publications, Thousand Oaks, 1998.

69 Janet Halley, *Split Decisions: How and Why to Take a Break from Feminism, op.cit.*, y Katherine Franke, "Theorizing Yes: An Essay on Feminism, Law and Desire", *101 Columbia Law Review* 181, 2001.

70 Janet Halley, *Split Decisions: How and Why to Take a Break from Feminism, op.cit.*

in the ambit of marital relations by virtue of the so called "marital duty" or the obligation of each spouse to satisfy the sexual needs of the other.[71] Instead, non-compliance with the marital duty has been indeed contemplated as a ground for divorce, since it can be considered a "grave and unjustified non-compliance" of the marital duties.

In the last decade, however, Latin American countries have expressed their concern about the physical and sexual violence against women in their homes, and have acted accordingly: they adopted the Belém do Pará Convention, in the context member countries of the Organization of American States adopted the Belém do Pará Convention, and passed domestic legislation to render violence in the home a visible issue and provide tools to protect women. Most of these laws made family violence a felony and established civil mechanisms through which women can request various options: the expulsion of the abuser from the family residence, the necessary police protection to avoid his return to the home, repair for damages caused, and settlement of child support installments.

Legal regulations on sexual violence and marital duty, however, have been generally interpreted by the judges in the light of social norms that invite women to support significant doses of abuse before ending a relationship, especially if there are children involved, and of questioning of the victim's behavior and plaintiff. Additionally, police have few resources made available to them to effectively deal with calls from women who ask for help when their spouses' or partners' behavior threatens their lives. The chapter of this book titled "Violence" develops this subject in depth; here we present only rulings and doctrine revealing some of the most important tensions in this discussion from the family's perspective. These have been grouped around two problems: resignation to violence to protect the family and blaming of the victim.

3.4.1 Resignation in the Face of Violence as a Means of Protecting the Family

In spite of the legislative commitments assumed by Latin American countries, women are still faced with the option of resignation as a possible attitude in the face of domestic violence. Two arguments are brought forth as justification: that family unity has such value that only considerable levels of physical violence may justify destroying the marital relationship of the couple; and that in order to establish what types of violence justify the intervention of legislators and judges it is necessary to take into account that family intimacy is a value protected by legal systems.

Although the law on inter-family violence aims precisely at weakening these arguments, they still continue to have great weight, as revealed by the cases

[71] *See* Pablo Rodríguez, *Sentimientos y vida familiar en el Nuevo Reino de Granada*, Ariel, Bogotá, 1997, and Sonia Lipsett-Rivera, "La violencia dentro de las familias: formal e informal", in Pilar Gonzalbo Aizpuru and Cecilia Rabell Romero, eds., *Familia y vida privada en la historia de Iberoamérica*, El Colegio de México and Universidad Autónoma de México, Mexico D.F., 1996.

presented herein. The justices, in opposition to the appellant women, consider that the situation they are living in is tolerable or susceptible of negotiation and reconciliation. In both cases they propose the intervention of psychologists or psychiatrists, and in the second case, in addition, the matter is directed to the bureaucratic apparatus in charge of resolution of family conflicts.

Supreme Court of Justice of Peru
Luisa Lizárraga Prat de Kaelin v. Óscar Guillermo Kaelin Cavenecia
January 10, 1997

Main Legal Issue:
Is the male privilege of exerting violence protected when a woman is denied a divorce for not having shown that the exerted violence against her was "permanent"?

Facts:
The plaintiff requested divorce based on psychological harm, claiming to have been repeatedly insulted and physically abused.

Court Ruling:
The Court denies divorce and orders that the family nucleus, spouses and children, enter group therapy with a professional psychologist who is charged with assessing and diagnosing the problem and of re-conducting the behavior and ways in which family members treat each other.

Extracts:
[…]
[A]lthough it is true that the plaintiff has presented elements of proof […] such elements do not fulfill the aim of producing conviction or certainty regarding the "permanent" contempt, insults and verbal abuse of which she claims to be a victim, these being, as expressed by the plaintiff herself, both in her written complaint and in her oral declaration during the hearing of February the fifth of the present year […] of reactions motivated by certain behaviors of the same "decision adopted on March the third of one thousand nine hundred and ninety five of interrupting co-habitation, a reaction derived from a fight occurred on the twelfth of that same month and a reaction having occurred on the sixteenth of June of the same year, following presentation by the plaintiff's attorney of a proposal of agreement of conventional separation".

[…]

That, as a result, not having the plaintiff proven the ongoing contempt, the alleged insults and verbal abuse which sustain her pretense for divorce, the claim must be declared groundless.

[…]

It is necessary to specify that in family law the role of the judge is fundamental, since in cases such as the present one, when informed of the existence of a family conflict, the judge cannot adopt a posture of mere spectator, while it is his duty to attempt to re-establish the disrupted balance and strengthen the family nucleus, the superior interest which advocates for the preservation of the integrity of the family and its members.

[…]

That consequently, it is necessary to dictate a therapeutic measure, while the collaboration of the members of the family nucleus is essential, all the more so taking into account that the minor children of the couple [...] have witnessed the incidents, according to the declaration of the parties in the claim and the response to the said claim.

Constitutional Court of Colombia
Ruling T-062 of 1996

Main Legal Issue:
Is the male privilege to violence against women in the framework of the family exerted when a husband attacks his wife's handicapped brother who lives with them?

Facts:
The plaintiff's husband, upset by the presence of the plaintiff's handicapped brother in the marital home, attacks and insults him.

Court Ruling:
The Court orders to protect the rights to personal integrity and dignity of the plaintiff's brother, but also that the handicapped person's family takes charge of him, so that the plaintiff's husband is not forced to support an unjustified burden.

Extracts:
[...] The plaintiff states that her brother is [50] years old, has suffered from epilepsy for the last 35 years and is an orphan of father and mother, and for this reason for the past three years she has hosted him in her home and fed him. She states that when he is not ill, he runs errands and collects firewood, with which he earns some money to pay for his medical expenses. She adds that the sick person has other brothers who live in the city of Cali, but who lack the capacity to take care of him.

[...] The evidence contained in the records of the case does not show a situation of violence within the family. Although the fact that at a certain moment physical or verbal actions of some intensity may have occurred cannot be ruled out, what is undoubtedly the case is that a grave family conflict around the presence and maintenance of the plaintiff's brother and whose voice she assumes with the aim of granting him, on behalf of her husband, a quiet accommodation basically appropriate to his personal conditions.

[...] The Court has reiterated that the mere family disagreements, which are not expressed through acts of violence, must be resolved according to moral and social criteria valid for the group and pursuant to the will of its members, except if issues which are relevant to and are regulated by the law are involved. In this respect, the Constitutional Court has pointed out: "From the intra-family perspective, the constitutional jurisprudence has focused on the infringements on the fundamental rights that are verified within the context of the family sphere".

[...]

The simple non conformity of the defendant with the relative's stay in the home, as well as his apparent intention of expelling him in some future time, do not *per se* infringe on any fundamental right. Persons are free to feel irritated and upset and to express such feelings, provided they do so without resorting to violence. In turn, if this situation should cause the other spouse and the rest of the family members to feel upset and annoyed, the case cannot be filed before the law, least of all in the form of an action for protection, to achieve the suppression of the forms in which the annoyance is translated or to resolve on the causes when these lie in the sphere of intentions.

[…] The decision on the continuation of what has been a prolonged stay of the relative of one of the spouses, on account of the implications of this situation on intimacy, privacy and the economic situation of the family, corresponds to the type of determinations reserved to the couple and cannot depend on only one of its members.

[…]

The way to follow, once a family conflict is verified, cannot be suggested by the Constitutional Court which, for the time being, is limited to establishing that the fundamental rights of the wife's relative who has stayed in her home for a period of time are not infringed on by the husband who refuses to continue offering hospitality to the relative, both for economic reasons and for the disruption of family intimacy it represents. […]

Consequently, it is stipulated that while the spouses arrive at an agreement on the interruption or extension of Melquisedec's permanence in their home, or his other relatives establish the way of contributing equitably to his support and maintenance should this be necessary, the defendant shall abstain from offending him and, in general, from carrying out acts of physical or verbal violence.

3.4.1.1 Matters for Debate

The rulings included in this section reveal the importance that is still assigned to family unity, even in contexts of aggression against women. In both cases the settlement of dispute is left in the hands of persons other than the judges: in the first ruling it is recommended to the spouses that they engage in family therapy; in the second, the intervention of juridical operators without judicial functions and who are members of the administrative body in charge of surveillance and support of families is requested. In both cases the woman's concern is minimized and she is invited to negotiate once again, as if it were not the exhaustion of all available remedies that generally leads to the search for a judicial solution. In both cases, the judges were competent to decide on the main issue of the suit and in favor of the woman.

3.4.2 Women's Accountability

There is another way of denying women the protection they seek against the husbands' aggressions: it occurs when the judges point out that these aggressions respond to some "guilt" of the victim – a "disobedient" behavior or a "defensive" attitude – and are therefore justified.

If the interpretation of domestic violence supports a masculine privilege aimed as disciplining women, it would result that in *all cases* men would use physical violence to obtain obedience, both during cohabitation or after it. Thus, the law would reinforce that privilege when considering that not remaining defenseless in the face of violence would be "guilt" of the victim that excludes her from the special protection granted to "defenseless" women.

It is worth highlighting that, once again, in both cases below, the Colombian Constitutional Court protects children's rights on account of considering these as "blameless" victims of the situation that the parents are going through.

Constitutional Court of Colombia
Ruling T-420 of 1996

Main Legal Issue:
Is the male privilege to violence reproduced when a woman threatened to death by her husband is denied protection, alleging that she no longer lives in the same city as her husband and in spite of the fact that the threats against her life occurred in the city where she is now living?

Facts:
The plaintiff becomes legally separated from the defendant because of the ill treatment he inflicted upon her. Although the woman moves to another city, he follows her there, takes their children away without prior notice, threatens to kill her, fires some shots in the air and breaks into her new home to steal from her.

Court Ruling:
The Court does not grant the plaintiff's request for protection because other judicial mechanisms have proven to be effective and because it believes that, upon moving to another city, she is not defenseless.

Extracts:
[…]
In early 1996, the petitioner settles in Montería, where she initiates law studies in the night shift; however, she states that her former partner continues to coerce her, insulting her and threatening her with forcing her to go back to live with him. "Among the ways of coercion – she clarifies – is the fact that at any time he would arrive and take the children away for several days, causing them damage in their classes and serious moral harm. Also, as a form of coercion, he threatens with killing me and beating me and on one occasion he even fired a shot at me and missed. I have filed a complaint on it at the Buena Vista police inspection, where the incident happened".

Indeed, the petitioner filed a complaint against YY […] for the offense of attempted murder. In such complaint she narrated the way in which the actions consisting of the defendant firing shots at her and missing when she was in the company of one of their children, occurred.

[…]

As explained […] defenselessness as a requisite for the appropriateness of the action for protection based on motives of intra-family violence requires to be considered a determining factor that such violence be exerted in the domestic space of the home. Thus, as it has been determined in the case under analysis that the claimant does not cohabitate with the defendant and that they have even established residence in different municipalities, the Court estimates that a true status of defenselessness, which would make the legal action prosper, does not exist, since it is directed against a private individual.

It is true that the behavior of the defendant infringes on the fundamental rights for which the plaintiff requests protection. But not every infringement on the fundamental rights implies *per se* that the procedure for protection is the appropriate juridical manner in which to achieve its protection. There are numerous juridical mechanisms which are appropriate for the defense of fundamental rights, reserving the action for protection as the residual and subsidiary procedure, that is, as the one called as a last resort, only in the absence of an alternative medium.

In the present case, in addition to not meeting the requirements for a status of true defenselessness in the person of the complainant […], the Court notes that she was expeditiously availed of the penal actions to repel the aggressions against her life and her intimacy which had been carried out by her former partner, as well as to file claim with regard to the facts that configure offenses against property. Therefore, although aware of the seriousness of the facts described, the Court shall be compelled to deny the protection requested, with regard to the rights referred to by the plaintiff. […]

Constitutional Court of Colombia Ruling T-199 of 1996

Main Legal Issue:
Is there a male "privilege" of resorting to violence against wives and permanent partners when the violence is excused and is sought to be justified by alleging that the woman defended herself with physical aggression as well?

Facts:
The plaintiff has cohabited for over thirteen years with the defendant. She claims that during that period of time she was a victim of physical and psychological aggressions; that on the last occasion the aggression handicapped her and she was unable to work for a period of fifteen days. The plaintiff claims that she defended herself from the defendant by throwing boiling water at him and physically attacking him in other ways.

Court Ruling:
The Court decided to protect the right of children to live in a home free of violence and ordered both spouses to stop the mutual aggressions.

Extracts:
[…] Mrs. Eulides Esther Tesillo states that for the last three years, when she initiated *de facto* marital life with the defendant, she and her two minor sons have been the object of constant abuse by the said defendant, which has caused them to suffer from a psychological condition and placed their lives at risk since "[…] it has not been enough for this man to abuse her verbally, but he has also beaten her with objects in different parts of her body, and only by some miracle these beatings have not caused her death".

[…] As can be observed, the role of social supervision of the State must be exercised when internal harmony, which should be a constant in the development of family life, cracks, placing the individual integrity of its members at risk. In similar cases, the authority must act accordingly and take the necessary measures to avoid the concretion of irreversible damage to the members of the social nucleus. This must be so, taking into account the priority and recognized attention that must be paid to the affected minors who, on account mainly of the incapacity that limits them, are unable to exercise the defense of their rights themselves. […]

[…] From the claim filed by the plaintiff, it is possible to verify, *prima facie*, that her permanent partner has exerted, in addition to psychological abuse, actions of physical violence against her, which are also damaging to her children's integrity.

[…]

Once verified, according to the declarations recorded in the file of the case, that the abuse actually occurred, the Court must then decide whether the requirement of being in a state of defenselessness has been fulfilled, since it is a requirement of the regulation in order for the pretenses claimed through the writ for protection to be deemed viable.

[…]

The concept of defenselessness is related to the particular conditions of those involved in the relationship, so that in each case a detailed analysis must be carried out with the aim of assessing if, on the basis of the consideration of each individual's strength, it may be deduced that one of them overpowers the other, in such a way as to prevent him/her from exercising the right to legitimate defense. The Constitutional Court has supported this criterion when expressing it in the following terms: "The situations of subordination and defenselessness referred to in article 42 contain the condition that the person who claims protection depend on the private organization or on the person who effectively controls the claimant, or that the claimant lack the media for defense from the attacks against the claimant's fundamental rights or insults that are committed by the private individual being accused of them. The status of defenselessness or powerlessness must be analyzed taking into account the circumstances of the concrete case, the persons involved and the relevant facts. The concept of defenselessness is relational. This means that the status of defenselessness in which the citizen finds himself in relation to another has to be determined according to the type of bond that exists between both".

In the opinion of this Court, the alleged state of defenselessness suffered by the claimant with regard to her permanent partner is not presented clearly enough, since the aggressions are not unilateral but mutual, which indicates that their relationship is not established in terms of superiority of one of the parties over the other, and consequently, of defenselessness of the other party. […]

As evidenced, the parents, who are the persons mainly responsible for conserving the internal family order, have constantly failed to fulfill this obligation of maintaining the inner harmony of the home imposed by reason, the law and society. Their behavior is therefore far from setting an example to their children and enriching for the relationship, because, as mentioned before, it is incumbent upon the State, when exercising the responsibilities incumbent upon it in accordance with article 42 of the Political Constitution, to watch over the maintenance of the family nucleus's unity, and that the protection of their fundamental rights and that of respect for their dignity be guaranteed to the children begotten within it. Since those directly in charge of correctly managing the home do not seem committed to achieving this, the State must set in motion the mechanisms available to it for achieving the constitutional mission.

[…]

Therefore, this Court considers that the pretenses of the plaintiff related to the protection of her fundamental rights to life and physical integrity should be rejected, and that on the contrary, the fundamental rights of the minors born from the *de facto* marital union should be protected instead, even when this has not been requested in a direct manner, as it is glaringly evident from the case study, since it is them who are directly or indirectly suffering the consequences of the conflicts between their parents. […]

3.4.2.1 Matters for Debate

In these last rulings, the justices have decided to protect the children, placing the burden of violence on the woman in order to favor the family. The justices' argument, however, has the peculiarity of suggesting that the plaintiffs' behavior does not make them worthy of obtaining the protection that other women do receive. In both cases, the fact that the women have reacted in the face of domestic violence, defending themselves, is central. The justices obviate, however, the fact that the woman's defense has resulted in an escalation of violence, and that in every case, she is the one who has lost.

The fact sexual violence does not appear to be an issue in any of the cases, and that when it does arise, it is generally to reinforce the general pattern of violence and not as a matter deserving special or distinct treatment, is significant. This is so in spite of the fact that Courts have determined that marriage duties do not authorize the use of sexual violence.

Chapter 4
Health

Lidia Casas

The conceptualization of the right to health originated, like most social, economic and cultural rights, as a consequence of its inclusion in the most important instruments of international law on human rights, whose normative antecedent is the Universal Declaration on Human Rights. The general content of this international obligation is enshrined in article 12 of the International Covenant on Economic, Social and Cultural Rights (ICESCR) of 1966; later treaties establish its legal scope for specific populations. In the case of women, the Convention on the Elimination of all Forms of Discrimination against Women (CEDAW), consecrates the right to heath, especially associated to the problems of maternal morbidity and mortality and to the regulation of fertility.

A historic review of the right to health reveals that it has been closely linked to the right to social security. Thus, the protection against, and the way of facing, diseases was considered a contingent risk that economically weaker persons had to face.[1] On this same level are unemployment, disability, work accidents, and even widowhood; all situations faced by employees and their dependents and which, if left to depend on private philanthropy, became unsustainable. In this context, social and trade union organizations established benefit societies or mutual aid societies as a collective response to the health needs of their members.

The German social laws of Otto von Bismarck of the late 1800s – of social insurance, work accidents, disability, and seniority – are the first precedents of state intervention in the protection of health as a contingency or social risk and served as a model in Latin America.[2] The rise of these types of laws, although beneficial, was a gravestone

[1] *See* Alfredo Bowen, *Introducción a la Seguridad Social*, Editorial Jurídica de Chile, Santiago, 1992.

[2] *See* Héctor Humeres Noguer, *Derecho del Trabajo y de la Seguridad Social*, Tomo III, Editorial Juridica de Chile, Santiago, 2005, p. 85.

L. Casas (✉)
Facultad de Derecho, Universidad Diego Portales, República 112, Santiago, Chile
e-mail: lidia.casas@udp.cl

C. Motta and M. Sáez (eds.), *Gender and Sexuality in Latin America - Cases and Decisions*, Ius Gentium: Comparative Perspectives on Law and Justice 24,
DOI 10.1007/978-94-007-6199-5_4,

for the mutual aid movement and for the collective efforts of labor protection: social security would then become a "social matriarchy of the State, built in the image and likeness of the 'huge mothers.'"[3]

Irrespective of the analysis on whether social laws broke up the movements that sought a more radical social change, the relevant matter is that the protection of health rested, and rests, on various models of financing that have left aside a great number of persons who do not have work contracts supporting labor relationships. Currently, the processes of reform of public health systems, in spite of being motivated by a discourse of equity, have left thousands of persons without healthcare coverage.[4] There have been attempts to revert, through systems of guaranteed basic healthcare coverage, some of the problems detected; that is, through the guaranteed delivery of packaged services for all persons, irrespective of the regime of social protection they are under. Even though this manages to solve the problem of access, it also reveals that one of the urgent problems is the ability to demand the right to the protection of health, since the traditional doctrine perceives them as programmatic norms.[5]

At the international level, the signatory parties to CEDAW have committed themselves to ban all forms of discrimination that could arise from both State officials and private agents, and to adopt positive measures to ensure the enjoyment of all the rights enshrined in the Convention. General Comment 14 of the Committee of the International Covenant on Economic, Social and Cultural Rights (ICESCR) captures this obligation, which establishes that the right to health is closely related to and dependent upon the realization of other fundamental human rights. However, local courts do not always recognize the relationship between the right to life and the right to health. This lack of recognition manifests, for example, in various lawsuits claiming access to drugs treating HIV/AIDS, or claiming high cost treatments in different countries of the region.

The definition of health as a "state of complete physical, mental and social well-being and not the mere absence of infections or diseases" was adopted at an early stage in the Constitution of the World Health Organization (WHO). Despite being dubbed utopian, a person's health depends on a series of factors, among these the biological, genetic, environmental and socio economic characteristics of each individual, for which reason the Committee of the ICESCR has stated that the right to health is not synonymous with "being healthy." These definitions, even with

[3] G. Salazar y J. Pino, o*p.cit*, p. 155.

[4] Luz Stella Álvarez Castaño, "El derecho a la salud en Colombia: una propuesta para su fundamentación moral", *Revista Panamericana de la Salud Pública*, Vol. 18, No. 2, August 2005, http://www.scielosp.org/pdf/rpsp/v18n2/27145.pdf; and Susana Checa, "Salud y Género: Aproximaciones a la Problemática de Salud de la Mujer" in Ana Lía Kornblit comp., *Ciencias Sociales y Medicina. La Salud en Latinoamérica*, Instituto de Investigaciones de la Facultad de Ciencias Sociales de la Universidad de Buenos Aires, Buenos Aires, 1994, p. 197.

[5] Víctor Abramovich and Christian Courtis, "Apuntes sobre la exigibilidad judicial de los derechos sociales, in Derechos Sociales. Instrucciones de uso", Victor Abramovich, Maria José Añón, Christian Courtis comp., *Doctrina Jurídica Contemporánea*, D.F. México, 2003, pp. 55–78.

their differences, allowed, from a legal point of view, to establish that the fulfillment of the right to health encompasses not only the healing of the body's ailments (physical health), but also the inclusion of conditions related to elements of mental health and of each person's environment. The WHO's definition incorporates, in turn, those factors that have incidence on the general health conditions of the population, such as the preventive dimension.

4.1 The Right to Life and the Right to Health

The relationship between the right to life and the right to health arises when the doctrine and the decisions of international bodies argue that the right to life extends to something more than the protection against the arbitrary deprivation of life, as traditionally understood. The basic example is the death penalty, which in order to be applied, must be found through a prior due process.[6] This restrictive interpretation of the right to life has been questioned for being considered man-centered,[7] that is, for assuming an interpretation based on the male experience, obviating the fact that the international obligations must include something more than the non interference by the State to ensure the protection of life. A broader interpretation of the international obligations understands that it must adopt concrete measures to prevent the loss of lives for foreseeable reasons. An inclusive reading of gender in the protection of the right is the one provided by the U.N. Committee on Human Rights, when it concludes that women die from avoidable causes, generally associated to maternity.[8]

The aim of this chapter is to study the manifestation of the right to health in its relationship with sexual and reproductive rights. The theoretical discussion takes the approach in which its slow conceptualization in law has allowed it to be a hinge between two aspects: the right to self determination and the exercise of health as a basic condition to exercise reproductive autonomy.[9]

The following pages present four subjects related to women's right to health. Each one of them studies specific problems that case law, doctrine, and international law should have faced.

---

[6] IHO, *Human Rights in Relation to Women's Health*, Geneva, 1994, p. 30; Cecilia Medina, *La Convención Americana: Teoría y Jurisprudencia. Vida, Integridad Personal, Libertad Personal, Debido Proceso y Recurso Judicial*, Centro de Derechos Humanos, Facultad de Derecho, Universidad de Chile, 2003, p. 61; Peter van Dijk, *Theory and Practice of the European Convention on Human Rights*, Kluwer Law International, 1998, pp. 296–299.

[7] IHO, *Id.*

[8] General Comment No. 6: *The Right to Life* (art. 6). 30/04/82, CPPR. http://www.unhchr.ch/tbs/doc.nsf/(Symbol)/84ab9690ccd81fc7c12563ed0046fae3

[9] *See* S. Correa and R. Petchetsky, *op.cit.*

4.2 Women's Health

From a gender point of view, it can be stated that men and women share similar biological and physiological conditions, so that they experience similar health problems. It is often argued that women have more longevity, but this says nothing about their health situation or quality of life. In fact, despite their tendency to live longer, women die in greater proportions from avoidable diseases related to maternity.[10]

Women's fertile life cycle gives a new meaning to the biological differences and introduces specific causes of morbidity. Some of them are the product of a set of stereotyped notions about women in which the allocation of roles, of attributes of a cultural and social nature, directly influence their health and reproductive capacity. At the same time, maternity, or its potential, introduce costs or negative externalities that only women assume. For example, health care insurances can be more expensive for women, work contracts are more unstable and discriminatory for women, and salary inequities are often based on arguments related to the nature of maternity.

Care and protection of health are awarded, on occasion, in honor of maternity, under the idea that maternity is innate to women's role. The exercise of sexuality, related to health, is scarcely dealt with and, in the case of sexuality, different from the hegemonic one, it generally constitutes a right susceptible of protection only to the extent viewed as a deviation. From this latter perspective, the State keeps watch to reverse the "deviate's" situation when it involves a health problem.

While the first feminists incorporated their concern for women's health, their emphasis was placed on women workers and the problems to regulate their fertility as well as on the need to reduce infant mortality caused by malnutrition; factors perceived as directly related to poverty.[11] In turn, this gaze on poverty and the regulation of fertility converged with a vision that public health had the objective to fulfill the health needs of populations in specific socio-epidemiologic contexts. A reflection of this was the sanitary response in the face of child malnutrition and the role women played in ensuring their children's food through maternal breast-feeding. For example, the Chilean Sanitary Code's regulations award and ensure protection to pregnant women.

It could be said that the State's concern for women has focused on their condition of breeders of the species. Thus, the legal obligation to ensure that women have time to breast-feed responds to a sanitary-nutritional axis, which attempts to avoid that

---

[10] Mirta Roses,"Desigualdades Ocultas," in Bernardo Kliksberg ed. *La agenda ética pendiente de América Latina*, FCE, México, 2005, pp. 149–154, http://www.paho.org/Spanish/D/BID_Artículo_GeneroySalud.pdf. *See also* José Barzelatto and Aníbal Faúndes, *El Drama del Aborto. En Busca de un Consenso*, Tercer Mundo Editores, Bogotá, 2005, p. 65.

[11] Ximena Jiles, *De la Miel a los Implantes. La Historia de las Políticas de la Regulación de la Fecundidad en Chile*, Corporación de Salud y Políticas Sociales, Santiago, 1992, pp. 104–105. *See also* Claudia Rojas Mira, *"Historia de la Política de Planificación Familiar en Chile: un caso paradigmático,"* Debate Feminista Año 5, No. 10, September 1994, pp. 138–148.

poor women become wet nurses neglecting their own children, placing the latter's health at risk. However, it can also be that in this approach there is an underlying prescription on the mother's role and the obligations it imposes: maternity and mandatory breast-feeding. This way, women turn into means for developing government promoted policies.[12]

The feminist claims of the early twentieth century included the need to have the adequate tools to protect families. This is to say that, women viewed their claims as intimately related to the needs of others. At the same time, their own needs were linked to the authority of being able to regulate and control the number of children one wished to have and to moderate the consequences of unwanted pregnancies and clandestine abortions.[13] Despite this strategy, the use of contraceptive methods has evolved hand in hand with a policy of state control and has limited the female citizens to such an extent that the use of coercion, surveillance, and submission are still a part of women's experience at the moment of giving birth.[14]

The fight for legal abortion and the use of methods to regulate fertility has been a crucial part of feminist claims, and in the 1980s, feminists and health experts coined the concept of sexual and reproductive health. This allowed to make visible the fundamental aspects of women's health associated to reproduction and sexuality, which would be at the basis of sexual and reproductive rights.[15] This new approach represents a significant change of paradigm. Matters associated to health and the exercise of sexuality focused on the sanitary axis (diseases or the infections they produce) and in reproduction and the gifts associated to a thesis of care of women. Until recently, the governments' health policies of the region kept maternal healthcare as part of the mother-child pairing. This excluded women who by choice or incapacity were not mothers, those who were not of reproductive age, and those who suffered problems related to sexuality but not to human reproduction. Women's health, traversed by maternity, leads to their not being recognized as subjects. If women are bodies that permit reproduction, State policies – and those of the biomedical community – will be strongly inspired by the power to control those bodies: to define the number of children in accordance with objectives of population regulation, national security, and poverty reduction. History shows that the concern

[12] Juan Guillermo Figueroa, "Comportamiento Reproductivo y salud: reflexiones a partir de la provisión de servicios," in Gloria Careaga, Juan Guillermo Figueroa and María Consuelo Mejía, comp., *Ética y Salud Reproductiva*, Porrúa, D.F. México, 1996, p. 292.

[13] *See* Sonia Correa and Rosalynd Petchetsky, "Reproductive and Sexual Rights: A Feminist perspective," in Gita Sen, Adriana Germain and Lincoln C. Chen, eds. *Population Policies Reconsidered: Health, Empowerment, and Rights*, Harvard Center for Population and Development Studies, Boston e International Women's Health Coalition, New York, 1994, p. 108.

[14] Roberto Castro and Joaquina Erviti, "Violations of Reproductive Rights during Hospital Births in Mexico," *Health and Human Rights: An International Journal,* Vol. 7, No. 1, p. 102.

[15] Rebecca Cook, Bernard Dickens and Mahmoud Fathalla, *Salud Reproductiva y Derechos Humanos. Integración de la medicina, la ética y el derecho*, Oxford and Profamilia, Bogotá, 2003, pp. 9–12.

for women can be presented in discourses coated with welfare aims, be it for population policies or the protection of health, but they ultimately deprived women the autonomy to choose for themselves.[16]

The feminist movement, accompanied by a progressive change in the focus of medicine, has gradually constructed a discourse capable of breaking with the sexuality-reproduction pairing, and, with the aim of ensuring that women and men can make decisions on central aspects of their lives, developing a notion of reproductive rights different from the sexual ones.[17]

4.2.1 Sterilization, Health, or Autonomy?

Sterilization is a surgical procedure of a permanent nature that entails risks because of the use of anesthesia and more invasive procedures (when the mini laparoscopy technique is not applied). The decision to practice this procedure must be, therefore, conscious and voluntary. Sterilization is frequently considered a preventive measure that may safeguard women's health. As such, where a new pregnancy might place the woman's health or life at risk, it is practiced by medical prescription. At the same time, it represents a pillar for the exercise of reproductive autonomy of persons.

The prevalence of this form of fertility regulation shows that in Latin America the use of the pill was displaced by sterilization. Indeed, depending on the country, today this method occupies the first or second place as a method of reproduction control.[18] Women's access to contraceptive methods is determined by class, race, and ethnic group.

The recent history of Latin America has shown how States use sterilization to reduce population growth or poverty. An eloquent example is Peru during Alberto Fujimori´s administration.[19] With the adoption of the Program of Reproductive Health and Family Planning (1996–2000) came a series of cases of women who had

[16] *See* Silvina Ramos, Mónica Gogna, Mónica Petracci, Mariana Romero and Dalia Szulik, *Los Médicos frente a la Anticoncepción y el Aborto en la Argentina: ¿Una transición ideológica?*, CEDES, Buenos Aires, 2001, pp. 32–37; Human Rights Watch, *Decisión Prohibida: Acceso de las Mujeres a los anticonceptivos y al Aborto en Argentina*, June 2005, Vol. 17, No. 1 (B); Lidia Casas, "Del Control a la Autonomía," *Informe de Investigación,* No. 18 año 6, Facultad de Derecho, Universidad Diego Portales, Santiago, 2004.

[17] S. Correa and R. Petchetsky, *op.cit.*, pp. 107–123.

[18] Cynthia Stelce and Terrence Jezowski, *Esterilización Voluntaria en América latina/Salud Reproductiva en las Américas*, Pan American Health Organization, Washington, DC, 1992, p. 300.

[19] Luisa Cabal, Mónica Roa and Lilian Sepúlveda-Oliva, "What role can International Litigation Play in the Promotion and Advancement of Reproductive Rights in Latin America?" *Health and Human Rights*, Vol. 7, No. 1, p. 63.

been sterilized without due consent and surrounded by a series of irregularities.[20] Women had scarce information on the utilized method; some found out that it was irreversible only after it was performed and, apparently, other women had received food in exchange for allowing sterilization.[21] The feminist movement has denounced this problem, especially when women are subjected to experimental procedures or sterilizations without their prior consent.

Superior Court of Justice of Corrientes, Argentina
Falcón María Liliana v. Hospital Vidal of Corrientes City
April 12 of 2006

Main Legal Issue:
Is the right to autonomy infringed upon when a woman must obtain judicial authorization to access a sterilization procedure?

Facts:
A woman filed a writ of amparo against a hospital for refusing to perform a procedure of tubal ligation. The amparo was granted in the first instance, but appealed by the State. She seeks legal authorization to perform the procedure after giving birth to her child.

Court Ruling:
The decision of limiting procreation adopted by a woman constitutes a moral action free of State sanction and exempted from all prohibitions.

Extracts:
[...]
In Article 20, paragraph 18, the national law establishes ... the prohibition of medical professionals to "practice interventions which provoke sterilization without a perfectly determined therapeutic indication."

If, on the part of the professional in the art of healing, a "determined therapeutic indication" does exist, the situation of prohibition contained in the norm disappears, so that consequently the physician will find himself entitled to perform those surgical acts when therapeutic reasons so advise it, therefore not needing authorization to perform them.

[...]

[T]he plaintiff presents a state of apparent general good health, and no pathologies have been detected; it is not a high risk pregnancy and therefore the interruption of the pregnancy is not a possibility to be considered in this case; that the pregnancy that she carries does not constitute a risk on the mother's or the baby's life; that there are no risks or dangers in case of a new pregnancy; ... the patient does not present a medical reason to opt for tubal ligation as a method of birth control, and the autonomy of the patient will be respected and the contraceptive practice be authorized.

---

[20] "Anticoncepción quirúrgica voluntaria I. Casos investigados por la Defensoría del Pueblo," *Informes Defensoriales*, No. 7, Lima, 1998.

[21] *Op.cit.*, p. 81.

For her part, the professional in Psychology … informs that the interviewed plaintiff understands the scope of her decision of having a tubal ligation performed and maintains her decision to do it; that she lives her pregnancies with great fear, with episodes of anguish, anxiety, and even of panic crises; she considers it a great responsibility that is hard for her to assume because of her economic situation; that for a long time she has wished for an effective method of birth control; the professional concludes that although a new pregnancy would not entail risks to her physical health it could however have an unfavorable effect on nuclear family since it would compromise the precarious balance of human and economic resources barely obtained.

[…]

As well stated in the *a quo*, health constitutes a fundamental human right and must be conceived according to the definition of the World Health Organization, which makes reference to a state of complete bio-psycho-social well-being. It is a non transferable function of the State to guarantee health to all the inhabitants. It must be understood as "a state of complete physical, mental and social well-being, and not merely the absence of disease or infirmity" (Constitution of the World Health Organization).

[…]

Constitutional Court of Colombia
Judgment T-248 of 2003

Main Legal Issue:
Is sterilization a feasible health service when the reasons to prescribe it do not respond to a need to remedy an underlying pathology? How does the State ensure the right to raise a family and procreate of a disabled woman?

Facts:
An underage girl suffers from "epilepsy, mental retardation or with mental disability." Her psychiatrist ordered that she undergo a tubectomy. In spite of the prescription of sterilization, the procedure was not carried out due to the inexistence of contracts and budgetary reasons. The minor's mother filed a writ of amparo against the Ministry of Health and Social Security.

Court Ruling:
The rulings that denied the plaintiff's claims are upheld and the Colombian Family Welfare Institute is ordered to inform the plaintiff about the necessary processes that must be undertaken with the goal of asking a judge to order a tubectomy. Social Security is ordered to abstain from practicing tubectomies or procedures that affect the personal autonomy of persons with mental limitations, until such time as the respective judicial authorization has been obtained or when faced with a situation of urgency or pressing need.

Extracts:
[…]
"Article 554 of the Civil Code provides:

"The insane person shall not be deprived of his/her personal freedom, except in those cases in which it is feared that by making use of it he/she may harm him/herself or might constitute a danger or cause discomfort to others.

Neither can the person be transported to a mad house, locked up, or tied up except momentarily, while upon request from the curator or from any person from the town, a judicial authorization to carry out any of these measures is obtained."

A literal interpretation of this provision would suppose that it only refers to the protection of the personal freedom of the insane person. In the absence of provisions regulating matters related to the protection of the fundamental rights of persons who have mental problems, one could wonder whether this provision can be extended to them.

[…]

When updating the interpretation of article 554 of the Civil Code, to adapt it to the regime of a constitutional democracy like the Colombian one and in the face of the precise mandates of the Constitution, it must be understood that the *ratio legis* of the norm would be the indispensable judicial intervention when it were necessary to limit or severely affect a constitutional right (the reference to a restriction of freedom would have a mere indicative character) of a person with mental problems. This interpretation, besides satisfying the mandate of article 28 of the Constitution, expands article 13 as relates to State protection of persons in circumstances of evident weakness.

Accordingly, the minor's mother had the obligation to obtain a judicial authorization to carry out the surgical procedure ordered by the doctor in charge of treating her. […]

[…]

The right to raise a family and to decide on the number of children. Projection of individual autonomy

In the particular case of a tubectomy, informed consent implies that the person has the capacity (a real one) of understanding that such a procedure will limit or annul the possibility of having children and of raising a family (by way of offspring). The informed consent is not limited to authorizing the performance of the procedure, but also comprises the knowledge and acceptance of the consequences derived from the same, even if they are temporary.

Along these lines, the inexistence of the possibility to grant informed consent to carry out the tubectomy, implies that there is also an impossibility of deciding on the formation of a family and on the number of children the person wishes to have. That is to say, the rights in question could not be limited or annulled, because the person is not in capacity to exercise them.

[…]

To subject a woman with serious mental problems that prevent her from making decisions on the number of children or on the raising of a family to the obligation of having a child and, consequently, of raising a family, results extremely disproportionate. In this case, the autonomy – making decisions on her own body – is reduced to its minimum expression, turning it into a forced pregnancy…. The protection of autonomy demands the protection of the right to decide on her own body which, in the absence of a real capacity to decide on the intention of becoming a mother, cannot be based on the prejudice according to which every woman wishes to be a mother, for biological reasons. If this thesis is accepted, we would once again be facing a biologically determined pseudo-autonomy. That is to say, the person's degradation to the mere condition of a human being capable of reproducing. In light of the possibility of reaching such a situation, there is no other option, with the aim of providing an effective protection to a person in a situation of evident weakness and for the sake of a genuine respect for women's rights, than the judge authorize, if there are reasonable arguments (e.g. personal security), the practice of a tubectomy, in spite of the absence of prior consent.

[...]

To order that through the Colombian Institute of Family Wellbeing, the plaintiff be informed on the administrative procedures, in the terms indicated in the present holding, that she must carry out with the aim of being able to request a judge of the Republic to authorize the practice of a tubectomy in her daughter [...].

[...]

[T]o order Social Security that in the future it abstain from practicing tubectomies or procedures that affect the personal autonomy of persons with mental limitations, until such time as the respective judicial authorization has been obtained or if the situation is one of urgency or pressing need."

4.2.1.1 Matters for Debate

Voluntary sterilization, when the procedure is not aimed at healing or alleviating an underlying pathology, is considered an intervention that does not alleviate a sickness or is not therapeutic. Arguably, this intervention leads to the atrophy of the natural capacities of the individual to procreate, which has a mutilating character on the body, and because of this, it should not be permitted.

Court cases regarding the request for sterilization face yet another problem. If the concept of health is understood under a remedial reading, sterilization could be left outside of the medical procedures covered by the social security system when the intervention does not respond to resolve a pathology or a specific medical condition. Consequently, the discussion around voluntary sterilization has the potential of obscuring the fact that reproductive rights require enabling conditions so they may be exercised.

4.2.2 The Religious Beliefs of Healthcare Providers

Another problem in access to health services by men and women is the influence of ethical or religious beliefs of the healthcare staff when they superimpose on the patients' rights. This conflict is generally identified as a conscientious objection. The conscientious objector is a person who abides by the law, but who does not comply with providing the service that he/she is required to provide because he/she believes that it interferes with his/her profound moral or religious beliefs.

In these situations, the right to freedom of conscience of the healthcare providers is in tension with the patients' right to protection of life and health. Every individual has the right to freedom of thought, conscience, and religion and the State cannot interfere in the beliefs of persons. However, the expression of beliefs is subordinate to other interests, such as security, order, health, or public morals or the rights and freedom of others. The CEDAW Committee has expressed in various reports that the conscientious objection cannot constitute a limit to the exercise of women's right to health.[22]

In some countries, the objection in health matters is especially dealt with by law or in technical norms and this allows those providers directly involved providing services to abstain from carrying out actions that might be against their ethical conscience or religious beliefs. However, only natural persons, not institutions, can invoke the conscientious objection; although, on some occasions the law permits institutional providers be exempted from compliance with certain obligations.

Correctional Court of the First Instance Number 1 of Paraná, Argentina
E. N. B. v. San Roque Hospital
and/or Secretary of Health and/or Provincial State of Entre Ríos, Argentina
November 29 of 1996

Main Legal Issue:
Can a public institution be required to perform a surgical procedure that will not prevent or heal a disease and the professionals who would provide said service consider it contrary to their moral convictions?

Facts:
Mrs. N. B. E. files a writ of amparo against a hospital with the aim of having a surgical procedure of tubal ligation. The hospital refuses to perform the procedure, alleging that, absent a pathology, "it cannot be forced in the ethical, legal, and moral framework in which it carries out its professional activity, to practice the requested procedure."

Court Ruling:
The judge accepts the *amparo* action and orders that the surgical procedure be performed.

Extracts:
[…]
The National Constitution in article 19, first part, expresses "The private actions of men which in no way offend public order and morals, nor offend third persons, are reserved only to God and not subject to the authority of magistrates." This norm

[22] CEDAW, Croatia, 14/5/98, U.N. Doc.A/53/38, Rev. 1, par. 199 and Italy 17/07/97, U.N. Doc.A/52/38, Rev. 1, par. 353.

refers to those voluntary actions that are part of the person's self reference, an area of freedom in which the State cannot interfere by indicating how we should live in order to be virtuous or what we should plan or profess, since choosing a personal life project only concerns the individual [...]

It is probable that Mrs. E.'s claim collides with the moral demands of other persons in different spheres; this is so, to the extent that we are all different and for being thus – different – we tolerate one another. Here resides, then, the sense of the constitutional guarantee that we commented: the non imposition of private morals which as an exteriorized action must be accepted, as long as it does not cause damage to third persons....

[...]

4.2.2.1 Matters for Debate

The application of the conscientious objection in matters of health is relatively recent in Latin America. Establishing exceptions to the compliance of professional duty in the sphere of health, through the conscientious objection, could be viewed as a form of strengthening and perpetuating the asymmetry of power between the users of the health system and the professionals of the area. For this reason, it is relevant to analyze the conditions and the context of the exercise of the conscientious objection with the aim of ensuring the right to health to all persons.

In the realm of health, the phenomenon of outsourcing, or delegation of functions (or externalization) in providing health services has occurred. The State signs contracts for third parties to provide some services. This situation turns the analysis of the limits of conscientious objection of providers more complex, since it is possible that the mission and vision of the private person collides with people's right to health, especially in the field of sexuality and reproduction.

4.3 Abortion

One of the most severe health problems for women in Latin America and the Caribbean is mortality provoked by clandestine abortions. Most countries in the region define abortion as a crime; notwithstanding, its practice is massive. For example, in Mexico, an estimated one million women and girls resort to illegal abortions every year.[23]

The mortality figures resulting from this practice fluctuate among the different countries and continents, and lethalness is directly related to its illegality. In the United States, mortality due to abortions is 0.6 per 100 thousand procedures, while

[23] Human Rights Watch, *Víctimas por Partida Doble, Obstrucciones al aborto legal por violación en México*, 2006, Vol. 18, No. 1 (B), p. 32.

in developing countries this rate can be a hundredfold higher. However, due to the clandestine and illegal nature of abortion in the region, the figures are only estimates. The situation in Latin America and the Caribbean – with the exception of Cuba and, to a lesser extent, Puerto Rico – is defined by the crime and punishment axis, while, in the rest of the countries, the growing trend is to consider it as an option to preserve women's health and life.[24]

The discourse on abortion in the region has been, to a large extent, marked by the great influence that the Catholic Church has had, and still has. The inadmissibility of abortion from the religious point of view has been the necessary assumption to prohibit and punish it.[25] Law has thus become a sort of military arm of Catholic morals, putting aside the diverse moral conceptions that co-exist in a society.[26]

From a philosophical point of view, the punishment for abortion is grounded on the idea that the *nasciturus* is a person from the moment of fertilization.[27] The argument of the sacred nature of the right to life, understood as inviolable and absolute, turns any other argument irrelevant, even when the pregnancy is the product of rape, the fetus has serious congenital malformations, or the pregnancy places at risk the woman's health or life. Liberalism and feminism deal with abortion from the perspective of women's right to autonomy on their own bodies[28] and the right to draw up their own life path.[29] The arguments in favor of regulating abortions are based on diverse premises. On the one hand, some arguments are based on rejecting the identity of the fetus as a person, concluding that women's right to autonomy prevails over any other consideration. For some authors, whether the fetus is or is not a person constitutes an individual ethical valuation. However, the perspectives that are constructed based on the quality of person of the zygote, embryo, or fetus, end up hiding the question on the moral capacity of women to decide and exercise their right to bodily integrity.[30]

Even if the discussion is constructed based on the assumption that both the fetus and the woman share the condition of person, it is still not clear why the woman's life now has less value and protection because she is carrying a pregnancy. If the fetus and the woman are considered equals, the woman could invoke legal concepts such as self-defense, the unenforceability of another conduct or the state of necessity

---

[24] Rebecca Cook and Bernard Dickens, *Dinámicas de los derechos humanos en la reforma de las leyes de aborto*, http://www.gire.org.mx/phpnuke/modules.php?name=prueba&opgire=61

[25] Luigi Ferrajoli, "La cuestión del embrión entre derecho y moral," *Revista Jueces para la Democracia*, Vol. 44, 2002, p. 3.

[26] *Id.*

[27] Margarita Valdés, "Aborto y personas," in Margarita Valdés comp. *Controversias sobre el Aborto,* Instituto de Investigaciones Filosóficas-UNAM and Fondo de Cultura Económica, México, 2001, pp. 70–74.

[28] Margarita Valdés, *op.cit.*, p. 74.

[29] *See* Lynn Smith, "An equality approach to reproductive choice: R. v. Sullivan," *Yale Journal of Law & Feminism*, Vol. 4, No. 1, 1991, pp. 93–99.

[30] Beverly Wildung Harrison, *Our Right to Choose: Toward a New Ethic of Abortion*, Beacon Press, Boston, 1984, pp. 193–199.

to protect her own life or integrity. This premise is obviously limited: it does not provide a satisfactory argument in cases of interruption of pregnancy in which the indicated justifications cannot be applied.

On the other hand, the debate on abortion, focused exclusively on the rights of women, could turn into a pyrrhic victory if governments are not willing to pay for legal abortion services.[31] This point is made more evident when abortion is constructed based on the idea of State non interference, since it could imply that it is not the State's obligation to finance this practice.

In the United States, since the 1973 decision of its Supreme Court in Roe v. Wade, there have been attempts to curtail the right of women to decide through legislation or judicial rulings.[32] For this reason Canadian feminists, for example, have grounded decriminalization of abortion on equality, respect for women's right to life, security, and personal freedom.[33]

On the other hand, to assume that abortion is a problem of rights means that these must be weighted when they come into tension. If this is so, women's position is weaker when, for example, the issue of fetal viability is treated.

At the International Conference on Population and Development in Cairo, a consensus was reached on the fact that abortion cannot be promoted as a method of family planning. States must commit to provide a humanitarian treatment and to guide those women who have resorted to this practice. The current trend in international law on human rights is to consider punishment of all forms of abortion as a serious violation of women's human rights, whether it be on their integrity, their right to survival, or the right to access the health services in confidentiality. For example, it is understood that there is an infringement of women's rights when they are notified in hospitals, in the face of complications of an induced abortion, or when the State does not deliver the services of non-punishable abortions.

Notwithstanding the above description, the situation of the region is in a process of change. Example of this are the modifications experimented in Mexico, since the Paulina Ramírez case,[34] the interpretation made by the medical profession in Uruguay when facing complications of abortion, and the recent holding of the Colombian Constitutional Court that partially de-criminalized it.[35]

Despite being one of the crimes of greater inefficacy, abortion has a high symbolic power because it gives an image of moral order in spite of the high number of clandestine abortions carried out in the continent.[36] Thus, in this case, the law operates as a mechanism that relieves the consciences of some, under the premise that the life of the unborn child is protected.

---

[31] *See* Carol Smart in, *Feminism and the Power of the Law*, Routledge, London, 1989, pp. 143–144.

[32] *See* Marlene Gerber Fried, "Abortion in the US: Barriers to Access," *Reproductive Health Matters*, No 9, 1997, pp. 37–45.

[33] Smith, *op.cit.,* pp. 93–99.

[34] *See* GIRE, "Paulina en el nombre de la ley", *Temas para el Debate* 2, DF México, 2000 in http://www.gire.org.mx/publica/paulina.pdf

[35] C 355/06.

[36] The Alan Guttmacher Institute, *Clandestine Abortion: A Latin American Reality*, New York, 1994, p. 23.

It is also possible to consider that the illicitness of abortion leads women to resort to it when a greater length of the pregnancy has elapsed. This exposes them to higher risks, for they must obtain the information and economic resources to be able to access to a clandestine procedure, after looking for the one which implies less risks for their health.[37] Finally, from a utilitarian point of view, the consequence of illegality lies in the high costs both for the women who suffer them directly and for the health systems which have to provide attention when complications arise.

4.3.1 The Right to Confidentiality and the Obligation to Report

Effective penalization, in the few cases in which it occurs, generally falls on women of more economically vulnerable sectors.[38] Penal prosecution in most cases results in reporting of the *noticia criminis* at health facilities where the women are treated because of post-abortion complications. The exercise of medicine and the related professions require, in most cases, that a bond of trust be established between the patient and the professional. Healthcare service providers are required, on account of their profession, to deploy a series of actions leading to the recovery and maintenance of health, for which they need a propitious environment that allow the person who requests the services to deliver complete information of what he/she is suffering from. Actions in healthcare are guided by the four principles of bioethics: those of beneficence, non-malfeasance, autonomy or respect for the patients and justice.[39] Medical confidentiality responds to the observance of the principles of beneficence and non-malfeasance of bioethics. The principle of beneficence obliges health professionals to advance the greatest welfare of their patients whereas that of non-malfeasance imposes the obligation that healthcare not produce harm.

One of the juridical problems arising from the matter of the treatment of incomplete abortion is the conflict between two mandates: the obligation to keep professional secrecy (which can be penalized) and the obligation to report women who have gone to the hospital with signs of a provoked abortion. For example, the General Health Law of Peru rests on the pillars of respect for the right of persons to decide on the number of children they wish to have, but at the same time, it establishes that doctors are exempted from the secrecy of medical confidentiality when they are

---

[37] J. Barzelatto and A. Faúndes, *op.cit.*, p. 71.

[38] Lidia Casas, *Mujeres Procesadas por Aborto*, Foro Abierto de Salud y Derechos Sexuales y Reproductivos and Center for Reproductive Law and Policy, Santiago, 1996; Foro Abierto de Salud y Derechos Sexuales y Reproductivos and Center for Reproductive Law and Policy, *Encarceladas. Leyes contra el Aborto en Chile. Un análisis desde los Derechos Humanos*, Canadá, 1998; Centro Legal para Derechos Reproductivos y Políticas Públicas (CRLP), *Perseguidas. Proceso político y legislación sobre aborto en El Salvador: un análisis de derechos humanos*, Nueva York, 2000.

[39] R. Cook, B. Dickens and M. Fathalla, *op.cit.*, pp. 64–69.

summoned by the Police or the Attorney General, being required to denounce any situation in which there are signs of a provoked abortion.[40] Similar provisions are found in the legislation from Mexico, Chile, Costa Rica, and Argentina.

In some cases, legislation foresees that those persons, who on account of their status, profession, or legal function – as doctors – have a duty to keep the secrecy of matters entrusted to them, may abstain from declaring, but only as concerns to that secrecy.

The doctrine has understood that secrecy is a professional duty that falls on certain persons on account of their profession or trade. It includes doctors, lawyers, notaries or priests and consists in not revealing to third parties facts they have come to know in the exercise of their profession or trade.[41] The protected information is all the information which the affected person wishes to shield and, which allows the professional to adequately perform his/her function, avoiding their discretion in appreciation of the scope of the secret. It would be absolute if it cannot be divulged under any circumstance and, relative when there are circumstances or a legal provision in which the revelation is justified or legitimized.[42]

The Inter-American Court, in the case of De la Cruz Flores v. Peru, declared that the principle of legality is infringed upon when a healthcare professional is incriminated for having provided medical assistance and not having reported the possible criminal acts that the treated patients may have been involved in. The Court considered that the doctors "have a right and an obligation to protect the confidentiality of the information to which, as physicians, they have access" and among other cases, imposing on doctors the obligation of reporting possible criminal conducts of their patients based on the information they may obtain while exercising their profession produces a violation of article 9 of the American Convention on Human Rights (American Convention). The Court reaffirmed the observation of the Committee on Human Rights on the matter, which established that the States incur in international responsibility when they violate professional secrecy incriminating a person, and recommended modifying legislation with the aim of protecting the confidentiality of medical information.

The rationale of Judge Sergio García Ramírez, in his vote, discussing the obligation of secrecy of the medical act, cautions that its protection does not mean not investigating or prosecuting criminal situations. It is the duty of the attorney and the prosecutor to fulfill their functions but they cannot make use of the doctor-patient relationship to achieve their aim, since turning the professional into the attorney's assistant would not only generate a crisis of professional and social roles, but would mean a tacit incorporation of doctors, defenders, and priests to the ranks of the police force. "If confidential communication between the lawyer and the accused,

[40] CLADEM and CRLP, *Silencios y Complicidades. Violencia contra las Mujeres en los Servicios Públicos de Salud en el Perú*, Lima, 1998, p. 37.

[41] Basile García Maañón, *Aborto e Infanticidio*, Editorial Universidad Buenos Aires, 1990, p. 162.

[42] Hernán Silva Silva, *Medicina Legal y Psiquiatría Forense*, Tomo II, Editorial Jurídica de Chile, Santiago, 1995, p. 615.

which is sheltered from interferences, is protected, and it is accepted that the priest is not required to violate the secret of confession –which even constitutes an essential feature of this specific communication that believers consider sacramental– the same consideration, at least, must be accepted in the relationship between the doctor and the patient."

Human Rights Watch
Prosecution for Illegal Abortions

Yes, of course we implement [the penal sanctions for illegal abortion] .... If anyone goes to jail, it is the woman.

Deputy Attorney General, San Luis Potosí.

Officials in most states told Human Rights Watch they do not maintain specific data on the number of women in prison for the crime of abortion. It is likely that only a small portion of the estimated hundreds of thousands of girls and women who undergo clandestine abortion in Mexico each year go to jail. Nevertheless, prosecutions of girls and women who have had illegal abortions are not unknown "From August to December 2005, we have had ten women here [charged] for illegal abortion," said Carmen Hernández Rosas, head of the forensic medical team in Guadalajara, Jalisco.

In stark contrast to the dismissive attitude and delays victims of domestic and sexual violence experience when they seek redress for crimes committed against them, justice seems to be relatively swift when the state decides to prosecute for illegal abortion. In Guanajuato, a public official who spoke on the condition of anonymity, said:

> There are five women [currently] in jail for abortion [in Guanajuato]. ... [In one case] a woman ... gets to the hospital with very strong hemorrhaging, and the first thing the doctor does is to report her [to the authorities]. ... They arrest her very fast, and they sent her to jail for a week [pre-sentence detention]. Why is it that when it is a rape case, everything is so negative, [and] they do not do anything. ... And in those cases [of illegal abortion], everything is so fast?

Guanajuato's attorney general denied that any women have been sentenced for abortion over the past five years in that state or are currently in jail for that crime.

"Ana Díaz," a twenty-nine-year-old woman from Yucatán personally experienced the priority authorities give to investigations of presumed illegal abortions as compared to reports of domestic violence. When she attempted to file a complaint against her now ex-husband for domestic violence, the public prosecutor told her that there was not enough proof, despite the fact that "I was all black and blue, all beaten up." The public prosecutor took her declaration once, and, according to Díaz, then did nothing. In contrast, one year later when she went to a public hospital with hemorrhaging, the public prosecutors suspected an illegal abortion and seemingly spared no effort to prove her crime:

> At 7:30 p.m. they [the doctors] did the curettage [to clean me out]. ... And then it all started, the hardest part. ... I was still more or less sleepy after the anesthesia. ... I saw a person, he said can I ask you questions, and I said yes. ... [I said] I didn't know that I was pregnant. ... In fact, I had gone four times to [the health center linked to my] social security and they had

told me it was my colon [that made my stomach hurt]. … [The public prosecutors] took my declaration, one time. … Then two more persons came, one was a chemical expert from the public prosecutor's office, and another person also from the public prosecutor's office, and once more I had to give the whole explanation. … Then two-three hours later, again. I think they came back four or five times. … At 6:30 in the morning they were still there. … They signed me out at about 10 o'clock and I still had to go to the public prosecutor's office to see where they had the [fetal remains]. … There I had to do another interview with who-knows who. … He said that I couldn't leave because they might need me for another declaration. … I said that I just wanted to be with my family. From 10 o'clock in the morning until 6 o'clock at night, they finally let us out. … My sister says that when they came [to my home] to inspect the bathroom, they measured it, they looked through the trash, they collected water from the waste-pipe, to see if there were remains of blood. … Look at the difference [from when I declared against my husband]!

Criminal and Correctional National Chamber of Appeals
Buenos Aires, Argentina
Natividad Frías
August 26 of 1966

Main Legal Issue:

Can a woman be sued for the crime of abortion when the authorities learned of this through her self-incrimination? Must the doctor who treated the woman, denounce her when he learned the facts from the women's confession?

Facts:

A woman who performed an abortion, suffered complications, and went to a public hospital in search of medical assistance. She was denounced to the authorities by the hospital staff. She was sentenced in the first instance but her defense requested the nullity of the criminal process since the criminal proceedings were initiated because the woman had incriminated herself by revealing her condition of post abortion.

Court Ruling:

The Chamber holds that the lawsuit against the defendant violates laws that prohibit self-incrimination, and, as a result, cannot be the basis of any process against her.

Extracts:

[…]

On art. 156 of the Penal Code which orders the disclosure "of a secret whose revelation may cause harm" when there is no "just cause," I shall say, like so many other times, that this case is exclusively legal. That is, that only a law may exempt from keeping due secrecy, turning its violation into an obligation.

In no case can the simple public interest be the just cause because that interest would always play so as to bugger up all secrets. Nothing would justify the secrecy of the priest or of the lawyer or of any other professional and not that of the versed in the art of healing, since confession or the knowledge that these obtain are generally conditioned by a greater and more urgent pressure.

Article 18 of the National Constitution states that "no one can be obliged to declare against himself," and a concealed form, cruel and ignoble of breaching the precept is to utilize the vital desire of the woman who has had the abortion to denounce her crime, a crime that is made known through a confession that has been practically snatched from her, or due to the state of physical and spiritual helplessness which should not be taken advantage of to serve these ends, as other situations which should not be taken advantage of, like the use of drugs, for example.

[…]

The exercise of an official position does not exempt from the duty of keeping secrecy. … In prior holdings I have also said over and over again that a preliminary investigation cannot be carried out based on a criminal denunciation because the legal system is airtight and it does not permit its own violation.

Besides, public interest could not justify this inhuman dilemma: death or prison.

[…]

It is necessary, before all else, to clearly understand what the secret is, and what those revelations are. We cannot admit, in any way, that the law demands the secrecy to have been expressly requested. The sick person who seeks the help of a doctor thinks that he does so with the certainty that his ailments will not be divulged, because they are guarded by the strictest secrecy. It is something that is implied, that it is not necessary to renew in each visit or assistance. To think differently would be like admitting that the faithful who approach the confessional booth, in search of relief of their conscience and forgiveness of their sins, had to request the same secrecy to the confessor. This would be simply absurd, since as noted by doctor Sebastián Soler, the secret is the same, whether it be communicated or informed, or not.

[…]

[W]hoever resorts to a doctor because of a self-inflicted condition, even a criminal one like abortion, enjoys the security that his/her secret will not be made public; instead, the same does not happen when the attack has been produced by a stranger, since that action is strange to the relationship between the doctor and the patient, which is the one covered by the law. In these cases the physician must report the criminal action executed by third persons, except in cases such as those of crimes against honesty, in which the viability of the action depends on the private instance, to cover the risks of the "*strepitus fori*."

It is true that a distinction between the doctors who exercise their profession in a private way and those who do it in a capacity as public employees or officials, whose conduct in the face of knowledge of a criminal act could be regulated by article 164 of the Code of Procedures and to which article 167 of the same code would not be referring, could be made.

The approach is, in my opinion, more apparent than real, since the law, in the first of the quoted texts, would not seem to have included doctors, instead, including them in a specific way in art. 165. In this functional duality – doctor and official – factors of a professional nature necessarily predominate originating in moral and juridical norms, which govern the exercise of medicine, as a profession, in which public order is involved.

On the other hand, a contrary solution would take us to the absurd of admitting that one same doctor would be obliged by professional secrecy, depending on whether he acted in his private office or in the public ward.

4.3.1.1 Matters for Debate

Confession, in the framework of a criminal prosecution and especially of a police investigation, has been the object of criticism for violating the individual guarantees of the investigated person before the punitive power of the State. Women's experience with induced and illegal abortion raises the problems and scope of the guarantee of non self-incrimination when they resort to a health facility in search of medical help. The obligations to accuse, imposed on professionals or public employees in the face of the commission of a crime, is contradictory with the duty of keeping confidentiality. This conflict is still more evident when the professional is a public employee, and leaves in a situation of special vulnerability those women who resort to public services for medical care.

4.3.2 Legal Insecurity of Non Punishable Abortion

Generally speaking, Latin American legislation prohibits abortion with the aim of protecting the lives of those who are not yet born, the social, moral and family order. In spite of the punitive or surveillance emphasis, with the exception of Chile, El Salvador and recently Nicaragua, the legislation of the region foresees some hypotheses of non punishable abortions: pregnancies which are the result of a rape or the rape of a minor, the pregnancies that pose risks to the woman's life or health, or when there are serious fetal malformations which are not compatible with life outside the uterus. These exceptions demonstrate that even the most conservative views recognize that in these cases there is an infringement of women's basic rights. After all, criminal law does not establish norms for heroes or heroines, since superfluous norms are not enforceable. However, when dealing with abortion, that maxim becomes imprecise. In the opinion of one of the drafters of the Chilean Constitution of 1980, women are called to martyrdom.

The exceptions in law have not been, however, a guarantee for women complying with the requisites to access safe and legal abortions in facilities providing public health services. Access to safe abortions with no risks depends on a variety of factors, one of them being the diversity of opinions – or interpretations – that the medical community has regarding the law and the risk assessment carried out by a medical team. Ultimately, the decision will not be subject to what the woman determines but will be in the hands of a group of professionals whose religious or ethical convictions could infiltrate their decisions.[43] Something similar happens in rape cases where the values or positions of the medical profession tend to hinder and limit a raped woman's right to abort.[44]

In countries like Argentina or Peru women are required to seek judicial authorization to disrupt a pregnancy. It is claimed to be a practice of hospitals and their professionals resulting from the fear of the consequences that the procedure could entail and of being sanctioned.[45] In the case of Argentina, where the law provides for non punishable abortions in therapeutic cases and in case of rape of a woman with mental disabilities, courts have gradually established the doctrine that judicial authorization is not necessary when the situation is expressly established by the law.

Those who deny even therapeutic abortions do not believe on the thesis of self-defense "because self-defense implies that someone, to defend him/herself from an unfair gestation, may provoke a harm that does not necessarily imply the death of the aggressor, and also because the child could never be considered an aggressor; he/she is in a condition of dependence on the mother, who on the other hand, has caused the pregnancy. The child is absolutely innocent."[46] Thus, facing a request for a therapeutic abortion, a judge pointed out: "Maternity and paternity have a risk. Love is a risk. [...] (Every day workers fall from the scaffolding of the building work...there are many men, women who die, in different places, taking the risks on their lives...)."[47]

Requirement of Prosecutorial Inquiry Number 1 referred to the death of Ana María Acevedo
Criminal Correctional Court of the First Instance of the Fifth District Court Santa Fe Province, Argentina 2008

Facts:
A 19 year-old young woman visits a health center where she is diagnosed with cancer. When the radiation treatment was about to begin, the doctors discover that she was carrying a one-month pregnancy; the radiotherapist expressed that the treatment should not be carried out because of the harmful effects that it could have on the fetus. The young woman's parents request a therapeutic abortion, permitted under article 86 of the Penal Code, but it is denied by the doctors of the hospital. At 22 weeks of pregnancy she undergoes an urgent cesarean section. The baby died and twenty days later the young woman died. The family reports the doctors for negligent injury and misconduct in office.

---

[43] J. Barzelatto and A. Faúndes, *op.cit.*, pp. 74–75.

[44] IACHR, Paulina Ramírez v. México. *See* L. Cabal, M. Roa and L. Sepúlveda-Oliva, *op.cit.*, pp. 67–69; and Marcela Serrano, "Sin Dios ni Ley", *Un Mundo Raro: Dos relatos mexicanos*, Mondadori, México DF, 2000, pp. 61–94.

[45] Human Rights Watch, *Decisión prohibida*, *op.cit.*, p. 51.

[46] Mauricio Besio, Fernando Chomalí, Jorge Neira and Ángela Vivanco, *Aborto Terapéutico. Consideraciones médicas, éticas, jurídicas y del magisterio de la Iglesia Católica*, Facultad de Medicina, Centro de Bioética, Pontificia Universidad Católica de Chile, Santiago, 2002, p. 24.

[47] Judge De Negri, Supreme Court of Justice Buenos Aires (Province) C.P. de P. A.K. Authorization, La Plata June 27 of 2005.

Court Ruling:
The court condemns the chief doctor of the hospital's oncology service for the crimes of malpractice derived in negligent injury and misconduct in office, the radiotherapist for the crime of misconduct in office. Additionally the court orders the seizure of the property of both in order to compensate the family. It recognizes that a therapeutic abortion would have been legal, at any time of the gestation period.

Extracts:
[T]wo aspects should be dealt with in order to define the penal responsibility of the accused, one of a strictly medical nature [...] and the other, related to the provision of a State healthcare service. [...]

[...] Knowing of the existence of the patient's pregnancy, from the beginning of gestation itself, the seriousness of the mother's illness, the danger on her life and the consent provided, "not to have offered" the interruption of the pregnancy as an alternative to perform the therapy against the tumor, knowing that without that it would be impossible to carry the pregnancy to term, to induce childbirth. [...] the positive omission of the demanded conducts of knowledge and prudence, have caused a serious damage to the health, negatively affecting the patient's chances of a better quality of life, being obliged to foresee it, or if foreseen, obliged to avoid it, as the duty of seeking the health welfare of the patient.

[...]

Now, having to make the legal qualification of the claimed fact, I uphold the one opportunely made when the prosecution of the appellants was ordered since we have found that the medical professional performance of César Raúl Blajman constitutes "malpractice," so that he is held criminally liable of the crime of Negligent Injury.

[...]

4.3.2.1 Matters for Debate

In the few cases in which the detractors of all justifiable forms of abortion recognize the risks to life, they formulate an authorization of *sui generis* law in the sense that they permit a morally acceptable action –for example chemotherapy during pregnancy- that would entail an abortion. These situations are termed "interruption of pregnancy," or "indirect abortion," since the fetus dies as a consequence of a health action which does not pursue abortion. In these cases, they point out, "there is no willful misconduct or abortive malice, but compliance with the medical duty, in the sense of utilizing the means available to save those who are susceptible of it."[48] This is what is known as the theory of the double effect, since the death of the fetus is not sought, as would happen in therapeutic abortion, but the application of certain medical conducts that could result, as a consequence of these, in the fetus' death.

[48] D. Basso, Nacer y Morir con Dignidad, *op.cit.*, p. 24.

4.3.3 *Anencephaly*

Anencephaly is a condition or anomaly in a fetus. It consists in the failure of one end of the neural tube to close, implying the absence of the cerebral hemispheres and the bone structure of the skull.[49] These cases are always incompatible with extra-uterine life and, if born alive, the babies die during the first days after birth.[50]

Some claim that the consequences for the pregnant woman and even for the rest of the family would permit to classify this case –medically and ethically- within the cases of therapeutic abortion.[51] Anencephaly increases the risk during pregnancy and childbirth because of the presence of "polyhydramnios [an increase of amniotic fluid] with all the complications derived from it (difficulties for breathing, hypotension in dorsal decumbent position, uterine rupture, amniotic fluid embolism, placental abruption, post-birth uterine lack of muscle tone, etc.)"[52]

The Juridical and medical position that questions the acceptance of "therapeutic" as a classification of abortion in these cases affirms that "provoked abortion, even when its intention is to protect the mother's life or health, is exactly the opposite: to deprive an innocent of his/her life. In this case there is no therapy, since if it existed, it would imply that the medical-surgical intervention directly seeks to eliminate the sick part of the body, and in this case, on the contrary, the suppression of the fetus is sought to avoid that the mother's health worsens or her life is at risk."[53]

United Nations Human Rights Committee
Karen Llantoy v. Peru
U.N. Doc. CCPR/C/85/D/1153/2003 (2005)
October 24, 2005

Main Legal Issue:

Is it a violation of international law under Optional Protocol to the International Covenant on Civil and Political Rights to deny a woman the possibility of a therapeutic abortion?

Facts:

The author became pregnant in March 2001, when she was 17. On June 27, 2001 she was examined at the Archbishop Loayza National Hospital in Lima, part of the Ministry of Health; the exam showed that she was carrying an anencephalic fetus.

On July 3rd, Dr. Ygor Pérez Solf, a gynecologist and obstetrician at the hospital, informed the author of the fetus abnormality and the risks to her life if the pregnancy continued. Dr. Pérez said that she had two options: to continue the pregnancy or to

[49] Pedro Hooft, "Anencefalia: Consideraciones Bioéticas y Jurídicas. La ausencia de un substrato biológico mínimo ¿genera" diferencia moral?, *Acta Bioética*, año VI, No. 2, 2000.

[50] *Id.*, pp. 269–270.

[51] *Id.*, p. 273.

[52] *Id.*, pp. 270–271.

[53] M. Besio, *op.cit.*, p. 10.

terminate it. He advised termination by means of uterine curettage. The author decided to terminate the pregnancy, and the necessary clinical studies were carried out, confirming the fetal abnormality.

On July 19th, when the author reported to the hospital together with her mother for admission preparatory to the operation, Dr. Pérez informed her that she needed to obtain written authorization from the hospital director. Since she was under age, her mother, Ms. Elena Huamán Lara, requested the authorization. On July 24th, Dr. Maximiliano Cárdenas Díaz, the hospital director, replied in writing that the termination could not be carried out as to do so would be unlawful, since under article 120 of the Criminal Code, abortion was punishable by a prison term of no more than three months when it was likely that at birth the child would suffer serious physical or mental defects, while under article 119, therapeutic abortion was permitted only when termination of the pregnancy was the only way of saving the life of the pregnant woman or avoiding serious and permanent damage to her health.

On August 16th, Ms. Amanda Gayoso, a social worker and member of the Peruvian association of social workers, carried out an assessment of the case and concluded that medical intervention to terminate the pregnancy was advisable "since its continuation would only prolong the distress and emotional instability of Karen and her family." However, no intervention took place owing to the refusal of the Health Ministry medical personnel.

On August 20th, Dr. Marta B. Rondón, a psychiatrist and member of the Peruvian Medical Association, concluded that "the so-called principle of the welfare of the unborn child has caused serious harm to the mother, since she has unnecessarily been made to carry to term a pregnancy whose fatal outcome was known in advance, and this has substantially contributed to triggering the symptoms of depression, with its severe impact on the development of an adolescent and the patient's future mental health."

On January 13, 2002, the petitioner gave birth to an anencephalic baby girl, who survived for four days, during which the mother had to breastfeed her. Following her daughter's death, the author fell into a state of deep depression. The petitioner also states that she suffered from an inflammation of the vulva which required medical treatment.

The petitioner has submitted to the Committee a statement made by Dr. Aníbal Faúndes and Dr. Luis Tavara, specialists from the Center for Reproductive Rights association, studied the author's clinical dossier and stated that anencephaly is a condition which is fatal to the fetus in all cases. Death immediately follows birth in most cases and endangers the mother's life. In their opinion, in refusing to terminate the pregnancy, the medical personnel took a decision that was damaging to the petitioner.

Regarding the exhaustion of domestic remedies, the petitioner claims that this requirement is waived when judicial remedies available domestically are ineffective in the case in question, and she points out that the Committee has laid down on several occasions that the petitioner has no obligation to exhaust a remedy which would prove ineffective. She adds that in Peru there is no administrative remedy which would enable a pregnancy to be terminated on therapeutic grounds, nor any judicial remedy functioning with the speed and efficiency required to enable a woman to require the authorities to guarantee her right to a lawful abortion within the limited period, by virtue of the special circumstances in such cases. She also states that her financial circumstances and those of her family prevented her from obtaining legal advice.

The petitioner states that the complaint is not being considered under any other procedure of international settlement.

Committee's opinion:
In opinion of the Committee, the State omission, by not authorizing the petitioner a therapeutic abortion was the cause of the suffering the adolescent girl suffered. In General Comment N. 20, the Committee has indicated that the right protected under Article 7 of the Pact not only refers to physical pain, but also moral suffering, and that this protection is even more important in the case of under aged individuals.

Extracts:
The Human Rights Committee has considered the present complaint in the light of all the information received, in accordance with article 5, paragraph 1, of the Optional Protocol.

The Committee notes that the author attached a doctor's statement confirming that her pregnancy exposed her to a life-threatening risk. She also suffered severe psychological consequences exacerbated by her status as a minor, as the psychiatric report of 20 August 2001 confirmed. The Committee notes that the State party has not provided any evidence to challenge the above. It notes that the authorities were aware of the risk to the petitioner's life, since a gynecologist and obstetrician in the same hospital had advised her to terminate the pregnancy, with the operation to be carried out in the same hospital. The subsequent refusal of the competent medical authorities to provide the service may have endangered the petitioner's life. The author states that no effective remedy was available to her to oppose that decision. In the absence of any information from the State party, due weight must be given to the author's claims.

The author also claims that, due to the refusal of the medical authorities to carry out the therapeutic abortion, she had to endure the distress of seeing her daughter's marked deformities and knowing that she would die very soon. This was an experience which added further pain and distress to that which she had already borne during the period when she was obliged to continue with the pregnancy. The author attaches a psychiatric certificate confirming the state of deep depression into which she fell and the severe consequences this caused, taking her age into account. The Committee notes that this situation could have been foreseen, since a hospital doctor had diagnosed anencephaly in the fetus, yet the hospital director refused termination. The omission on the part of the State in not enabling the petitioner to benefit from a therapeutic abortion was, in the Committee's view, the cause of the suffering she experienced. The Committee has pointed out in its General Comment No. 20 that the right set out in article 7 of the Covenant relates not only to physical pain but also to mental suffering, and that the protection is particularly important in the case of minors. Consequently, the Committee considers that the facts before it reveal a violation of article 7 of the Covenant. In the light of this finding, the Committee does not consider it necessary in the circumstances to made a finding on article 6 of the Covenant.

The petitioner states that the State party, in denying her the opportunity to secure medical intervention to terminate the pregnancy, interfered arbitrarily in her private life. The Committee notes that a public-sector doctor told the petitioner that she could either continue with the pregnancy or terminate it in accordance with domestic legislation allowing abortions in cases of risk to the life of the mother. The conditions for a lawful abortion as set out in the law were present. In the circumstances of the case, the refusal to act in accordance with the petitioner's decision to terminate her pregnancy was not justified and amounted to a violation of article 17 of the Covenant.

The petitioner claims to have been a victim of violation of articles 2 of the Covenant on the grounds that she lacked an adequate legal remedy. In the absence of information from the State party, the Committee considers that due weight must be given to the petitioner's claims as regards to the lack of an adequate legal remedy and consequently concludes that the facts before it also reveal a violation of article 2 in conjunction with articles 7, 17 and 24. 7. The Human Rights Committee, acting under article 5, paragraph 4, of the Optional Protocol to the Covenant, is of the view that the facts before it disclose a violation of articles 2, 7, 17 and 24 of the Covenant. In accordance with article 2, paragraph 3 (a), of the Covenant, the State party is required to furnish the author with an effective remedy, including compensation. The State party has an obligation to take steps to ensure that similar violations do not occur in the future.

Bearing in mind that, as a party to the Optional Protocol, the State party recognizes the competence of the Committee to determine whether there has been a violation of the Covenant, and that, under article 2 of the Covenant, the State party has undertaken to ensure to all individuals within its territory and subject to its jurisdiction the rights recognized in the Covenant and to offer an effective and enforceable remedy when a violation is found to have occurred, the Committee wishes to receive from the State party, within 90 days, information about the measures taken to give effect to the present Views. The State party is also requested to publish the Committee's Views.

Supreme Court of the Argentine Nation
Silvia Tanus v. the Government of the City of Buenos Aires
January 11 of 2001

Main Legal Issue:
Is it possible to circumvent the matter of abortion when the interruption of a pregnancy of an anencephalic fetus is considered an induction of birth? Is there conflict of rights in the abortion of an anencephalic fetus?

Facts:
A woman was authorized to have labor induced to end the pregnancy of an anencephalic fetus. The court of first instance authorized the hospital to do so, and the General Advisor of Persons with Disabilities filed an extraordinary appeal requesting that the authorization be revoked, taking into account the constitutional norms, the American Convention on Human Rights, the International Covenant on Civil and Political Rights and the Convention on the Rights of the Child.

Court Ruling:
The court authorizes the procedure for considering that what will be done will be to induce birth and that the fetus will not die as a result of the procedure but because of its condition as anencephalic.

Extracts:
[…]
The birth will only evidence that the baby cannot survive in an autonomous way, while the solution here adopted will not affect the protection of the baby's life since conception, as established in article 2 of law 23849 which approves the Convention on the Rights of the Child – and article 4 of the American Convention on Human Rights, Pact of San José, Costa Rica. […]

The causes and effects of the facts that lead to the death qualified as inevitable are part of a biological process whose course cannot be altered by scientific means nor, as is evident, by any judicial decision.

[…]

It must be stated, as a summary of what has been noted here, that it is not a case of abortion, or of eugenic abortion […], or of a sort of euthanasia, or of a being that is not –to exclude the protection of its life- a person, nor of the freedom of procreation to justify the interruption of its life.

Indeed, such actions appear aligned with a human action aimed at provoking the child's death during gestation.

On the contrary, what is authorized here is the induction of childbirth once the moment is reached when the progress of the pregnancy ensures –within the margin of every vital situation– the birth of a child with full possibilities of developing and living.

[…]

[Dissenting opinion of Minister Boggiano:]

In the first place, that the anencephalic unborn child have a right to life is not only an imperative derived from the letter of the provisions transcribed but the harmonization of these with the rest of the constitutional system in force in matters of human rights […] that is so, because there is not a single norm in that ambit, which, as concerns the right in question, makes any distinction limiting it, for example, to certain types of infants with certain phenotypic, physiognomic characteristics or, in sum, distinguishable from the field of medical science; neither is it perceived that the protection of the life of children is restricted to a determined class of situations or else that, plainly and simply, it is excluded in cases like the one now before us.

With that understanding it is not pertinent for the judges to create – under pretext of filling non existing legal gaps – situations of exception that reduce the subjective ambit of the alluded right; and that, not only because if they acted thus they would be overflowing the channel within which the Constitution mandates them to perform their function, but because in addition, they would incur in a biased exegesis of the international treaties on human rights which is contrary to the specific hermeneutical norms; thus, for example, it is prohibited to "permit any State Party, group, or person, to suppress the enjoyment or exercise of the rights and freedoms recognized in this Convention or to restrict them to a greater extent than provided for herein" at the same time as it is prohibited "to restrict the enjoyment or exercise of any right or freedom recognized by virtue of the laws of any State Party or by virtue of another agreement to which one of the said states is a party (conf. art. 29, sections a) and b) of the Pact of San José, Costa Rica)…."

4.3.3.1 Matters for Debate

In the majority of cases of anencephaly an *ad litem* curator is designated in representation of the one who is to be born, whose main argument in this and other cases is that, recognizing the effects on the woman's health, the sole induction of labor means shortening the life of the unborn, which would be contrary to the American Convention. The development of case law in higher courts has been to consider the authorization of induction of childbirth as licit. Hooft cautions that in addition to the certainty of the medical diagnosis, the gestational age of the fetus is relevant, adding that anencephaly constitutes a substantive moral difference, for which reason there is no problem in the authorization of abortion, and that he shares the opinion that "it is not appropriate in this case to speak of 'abortion,' because of all the ethical, social and legal connotations that this term entails."[54]

The cases of anencephaly that could lead to abortions for therapeutic indication, – if the objective is aimed at protecting the woman's health (physical or mental) – or eugenic, are often termed "authorization for the induction of labor."[55] This way, to resolve a case, the judges seem to opt for the medical language rather than a legal language. In sum, the operators seek to give concrete answers to pressing situations for women, and one way is to avoid that the situation be labeled as abortion. These situations have hindered the development of a jurisprudence that takes care of the facts that lie at the basis of the case, that is, the non punishable abortion under certain circumstances. At the same time, to the extent that these cases are treated like induced labor, the discussion focuses on the recognition of the unborn as a person in contrast with the rights of the born person – the woman.

[54] P. Hooft, "Bioética y Jurisprudencia", *op.cit.,* p. 224.

[55] P. Hooft, "Anencefalia: consideraciones bioéticas y jurídicas. La ausencia de un substrato biológico mínimo ¿genera diferencia moral?" *op.cit.,* p. 272.

4.4 Health, Technology, and Contraception

For some decades now, courts of justice have become spaces of discussion on the right of persons to decide. The legal actions, in some cases, have been promoted by men and women whose right to self-determination is questioned as a result of the actions or omissions of health officials or professionals, and who search, through litigation, the reaffirmation and exercise of the infringed upon rights.[56]

However, Latin America has also witnessed how public policies developed by governments and regulations regarding health, particularly sexual and reproductive health, are judicialized when they contradict positions that reject the notion of autonomy. While the emergence of detractor militant groups of modern contraceptive methods has taken to judicial platforms the authorization to deliver, commercialize, or distribute emergency contraceptives drugs, the utilization of new assisted reproductive techniques have also been affected.

The authorization for the registry, delivery and sale of emergency contraceptive drugs has been litigated in Argentina, Chile, Colombia, Ecuador, Mexico, and Peru. In some cases, the legal actions have been promoted directly by the Church (as the case of the administrative process against Profamilia in the INVIMA)[57] or Catholic organizations close to the ecclesiastical hierarchy, like the organization Portal de Belén in Argentina.

The objections to these methods lie in the fact that for their detractors they do not operate as contraceptive methods. They claim that preventing the implantation of a fertilized egg in the lining of the uterus wall would be equivalent to an abortion. They also add that the *conceptus,* if exists, would have a special protection in the American Convention, under article 4.1 and the Convention on the Rights of the Child, to the extent that the latter understands that every human being under the age of 18 is a child.

In a similar way, this rationale questions assisted reproduction techniques. The manipulation and death of pre-implanted embryos is objected too. The arguments in both cases are similar:

> For those who want to argue that the unborn, particularly during the first trimester of gestation, is not an integral human being because it does not possess the characteristics of self-conscience, intuition, thought, memory, imagination, and therefore does not deserve the same rights and protections awarded to the newborn, it must be said that even though such characteristics are not yet developed in the zygote, they are present in the genes for the development of the brain, where these capacities are located.[58]

From this rationale they claim that the conceived is a person: "it is no more – and no less! – than to make a reality of that which Andrés Bello established in our Civil

---

[56] *See* Lucia de Lourdes Ferreira da Costa, Ellen Hardy, Maria José Duarte Osis, Aníbal Faúndes, "Termination of Pregnancy for Fetal Abnormality Incompatible with Life: Women's Experiences in Brazil," *Reproductive Health Matters*, Vol. 13, No. 26, 2005, pp. 139–146.

[57] *See* L. Cabal, M. Roa and L. Sepúlveda-Oliva, *op.cit.*, pp. 51–88.

[58] Eduardo Rodríguez Yunta, "Derechos del cigoto desde una perspectiva biológica y metafísica," *Revista Chilena de Derecho*, Vol. 28, No. 2, 2001, pp. 263–264.

Code (art. 55 of the Civil Code of Chile) in a really vanguard norm, still challenging today: 'All the individuals of the human species, whatever their age, sex, lineage or condition, are persons.'"[59]

The objection is based on sustaining that any interpretation of the substantive or procedural norms must be made in the light of the international obligations on the respect for life.[60] However, it ignores the interpretation made by the Inter-American Commission on Human Rights on the right to life in the "Baby Boy" case. The majority of the Commissioners, making use of the preparatory works as an auxiliary source of interpretation of treaties, established that the literal formula used in article 4.1 of the Convention did not have the purpose of prohibiting abortion, but that it left in the hands of each State the future regulation of this matter. This way, the authorization of abortion, in accordance with domestic legislation, could not be considered contrary to the Convention. The Commission pointed out that "the interpretation that the claimants assign to the definition of the right to life formulated by the American Convention is incorrect. The addition of the phrase "in general, from the moment of conception" does not mean that those who formulated the Convention had the intention of modifying the concept of right to life that prevailed in Bogotá, when the American Declaration was adopted…"[61]

Sometimes those who support their positions in the protection of the right to life since conception, alter the language utilized in the Convention itself. As pointed out by Alejandro Montiel, the legal implications of the clause that points out that "in general, from the moment of conception" are very different from those that would be implied if it said "from the moment of the conception."[62] It would be erroneous to sustain –considering the deliberations that surrounded the origin of this particular phrase – that the right to life establishes an absolute prohibition of abortion.[63] The formulation of this clause, just like the minority vote in the Baby Boy case,[64] reveals the influence of the religious convictions both of those who participated in the drafting of the Convention and of the commissioners. We could sustain that this problem is reproduced time and again in decisions of Latin American courts, ignoring the basis of the separation between State and Church,[65] and renouncing to a valid argumentation among those who profess different creeds or beliefs. It is worth noting that most Latin American states have made a distinction between State

[59] Eduardo Rodríguez Yunta, "Derechos del cigoto desde una perspectiva biológica y metafísica," *Revista Chilena de Derecho*, Vol. 28, No. 2, 2001, pp. 263–264.

[60] Hernán Corral, "Biotecnología y Procreación artificial: Hacia una regulación jurídica respetuosa del ser humano," *Revista de Derecho Universidad de Concepción*, No. 196, Year LXII, July–December, 1994, p. 58.

[61] IACHR, Resolution 23/81, Case 2141, United States, March 6, 1981.

[62] *Id.*

[63] Alejandro Montiel Argüello, "El Derecho a la vida y la Convención Americana sobre Derechos Humanos," in Rafael Nieto, ed., *Corte Interamericana de Derechos Humanos, La Corte y el Sistema Interamericano de Derechos Humanos*, San José de Costa Rica, 1994.

[64] *Id.*

[65] C. Medina, *La Convención Americana: teoría y Jurisprudencia, op.cit.*, p. 69.

and Church. Even when such separation is not made, like in Argentina, where the Constitution establishes, *inter alia,* that the official religion of the federal government is the Catholic, apostolic and Roman faith, the citizens of that country enjoy, nonetheless, the right to freedom of conscience and religion.

The conflicting views on the authorization of contraception both in Chile and in the rest of Latin America is deployed through a judicial strategy, demanding that the health authorities authorize the method or repeal the norms that include this method among the contraceptives of the national programs of responsible procreation. Emergency contraception, also known as "the morning-after pill," is a method that can be used up to 72 hours after coitus with no contraceptive protection, failure of the contraceptive method used, or sexual aggression. It is not a method of regular utilization since as its use increases, its efficacy decreases. The questioning lies in the fact that there is apparently no certainty regarding a possible anti-implanting effect which, should it occur, would be, for its detractors, equivalent to an abortion. The arguments that reject assisted reproduction techniques are similar: manipulation of embryos and loss of lives.

4.4.1 Emergency Contraception

The polemics around this contraceptive method have been similar and constant in all of Latin America. In March of 2002, the Supreme Court of Justice of Argentina prohibited, upon request of anti-abortion organizations, the sale of the pill for considering it abortive.[66] In April of 2004, the Colombian Ministry of Social Planning ordered the local authorities to proceed with the distribution of the drug in spite of the explicit rejection and direct intervention of the Catholic Church, which generated a litigation around the legality of the drug. In Mexico, its detractors filed a claim of unconstitutionality against the adoption of the technical norms of regulation of fertility that included emergency contraception, a case that was finally dismissed by the courts, which alleged lack of active standing of the plaintiff. A similar situation occurred in Chile, when in September of 2006, a group of deputies filed a claim of unconstitutionality before the Constitutional Court against the National Norms for the Regulation of Fertility,[67] in spite of the fact that a holding of the November 2005 Supreme Court declared that there were no antecedents that might invalidate, for constitutionality reasons, the pharmaceutical register of a commercial brand of contraceptive.

In Peru, in October of 2004, a group of congresspersons constitutionally accused the Minister of Health for permitting the distribution of a drug considered by many

[66] Arturo Fermandois, "La Píldora del día después: Aspectos Normativos," *Revista Estudios Públicos*, No. 95, 2004. http://www.cepchile.cl

[67] Profamilia, *Anticoncepción de Emergencia. Un derecho de la Mujer. La experiencia colombiana*, International Planned Parenthood Federation and Profamilia, Bogotá, 2001.

to be abortive. At the same time, a group of women judicially urged the compliance of the technical health norms that expressly included the emergency hormonal pill among the contraceptives in the health plan of that public institution.[68]

The aim in each one of these cases was to declare unconstitutional those acts that led to the authorization of registering, commercializing or distributing the contraceptive. In contrast, from the point of view of the right of persons to decide, it has been argued that denying access to this contraceptive infringes upon the basic principle of self-determination of regulation of fertility, *inter alia*, the right to health.

Constitutional Court of Peru
Case File N° 7435-2006-PC/TC
Susana Chávez Alvarado et al.
November 13, 2006

Main Legal Issue:

Is it a violation of human rights and arbitrary discrimination that women can access contraceptives in private health institutions but these are not freely administered in public institutions?

Facts:

In 2001, Peru's Department of Health approved the emergency oral contraceptive. There is an obligation to provide it at no charge throughout the nation. In cases of repeated noncompliance to this resolution, plaintiffs may initiate a legal action for noncompliance. The trial court judge renders judgment in the plaintiff's favor and obligates the Department to comply with the resolution. Nonetheless, the Department appeals this decision before the Third Superior Civil Court of Justice, who decides to close the case, arguing that the resolution that established supplying the contraceptive had been revoked by a later resolution. The plaintiff, Susana Chavez Alvarado, presents a Constitutional Petition for damages against the judicial disposition that closed the case, arguing that the new resolution, before revoking the earlier one, expanded and developed it, and for that reason its fulfillment is still demandable.

Several national and international organizations, among them the World Health Organization (WHO), the Panamerican Health Organization (PHO), and the United Nations Population Fund (UNFPA) presented amicus curiae in support of the plaintiff.

Court Ruling:

The obligation of providing information and distributing emergency birth control is based on constitutional rights to equality, self determination, life, and health, and is only complied with when states provide extensive and accessible information and ensure free and effective distribution.

---

[68] Susana Chávez and Anna Brito Coe, "Emergency contraception in Peru: Shifting government and Donor policies and influences," *Reproductive Health Matters*, Vol. 15, No. 29, 2007, pp. 139–148.

The petitioners allege that the mandates whose compliance is required are:

a) To ensure free choice and informed access for the person regarding the contraceptive that she wishes to use.
b) That service and furnishing of information and/or supplies for contraceptive methods are free and with instructions available to the public sector
c) That emergency oral contraception (EOC) is one of the contraceptive methods accepted in the technical norms for Family Planning
d) Fulfillment of the described requirements is required for the Regional Health Offices and public and private health centers that carry out Family Planning activities.

Extracts:
In effect, this court believes that the first point of the petition should be guaranteed, in the sense that the Department of Health should make information on EOC as well as information regarding other contraceptive methods readily available to citizens. The petitioners have proven, additionally, that the Department of Health fails to comply with the mandate to permanently place free EOC supplies at the disposal of male and female citizens equally as well as are other contraceptive methods. […]

[…]

Concurrence of Magistrate Mesía Ramírez's Vote:
If I were to make public in its entirety the legal foundations and the decision adopted by the Plenary Session of the Tribunal, I believe that the judgment could have been complemented and reinforced with a pronouncement from the point of view of human rights.

The right to equal treatment
The plaintiffs state that reluctance on the part of the Department of Health to comply with Department Resolutions leads to discrimination with prejudice to poorer women who are not able to access the use of EOC by purchasing it in pharmacies. I do not agree with that opinion because the state's decision not to distribute EOC is not aimed at a particular segment of the population, but rather at the population at large. This is not a refusal to give the pill to a certain class of women, but rather it is a decision not to distribute it to anyone.

Nevertheless, I do not find it reasonable that if the EOC is freely sold in pharmacies, the State should refuse to give them out at the state health centers to women of every social, economic, and cultural condition, after information has been posted on the national health and family planning notice boards. More so when there is a law in force that requires it.

The refusal of the State to inform and to place EOC materials at the disposal of those who need them may signify, in certain cases, unjust treatment that may be avoided with its simple distribution. Indeed, without it being dealt with as an act of discrimination, the state's unwillingness may contain a degree of inequality, at least, if one considers: a) that women of few economic resources cannot access this method of contraception in private and commercial establishments nor even in public health centers, b) that women, girls, adolescents, and teenagers with little or no information are impeded from accessing knowledge on the scope and benefits of various methods of family planning.

The right to receive information

[...]

As far as what is material in the procedure, the right to information on all of the different birth control methods is the basic assumption for the exercise of women's reproductive rights consecrated in Article 6 of the Constitution. But at the same time, it is a genuine constitutional principle that obligates the State to offer the information needed in order that paternity and maternity develop under conditions of responsibility, and so that people become conscious of the implications and transcendency of bringing a child into society. Consequently, the right to information on birth control methods constitutes a way to concretize the principle of dignity of the human being and forms part of the essential elements of a democratic society because it allows the exercise of sexual rights in a manner that is free, conscientious, and responsible.

The right to reproductive self-determination as an implicit right of free development of personality and autonomy

I think that the right to reproductive self determination is an implicit right contained in the most generic right to free development of personality. This right consists of the autonomy to decide those affairs that concern that person only.

[...]

Consequently, every woman has a right to freely chose her method of contraception, which is directly related with the decision regarding how many children she wants to have, with whom and when [...]

I do not aspire to legalize abortions with these interpretations, as it is obvious that there are substantial differences between the use of EOC, which is ingested during a time of incertitude because the woman is not scientifically certain if she is or is not pregnant; and a behavior described by law as illegal and culpable as is abortion, which ends in the violent expulsion of the unborn. This deals with situations that have a different connotation and scope and that should receive different treatment under constitutional and criminal law.

The use or not of EOC is a matter of freedom of conscience, a situation in which the State cannot intervene. Nevertheless, its use can be restricted in public health centers, making its use conditional within a system of instructions which will be the legislator's responsibility to determine. This system may be based on the following events:

- Therapeutic or medical reasons: to prevent the pregnancy causing serious danger to the life or health of the mother.
- Crime related reason: to avoid pregnancy resulting from rape.
- Eugenic reasons: when it is probable that the fetus will suffer serious physical defects at birth

According to recent numbers from the National Institute of Statistics and Information Science, in 2005 there were 6,268 accusations of rape, an average that has held even for the last seven years, but, when compared to 1998, has increased given that in that year only 4,677 cases were reported. Of the women who were raped, 73% were minors, younger than 18, compared to 21% who had already reached legal age.

This social and economic situation that places women in a serious state of indefensibility cannot escape interpretation of the Constitution. The rights of a woman cannot be defended in the venue of constitutional law if the person who is called upon to defend her fails to take into account the social, constitutional, and cultural aspects that determine those rights.

A woman's right to life and physical, psychological, and moral integrity
The United Nations has declared that the rate of maternal mortality could be reduced by 20% and 35% if involuntary pregnancies were prevented by access to family planning.

Social reality imposes an objective obligation upon the State to do everything in its power to avoid women dying because of illegal abortions. The EOC can play a central role in this sense. Consequently, if rape affects the psychological, social and existential sphere, criminal abortion, when the use of EOC is permitted, obviously contributes additional damage along with the serious trauma that unwanted sexual treatment signifies. Therefore it is not reasonable for the State to allow double the suffering to women whose purchasing power is insufficient to allow their access to pharmacies where EOC is freely sold with the acquiescence of public services.

The right to health
I believe, finally, that the right to health is directly linked to the right to life, when the state's family planning policies sidestep a manifestly obvious reality as is the practice of indiscriminate, clandestine, and insalubrious abortions that entail non-compliance to Article 11 of the American Declaration of the Rights and Duties of Man which says exactly: "every person has the right to the preservation of his health through sanitary and social measures."

Those pregnancies that put the life of the mother at risk; those that carry a congenital malformation that is incompatible with uterine life; those that have resulted from sexual abuse; or those that exist because of artificial insemination or transfer of ova without consent, to the extent that they place the physical, psychological, or moral integrity of the mother at risk also constitute an attack on her health.

These are various aspects that could be developed in this case and whether or not the majority has thought it unnecessary to pose them, I propose them for consideration of the citizenry as a contribution to the theme of reproductive rights from the perspective of Constitutional Law.

4.4.1.1 Matters for Debate

Public health policies were developed starting in the 1970s, as a way to face the population's health problems, controlling birthrates or reducing poverty. In this context, contraceptive services and contraceptive technology entered into the healthcare services of Latin America and the Caribbean without the need to ensure or consecrate its access at the normative level, and in spite of the claims of ecclesiastical sectors on the use of methods for regulating fertility. History reveals that there was no judicialization in the access to contraceptive methods in Latin America.

The market for contraceptives, in turn, supplied the population in drugstores. The registry and authorization for contraceptive technology, initially, found no obstacles. However, the gradual growth and power of social and political sectors against the use of these methods have created an atmosphere such that, their use in the public healthcare services began requiring an express, specific regulation, even when the method in question was available in the market. An inefficient or highly bureaucratized state apparatus or the presence of reluctant authorities may constitute barriers to access to contraceptive methods and perpetuate the infringement of women's right to equality.

4.4.2 Assisted Reproduction

Assisted reproductive techniques manifest the development of science in the face of fertility that do not necessarily correspond to any pathology. In the case of women, some of the causes that underlie acquired infertility are sexually-transmitted infections such as Chlamydia, gonorrhea, or chronic pelvic infections.[69] Conceived as "an essentially therapeutic technique medically indicated to give offspring to a couple that cannot procreate," it should not be the object of strong moral objections.[70] However, the resistance to understand it as a morally acceptable technique arises from reasons associated to the alleged violation of the dignity of human life when embryos are manipulated, frozen, and eventually discarded. Likewise, those who see assisted reproduction as a moral problem condemn its use by women who are alone, or by lesbians.[71]

It should be noted that health goes beyond aspects associated to healing disease. For this reason, from a wider interpretation, it is possible to sustain that access to these techniques should be legally protected because they compromise the right to enjoy scientific progress and to health; both recognized in the ICESCR. Additionally, it would otherwise infringe on the right to raise a family, recognized in the International Covenant on Civil and Political Rights (CCPR) under its article 23 and article 17 of the American Convention.

In spite of this recognition, some authors sustain that the use of assisted reproductive techniques can be conceived as a negative right, of non-interference, given the high cost of the procedure and the scarce resources available to any exchequer

[69] R. Cook, B. Dickens and M. Fathalla, *op.cit.*, p. 298.

[70] *Id.*, p. 299.

[71] H. Corral, *op.cit.*, p. 47.

for the health budget.[72] This could mean that these procedures on the part of public services, should they exist, would be highly selective, and their financing restricted, without necessarily configuring an arbitrary discrimination.[73] However, the reasons of the health authorities for ensuring some healthcare services and not others are not always crystal-clear. An example of this is Colombia, where the Constitutional Court protected the inclusion of Viagra for the men to be able to fully live their sexuality, but did not guarantee fertility treatments.

The regulation of the use of assisted reproductive techniques has virtually remained in the hands of the medical practice, since the various attempts at regulating have proved unfruitful.[74] In Chile, a bill was lodged in the Senate which pointed out that "the techniques could only be used in cases of spouses with difficulties to procreate, and when other therapies have been discarded on account of their inefficacy."[75] A lack of consensus in the Senate blocked the initiative.

In Costa Rica, the executive branch decreed to regulate assited reproductive techniques: the decree was declared unconstitutional.

Supreme Court of Justice of Costa Rica
Action of Unconstitutionality
March 15, 2000

Main Legal Issue:
Does in vitro fertilization infringe upon the right to life?

Facts:
A citizen requested the declaration of unconstitutionality of the Executive Decree on in vitro fertilization and embryo transfer (IVFET). He alleges that the practice of artificially implanting—in a laboratory—fertilized ovules in a woman's uterus to achieve a pregnancy, is lucrative practice that infringes on the right to life of those conceived and on the dignity of human life.

Court Ruling:
The Court declares the challenged decree unconstitutional because in spite of the restrictions contained, the implementation of IVFET infringes on human life.

Extracts:
[…]
The principle of inviolability of life derives from various corollaries and annexed rights. Among them, it is worth noting that, since the right is declared in favor of all, without exceptions, – any exception or limitation destroys the content itself of the principle –, the right should be protected in the already born being and in the unborn one, from where derives the illegitimate nature of abortion or the restitution of the death penalty in the countries where it no longer exists. The international normative

---

[72] *Id.*

[73] R. Cook, *op.cit.*, p. 304.

[74] L. Cabal, J. Lemaitre and M. Roa, *op.cit.*, p. 470.

[75] *Id.*, p. 67.

body, although not very neat, establishes solid guiding principles in relation to the subject of human life. [W]e can say that the value of human life finds international normative protection in article I of the American Declaration of the Rights and Duties of Man […]

[…]

The Court circumscribes the matter to the analysis of the technique of in Vitro fertilization in relation to the right to life and the dignity of the human being […] This Court accepts that the scientific and technological advances in the field of medicine, in general, tend to the improvement of the human being's life condition. The development of assisted reproductive techniques has made it possible for many infertile couples around the world to have children. However, it is necessary to reflect upon whether all that is scientifically possible is compatible with the norms and principles that guard human life, in force in Costa Rica, and to what extent the human person admits to be the object or result of a technical procedure of production. When the object of the technical manipulation is the human being, as in IVFET, the analysis must go beyond the technically correct or effective. The ethical criterion that inspires the instruments of Human Rights that our country has subscribed must prevail: the human being can never be treated as a simple means, since it is the only one that has value in itself and not by reason of another thing. If we have admitted that the embryo is a subject of rights and not a mere object, it must be protected just as any other human being. Only the contrary thesis would permit to admit that it be frozen, sold, submitted to experimentation, and even discarded.

[…]

This Court knows that the advances of science and biotechnology are so vertiginous that the technique could be improved in such a way, that the objections here noted eventually disappear. However, the conditions in which it is applied today lead to the conclusion that any elimination or destruction of those conceived, voluntarily or as a result of the incompetence of those who execute the technique or of its inaccuracy, violates its right to life, so that IVFET is not consistent with the Right of the Constitution and therefore the challenged regulation is unconstitutional for infringing article 21 of the Political Constitution and 4 of the American Convention on Human Rights. […]

4.4.2.1 Matters for Debate

The utilization of assisted reproductive techniques has opened the way for ethical debates on manipulation of human embryos, especially if they imply discarding embryos. The law, and particularly penal law, has been the forum for this debate: for some, the consequences of the use of these techniques that lead to discarding embryos can be comparable to homicide or abortion.

As background, the opposition to the use of techniques invokes international human rights law, and particularly the American Convention, which holds that the protection of life, begins at the "moment of conception."

4.5 The Right to Health and Adolescence

Judges and public policy decision makers have generally read a limited notion of sexual and reproductive health. This is especially problematic when the holders of the right are persons whose capacity to choose is reduced for being underage. Historically, children and teenagers have been treated more as objects than as subjects of concern. They are defined based on their deficiencies – such as legal capacity – and not so much on the rights of which they are holders.[76]

Even though the Convention on the Rights of the Child changes this paradigm, some adults insist in considering children as easily molded clay in the hands of the aspirations and demands defined by adults,[77] or that the adult-child relationship rests on the basis of love, care, and altruism, so that the family space must escape the State intervention.[78]

The idea of the teenager as holder of rights collides, very frequently, with the parents' wishes.[79] The institution of parental authority is partly responsible for this situation. As interpreted, parental authority is not only protection but also domination.[80] An illustrative example is the provision in the first edition of the Chilean Civil Code, which established that the father had the authority of moderately chastising the son "and, when this would not suffice could impose the penalty of detention of up to 1 month in a correctional facility…."[81]

The Convention on the Rights of the Child is based on the premise that boys, girls and youths have rights, but, in certain circumstances, cannot act by themselves and are therefore endowed with a supra protection – or complementary protection.[82] Now, who and how the rights of children are reclaimed, when they are infringed upon, is a debatable matter.[83]

In matters of health, *inter alia,* it is recognized that adolescents are the holders of rights. For the right to health, the scope of the right of girls and boys to obtain from the State all the prevention care, vaccines, or necessary medical treatments is unquestioned. These are clearly required of the State and nobody questions it.

---

[76] Miguel Cillero Bruñol, "Infancia Autonomía y Derechos: una cuestión de Principios," in AA.VV. *Derecho a Tener Derecho. Infancia, Derecho y Políticas Sociales en América Latina y el Caribe*, Tomo IV, UNICEF-IIN, Montevideo, 1999, p. 3. http://www.inau.gub.uy/Biblioteca/cillero.pdf

[77] Gabriel Salazar and Julio Pinto, *Historia Contemporánea de Chile V. Niñez y Juventud,* LOM, Santiago, 2002, p. 7.

[78] Michael Freeman, "Tomando más en serio los derechos de los Niños," *Revista de Derechos del Niño*, No. 3–4, 2006, pp. 257–258.

[79] Robert Burt, "El tratamiento de menores sin el consentimiento de los padres," in Mary Beloff comp., *Derecho, infancia y familia*, Gedisa, Barcelona, 2000, pp. 189–190.

[80] Benito Alaez Corral, *Minoría de Edad y Derechos Fundamentales: Temas Clave de la Constitución Española*, Tecnos, Madrid, 2003, p. 33.

[81] Chile, Art. 233 Civil Code 1856.

[82] M. Cillero Bruñol, *op.cit.*, p. 6.

[83] M. Freeman, "Tomando más en serio los derechos de los Niños," *op.cit.*, p. 261.

In some cases, however, the measures that the State promote can diffuse the intervention on the parents child-rearing labor. An example of this are the treatments or interventions contrary to the beliefs of the parents. The cases in which parents could put their children's health at risk for the sake of their own convictions, are intensely debated.[84] This is the case of Muslim girls in some regions of Africa where they are subjected to genital mutilation or, in the much less traumatic but equally applicable case of the procedure of circumcision in boys practiced in the Jewish and Muslim religions. In this latter case, the mutilation is accepted for reasons of hygiene or for religious reasons even when there is a specific norm contrary to mutilation.[85] It is important to point out that the effects on health in the case of circumcision are not at all comparable to those associated to female genital mutilation. Another important example is that of parents who are Jehovah's Witnesses, who do not accept that their children be submitted to surgical procedures or receive transfusions.

In the case of teenagers, the recognition of fundamental rights becomes more controversial when these correspond to the field of sexuality or reproduction. Many times, the rights of teenagers are rejected invoking the Convention on the Rights of the Child, which recognizes the progressive autonomy as a transversal pillar but also guarantees the special relationship between parents and children. Parents have the duty to orient their children, to provide them with direction so that they can exercise their rights.

What is the limit? Where is the boundary between the protection of the child and the parent-child relationship recognized by the Convention on the Rights of the Child? These questions are key issues in the subject of sexuality and reproduction of the teenage population, and the law or the rules of the Convention on the Rights of the Child themselves do not always seem to deliver clear guidelines for action. In fact, the tradition of Western law has been of *laissez faire*, for it has recognized to the family a sort of sovereign state condition, establishing minimum intervention.

4.5.1 Progressive Autonomy

The idea of progressive autonomy, the transversal and guiding principle of the Convention on the Rights of the Child, accounts for a factual matter: the exercise of citizenship by children and youths is a gradual process dependent on the evolution and maturity of the adolescent. It is therefore, the duty of parents and, alternatively, of the State, to provide appropriate orientation and correction for the child to exercise the recognized rights.

---

[84] G. Gómez, *op.cit.*, pp. 277–278.

[85] R. Cook, *op.cit.*, p. 263 and Geraldine Van Bueren, *The International Law on the Rights of the Child*, Martinus Nijhoff Publishers, The Hague, 1998, p. 308.

If we understand adolescence as a period characterized by quick physical, cognitive, and social changes, including sexual and reproductive maturity, we must understand that, at the same time, adolescents gradually acquire conducts and functions of adults that demand new obligations and theoretical and practical knowledge, which are not always available to them.

An example, is the experimentation and exercise of sexual relations among young persons. Chile, for example, estimates that about 15% of the teenage population under the age of 16 is sexually active.[86] Participation in consented sexual activities is something that happens independent of the parents' non-consent, of social rejection, or of the existence of a norm that makes it punishable. If we understand the capacity to act not only as effective, but also as potential, which necessarily implies the possibility of making mistakes, we must face the question of what the parents can do and to what extent they can protect their children from irrational acts – as some groups consider pre-marital sex. The problem, as suggested by Freeman,[87] is that rationality must be defined in neutral terms, capable of accommodating pluralist visions of good, so that the intervention is always justified to the extent of avoiding immediate damage to the minor.

If we start from the premise that all teenagers and children have the right to health, it is understood that the role of health professionals to protect it and, consequently, their task includes providing orientation and access to the information that allows adolescents to make responsible decisions in an appropriate and respectful way. Besides, it must be remembered that maternity in adolescence does constitute a risk in itself. As collateral effect, a precocious and unplanned maternity may in many cases entail the repetition of the circles of exclusion and social marginalization due to lack of education and economic resources.

The position of persons who deny the right of the young to information and services on reproductive health, often reveal a fear that consists in believing that facilitating access to such services is a way to promote or speed up their sexuality.[88] To complement, it is argued that these policies or programs may propitiate the rupture of the link between sexuality, love, commitment, and reproduction. Those who oppose free access to integral healthcare services for the young invoke the child's best interest, enshrined in the International Convention on the Rights of the Child. They have reconstructed the concept starting from a vision that children and adolescents remain the object of protection and control by their parents or other adults. This is what Cillero terms a paradox: the denial of the autonomy to ensure the rights of the adults. But, if the State has the obligation to strengthen the educational mission of the family, the latter should seek to guarantee that the raising and education of children develops to reach autonomy and not tend to deny it.

[86] Libertad y Desarrollo, "Píldora del Día Después y Embarazo Adolescente," *Temas Públicos*, No. 788, 15 de September, 2006, p. 2. http://www.lyd.org

[87] M. Freeman, "Tomando más en serio los derechos de los Niños," *op.cit.* p. 272.

CONASIDA· National Survey on Sexual Behavior, Chile, Ministry of Health, 1998.

[88] M. Cillero, *op.cit.*, p. 60.

The concept of "best interest of the child" is imprecise and the Committee of the Convention on the Rights of the Child has delivered a guideline that allows endowing it with normative content. It has established that the authorities must evaluate the effect of their policies, programs, decisions, and laws proposed and in force, on children's rights. The concurrent vote of the Inter-American Court on Human Rights' Advisory Opinion 17 establishes that children's lack of full legal capacity to act does not imply that they be deprived of their condition as subjects of rights.[89] This means that the State must guarantee to children the right to create and develop their own life plan, through, for example, education.

Taking the idea of progressive autonomy seriously means allowing youths to gradually exercise their rights and faculties, which prepare them to become adult individuals that can respond for their actions.[90] This evolution or progressive autonomy was recognized as a principle even before the entry into force of the Convention on the Rights of the Child and has been adopted by legislation and comparative jurisprudence.[91]

The Chamber of Lords, in a historical judgment that has permeated the doctrine of common law countries, consecrated the principle of competence, a concept distinct from legal capacity in adolescents. Out of Gillick v. West Norfolk & Wisbech Area Health Authority,[92] arose the concept of competence, which refers to having enough discernment to adopt decisions of one's own understanding, their meaning, and repercussions. The English Court pronounced itself in the face of a lawsuit filed by a mother of five daughters, who requested a declaration of illegality of a clinical guide dictated by the health authority on the regulation of fertility. The guide established that the services of family planning should be available to the young persons of all ages. It further indicated that a young woman should be persuaded to inform her parents or tutors, but that the services would be delivered even without the parents' consent.

The claimant also argued that the doctors and healthcare professionals who prescribed contraceptive methods infringed upon the rights of parental authority and that, by providing contraceptive services to minors under the age of 16, they incurred in criminal responsibility for their collaboration in committing a crime (encouraging unlawful sex with a minor). Lord Fraser pointed out that the capacity and autonomy of the young must be understood in accordance with the social context, and that it is not possible to sustain that English teenagers, in 1980, are under strict parental control until they become of age and only from then onwards do they acquire independence.

---

[89] *Id.*, p. 52.

[90] Verónica Undurraga Valdés, "Anticoncepción de Emergencia: Autonomía de las Adolescentes y Derechos de sus Padres," *Anuario de Derechos Humanos*, 2007, pp. 163–171.

[91] Rebecca Cook y Bernard Dickens, "Recognizing Adolescents 'Evolving Capacities' to Exercise Choice in Reproductive Healthcare," *International Journal of Gynecology and Obstetrics*, Vol. 70, No. 1, 2000, p. 14.

[92] Gillick v. West Norfolk and Wisbech Area Health Authority (1985) 3 All ER 402 (HL). http://www.hrcr.org/safrica/childrens_rights/Gillick_WestNorfolk.htm

Civil, Commercial, Mining and Labor Chamber Number 2, San Luis, Argentina Family and Life Civil Association v. Provincial State of San Luis March 21 of 2005

Main Legal Issue:

Can parents intervene to prevent teenage children under their custody from accessing contraceptive services? Can these healthcare services be delivered without the parents' consent?

Facts:

The Civil Association Family and Life filed a writ of amparo against the provincial State requesting the declaration of unconstitutionality "erga omnes," of law 5344 for violating the institution of "parental authority" and the right to life, for allowing the prescription of abortive methods.

Court Ruling:

The Court holds unconstitutional articles 1 and 2, paragraph c) of law 5344 because they allow healthcare services provided by the Provincial State that threaten the life of unborn persons and because they dispense with a possible intervention by the parents when minors are who receive these services.

Extracts:

[…]

[I]t is known that under the term "parental authority" reference is made to the assemblage of rights and duties that correspond to the parents in relation to the persons and the assets of their non emancipated underage children […] Thus, "parental authority" is, currently, no longer characterized simply as paternal authority, but as an institution of family law that tends primarily at the protection of the minor children, their education and their preparation for life…. From this it may be inferred that the indissoluble assemblage of duties and rights that make it up have as an aim not only the child and the father, but also society.

[…]

In agreement with this concept of "parental authority," the Civil Code establishes that minor children are under the authority and power of their parents, who have the obligation and the right to raise them, choose the profession they will exercise, feed and educate them […]

Currently, a growingly prevailing doctrine in the jurisprudence, sustains that parental authority conceived in the enacted law as the assemblage of duties and rights that parents have regarding their minor children with the aim of the protection and integral formation of the latter (art. 264, Civil Code), should be complied with by its holders and, eventually, by the State, recognizing the child as a "*subject of rights*" rather than an "object *of protection*" of his parents and the State.

In this understanding, the guideline for interpreting the legislation and the judicial decisions, whenever a minor and his/her family are involved, must always be the best interest of the child.

[…] It has been said, in this respect, that access to information, to healthcare, to the methods and services necessary for the exercise on the part of the adolescent of his/her sexual and reproductive rights, is a very personal act that cannot be replaced by the parents' will. The latter have the duty and the right to advise their children, form and educate them according to their convictions, they cannot prevent them from resolving such a private and personal issue by themselves, according to their possibilities, life plan and beliefs [...]

[...]

However, also from this doctrinaire conception, it has been admitted that the recognition of the principle of self-determination of the child in this matter, does not prevent the parents from exercising, with respect to them, their responsibility of educators and primary providers of guidance, but it clearly favors the development of children and adolescents in an egalitarian family milieu, where respect and intra family human rights are promoted, within the context of a democratic State [...] In this context, it is undoubted that the parents have, in relation to their children, a socializing function, aimed especially at, in the face of the lack of maturity and the child's evolutionary nature itself, protecting them from their own acts and from the acts of third parties that could damage them.

[...]

The authorization of the parents, while exercising the parental authority and as legal representatives of their underage children is also required by statutory law with reference to other very personal acts such as when the minors under eighteen decide to be donors in the cases of bone marrow transplants (art. 15, law 24193, of "Transplants of organs and anatomic materials").

[...] From this point of view, it does not seem reasonable and much less, legitimate, that the provincial State, through law 5344 and its regulations, provided that underage children exercise their rights relative to sexuality and procreation, receiving education and assistance from the State with absolute abstention of the responsibility that the parents have as holders of the parental authority.

[...]

Thus, it can only be concluded, without hesitation, that the entry into force of law 5344 places the minors in imminent and certain danger, by reason of the possibility that in the ambit of application of said law, they can (induced or not) make transcendent decisions for their lives, away from the bosom of their home and in the absence of their parents who, in this way, would see themselves deprived of having the intervention and/or the knowledge to which they have legitimate right as holders of the parental authority and are therefore responsible for imparting to their children the appropriate direction and guidance for them to exercise the prerogatives recognized to them in the Convention on the Rights of the Child in keeping with the evolution of their faculties (sic, art. 5, Convention on the Rights of the Child) [...]

4.5.1.1 First Matter for Debate

The concept of intensely personal right is frequently analyzed from a civil law tradition perspective, especially when dealing with the rights of certain groups that have historically been deprived of rights. Under the paradigm of the International

Convention on the Rights of the Child, boys and girls have a framework of supra protection. The question that should be asked is if they are linked exclusively to the very personal rights, and if these reach the threshold of fundamental.

4.5.1.2 Second Matter for Debate

It is a proven fact that healthcare services for adolescents must break with innumerable cultural barriers that pose obstacles for the exercise of the right of these to health and also to access to information.[93] The most efficacious programs are those that take into account the reality of youth, and prepare them for active life and provide adequate preventive tools. To this end, States must abstain from deliberately distorting, concealing and censuring the information related to health and sexuality.

The problems associated to the rupture of the doctor-patient relationship are very delicate, especially because Latin American legislation on the matter is not clear. When a sexually active adolescent, or an adolescent in the process of becoming sexually active, resorts to a healthcare service to obtain advise on the regulation of fertility and finds out that his/her decisions in that respect shall not be treated with medical confidentiality, he/she will probably not request assistance again, or he/she shall not resort to the healthcare system any more.[94] When such a thing happens, young girls are exposed to unwanted pregnancies and sexually transmitted infections, both preventable situations.[95]

Some criticize the Gillick doctrine, since it insists on a biomedical parameter by leaving the decision of delivering services to other adults: the medical community.[96] Notwithstanding, and despite of the conservative current that questions the youth's capacity to receive information and services from the health professionals, the United Kingdom has reaffirmed as doctrine, the thesis of competence developed by Gillick.

In the case of Axon v. Ministry of Health,[97] the plaintiff, filed an action similar to Gillick's action, requesting the declaration of illegality of the 2004 technical and clinical norms on contraception and abortion for minors under the age of 16. Axon argued that adolescents do not have the same right to medical confidentiality in the same terms as adults. The judge affirmed the Gillick doctrine on competence of

---

[93] Report of the Special Rapporteur, Paul Hunt, "The right to the enjoyment of the highest attainable standard of physical and mental health", E/CN.4/2004/49 16 February 2004, pars. 14, pp. 39–40.

[94] Jocelyn Lehrer, Robert Pantell, Kathleen Tebb and Mary-Ann Shafer, "Forgone Health Care Among U.S. Adolescents: Associations between Risks Characteristics and Confidentiality Concern," *Journal of Adolescent Health*, Vol. 40, 2007, pp. 218–226.

[95] R. Cook, B. Dickens and M. Fathala, *op.cit.*, p. 115.

[96] Michael Freeman, "Rethinking Gillick," *The International Journal of Children's Rights*, Vol. 13, 2005, pp. 201–217, 205.

[97] Sue Axon v. The Secretary State of Health, [2006] EWHC 37 (Admin), 26 January 2006.

adolescents to consent on medical decisions related to their sexual and reproductive health. On the matter of confidentiality, he pointed out that it was a cornerstone in the medical profession, as sustained by the European Court on Human Rights. If someone needs assistance, he/she could not request it if he/she perceives that his/her situation shall be revealed, thus placing others and him/herself in a situation of risk.

4.5.2 *The Best Interest of the Child, the Right to Identity*

Melinda Jones points out that Gillick provides not only a functional standard, since it is not the age of an adolescent that is relevant to qualify him to consent to a treatment or medical action, but the fact that he may understand the background and the consequences of the course of action to be taken.[98] This way, an adolescent could be considered competent to decide on certain spheres, and not be in condition to decide in others.

One of the pillars on which the International Convention on the Rights of the Child rests is the best interest of the child. The concept is very vague; any decision can be defended by claiming that it protects the best interest of the child.[99] Sometimes it is not possible to clearly perceive whether decisions on the adolescents' health – or on persons whose capacity to express themselves is diminished – are adopted taking into account their interests, those of the parents, social interests, or the institutional ones.

A matter that intersects aspects of health and the right to identity are the cases of sexual or genital ambiguity, also known as hermaphroditism. In medicine several classes of sex are considered: chromosomal sex or genotype, defined by the sexual chromosomes (46 XY for the male and 46 XX for the female); the phenotype, determined by the aspect of the external genitals (vagina and penis); the gonadal sex, determined by the type of gonads (testicles or ovaries); the legal sex, what appears on the birth certificate for the identification of a person (male or female); the attributed sex from child rearing, the one induced by the family and the home environment; and the psychological sex, acquired according to the social milieu or the genetic, anatomical or social conditions.

It is claimed that hermaphroditism is a serious health condition because of the possible psychological effects it may have on the girl or boy born with the ambiguity that would be aggravated by the social, family, and cultural consideration on a person's identity. As the individual grows up, he/she would develop an anxiety because of the conflict between his/her personal, sexual, and legal identity, which would affect his/he right to health.

---

[98] Melinda Jones, "Adolescent Gender Identity and the Courts," *The International Journal of Children's Rights*, Vol. 13, 2005, p. 121 y pp. 130–132. *See* M. Freeman, "Tomando más en serio los derechos de los Niños," *op.cit.*, p. 273.

[99] M. Jones, *Id.*, p. 135.

In terms of the family impact, some parents may prefer that a girl undergo surgery at an early stage, but in other cases the young persons themselves shall be the ones to request the surgical procedure to define a given sexual condition. The surgical procedure is understood as an invasive procedure which includes, in the case of women who wish to identify themselves as males, removal of the uterus, ovaries, breasts and, undergoing a hormonal therapy to suppress the female characteristics and release the male features.

Constitutional Court of Colombia
T- 477 of 1995

Main Legal Issue:
Is autonomy grounded in the legal capacity to consent a health treatment? What is the limit of the parents or of those responsible for a child to give consent for a health treatment? How is progressive autonomy understood in the rejection of or the request for a medical treatment?

Facts:
According to the version of the parents of the minor N.N., when he was six months old, in a rural area, and finding himself locked up and alone with a small female dog in his room, the animal had cut off the penis and the testicles. The parents walked to nearest hospital, eleven hours away, where it was determined that the mutilation had been carried out with a sharp pointed instrument. It could not be determined whether the parents were responsible. The parents authorized an operation of meatotomy for a change of sex. When the girl reached puberty, she rejected the treatment and requested to return to her condition as a male.

The Court of Antioquia announced the ruling of first instance denying the petition of protection, considering that "the Hospital acted with extreme diligence and care and placed at the disposition of the minor all the technical and human resources available at that time to give to the case the best solution, or the less burdensome that medicine could at that time provide."

Court Ruling:
The Court revokes the decision of the Tribunal, orders to protect the right to sexual identity, free development of the personality and the right to equality of the minor and to constitute an interdisciplinary team to deal with the case and provide psychological and social support necessary for the child and the parents. This team…. shall have the task of determining when the minor has reached enough autonomy to give informed consent for performing the surgeries and carrying out the hormonal treatments, if that is the child's option.

Extracts:
[…]
The problem of consent acquires legal relevance when, as in the episode that has given rise to this ruling, something as important as a person's sex is at stake. Therefore, we shall have to affirm that in this case the consent must come from the patient himself in person, with full capacity and even with the fulfillment of some formalism such as written consent.

On many occasions the doctor has to face specially grave events that need an urgent treatment.

[…] Once the urgency has been foreseen by the legislator himself, the doctor has the obligation to act in defense of the person's life and integrity, being the patient's consent substituted by the objective reality of an intervention that is necessary to preserve the person's life, there is no doubt about this. The discussion can arise in the explanation that is given to the expression "integrity of the person"; this demands a rigorous, objective appreciation, closely linked to the requirement of immediate attention to avoid an irreversible damage, and in no case must respond to the wish of the doctor of performing scientific experiments however publicized they may be.

In the case concerning the present action of protection, there were two operations: an initial one, the "meatotomy" practiced a month and ten days after the mutilation, and the second, of "sex re adaptation," six years later. Then, expressed immediate attention would not be applicable, we would not be facing a situation of urgency that might place the patient's life at risk and that would substitute the patient's consent. And the situation was so, that the doctors sought a prior "authorization" of the parents and only after they had given it in writing did they proceed with the operation.

[…]

Indeed, in specific cases, it is legitimate for the parents and the State to take certain measures in favor of the minors, even against the apparent will of the latter, if considering that they have not yet acquired the sufficient independence of criterion to design in an autonomous way their own plan of life and to have full conscience of their interests. … However, this does not mean that the parents can make, in the name of their son, any medical decision regarding the minor, since the boy is not a property of his parents but he is already developing liberty and autonomy that then has constitutional protection.

[…] Children are not anyone's property: they are not their parents' property, or the property of society. Their life and liberty are of their exclusive autonomy.

[…]

Sex constitutes an unchangeable element of identity and a determined person and only that person, with full knowledge and duly informed, can consent in a re-adaptation of sex and even of "gender" (as doctors call it) because man cannot be a toy of depersonalized experiments nor can his identity be disfigured so that the environment in which he lives gets used to the idea of the "gender" that some doctors determine with the excuse that it was the "less bad one." […]

[…] If we are not in the presence of a transsexual, bisexual, hermaphrodite, or pseudo hermaphrodite, the Natural and Personal Truth must be respected. A fortuitous case, completely strange to the person, beyond his control, does not have enough cause to alter that truth, that nature. When the mutilation appears, the patient has the possibility to decide. If he has not done so before, he can do it now that he has use of reasoning.

It is inhuman that if the penis and the testicles were cut off, the solution is to transform the victim into a woman. This is a degrading treatment.

[…]

The Colombian Family Wellbeing Institute, represented by its Director, is ordered to convey to the injured person … the adequate protection consisting in the integral physical and psychological treatment required for the re-adaptation of the minor, with prior informed consent, and in relation to the mutilation suffered and which has been referenced to in this judgment. This integral treatment could have continuity beyond the age of 18 provided that an interinstitutional scientific group deems it convenient. […]

4.5.2.1 Matters for Debate

One of the problems that the transsexual population must face is the prejudices of the body of health professionals when faced with an individual who does not "share sexual normality." Transsexuals do not present sexual or genital ambiguity from the strictly biological point of view, as would happen with the cases of hermaphroditism; the transsexual individual identifies him/herself with a gender different from his/her biological sex.[100] This can mean that, even when being able to carry out the procedures, this is not done because of the cultural resistance to homosexuality and transsexuals. This resistance leads to a situation in which transsexuals in search of a sexual identity many times end up having risky and rudimentary surgical procedures performed on their bodies, from silicone injections to breast implant.

The biomedical intervention could be paradoxical in these cases, since when providing guidelines for action toward normalization, it does so without there necessarily existing understanding of the needs inherent in this group, related to identity and life experience as a transsexual. For this reason, the request for sex change, irrespective of the medical considerations, requires a gaze that is able to challenge the gender roles and the sexual identities that control, classify, and normalize persons according to their genital characteristics.

[100] M. Pecheny and M. Petracci, *op.cit.*, p. 57.

Chapter 5
Property

Helena Alviar

In Latin America, the participation of the feminist theory in the legal debate on property has developed, mainly, through three manifestations.

The first one, as a movement of activists and academics[1] promoting the consecration of formal equality through the recognition of women's rights. From this principle, stem multiple legal developments: equal access to education, health, pensions and property. Among these legal developments are agrarian reforms,[2] regulation of communal property[3] and access to urban housing. Another current has promoted the study of social, economic, or cultural impediments that women face when they

[1] *See* Mary Wollstonecraft, *A Vindication of the Rights of Women*, Carol H. Potson, ed., W.W. Norton, New York, 1975; Amy Gutmann, *Liberal Equality*, Cambridge University Press, New York, 1980; Alison M. Jaggar, *Feminist Politics and Human Nature*, Rowman & Alanheld, Totowa, 1983; Frances E. Olsen, "The family and the Market: A study of ideology and Legal Reform", *Harvard Law Review*, Vol. 96, No. 7, 1983, pp. 160–78; Joanne Conaghan, "The invisibility of women in labour law: gender neutrality in Model- building", *International Journal of the Sociology of Law*, Vol. 14, No. ¾, 1986, pp. 377–92; Mary Joe Frug, *Women and the Law*, The Foundation Press, New York, 1992.

[2] Heidi Tinsman, *Partners in Conflict: The Politics of Gender, Sexuality, and Labor in the Chilean Agrarian Reform, 1950–1973*, Duke University Press, Durham, 2002.

[3] Magdalena León de Leal, comp., *Poder y empoderamiento de las mujeres,* Tercer Mundo Editores, Santafé de Bogotá, 1997; Magdalena León de Leal, Eugenia Rodríguez Sáenz, ed., *¿Ruptura de la inequidad? Propiedad y género en la América Latina del siglo XI*, Siglo del Hombre Editores, Bogotá, 2005.

H. Alviar (✉)
Facultad de derecho, University of Los Andes Law School,
Carrera 1# 18A-10, Bogota, Colombia
e-mail: halviar@uniandes.edu.co

C. Motta and M. Sáez (eds.), *Gender and Sexuality in Latin America - Cases and Decisions*, Ius Gentium: Comparative Perspectives on Law and Justice 24,
DOI 10.1007/978-94-007-6199-5_5, © Springer Science+Business Media Dordrecht 2013

attempt to have access to property.[4] By social and economic impediments we mean the conditions of class or regional situations that have prevented women from exercising property rights; when they are tenants or have been displaced for reasons of violence. By cultural factor, we understand the analysis of how the construction of 'the feminine' and 'the masculine' has limited the possibilities of access to some types of property. Many of these studies have been fundamental in understanding the difficulties encountered by women with respect to the right to property in spite of its legal enshrinement. This second category includes the reports that differentiate the consequences that armed conflicts[5] and forced displacement have had for women and girls; texts that highlight the legal gaps produced as a consequence of the patriarchal structure of society; and studies showing the reality and the effects of domestic violence on the possibilities of women to access employment[6] and property.

Lastly, a feminist current critical of law in the region has analyzed diverse norms to establish how, in spite of the different regulatory efforts, the interpretation of these norms and their implementation through public policies has been less generous for women. In this case, feminist theory has been critical both of the legal system as a whole, and of the laws and reforms proposed by feminists of different ideological inclinations.

This chapter will discuss the different ways in which case-law has reiterated or increased inequality in the region. It will also describe some exceptional cases in which the laws, public policies or the work of the courts have transformed such inequality. This in turn will examine the main characteristics of the legislation that promotes access of women to property and its limitations, and the judicial interpretation it has entailed. The cases to be analyzed cover three thematic axes: (1) the positive and negative consequences of linking feminine identity to maternity and access to property; (2) the configuration of privileged access to property; and, (3) the tensions among excluded groups.

Before initiating the debate on gender perspective and property, it is important to make some precisions on the definition of this right in the region itself. Right to property is part of what in the legal doctrine is termed "the theory of goods" and along its history, it has evolved from an absolute right to a right with the limitations imposed by its social function.[7]

For purposes of this chapter, we define the right to property as the capacity to enjoy, use and dispose of a good in accordance with the limitations imposed by law,

---

[4] *See* Nancy Holmstrom, "A marxist theory of women's nature", *Ethics,* Vol. 94, No. 1, April 1984, pp. 456–73; Lise Vogel, *Marxism and the Oppression of Women: Towards a Unitary Theory*, Rutgers University Press, New Brunswick, 1983; Annette Kuhn, Ann Marie Wolpe, eds., *Feminism and Materialism: Women and Modes of Production*, Routledge & Kegan Paul, Boston, 1978; Ann Foreman, *Femininity as Alienation: Women and the Family in Marxism and Psychoanalysis*, Pluto Press, London, 1977.

[5] *Primer Avance del Informe Sobre Violencia Contra las Mujeres y las Niñas en el Conflicto Armado Colombiano*. Informe Especial de la Red de Solidaridad Social, August 31, 2001, http://www.mujeryconflictoarmado.org/pdfs/mca_1er_avance_2001.pdf

[6] *See* Heidi Tinsman, *op.cit.*

[7] Steven E. Hendrix, *Property Law Innovation in Latin America with Recommendations*, 18 B.C. Int'l & Comp. L. Rev. 1 (1995).

among them the subordination to the interest of society. Additionally, the right to property includes the possibility of accessing the resources of a society without legal impediments to free access. In this sense, the right to property includes the possibility of producing wealth through work, so that the analysis will also include access to wealth, to rural land, urban property and business premises.

5.1 The Positive and Negative Consequences of Linking the Feminine Identity to Maternity and Access to Property

The enshrinement of property as a right has been one of the fundamental pillars of the exercise of freedom within classical liberalism. This relationship between property and freedom has been brought forth as one of the very justifications of the social contract. In other words, one of the reasons why citizens abide by the rules dictated by a State is to receive in exchange, protection of individual property.

With the aim of delimiting the role of private property within the classical conception of liberalism, the following presents a brief summary of its basic principles. Liberalism, in its wider sense, can be understood as a philosophical position that encompasses a conception of the individual and his values, as well as a political tradition that contains an assemblage of assumptions on the adequate functioning of government, the economy, and the law.

For the purpose of its relation to property, liberalism shall be considered as a thought process within a political tradition. In the opinion of classical liberals, there exists a defined conception of the human being and society. This conception is individualistic, since it places persons in a privileged position in the face of the demands of a collective society; it is egalitarian, because the laws must be applied to all and because it prohibits, within a certain political and legal order, the inclusion of differences at the time of valuing human beings; and it is universalistic, since it ignores historic conditions, and gender, class, race or cultural differences.

The ideal political structure translates into the consecration of a series of civil freedoms: freedom of thought; freedom of expression and of association; the protection of private property and the control of public institutions through an informed public opinion. The division of powers, with clearly established functions, as well as the system of checks and balances, leads to providing guarantees to freedom of thought, expression and association. A series of rights that guarantee freedom and privacy, and allow cohabitation in society form part of the political system. The only restrictions on freedom must come from some norms whose justification is solely their usefulness for the largest number of members of a society.[8]

[8] This is the perspective held by Jeremy Bentham: "A measure of government (which is but a particular kind of action, performed by a particular person or persons) may be said to be conformable to or dictated by the principle of utility, when in like manner the tendency which it has to augment the happiness of the community is greater than any which it has to diminish it." Jeremy Bentham, "An Introduction to the Principles of Morals and Legislation" in Peter Gay, ed., *The Enlightment: A Comprehensive Anthology*, Touchstone Press, New York, 1973, p. 664.

Alternatively, and as an evolution of the principle of legality and due process, the State is obliged to respect this right and in the exceptional cases of expropriation, it must abide by the consecrated legal procedures. The principle of legality guarantees that all citizens have equal rights; that they accept on equal terms a system of norms that must be stable and that applies to all, including the government, with impartiality and neutrality. Due process guarantees that if some of the rights are limited, there exist a legally consecrated process that guarantees that citizens may know, dispute and defend their interests when facing these limitations. These two guarantees are essential for the right to property because on the one hand, access to property is universal, impartial, and neutral and, on the other hand, in the cases in which this right must be limited, the corresponding procedure is legally consecrated. Because of its importance in a State under the rule of law, free access to property is a fundamental part of modern constitutions in the region; neutrality in the consecration of this right has been one of its fundamental characteristics. However, access to property has been historically limited on account of race, class or gender, and extensively shown by economists and sociologists.[9]

In the specific case of women, neutrality has not been a guarantee, since in most countries women have had less access to property than men. Even though accurate data is difficult to find, Magdalena León and Carmen Diana Deere in their extensive study on property and gender in Latin America, state the following:

> Unfortunately, few studies on the distribution of property by sex have been carried out. Frequently quoted data indicate that women constitute half of the world population, occupy one third of the official records of the workforce, carry out two thirds of the work, but earn only one tenth of the world income and own only 1% of the world's property.[10]

Consequently, the consecration and exercise of the right to property in universal and neutral terms do not necessarily bring about equality of conditions to access property. This section, based on the cases developed, will show that identifying women as providers of care, love, and values, as opposed to men as economic providers, sometimes limits their possibilities of being owners. In other cases, the judges have taken into account the reproductive work and allowed access to property when the aim of legislation has been to protect the children of a family, as in the cases of dissolution of the community property regime.

[9] *See* M. León, E. Rodríguez ed. *op.cit.;* Carmen Diana Deere y Magdalena León, *Género, Propiedad y Empoderamiento: Tierra, Estado y Mercado en América Latina*, Tercer Mundo Editores, Universidad Nacional de Colombia, Bogotá, 2000; Silvia M. Arrom, "Cambios en la condición jurídica de la mujer mejicana en el s. XIX", in Jose Luis Soberanes Fernández comp., *Memoria del II Congreso de Historia del Derecho Mexicano*, UNAM, México D.F., 1981.

[10] C. Deere and M. León, *op.cit.*, p. 2.

5.1.1 *The Protection of the Family and of the Mother in the Distribution of Goods in the Community Property: The Recognition of Reproductive Work*

In family law, the patrimonial effects of civil unions, the administration of family property, and the norms regulating the dissolution of the community property affect, in a direct way, women's access to such property. At the moment of marriage dissolution and distribution of the community property, or of the dissolution of a partnership resulting from a *de facto* marital union, women are awarded ownership of certain goods assets. In some cases involving an immovable such as the marital home, the woman receives its ownership.

In this sense, the rulings presented below are examples of the legal recognition of the value of reproductive work in the distribution of community property. Reproductive work was a concept originally developed by Friedrich Engels in his book, *The Origin of the Family, Private Property and the State.* According to Engels, with the onset of industrialization and the establishment of private property, the forms of production filtered from the family nucleus to the public ambit. Men's access to the public sphere was facilitated because they did not have the obligations of family care. Gradually, productive work started to be valued in social and economic terms – done in exchange for a salary – , and the reproductive work – everything that is related with care, feeding and maintenance of the family members – was devaluated and disregarded as work. Women were pushed into and relegated to the private sphere, while men were promoted to the public sphere. This division of work effectively prevents women from accessing property and, consequently, makes them poorer and more dependent on men.[11]

In the first case that follows, the Court of Appeals of Puerto Montt, Chile, awarded economic compensation to the wife for domestic work. Together with the dissolution of the community property, an additional property right is recognized to the woman. In the Colombian case, there is an appeal for recognition of a woman's right to possession of an asset obtained within the *de facto* marital union. In addition to questioning the value of reproductive work over the right to property, these judgments invite us to reflect on the rights of good faith third parties.

Court of Appeals of Puerto Montt-Chile
Ruling 529-2006
June 20, 2006

Main Legal Issue:
Upon dissolution of the community property regime, should the wife be granted monetary compensation for having devoted herself to working in the home, in recognition of her impossibility to acquiring property on her own?

---

[11] Leslie Kurshan, *Rethinking Property Rights as Human Rights: Acquiring Equal Property Rights for Women Using International Human Rights Treaties*, 8 AM. U. J. GENDER SOC. POL'Y L. 353 (2000).

Facts:
Within a divorce proceeding for a marriage that has lasted 16 years, the wife, a 61 year old woman, counterclaims against her husband, demanding payment of monetary compensation for all the years she had devoted to domestic work, which had prevented her from pursuing studies in some technical career.

Court Ruling:
The Court recognizes the impossibility of the woman to access a property of her own during the duration of the community property regime because she had devoted herself to the care of her home. The woman is awarded the possibility of the property with a surplus, in addition to the result of the distribution of the marital property. The Court decides to grant monetary compensation to the petitioner.

Extracts:
[…]
The claimed economic compensation … corresponds to an institution of matrimonial right introduced by Law 19.947; and its objective is to compensate the spouse, who devoted him/herself to the care of the children or the domestic work of the common home, for the economic damage suffered as a result of not having been able to perform a lucrative activity or having devoted him/herself to one of a lesser extent …. In this way, it is not effective, as stated by the trial judge, that it has an assisted nature, but rather that the legislator's intent was of a compensatory content, which is why factors of indigence and dignity need not be protected, but rather those established in article 62 of the abovementioned Law, which are: a) duration of the marriage and of cohabitation; b) property situation of both spouses; c) good or bad faith; d) age and health of the beneficiary; e) situation of the said spouse as regards social security and healthcare benefits; f) professional qualifications and possibilities of access to the labor market; and g) collaboration in lucrative activities of the other spouse. Other equally useful criteria are not opposed to such prescription, provided that the mentioned aim is adequately taken into account, for example degree of commitment in the sentimental relationship (a marriage based on a poor or null bond of affection between the spouses introduces a bias regarding its duration), age and health status of the other spouse, economic capacities of the said spouse (which is not the same as taking into account his/her patrimonial situation), economic behavior during cohabitation and during separation preceding divorce, among others.

[…] That the claimant could have pursued a technical career and even obtained some income from these studies, which have not been valued in quantity and importance, does not at all disprove the essential factual assumptions of the benefit itself if, as is the case of this ruling, it is not a matter of controversy that the woman devoted herself effectively and as her main activity to the care of the children (who in this case, were not even common children) and that this prevented her or at least restricted her from developing a full-time lucrative activity, which would have allowed her to face with greater calmness her sustainable future.

Constitutional Court of Colombia
Ruling T- 494 of 1992

Main Legal Issues:

Should domestic work be considered an in-kind contribution to the de facto marital property regime? Can possession be considered a fundamental right?

Facts:

A woman cohabited with a man for approximately 24 years. The petitioner possessed the house in which she has lived since 1970, when her partner, with whom she moved in with, acquired it. The partner died in 1990. As a result of the process of succession by inheritance, the only heir was the sister of the deceased and all the goods were allocated to her, including the house. In parallel to the process of succession, the cohabitant lodged a claim demanding recognition of the existence of the *de facto* marital union and its later dissolution upon her partner's death. The cohabitant opposes handing over the house.

Court Ruling:

The Court decides to instruct the judge to abstain from handing over the house to the heir and to respect the possession and the fruits of the work of the petitioner. Also, it establishes as the rule "that in all case similar to the cased at bar, by facts or circumstances, whenever there is domestic work in the relations between men and women, the enunciated constitutional jurisprudence shall be mandatory."

Extracts:

[…]

The [judge of first instance] seems to believe that the only contributions to a *de facto* marital union must be money or goods that are relevant in the market, so that the so-called in-kind labor contribution is totally discarded. It was surely for this reason that he abstained from considering, even for a moment, if the concubine's domestic work did or did not have enough economic significance to recognize, with all the ensuing consequences, her status as a partner. The non-recognition of the domestic work of the petitioner involved in the threat of eviction, without due process, from the immovable she inhabits today, acquired and gradually improved during the *de facto* marital union, and all this as a fruit of the joint effort of the cohabitants, openly infringes upon the constitutional rights to equality, due process and non-discrimination against women.

[…] The petitioner is, at least, the active titleholder of a possessory relationship, whose essential nature should be clarified, with the aim of determining whether it requires or not the specific protection that the 1991 Constitution bestows on the fundamental constitutional rights.

[…]

Among the classical reasons to justify the protection of possession, the most important one is that it is an externalization of property, one of its most efficacious forms of proof and advanced position of such right, with social and economic implications because of its impact on the creation of wealth.

[…]

"Feminine" domestic work and inequality
Among the mentioned and proven facts in the case file, are the diverse activities that the petitioner performed from the very moment when she initiated permanent relationships with her deceased partner..., which lasted a span of 24 years.

These were, among others, the domestic tasks inherent in the home, the collaboration in commercial activities in which two vehicles acquired during the *de facto* marital union were used, as well as in the joint exploitation of a house through renting of rooms to tenants....

It is also found that the petitioner permanently took care of her partner's health and that she fixed, washed, and ironed clothes outside the home to contribute to its maintenance.

[...]

The lower court agrees with those who believe that domestic work is "invisible" and as such, is devoid of any meaning in the market economy. This Court can do nothing but manifest its total disagreement with such vision inasmuch as it stimulates and deepens the inequality and the injustice in social relationships, makes economic development inequitable, and infringes upon the fundamental rights of the human person.

[...]

The traditional obligations of the woman, with regards to the family and her wageless work in the home, is seldom recognized despite these being economic activities that contribute to the home's income and hence to the national revenue.

These activities that bear no price tag, are not considered an important variable for development and are not taken into account in economic planning.

[...]

All of the above elements permit this Court to affirm that the non recognition of the domestic work of the petitioner involved in the threat of eviction, without due process, from the immovable which she inhabits today, acquired and gradually improved during the *de facto* marital union, and all of which was the fruit of the joint effort of the cohabitants, openly violates the constitutional rights to equality, due process and non discrimination against women [...]

5.1.1.1 Matters for Debate

Both in the Chilean and Colombian case, reproductive work is translated into an equivalent economic value. In the Chilean case, the economic compensation is recognized in favor of the petitioner, granting her the property of the movable assets. In the Colombian case, even though the Court does not decide on the property as such, the recognition on the right of possession in favor of the cohabitant allows her to remain in the house, forbidding the handing over of the good to the person who, by virtue of succession by inheritance, had obtained the ownership of the same. In other words, it placed possession of the property in a privileged site.

The recognition of a certain part of the feminine identity may be viewed as an affirmative measure in favor of women. It would be worthwhile to reflect, however, on the weight of constitutional principles in these cases. What juridical considerations allow them to argue in favor of recognition of feminine identity? Why don't they do it in favor of the absolute right to property?

5.1.2 The Feminine Identity, Reproductive Work and Access to Commercial Property

Individuals live in societies and between individuals and society, relationships are established which acquire forms, and with time differentiate one from the other. These can be termed relationships of sociability, and they account for the necessary dialogue among the individuals of a determined society. They are not equal in time; they depend on the place and time in which they develop. The conception that individuals have of the society in which they live and of their place in it, governs the way of living and of treating each other. The collective conceptions, unlike many individual representations, are a part of reality, and grounded in facts. This vision that conceives the individual and society as adversaries must be set aside and instead, understand the need that individuals have to forge, reinforce, and continuously affirm a place in society and maintain or expand their field of action. To this end, the concept of social configuration is pertinent.[12] It includes the study of the individual and society and is defined in the ways individuals relate, establish bonds, and belong to a network in which they are interdependent. Individuals may be distinguished but not separated from society; society precedes and succeeds them. Individuals are unique and unrepeatable, but they die. Society changes much more slowly, and although it does not depend on particular individuals, it does depend on them in general.[13]

Women's identification in current societies is defined precisely by the social configuration of a discourse in which legal and social norms converge. This discourse has been the basis for the construction of the status of women as political subjects, represented within a legal system in which they are intimately linked to regulated social relationships. In this sense, representation functions as an operative term within a political process that attempts to expand the visibility and the legitimacy of women as political subjects. This representation has the normative function of a language that, is said, reveals or distorts that which is considered true about women's category.[14]

---

[12] Max Weber, *Economy and Society*, University of California Press, 1978.

[13] Roger Chartier, *El mundo como representación: estudios sobre historia cultural,* Gedisa, Barcelona, 1995, p. 56.

[14] Judith Butler uses this concept in *1990: Gender Trouble: Feminism and the Subversion of Identity,* Routledge, 1990. She might have borrowed it from Sandra Harding, "The instability of the analytical categories of feminist theory", *Signs*, Vol. 11, No. 4, 1986, pp. 645–64.

Foucault points out that legal systems of power produce the subjects that they later represent. Subjects regulated by these legal forms, by virtue of their being governed by them, are formed, defined, and reproduced according to the requirements contained in these forms.[15] With certain legitimizing and excluding objectives, these political operations are hidden and naturalized through a political analysis that the legal structures take as their foundation to carry out the political construction of the subject. It is not enough to investigate how women can be more fully represented in language and in politics. The feminist critique should also understand how the structures of power themselves, through which emancipation is sought, produce and restrict the category of women.

If the construction of women's identity is discussed in relation to the term "women," said term denotes a problem and the tendency to think of a common identity in time and space. Instead of a stable signifier which demands the approval of those whom it pretends to describe and represent, the term "women" has turned problematic, a site for impugnation, a cause for anguish. This must then be analyzed in the light of social configuration in such a way that the peculiarities of certain places and historical moments be taken into account. Generally, gender does not only define a subject but also modalities of race, class, sex, ethnic, and region, of discursively constituted identities. Thus, the categories of identity that contemporary legal structures create, naturalize, and immobilize must be understood in this context.

Within access to property, it is worth reflecting upon the manner in which the resources to allow the exercise of access are acquired. Even though the right to work will be analyzed in a separate chapter, the possibility of acquiring the status of tradeswoman and of being able to have ownership of the goods derived from the trade, has an incidence on ideas such as those related to domestic work performed by mothers, who are heads of household, the conception of commerce as an anti-moral activity, and the function of women as makers of morals.

Supreme Court of the Nation of Mexico
Romero Rodríguez Avelina and other aggrieved parties
June 14, 1945

Main Legal Issue:
Is an administrative communication which prohibits women from being in charge of commercial premises that sell alcoholic beverages valid, even though there is no legal or constitutional provision supporting it?

Facts:
The Chief of Coordinated Services closes a commercial premise belonging to a woman by virtue of a communication he himself has issued.

Court Ruling:
None of the provisions of the Federal Sanitary Court, nor the Tlaxcala legislation, prohibit women from running or personally being in charge of commercial premises

[15] Michel Foucault, *La verdcd y las formas jurídicas*, Gedisa, Barcelona, 2003.

in which alcoholic beverages are sold. Therefore, the prohibition based on a communication from the chief of coordinated services has no legal support.

Summary:
Clause III of article 7 of the Regulations on the Sale of Alcoholic Beverages, and similar provisions of such regulations, refer exclusively to commercial premises that are the object of such regulations, but not to the grocery stores with a license to sell bottled alcoholic beverages; nor restaurants in which these kinds of beverages are also sold. For this reason, the pretended prohibition for women to own or manage these types of businesses is in this case illogical, since there is no reason to justify it.

Supreme Court of the Nation of Mexico
Leñero de Revilla Rosa María
September 24, 1954

Main Legal Issue:
Taking into account the prohibition on the management by women of commercial premises such as bars, due to their moral role within society, can a woman who is the owner of a restaurant request the license to sell inebriating beverages?

Facts:
Mrs. Leñero de Revilla is the owner of a restaurant. After successfully running it for many years, the license to sell alcoholic beverages is denied to her on account of the existing prohibition, which bans women from owning bars and related commercial premises.

Court Ruling:
Even though the Court recognizes the moral role of women within society, it establishes a clear distinction between running a bar and selling alcoholic beverages in a restaurant. On these grounds, the analysis takes into account and does not place the task of moral teaching exclusively on women.

Summary:
[…]
Article 7 of the Regulations on the Sale of Alcoholic Beverages, of the sixteenth of May of nineteen forty four for the Federal District imposes, in fact, in clause III, the prohibition for women, among other persons, and irrespective of their age, to own or manage commercial premises in which inebriating beverages are sold; but this prohibition is circumscribed exclusively to commercial premises such as bars and wineries, for which reason, this being a restaurant, where inebriating beverages are sold as a secondary aspect of the main business, the cited precept does not justify that a license be prohibited or denied to a woman for it to be applied in the restaurant or tavern of her ownership, premise that must be regulated not by article 7 of the said regulations, but by article 14 of the same legal disposition, which warns that in taverns and restaurants it will only be permitted to sell wines, liquors and beers, when these be consumed with food, and the corresponding license has been previously issued.

5.1.2.1 Matters for Debate

The cases discussed are a reflection of the moral, social, and cultural nature of the law. Even though these days it is very strange to encounter judgments that prohibit the exercise of some commercial activity to women because of their role within the family and as makers of public morals, these judgments have an historical interest: they reflect the role that society traditionally assigned to women. In the two cases analyzed, the judges questioned the legislative provisions that prohibit the management and ownership by women of commercial premises that sell inebriating beverages. While in the first case the judge circumscribes the discussion to a normative conflict resolved by virtue of the normative hierarchy, in the second, the judge upholds the principle of specialty to resolve the normative conflict.

Behind the normative conflict, however, the discussion on the cultural identity assigned to women in society and the legal regime that sustains this identity is important. At the time of these judgments, women were identified with the formation and preservation of public morals. The judge made his decision on the basis of these social assumptions. How would a judge decide today? Will these moral arguments continue configuring our identification of the feminine, but in more subtle ways? To what extent does gender equality also mean the dismantling of the stereotypes regarding what we understand as feminine? How did morals affect the distribution of property, especially with regard to commercial premises?

5.2 The Consecration of Privileged Access to Property

The assemblage of norms that attempt to correct the restrictions faced by women to access property are grounded on two theoretical currents: the discussion within liberalism regarding state intervention in resource distribution and the international feminist movement.

Both the consecration of property in absolute terms and its neutrality were analyzed, debated and re-configured during the first half of the twentieth century. In this way, the so-called modern liberalism was justified within a wider idea of state intervention in the economy and in society to achieve a better distribution of resources. Specifically, in relation to property, state intervention is necessary, since the neutrality of the norms and the *laissez-faire* did not guarantee the minimum human dignity to the excluded classes,[16] or access to property to some groups within society.

---

[16] *See* Louise A. Tilly, Joan W. Scott, *Women, Work and Family,* Routledge, London, 1989; Ivy Pinchbeck, *Women Workers and the Industrial Revolution 1750–1850*, Cass, London, 1969; Eric Hobsbawm, *The Age of Revolution: Europe 1789–1848*, Vintage Books, 1962; Maxine Berg, *The Age of Manufactures. Second Edition, Routledge*, 1994; David Landes, *The Industrial Revolution in Britain*, New York University Press, New York, 1969; Arnold Toynbee, *The Industrial Revolution*, The Beacon Press, Boston, 1961.

In other words, this reaction to classic liberalism is partly the product of the indignation of academicians and politicians regarding the inhuman conditions imposed on the industrial workers.[17] Given that one of the pillars of liberalism is respect for the individual and human dignity, it was necessary to review the philosophical, political-legal, and economic foundations of liberalism, particularly, its conception of freedom and of the role of the State in society.

John Stuart Mill, one of the most important theoreticians of liberalism, undertook the task of reformulating the definition of freedom and Bentham's utilitarian conception. For Mill, the individual's value lay in his capacity to fulfill himself in the conditions of a free society. In this sense, political and social freedoms are the fundamental tools that allow the individual who lives in society, to live his own life, develop his own features and personal abilities. A good society must be one that allows freedom and the opportunity of free and satisfactory ways of life; freedom is not only an individual good, it is also a social good.[18] It refers to a quality of the society and to a quality of the persons who comprise that society. For this reason it is impossible for a government to be liberal simply because it remains on the margins. The function of the liberal government is to support the existence of a free society and, even though the government cannot force people to acquire moral conducts by law, it can remove many of the obstacles that stand in the way of its moral development. Extreme poverty must be avoided, among other things, because it tends to provoke certain moral degradation[19] and avoids full participation in the political game. Mill's ethical theory was important for liberalism because it attempted to make it abandon selfishness, and disseminated the idea that social wellbeing is in the interest of all men.

These re-formulations of classic liberalism materialized in a new conception of the State and its capacity to intervene in society. The particular quality of the Benefactor State consists in the impersonal and general guarantee of being the recipient of services, irrespective of each individual's capacity to pay, to which the citizens have a right because of their condition as such. In this sense, the Benefactor State attempts to grant social rights to its members, situated at the same level, regarding rights to property. That is, such rights are inviolable and are assigned to individuals by virtue of being citizens and not according to their performance in society.[20] These services aim principally at the maintenance of a minimum level of

---

[17] *See* Louise A. Tilly y Joan W. Scott, *Women, Work and Family,* Routledge, London, 1989; Ivy Pinchbeck, *Women Workers and the Industrial Revolution 1750–1850,* Cass, London, 1969; Eric Hobsbawm, *op.cit*; Maxine Berg, *op.cit*; David Landes, *The Industrial Revolution in Britain*, New York University Press, New York, 1969; Max Pietsch, Arnold Toynbee, *The Industrial Revolution*, The Beacon Press, Boston, 1961.

[18] Friedrich Engels, "Working Class in Manchester", in Robert C. Tucker, ed., *The Marx-Engels Reader,* Norton, New York, 1978, p. 583. "Passing along a rough bank, among stakes and washing-lines, one penetrates into this chaos of small one-storied, one-roomed huts, in most of which there is no artificial floor; kitchen, living and sleeping-room all in one. In such a whole, scarcely 5 ft long by six broad, I found two beds-and such bedsteads and beds!-which with staircase and chimney place, exactly filled the room."

[19] John Stuart Mill, *On Liberty*, Hackett, Indianapolis, 1978.

[20] *Id.* pp. 56–78.

income, independent of the fluctuations of employment and of the market in general. To this end, many countries created mechanisms that to a lesser or greater extent ensured education, health, and recreation and that took care of special family contingencies such as unemployment, old age, death, or lack of housing.[21]

The basis of the creation of the State itself must be transforming, since it is no longer the fruit of a contract between independent individuals, but the result of a quasi-contract or tacit pact among interdependent subjects who have reciprocal obligations and related needs. As opposed to the theory of addition of interests and individual needs, León Duguit,[22] among others, postulated social solidarity as a source of law and political power. The State is born from a debt or social obligation towards the citizens who, in turn, have mutual obligations to each other. Solidarity imposes duties on all individuals, precisely so that those individuals may develop all their possibilities. The State, in turn, has the primary obligation of creating the conditions for individuals to exercise and comply with their social duties: it is not only the holder of prerogatives derived from the public force and power but also the link that binds together the individuals in social solidarity through their functions of public use. For this purpose, the State must widely intervene in social and political matters with a criterion of service, derived from solidarity that equally governs the private individuals and the public sector.

In the case of property, State intervention to improve its distribution materialized in three ways. First, the social function weakened its identification as an absolute right to re-configure itself as a right with limits. This idea was the basis of less radical agrarian reforms – the more radical ones dismantle private property – and justified the redistribution of great extensions of land in different countries. Additionally, the distribution of property permitted the institution of subsidies for urban housing. Secondly, and within the same spirit of equitable distribution of resources, there are the laws and public policies that designate a portion of the territory to be allocated to a minority.[23] Finally, there is the development of case law that configures an order of priority and a privileged procedure for members of vulnerable groups: indigenous people, peasants, women, women heads of household, displaced women, and victims of an armed conflict, among others.

Conversely, the regional feminist movements that were born in the early twentieth century, together with the international feminist movement that became established as a significant global force as of the 1970s, configured an assemblage of political vindications that led to the inclusion of women's rights in laws and public policies. In this sense, the agenda of feminism as a movement resulted in specifically relating norms at women that related to access to education, work, and property, among other issues.

[21] Gosta Esping-Anderson, *The Three Worlds of Welfare Capitalism*, Princeton University Press, Princeton, 1990, p. 21.

[22] *Id.* p. 19.

[23] León Duguit, *Las transformaciones del derecho público y privado*, Editorial Heliasta, Buenos Aires, 1975.

The following section will show how the re-distribution of resources inherent in the interventionist liberalism and in the feminist claims was interpreted by the judges.

5.2.1 Women as Victims of Displacement and the Need for Immediate Intervention by the State: Damage Compensation with Gender Perspective

One of the debates in the feminist theory has been the identification of women as defenseless, weak beings, who need the protection of others. This characterization is found in many academic texts that propose the strengthening of women's human rights. Leslie Kurshan characterizes Latin American women as victims in the following way:

> Acquiring property rights is a particularly important human rights issue because without property rights women are unable to effectively exercise other human rights. Inequality in property rights is a major hindrance to correcting internationally recognized problems women face such as generally inferior economic status, domestic violence, and female genital mutilation. Without property rights, it is difficult for women to be individual economic actors. (…)
>
> In many countries within the OAS, women do not have equal property rights in law and/or in practice. The denial of equal property rights is a violation of the Inter-American Convention on Human Rights.[24]

Postmodern feminist studies,[25] however, reject this description; they consider that the diversity among women is too wide for all women to be described as victims. At the same time, they caution that this identification paralyzes, limits the possibilities of action, and weakens.

In the following cases, which refer to internal displacement, there is the need to describe women as victims to be able to demand the immediate intervention of an absent and negligent State. Along these lines of ideas, identifying the mothers heads of household, the children and the elderly persons who accompany them as victims, strengthens the argument of the judges who demand redress with gender perspective.

State Council of Colombia
April 10 of 2003

Main Legal Issue:
Is the State responsible for not paying immediate humanitarian emergency attention to the displaced population, even when there are budgetary reasons for the delay?

---

[24] *See* Kurshan, *supra* note 12, at 357–58.

[25] *See* Arturo Escobar, *Encountering Development, The Making and Unmaking of the Third World*, Princeton University Press, Princeton, 1995; Marianne H. Marchand y Jane L. Parpart eds., *Feminism, Postmodernism and Development*, Routledge, Nueva York, 1995; Karen Engle, *Female Subjects of Public International Law: Human Rights and the Exotic Other Female*, 26 New Eng. L. Rev. 1509 (1992).

Facts:
Mrs. Díaz petitioned for a writ of *amparo* against the President of the Republic and various agencies because she was forced to flee from her land and her belongings on account of the continuous threats against her life. She was registered in the national registry of the displaced population but since then she has not obtained the emergency humanitarian help provided for in article 20 of Decree 2569 of 2000, due to lack of budgetary resources.

Court Ruling:
It is established that forced displacement implies the violation of economic, social and cultural rights of the persons subjected to it, as well as damage to their life conditions. The Council of State affirms the sentence of the lower court, demanding that the respective public entity repair the violated rights of the petitioner in 90 days.

Extracts:
[…]
It is a notorious fact that thousands of persons, as occurs with the petitioner, have been forced to abandon their places of residence and work because of the threats and the fear generated by the actions of illegal armed groups. This forced displacement implies the violation of the economic, social and cultural rights of those persons, and also affects their life conditions, as stated by the Constitutional Court in ruling SU-1150/00:

> The fact that forced displacement entails a multiple, massive and continuous violation of the rights of those persons forced to migrate is widely accepted. On the one hand, it is clear that these persons are forced to abandon their homes because of the risk they perceive on their lives and personal integrity, a danger that is derived from the direct threats against them or from the perception they develop because of the multiple acts of violence that take place in their dwelling places.

[…]

Emergency humanitarian aid, as provided in article 20 of Decree 2569 of 2000, includes "… the temporary and immediate help aimed at actions of aid, assistance and support to the displaced population, to mitigate the basic needs of food, health, psychological attention, housing, emergency transportation, elements of internal habitat and public health." This norm provides that this benefit be granted for a maximum period of three months, renewable, exceptionally, for three more months, in accordance with the criteria pointed out in article 21 of Decree 2569.

[…]

The request to extend the term for complying with the judgment to 180 days will not be granted, since for the effective protection of the fundamental rights awarded to the petitioner, the ordered measures must be adopted with swiftness and within a reasonable time given the special circumstances in which the petitioner and her minor children find themselves, as well as the budgetary difficulties of the Network of Social Solidarity. The established term of 90 days, mentioned in the challenged ruling, satisfies those conditions.

[…]

Consequently, to guarantee the protection of this right, the Court shall command the Inurbe agency to respond to the alluded request, if it still has not done so, within the term of forty eight (48) hours to be counted as from the notification of this resolution.

5.2.1.1 Matters for Debate

Forced displacement implies a violation of the right of nationals to choose their dwelling place, as well as their right to free development of the personality. Also, given the intimidating atmosphere that precedes the displacements, these persons see their rights to expression and free association infringed on.

The Colombian courts have justified the demand for immediate action by the authorities based on the description of the devastating outlook resulting from internal displacement. Specifically, the manifest weakness of the victims is the basis of the rationale and for this reason it focuses on the situation of women, children, and elderly persons who are forced to leave their homes and travel great distances facing all kinds of dangers, watching their accompanying family suffer and even die. The understandable flight is not a public order problem generated by those who wish to go on living but a problem of humanity that must be faced with solidarity by all persons, starting, as is logical, by State officials. Consequently, the Colombian Government, through Law 387 of 1997 has implemented integral programs aimed at providing aid to the displaced population, including the National System of Aid to the Displaced Population.

Even though such programs have been implemented, they are either insufficient or their development is incipient. This leaves victims without the receipt of support or humanitarian aid needed from the Government in an immediate, complete and efficacious way, and they must face long and cumbersome bureaucratic procedures that do not guarantee their re-settlement or their return to their original dwelling sites in better conditions. For these reasons, they are forced to file writs of *amparo*, seeking to obtain protection of their fundamental rights.

The Court has pronounced itself in numerous opportunities about the acceptability of the action for protection of fundamental rights in these cases, with the aim of obtaining from a judge, an immediate order that re-establish the violated rights. It has sustained that the writ for the protection of Constitutional rights assures a serious and rapid attention, and a more dynamic and supportive commitment from the institutions in charge of providing the requested humanitarian aid; it is a mechanism that achieves, guaranteeing in this way the respect and realization of the fundamental rights.

Indeed, the weak status of this population group justifies a special treatment by the State, implying the right to receive humanitarian aid in aspects such as food, personal hygiene, health care – including psychological attention – and decent housing. In the event that this does not happen, the action for protection to make these rights effective is appropriate. The State has the obligation to guarantee the welfare of the associates and to grant the displaced population not only minimum conditions to procure a decent subsistence, but also definitive solutions to their situation. Therefore, those who have the status of forced displaced persons cannot be abandoned or left adrift, and the State must deploy all the available mechanisms for efficiently providing humanitarian aid and for their re-integration into society, and that integral healthcare be provided to them.

5.2.2 *The Right of Mothers Who Are Heads of Household to a Decent Housing*

Within the consecration of privileged access to property, the measures in favor of mothers-heads of household have been key strategies for the exercise of the social function of property. The right to a decent housing was made effective for excluded sectors of society through this focal group of the population. Privileged access to property for women with special family burdens must be analyzed within the concept of family, protected by a legal system in accordance with the promoted concept of property.

Along these lines, one of the most important policies to achieve a better distribution of property and privileged access by women is access to housing for mothers who are heads of household. The following case shows how judge argued for this special treatment with the existing laws.

Constitutional Court of Colombia
Ruling T-950 of 2004

Main Legal Issue:
Can more expedited procedures be established for the formation of the family property, without infringing upon the equality that must exist among citizens, when the head of household is the mother?

Facts:
A woman petitioned for a writ of *amparo* against the Southern Zone Principal Registering Officer of the Office of Registry of Public Instruments, because she considered that the fundamental rights of her children to a decent housing, the right to a family as an essential nucleus of society, and the right to the special protection as a woman who is head of household, had been infringed.

Court Ruling:
The Court held that by virtue of the special protection granted to women who are heads of household, the formation of the family property should not be subject to the same requirements established for the family nuclei in which both parents are present.

Extracts:
[…]
On account of the special protection of the family and the minor, our Constitution established in favor of the family and especially of children, a minimum patrimony that enjoys protection in the face of coactive judicial debt collection and that cannot

be used, even by those who have constituted it, for aims different from the family home. Along these lines, the Political Constitution authorized the legislative power to define, in the performance of the social function of the property, under which aspects and conditions and with what scope should the inalienability and unseizability of the family property be understood.

[…]

The petitioner considers that the Registering Officer of Public Instruments […] ignored her fundamental rights to a special protection in her capacity as woman head of household, as well as the fundamental rights of the children, especially the right to a decent housing, by refusing to favorably resolve the petition filed before that entity by the petitioner as a woman who is head of household […] The challenged Registering Officer refused to grant the referred benefit to the petitioner because it considered that the regulations of the Law had not been issued, and that the procedure for its compliance was not established in it, that the immovable belongs to the petitioner in common and joint ownership with the man […] and that it is encumbered with a mortgage by deed of June 28 of 2001, and finally because the formation was not requested by public document.

[…]

First, Law 861 of 2003 did establish a procedure for its compliance and with special character for women who are heads of household to be able to constitute unseizable family property, since (i) it has determined that the woman is holder of a petition as head of household; (ii) it has designated the competent officer to act, that is, the Registering Officer of Public Instruments of the jurisdiction in which the immovable is situated; (iii) it has noted the necessary documentation that must accompany the request; and (iv) it has ordered the Registering Officer that, prior to checking through review the respective proofs, it record in the property registration folio of the corresponding immovable the inclusion of the same under Family Property. Along these lines, it cannot be claimed that a procedure established to comply with the provisions of Law 861 of 2003 does not exist, when the law itself establishes such procedure by prescribing how the constitution of the property before the Registering Officer of the respective jurisdiction should be advanced (articles 2 and 3 of Law 861).

Second, … it is clear that the requisite of public deed was discarded by the legislator … precisely to expedite the constitution procedure to the mother who is head of household, all of which was expressly consecrated in the antecedents of Law 861 of 2003.

Third, and also in accordance with the considerations of this Court of revision, given that the petitioner's partner passed away, leaving her in a condition of mother head of household, to which she attested by accompanying the pertinent declarations in compliance with Law 861 of 2003, it is not possible to argue that the property with status of the immovable of joint ownership with the petitioner's partner, now deceased, is a reason to deny the constitution of the property, precisely when such circumstance represents one of the causes for acquiring the status of woman head of household.

[…]

… The Court proceeds to revoke the decision of the judge of lower instance in the sense of granting the *amparo* regarding the request for constitution of the family property claimed by the plaintiff.

5.2.2.1 Matters for Debate

In Colombia, the legal and case law preservation of the rights in favor of the mother-head of household, illustrate the existing tension between the right to equality and the social function of property. The Court, through various judgments of constitutionality and protection of constitutional rights, has established and developed the special protection held by mothers as heads of household. This special protection for women heads of household is explained, in part, by the conditions of discrimination and exclusion to which women have been subjected to for many years and, on the other hand, by the significant number of women who for diverse reasons have become heads of household and must assume, in precarious conditions and without any sort of support, both the responsibilities of the home and those inherent in the activity that derives the family's maintenance. In this sense, a response is given to a growing need of the less favored population by applying a kind of positive discrimination.

The legal problems surrounding the allocation of housing to mothers who are heads of household also introduces the discussion on the conflict between the constitutional provision on the social function of property and the equally constitutional mandate for gender equality. In this sense, one should reflect on the meaning attributed to each of these provisions, as well as the legal weight that must be given to them, when they conflict in a given case. This way, the option for one constitutional provision or another would require weighing certain principles in specific social and cultural realities.

For the case of special allocation of urban housing to mothers-heads of household, in Colombia the positive discrimination in favor of women could be interpreted as if gender equality prevails over the social function of property. However, the justification of public policies in favor of women heads of household regarding allocation of urban property, are also based on the social function of property. The State conceives public policies, aimed at facilitating the acquisition of homes to a sector of the population usually marginalized and for which generally it is not easy to own a dwelling, with the objective of re-distributing the property. Available cases on this subject are characterized by women requesting that the special regime be applied to them, and consequently, that the bureaucratic procedure required to acquire property be diminished. From this simple fact, it could be concluded that even though courts in most cases grant the claims, in practice the institutions in charge of awarding the homes are not implementing the disposition.

In Argentina, decree 565/021 regulated the *Program of Heads of Household*, also known as *Family Law of Social Inclusion: Plan Unemployed Men and Women who are Heads of Household,* to be implemented until December 31, 2002, within the framework of emergency declarations of food, employment and health. The preliminary paragraphs of the decree pointed out that the establishment of the Family Law of Social Inclusion originated in compliance with the mandate contained in article 75, paragraph 22 of the National Constitution.[26] Due to the social emergency facing Argentinean society, government organizations and institutions were forced to supply the basic needs of the populations most affected by the crisis. The cases dealing with the generation and allocation of resources in the emergency housing programs are noteworthy for ordering the promptness of resource distribution, without heeding to the formal requisites for compliance. The questions that judges seem to be asking themselves are the following: To what extent does the consecration of general requirements guarantee the right to equality? Or on the contrary, how does the consecration of merely formal requirements hamper compliance with substantial rights? In the responses provided by the different courts, the special conditions of certain population groups such as mothers heads of household are taken into account.

5.3 The Tensions Among Excluded Groups

State intervention in re-distributing resources in favor of some groups has been criticized from at least three theoretical perspectives. For the classical liberals, this intervention is a violation of freedom and an erroneous definition of equality. For socialists, to establish a series of privileges for some given groups or persons does not thoroughly tackle the causes of inequality. Finally, interventionist liberals have pointed out the difficulties that develop when faced with having to choose between equality in universal terms and equality in favor of a group or individual.

The rationale of classical liberals, granting privileges to certain groups goes against one of the fundamental ideas of liberalism: equality before the law. In other words, equality is a starting point, but it does not guarantee the results because individuals are different in terms of abilities, ambition and luck, among other factors.[27] In establishing preferential rights for some groups, freedom is restricted since one of the fundamental freedoms of a person is the ability to differentiate ourselves from the rest and to obtain differentiated results according to our inclinations, options, and strengths.

For the socialists, the problem of inequity is not one that can be solved through the distribution of resources in favor of a given group, but by the radical transformation of resource distribution in a society. This way, equality, even equality based on distributive justice, is impossible to achieve as long as social classes exist. Finally, for liberal interventionists themselves, the granting of a special right to a group

---

[26] Art. 75, para. 22, Constitucion Nacional (Argentina) (establishing the constitutional hierarchy of international treaties and pacts, and expressly of the provisions of the International Pact on Economic, Social and Cultural Rights (IPESCR)).

[27] Robert Nozick, *Anarchy, State and Utopia*, Basic Books, London, 1974, p. 148

generates diverse contradictions inside the disadvantaged groups, which is contrary to the concept of equality.

This section discusses two cases in which this tension between the general aim of the State to achieve equality, and the specific needs of a disadvantaged group – women – become apparent. Indeed, these cases show the tensions that exist when a choice must be made between two excluded groups, and the difficult decision of privileging one group over the other.

5.3.1 Agrarian Reform and Gender Equality

The wave of agrarian reforms in Latin America occurred in the 1960s, in the framework of the US policy of "Alliance for Progress." In 1961, the Declaration of the Peoples of America, signed in Punta del Este, Uruguay, agreed to promote, within the peculiarities of each country, programs of integral agrarian reforms aimed at the effective transformation of the structures and unfair systems of tenure and exploitation of the land.[28]

However, during the whole of the twentieth century, agrarian reforms were carried out under different circumstances and contexts. The first reform was that of Mexico in 1917, followed by those of Bolivia and Guatemala, and that of the Cuban revolution, among others. In response to the Cuban communist reform,[29] and following the guidelines of the Alliance for Progress, 17 Latin American countries undertook agrarian reforms and created organizations or institutions of agrarian reform and colonization. The agrarian reforms of the Alliance for Progress with the greatest impact were those of the progressive military government of Peru, under the leadership of general Velasco Alvarado, and the Chilean socialist reform, under President Salvador Allende. After Alliance for Progress, the most extensive reforms that ensued were those of the Sandinista revolution in Nicaragua and those that occurred after the civil war in El Salvador.[30]

In this sense, agrarian reforms are perhaps the best example to explain the meaning of the social function of property. The majority of reforms occurred in Latin American countries in order to bring about a better distribution of resources; the intention was to divide the large land estates (*latifundios*) into smaller estates (*minifundios*) cultivated by families. The reforms privileged the right of possession as a requisite of property. With the exception of Costa Rica, the legislation of agrarian

[28] Organization of American States, *Official documents emanating from the especial meeting of the Inter-American Economic and Social Counsel at the Ministerial Level held in Punta del Este. Uruguay 5–17, 1961*, Washington, DC. General Secretariat of the OAS, 1961.

[29] *See* Richard L. Harris, "Marxism and the agrarian question in Latin America", *Latin American Perspectives*, Vol. 5, No. 4, 1978, pp. 2–26.

[30] *See* Rodolfo Stavenhagen, *Agrarian Problems and Peasant Movements in Latin America*, Double Day, New York, 1970.

reform provided that land be expropriated for purposes of social justice or whenever this contributed to the national interest.[31]

Even though the norms on agrarian reforms are not thought of in terms of gender discrimination, the following cases illustrate how possession is dismissed to give way to ownership by women. This lack of recognition of possession evidences the tension between the objectives of equality for peasants and equality for mothers who cannot own land because of their obligations of family care. In other words, it clearly shows the hierarchy generated among disadvantaged groups and the difficult decisions that must be made.

Supreme Court of the Nation of Mexico
Administrative Appeal Judgment 1950/41.
Zarazúa Jerónimo et al.
February 26, 1943

Main Legal Issue:
Taking into account the social function of the right property and recognizing the right to gender equality, may the effective and productive possession of a property be considered a requirement for awarding property rights, even when the woman is devoted to domestic work?

Facts:
The persons who cultivate the communal rural property allocated to a woman, who is head of household, request the transfer of the property claiming possession of the same. However, the plaintiffs have cultivated the land for years, recognizing the woman's ownership. The woman is devoted to domestic work.

Court Ruling:
The Court denies the plaintiffs' petitions.

Extracts:
Articles 14 and 16 of the Federal Constitution are not violated, if the owners of communal land plots are ultimately deprived of their rights to enjoy their land parcels, if they have exploited them by means of rural workers, sharecroppers or tenants, since article 139 of the Agrarian Code provides: "The communal landowners shall lose the rights they hold as members of a nucleus of communal land … for any one of the following causes: I. For the violation of the provisions contained in clauses I, II and IV of article 128," and the latter, in the pertinent section, literally states: "The owner of communal land shall enjoy the communal parcel, when the communal farmland has been divided in fractions, or if it has not, that of the minimum land parcel, governed by the following limitations . . .[i] t will not be the object of a contract of lease, of share-farming or of any other arrangement that implies the use of paid work by third parties, being exempted from this prohibition…." "If from a certified copy provided as evidence, it emerges that the complaining owners of communal land did not personally carry out the sowing, but that in some cases it

[31] C. D. Deere and M. León, *op.cit.*, p. 429.

was done by their relatives or family members, by paid peasants or by sharecroppers, undoubtedly constitutes a violation of clause IV of article 128 of the cited Agrarian Code, whose purpose is none other than to ensure that the owners of communal land themselves are the ones who cultivate their parcels, with the only exceptions established in that clause. For cases of women who are disabled as a result of domestic labor or caring for the children or minors depending on them…."

Supreme Court of the Nation of Mexico Judgment
12/97 Vicente Aviña Zaragoza y otro.
February 20, 1997

Main Legal Issue:
Do those who cultivate land and those who do not, have the same inheritance rights on communal land rights?

Facts:
Within a succession by inheritance process, the sons demand the allocation of the communal land of the father, since the sister has not cultivated it. The lower court ruled in favor of the plaintiffs.

Court Ruling:
The Court revokes the decision of the lower court, ruling that the invoked successive right is invalid because the deceased was not formally the holder of the communal land rights.

Extracts:
[…]
From the harmonious and systematic interpretation of articles 12, 14, 15, 16, 17 and 18 of the Agrarian Law, published in the Official Federal Gazette on the twenty-sixth of February of one thousand nine hundred and ninety-two … it is concluded that only the legally recognized agrarian rights are susceptible of transfer by inheritance, that is, those that belong to the holders of communal land rights, which is established by the corresponding certificates of agrarian land rights or common rights, issued by a competent authority, or by the judgment or relative resolution of the Agrarian Tribunal, given that such provisions, respectively, state: that the men and women who are holders of communal rights are owners of communal land; that the status of communal land owner is proven by the certificate of agrarian rights issued by a competent authority, by the land certificate or certificate of common rights, or by the ruling or resolution of the Agrarian Tribunal; that the communal land owner has the authority to designate the person who should inherit his rights on the parcel and the rights inherent in his status as communal land owner, for which it will suffice for him to elaborate a list of heirs in which the names of the persons and the order of preference according to which the allocation of goods must be realized upon his death, among which he may include the female spouse, the concubine or concubinary, whatever the case may be, one of his children, one of the ascendants or any other person; and that when the communal land owner has not designated heirs, or when none of the listed heirs can inherit due to material or legal impossibility, the agrarian rights shall be transferred according to the order established in article 18

of the said Agrarian Law. Therefore, the competent Unitary Agrarian Tribunal acted incorrectly when determining that the possessory communal rights are susceptible of being transmitted by inheritance, even when they have not been legally recognized.

5.3.1.1 Matters for Debate

Mexico underwent several agrarian reforms during the twentieth century[32] without this having necessarily meant either a better distribution of the land or an equitable access for women. The definition of possession is an important legal impediment: especially within the framework of agrarian reforms, the use of land grants formal ownership of the land. Along these lines, even though the formal requirements to grant a title deed are equal for men and women, in most cases, possession is defined in accordance with cultivation of the land, and this definition excludes reproductive work. Thus, the judgment refers to the work in the land as a necessary condition for obtaining communal land, even though there are some exceptions for women incapacitated because of domestic work or childcare, effectively awarding property to the women.

Due to the objective of agrarian reforms in the region to promote the social function of the property by giving more weight to possession and work, weakening that definition of possession implies risks in the face of distribution among classes. In this sense, legal institutions of the right to property and the social function of the same are in opposition. To the question of who can be the holder of the right to property, the Mexican rulings response is twofold. Although formally both men and women access it, they can do so, provided they comply with certain requirements, among those to toil the land without intermediaries. However, here, the conflict between the so-called social function of property and gender equality emerges.

In the case of allocation of rural lands, most agrarian reforms have been conceived in terms of re distribution corresponding to men; women were ignored at the beginning of the political debates. In this sense, women were viewed as the wives of landowners and not as in the Mexican cases, it was found that most involving women, are about succession of communal land or cases in which the man who cultivates the land requests the allocation of the same, ignoring the formal rights corresponding to women.

5.3.2 Special Access to Property for Male Specific Conditions

This last section will deal with a form of positive discrimination in favor of men, regarding the distribution of homes of a social interest. It is about legislative measures that establish a privileged condition for men because of the enshrinement of

[32] Arturo Warman, *La reforma agraria mexicana: una visión de largo plazo*. http://www.fao.org/docrep/006/j0415t/j0415t09.htm

especially masculine eligibility requisites for the acquisition of homes of social interest. The case faces a law that establishes a positive discrimination for members of a population group comprised mainly of men. The analysis of these measures allows us to review the question of what has been historically identified as masculine and feminine. The construction of stereotypes confirmed by a social reality shows that the requirements to obtain privileged access to property are met by men more than by women.

As regards the feminist theory, these types of cases challenge the usefulness and pertinence of the dichotomies of equality/difference and of identity/otherness. Thus, even though feminists are split because of the first dichotomy advocating either for equality of conditions between men and women or for the specialties of each gender without the establishment of a hierarchy that favors the masculine, a more viable theoretical possibility should opt for a vision that questions the dichotomy itself.[33]

The following judgment of the Constitutional Court of Colombia illustrates once more the difficulties faced by the judges when having to decide between two marginalized groups and scarce resources such as land. The judges find themselves at a crossroads and must decide which group to privilege at a given moment, awarding greater or lesser weight to the characteristics of the groups involved.

Constitutional Court of Colombia
Ruling C-423 of 1997

Main Legal Issue:
Does a provision, which enshrines that the Army, Navy, or Police reservists shall have priority in the programs of agrarian reform and housing of social interest, infringe on the principle of gender equality?

Facts:
Three Colombian citizens claimed the unconstitutionality of article 1 of Law 264 of 1996, since they considered that it infringed upon the preamble of the Political Constitution, and also of articles 2, 13 and 43.

Court Ruling:
The Court makes a balance to weight the social function of the property and the principle of equality arguing in favor of the special function of the right to property, and it declares the challenged norm enforceable.

Extracts:
[…]
For the distribution of goods to be practiced in accordance to fundamental objectives, and not subject to whims or personal proclivities of the competent official, some criteria need to be established. These criteria of distribution cannot be general,

---

[33] Joan W. Scout, "Deconstructing Equality Versus Difference: Or the Uses of Postestructuralist Theory of Feminism", en Frances Olsen, ed., *Feminist Legal Theory I: Foundations and Outlooks*, New York University Press, Nueva York, 1995, pp. 261–278.

applicable to all cases, but have to be determined according to the characteristics inherent in the goods or means to be distributed and the needs and aspirations that they satisfy.

[…]

Granting a privileged treatment to a given group regarding the distribution of a scarce good consists, by virtue of such treatment, in granting to the chosen group the right to access the specific good, without it having to comply with any special requisite. According to this position, the assets of the property would have to be allocated directly to the members of the privileged group, and only in the case in which the amount of resources were greater than the number of members of the mentioned group, would its residue be distributed among persons not included in the circle of preferential beneficiaries. Special treatment, which in the framework of a process of allocation of scarce goods, is granted to a group of persons, who are part of a conglomerate, is based on the fact that these individuals comply with the basic criteria established to access this service. That is, the privileged treatment may only be applied once the person, to whom a bonus within the process is recognized, fulfills the minimum necessary requirements to be able to compete for the allocation of the good. Only when these requisites have been complied with may the privilege enter into operation.

[…]

The need arises to distinguish between special treatment and the allocation of quotas in the distribution of a good in favor of certain social groups, inherent in the so-called positive differentiation. It has been noted that in the quota system, before proceeding to the distribution of resources, a specific minimal portion of the goods to be distributed will be awarded to a specific social assemblage that is identified according to certain characteristics or criteria. This signifies that the competition for the allocation of the means that correspond to that group will take place only among the members of the same and therefore, its members do not have to emulate with all the rest of the applicants for the allocation of the goods that have been set aside from the general distribution process. However, once all the means reserved for them have been allocated, the group member who has not been selected and still aspires to the allocation of the good shall enter into a competition with all the rest of the applicants, without being given a special treatment.

[…]

The system of prerogatives or preferences operates in the final moment of the distribution, whereas the quota system operates in the process of resource distribution. But, in addition, in the case of the special treatment, there are no limits to its implementation: all those who meet the conditions to be the object of special treatment may demand that such treatment be awarded them. This means that the use of the privilege is not restricted to a certain portion of the goods to be allocated, but that it can, in certain cases, even determine the process of allocation of all the resources to be distributed in a given opportunity.

[…]

The object of the norm is not to sanction those who have not performed military service, but to compensate those who have effectively performed it, assuming the risks and limitations entailed in it. Besides, the implementation of the prerogative does not seem disproportionate since it does not infringe on rights of a higher entity, of those not benefited by the provision. The challenged norm respects the basic parameters of allocation established by the programs of agrarian reform and social housing of an official nature, but introduces an additional criterion for the allocation of these scarce goods – which is applied in cases in which there is equality of conditions among the petitioners of the State subsidy-, which is that of holding the condition of reservist. Preferential treatment is granted for having held the status of conscript, whatever the branch in which the mandatory military service was performed. The exclusion of reservists of the Colombian Air Force from the benefit constitutes an infringement on the right to be treated equally.

5.3.2.1 Matters for Debate

This case highlights the importance of one of the major problems judges face: weighting principles of equal constitutional importance. The social function of property, in favor of special constitutional protection for the military, opposes to the right to equality. The preferential treatment conferred on one sector of the population for commendable reasons may result in discrimination against another group of citizens. The proportionality principle gains special significance if we consider that the distribution criteria cannot be general nor applicable to all cases, but rather should be determined in accordance with the characteristics inherent in the goods or means to be distributed and with the needs or aspirations that they are meant to satisfy. The Colombian Court decided in favor of the military. However, we should wonder what this tells us about the war related values of the government as a whole in a country where armed conflict has been present for decades.

Chapter 6
Violence

Julieta Lemaitre

The 1990s were a decade of legal reforms regarding violence against women. The countries of the region not only signed the only regional agreement on the subject, but also reformed their criminal codes and adopted new laws against violence within the family.[1] The reforms eliminated discriminatory norms, established equality between the sexes and determined the creation of new institutions.[2] Whereas the exact content of the norms varies among countries, they contain numerous similarities, which render their comparative study possible. This repertoire includes, among other reforms, the criminalization of intra-family violence, the creation of civil measures of protection for battered women, the creation of special institutional jurisdictions, increased penalties for sex crimes, and the elimination of discriminatory measures from penal codes.

At the theoretical level, these reforms correspond to three great stages in feminist conceptualization: U.S. radical feminism of the 1970s and 1980s; the feminism of Latin American women's organizations during that same period, and feminist

[1] For example, see Inter-American Convention on the Prevention, Punishment and Eradication of Violence Against Women "Convention of Belem do Para".

[2] Some of the statutes on violence against women are: Argentina, Ley 24.417, 1994; Bolivia, Ley 1.674, 1995; Colombia, Ley 294, 1996 reformed by ley 575, 2000; Costa Rica, Ley 7.586, 1996; Chile, Ley 20.066, 2005; Ecuador, Ley 103, 1995; El Salvador, Decreto Ley 902 de 1996; Guatemala, Ley 97–96; Honduras, Decreto 132–97; México, Ley de Asistencia y Prevención de la Violencia Intrafamiliar 1996 and Ley General de Acceso de las Mujeres a una Vida Libre de Violencia de 2007; Nicaragua, Ley 230, 1996; Panamá, Ley 27, 1995; Puerto Rico, Ley 54, 1989 (the first one in Latin America); Perú, Ley 27.306, 2000 amending ley 26.260, 1993 (the first one in South America); Dominican Republic, Ley 24–97; Uruguay, Ley 16.707, 1995; and Ley 17.514, 2002; Venezuela, Ley sobre la violencia contra la mujer y la familia, September, 1998.

J. Lemaitre (✉)
Facultad de derecho, University of Los Andes Law School,
Carrera 1# 18A-10, Bogota, Colombia
e-mail: jlemaitr@uniandes.edu.co

C. Motta and M. Sáez (eds.), *Gender and Sexuality in Latin America - Cases and Decisions*, Ius Gentium: Comparative Perspectives on Law and Justice 24,
DOI 10.1007/978-94-007-6199-5_6, © Springer Science+Business Media Dordrecht 2013

innovations in international law concerning human rights in the 1990s. Although the issue of "violence against women" emerges as a great banner of the transnational movement during this latter stage, it is impossible to understand this stage of activism and reforms without considering the previous theoretical frameworks, especially radical feminism and Latin American feminism.

Unlike liberal feminism, U.S. radical feminism assigned a prominent place to violence in its theoretical apparatus to explain sexual difference and women's subordination. For radical feminism, women's subordination does not correspond mainly to their exclusion from power, or to the effects of discrimination, but to their domination through different violent means. In the legal field, Catherine MacKinnon is perhaps the person who explains this in a more conclusive way, associating violence with the construction of sexual difference. In her opinion, sexual difference resides essentially in the dominance of women by men, and this is a dominion maintained through violent means.[3] In other words, for MacKinnon, the sexual difference, constructed as gender difference, is essentially a difference between dominating and dominated persons. The specific acts of violence that women are faced with in their personal lives, rape and physical violence, are instrumental in maintaining the dominion on individual women in individual cases, and in maintaining the subordination of all women in every sphere through fear.[4] Consequently, the fight against violence is a fight for women's liberation, to free women individually and to free all women from the climate of fear and impotence generated by the persistence and frequency of the acts of violence and their tacit legitimization in the dominant culture.

Although it is possible to trace some clear connections between radical feminism and legal reforms, the latter are not a simple reflection of the regional reception of radical feminism; they also correspond to the theoretical development carried out by various women's organizations and their interrelation in regional networks.[5]

---

[3] *See* Catharine MacKinnon, *Feminism Unmodified: Discourses on Life and Law*, Harvard University Press, Cambridge, 1987; *Toward a Feminist Theory of the State,* Harvard University Press, Cambridge, 1989. See also, Mary Daly Gyn, *Ecology: The Methaethics of Radical Feminism*, Beacon Press, Boston, 1978. Susan Brownmiller, *Against Our Will Men Women and Rape*, Simon & Schuster, New York, 1975.

[4] Catherine MacKinnon "State of Emergency: Who Will Declare War on Terrorism Against Women?" *Women's Rev. Books* 19, no. 6 (2002): 7–8 y "Women's September 11th: Rethinking the International Law of Conflict." *Harv. Int'l L. J.* 47, no. 1 (2006): 1–31.

[5] Sally Engle Merry, *Human Rights and Gender Violence: Translating International law into Local Justice,* University of Chicago Press, Chicago, 2006; Nancy Saporta Sternbach, Marysa Navarro Aranguren, Patrucia Chuchryk y Sonia E. Alvarez, "Feminisms in Latin America from Bogota to San Bernardo" in Arturo Escobar and Sonia E. Alvarez, *The Making of Social Movements in Latin America,* Westview Press, Boulder and Oxford, 1992; Nelly P. Stromquist, *Feminist Organizations and Social Transformation in Latin America*, Paradigm Publishers, Boulder, 2007; Norma Stoltz Chinchilla, "Marxism, Feminism and the Struggle for Democracy in Latin America" in Escobar and Alvarez, *op.cit.*; pp. 37–51; Margaret E. Keck and Kathryn Sikkink, *Activists Beyond Borders: Advocacy Networks in International Politics,* Cornell University Press, Ithaca and London, 1998; Francesca Gargallo, "El feminismo múltiple: prácticas e ideas feministas en América Latina," in María Luisa Femenías (comp), *Perfiles del Feminismo Iberoamericano*, Catálogos, Buenos Aires, 2002.

Feminists in the region encounter the problem of violence against women through different paths. In their work with working-class women, they witness male violence as a constant and verify its devastating effects on women's life.[6] Additionally, many of them, in their militancy against dictatorships and authoritarian governments, bring up how sexual torture demonstrates, once again, the depth of inequality between the sexes and its relationship with violence.[7] Both of these experiences, together with the reflection on personal life that feminism demands, lead to a conceptualization of patriarchy as a total system of domination that goes beyond the subordination of women and also includes, in addition to social injustice, militarism, authoritarianism, obligatory heterosexuality, homophobia, and obviously, the different forms of physical, sexual, and psychological violence against women.[8] This formulation of patriarchy is first outlined in the First Feminist Meeting in Bogotá, in 1981, and unfolds during the Second Meeting in Lima, in 1983. It was Latin American feminists who established, during the First Meeting, the International Day for the Elimination of Violence Against Women on November 25, in commemoration of the torture and assassination of the Mirabal sisters by the Trujillo dictatorship in the Dominican Republic.[9]

Despite the importance of both conceptualizations—those contributed by radical feminism and by Latin American feminism—the issue of violence against women materialized in large-scale legal reforms only after a third major conceptual contribution: the notion that violence against women is a violation of human rights. This idea began to circulate in the early 1990s, especially in an article by Charlotte Bunch,[10] and it was enthusiastically received by feminists from different countries who understood its explanatory and mobilizing power. Indeed, categorizing the different forms of violence against women as violations of human rights establishes the responsibility of the State as guarantor of the mentioned rights.

Thus, under the fortunate slogan "women's rights are human rights," transnational feminist networks have pressured countries and multilateral organisms to produce a series of agreements and documents that consider violence against women a serious infringement on the rights to equality, dignity and life, and formulate the right to a life free from violence implicit in the aforementioned rights.

This formulation once again reinforced the region's feminist movements, which promoted legal reforms and the formulation of public policies, often with funding and support from a transnational feminism. It also allowed a rapprochement with the State, which coincided with the strengthening of democracies, the end of the Cold War, and a new readiness on the part of feminist organizations to work jointly with the State.

---

[6] S.E. Merry, *op.cit.* p. 24.

[7] F. Gargallo, *op.cit.* p. 117; K. Sikkink y M. E. Keck, *op.cit.* p. 176.

[8] F. Gargallo, *Ibid.* p. 118; S.E. Alvarez, *op.cit.* p. 210; K. Sikkink and M.E. Keck, *Id.* p. 175.

[9] M.E. Keck y K. Sikkink, *Ibid.* p. 178; S.E. Alvarez, *op.cit.* p. 218.

[10] M.E. Keck y K. Sikkink, *Ibid.* p. 165. Charlotte Bunch, "Women's Rights as Human Rights: Toward a Revision of Human Rights" in, *Human Rights Quarterly* 12 (1990): 486–498.

These circumstances led to important victories in the legal field and to the creation of international networks, but also to a new period of challenges and frustrations in the implementation of these norms. The first frustration was the difficulty to translate a complex conception of patriarchy like the one formulated by the feminists of the region, into legal norms. The immediate result is the simplification of the problem of women, especially of poor women, through privileging marital violence over the other forms of exclusion and violence they suffer. In societies that are so unequal, and in which the application of the law is uncertain, norms frequently do not have the expected results. On the one hand, because marital and sexual violence is one of many problems that poor women must face as individuals and as members of a family group. On the other hand, because even in the case of focusing exclusively on the problem of marital and sexual violence, the State fails because of lack of resources, lack of political will, and sometimes because it is simply absent.

In addition to these problems generated by the application of norms, or lack of application, there are a series of problems that are mainly juridical, and the focus of this chapter. The "mainly juridical" means that they are problems related to the formulation of norms and to their interpretation. In particular, this chapter highlights the tension that exists between the formulation and interpretation of norms and the emancipatory intentions of feminism, in three general issues: penalization as a mechanism of social change, the difficulties of including women's point of view in penal regulations, and the restrictive effects of norms in women's freedom and autonomy. These three subjects represent both the feminist contributions to traditional dogma and the difficulties faced by the feminist project when it pretends to use the law to advance its agenda. These are examples that do not exhaust the subject but rather offer a useful introduction to the relevant material and to a form of analysis that is at the same time feminist and critical.

6.1 The Paradoxes of Penalization

6.1.1 Feminism and Critical Criminology

Feminist criticism of the law supports the reforms introduced in penal codes, arguing that the law does not only discriminate against women, but that it also excludes their point of view. The reforms have therefore focused on eliminating sexist classifications, for example, the qualification of the passive subject of certain sexual crimes as "virgin woman" or "honest woman," as well as on including the point of view of women, for instance, that marital rape does exist as a form of sexual violence. The aim of the reforms is not only to improve the situation of women vis-à-vis penal law, but also to change the culture through the legitimizing effect of the law.

For critical criminology, this use of penal law is a monumental mistake of feminism, which, being an emancipatory movement, must not forge an alliance with the State in the exercise of a punitive power.[11] It is impossible for a power that due to its structure can only be exercised in a selective and discriminatory way, to be exercised in an anti-discriminatory way. That "the hierarchizing power of society, the most violent instrument of discrimination, the tool that underpins all discriminations, may become an instrument in the fight against discrimination," is questioned.[12]

These two perspectives provide a framework to the cases examined below. The first is the creation of the crime of femicide or "feminicide" to typify the torture and murder of young, poor women and the absence of investigation and punishment for these crimes. Several feminists from Central America, with some echo in the rest of the region,[13] advocate for the creation of this offense, defined as the killing of women because they are women. For instance, sexual murders committed as a way to impose "appropriate" wife or mother behaviors, or against a prostitute for being a prostitute, would constitute femicide. In particular, we consider its application in two very complex phenomena, namely, the serial murders in Ciudad Juarez, associated to legal economies (*maquilas*) and to illegal ones—drug trafficking, illegal immigration, human trafficking—in the Mexican border area, and those occurring in Guatemala, associated to gangs composed by young and poor adolescents, the "*maras*."

The second case concerns the responsibility of the State for rapes in the context of State terrorism or armed conflict. Feminists have advocated that the State, instead of assigning responsibility solely to the individual(s) who perpetrate sexual violence, assume the responsibility for such violence. What is questioned is the notion that rape be considered an act separate from other acts of repression, such as unlawful arrest and other forms of torture, and what is sought is that it be recognized as part of one and the same phenomenon infringing upon human rights. Very important in this respect is the decision of the Inter-American Commission on Human Rights in Raquel Martín de Mejía v. Peru, which recognized that sexual violence is a form of torture.

The question is whether it is productive to insist upon State responsibility for acts it is indifferent to, like sexual murder or sexual violence; whether insisting on such responsibility contributes to emancipate women and to change mentalities. The incapacity of penal law to protect women is evident in the region and is reflected outside the sphere of violence, for instance, in the inefficacy of the criminalization of failure to pay child support. The idea is not to totally reject the legal reform, but rather, to place it in a broad concept of activism, and consider that the time has come to evaluate not only its results but, also the difficulties in putting it into practice as a strategy for social change.

[11] *See* Elena Larrauri, *La Herencia de la Criminología Crítica,* Siglo XXI, Madrid, 1991; Regina Pereira de Andrade, *A Ilusao de Seguranca Juridica do controle da violencia a violencia do controle penal,* Livraria do Adrogado, Porto Alegre, 1997; Haydée Birgin (Comp.), *Las Trampas del Poder Punitivo. El Género del Derecho Penal*, Editorial Biblos, Buenos Aires, 2000.

[12] Eugenio Raul Zaffaroni "El discurso feminista y el poder punitivo" in Birgin, *op.cit.*

[13] *See* Centro de la Mujer Peruana Flora Tristan, *La Violencia Contra la Mujer: Feminicidio en el Perú*, Lima, 2005.

6.1.2 *Femicide or the Murder of Women Simply Because They Are Women*

The reports on torture and murder of women in the region, especially in Mexico and Guatemala, hold the different States responsible for the impunity and persistence of these crimes, and insist on the fact that they cannot be included in the general crime rate statistics. The reports affirm that these crimes reveal discrimination against women, not only because sex is their main motivation, but also because the authorities deliberately ignore them, repeat stereotypes—a recurring argument wielded by the authorities is that the missing girl must have run away with her boyfriend—and do not investigate the crime or punish the offenders. This has led many human rights organizations to accuse the State of failing to fulfill its obligations as guarantor of human rights.

A sector of the feminist movement also propounds the designation of this phenomenon as femicide, in order to identify female sexual homicides as a special type of homicide. The term was coined by Jill Radford and Diane Russell, following the shooting of a group of female engineering students by a young Canadian man who alleged his hatred of women, defined as the misogynist killing of women by men.[14] In Latin America, the prototype of femicide is not this kind of isolated case, but the 15 years of forced disappearance, torture, and murder of young women in Ciudad Juárez, Mexico. More recently, similar phenomena occurring in Guatemala have been included.

We are in the presence of a phenomenon that has at least three new dimensions in criminal law. Three dimensions which are new to the law. The first one is the murderers' motivation, which seems to be related to the young age and gender of the victims and to a hatred or contempt that itself through extremely violent behaviors of a sexual nature. The second dimension is the climate of distress and impunity that the accumulation of unresolved crimes creates over the years, and last, is the apathy, negligence, and occasionally, evident bad faith shown by the authorities in charge of investigating the crimes

In view of this situation, the feminist movement works on two legal fronts. On the one hand, it aims to create a new crime to define both the misogynous motivation and the general situation of distress and impunity of which criminals take advantage. The definition that has had greater diffusion is the one proposed by the Mexican congresswoman Marcela Lagarde to support her project of reform of the Penal Code. Lagarde defines feminicide as an attempt on the life and physical integrity of women when such an act is committed in a place where this type of attack is carried out in a systematic way, and where, also in a systematic way, such attacks remain unpunished. The second legal front involves denouncing the State for violating its obligations to protect and guarantee the validity of human rights in its territory, especially the right to life and access to an adequate administration of justice.

[14] Jill Radford and Diane Russell, *Femicide: The Politics of Woman Killing*, Open University Press, Buckingham, 1992.

Some of the problems that arise from both efforts, that of creating a new criminal offense and that of insisting upon State responsibility, are examined below.

Inter-American Commission of Human Rights
The Situation of the Rights of Women in Ciudad Juárez, Mexico: The Right to be Free from Violence and Discrimination[15]

1. This report addresses the right of women in Ciudad Juárez, Mexico to be free from violence and discrimination. It reports on the grave situation of violence faced by the women and girls of Ciudad Juárez, including murder and disappearance, as well as sexual and domestic violence, and offers recommendations designed to assist the United Mexican States ("State" or "Mexican State") in amplifying its efforts to respect and ensure those rights. [...]

3. During the visit, authorities in Ciudad Juárez presented information with respect to the killing of 268 women and girls since 1993. In a substantial number of cases, the victims were young women or girls, workers in the *maquilas* (assembly plants) or students, who were sexually abused before being brutally killed. These authorities also reported on over 250 missing person's reports filed during that period that remained unresolved. During the visit, representatives of civil society presented ample information, as well as a letter signed by over 5000 individuals demanding that the Mexican State provide an effective response to this situation. The letter expressed that: "Since 1993 women living in Ciudad Juárez have been afraid; afraid to go out into the street and walk the distance between their home and their job. Afraid at 10, 13, 15, 20 years old; it makes no difference if she is a girl or a woman...."

4. While the situation of women in Ciudad Juárez shares many aspects common to other cities in the United Mexican States and the region generally, it is different in certain important respects. First, the homicide rate for women experienced an unusually sharp rise in Ciudad Juárez in 1993, and the rate has remained elevated since that time. Second, as explained in more detail in the report, the rate of homicides for women compared to that for men in Ciudad Juárez is significantly higher than for similarly situated cities or the national average. Third, the extremely brutal circumstances of many of the killings have served to focus attention on the situation in Ciudad Juárez. A significant number of the victims were young, between 15 and 25, and many were beaten and/or subjected to sexual violence before being strangled or stabbed to death. A number of the killings that fit this pattern have been characterized as multiple or "serial" killings. Fourth, the response of the authorities to these crimes has been markedly deficient. There are two aspects of this response that are especially relevant. On the one hand, the vast majority of the killings remain in impunity; approximately 20% have been the subject of prosecution and conviction. On the other hand, almost as soon as the rate of killings began to rise, some of the

[15] IACHR, The Situation of the Rights of Women in Ciudad Juárez, Mexico: The Right to Be Free from Violence and Discrimination, OEA/Ser.L/V/II.117, Doc. 44, Mar. 7, 2003.

officials responsible for investigation and prosecution began employing a discourse that in effect blamed the victim for the crime. According to public statements of certain highly placed officials, the victims wore short skirts, went out dancing, were "easy" or were prostitutes. Reports document that the response of the relevant officials to the victims' family members ranged from indifference to hostility. [...]

7. While the high level of violence against both men and women is a source of concern for the Commission in more general terms, efforts to sanction past killings of women and prevent future such killings have been impeded by additional obstacles, most especially, discrimination based on gender. In this sense, it must be emphasized that, as the Inter-American Convention on the Prevention, Punishment and Eradication of Violence against Women ("Convention of Belém do Pará") makes clear, violence against women is a manifestation of the historically unequal power relations between men and women. Violence based on gender originates in and perpetuates those negative power imbalances. As the Beijing Declaration and Platform for Action adopted by the UN Fourth World Conference on Women sets forth, such violence "is one of the crucial social mechanisms by which women are forced into a subordinate position compared with men." The lack of due diligence to clarify and punish such crimes, and to prevent their repetition reflects that they are not perceived as a serious problem. The impunity in which such crimes are then left sends the message that such violence is tolerated, thereby fueling its perpetuation.

Amnesty International
Guatemala
No protection, no justice: Killings of Women in Guatemala[16]

"My 15-year-old daughter María Isabel was a student and worked in a shop in the holidays. On the night of 15 December 2001, she was kidnapped in the capital. Her body was found shortly before Christmas. She had been raped, her hands and feet had been tied with barbed wire, she had been stabbed and strangled and put in a bag. Her face was disfigured from being punched, her body was punctured with small holes, there was a rope around her neck and her nails were bent back. When her body was handed over to me, I threw myself to the ground shouting and crying but they kept on telling me not to get so worked up.

With the help of witnesses, the authorities identified two of the culprits and a luxury car and obtained details of the house where she had been held. The case has been passed to two prosecutor's offices but those responsible are still at liberty."[17]

The brutal sexual violence inflicted on Maria Isabel following her abduction and before her murder in 2001 is a characteristic common to many of the hundreds of killings of women and girls that have been reported in Guatemala in recent years.

---

[16] Amnesty International, Guatemala: No Protection, no Justice: Killings of Women in Guatemala, 9 June 2005, AMR 34/017/2005, *available at* http://www.unhcr.org/refworld/docid/45bf6e4d2.html

[17] Testimony of the mother of Maria Isabel Veliz Franco, aged 15, who was abducted and murdered in December 2001.

The failure of the Guatemalan authorities to subsequently detain and bring to justice those responsible for her murder is another characteristic of this case and many others. The suffering of many of the relatives of murdered women has been compounded by the knowledge that the government's failure to adequately address these cases by ensuring such crimes are thoroughly and impartially investigated means that they will almost certainly never have access to truth and justice. At a broader level, the Guatemalan Government's failure to prevent an escalation in the number of killings or to ensure effective prosecutions means that those responsible can continue to commit these crimes in the certainty that they will not be held to account.

Guatemalan authorities confirmed to the Inter-American Commission on Human Rights (IACHR) that between 2001 and August 2004 they had registered the deaths of 1,188 women. Nevertheless, the precise number of women who have been murdered is unknown and disputed. Figures vary among institutions and are based on different criteria. One official source is the National Police Force (PNC *policía nacional civil*) which recorded 527 cases of women violently killed during 2004. A number of factors, however, including relatives' fear of reporting a murder and lack of public confidence in state institutions, in particular in the administration of justice system to adequately respond to complaints, suggest that police figures could be conservative. Some observers have questioned or dismissed the seriousness of the problem relating to killings of women by arguing the statistics are the same or similar to statistics for the killing of women in other countries in the Americas region. Amnesty International believes, however, that the pattern of brutality, the evidence of sexual violence, which can amount to torture in some cases, and the increasing number of women killed requires the authorities pay immediate and urgent attention to the problem.

Most of the killings of women in Guatemala have occurred in urban areas of the country which have also witnessed a dramatic rise in violent crime in recent years often linked to organized crime, including drugs and arms trafficking and kidnapping for ransom, or to the activities of street youth gangs known as 'maras'. Men have also been affected by general levels of violence in the community and there has been a significant increase in the overall murder rate. Public security issues and breakdown in the rule of law are frequently cited as among the main concerns of the population at large.

Many women and girls in Guatemala live with gender-based violence: violence against women in the family, rape, and sexual harassment in the workplace are commonplace. Women and young girls are also the victims of commercial trafficking and sexual exploitation. Police officers have also been implicated in cases of sexual violence. A number of the victims of killings were under 18 years of age. Among the women killed over the last few years in Guatemala are students, housewives and professionals, domestic employees, unskilled workers, members or former members of street youth gangs and sex workers. While the murders may be attributed to different motives and may have been committed by both state and non-state individuals, a study of some of the cases shows that the violence is usually gender-based; the gender of the victim would appear to be a significant factor in the crime, influencing both the motive and the context, as well as the kind of violence suffered by the woman and the manner in which the authorities respond. [...]

Establishing a comprehensive picture of the extent of the violence perpetrated against women in Guatemala remains extremely difficult because of the lack of reliable official information. In particular, the almost total absence of sex-disaggregated data in official documents means that gender-related violence is generally under-recorded and often rendered almost invisible. For example, in the case of women who have been killed, the numbers presented by the police for 2004 attribute 175 deaths to gunshots, 27 to knife wounds, and 323 to "other causes." These categories, however, conceal the gender-based brutality and sexual nature of many of the killings in which victims present evidence of rape, mutilation, and dismemberment. The absence of official information represents a serious setback for research and policymakers since any examination of violence against women as a human rights issue needs to be based on data that is broken down by sex and to follow a methodology that addresses women's rights, gender and the victims [...]

Amnesty International acknowledges that some positive steps to prevent violence against women have been taken by the Guatemalan authorities including the ratification of international human rights treaties, the introduction of laws and creation of state institutions to promote and protect the rights of women. However, these measures have frequently not been effectively implemented, monitored or reviewed, and have therefore, seldom prevented women from suffering violence.

6.1.2.1 Matters for Debate

Definition of Femicide as a Crime

Both reports insist on the responsibility of the State in these murders, considering that it has violated its obligation to protect the victims' rights to life and access to justice.

Consider the impact the categorization of femicide in the criminal process would have, and whether it would serve as an effective pressure mechanism for individuals to modify their conduct.

The term femicide as a crime describes certain homicides of women motivated by the victim's gender. Thus, for instance, an aggressor who seeks a woman to rape and murder, does so because she is a woman. He would not commit the action if a man were involved because the situation would be different. This difference does not exist in the case of robbery, where the victim's gender can facilitate the offense if the perpetrator considers that women are weaker, but, the motive is monetary gain not her gender. Being killed for reasons of gender is something that occurs mainly to women—although it is certainly not the only type of murder motivated by the category to which the person belongs, since there are also murders of homosexuals, transvestites, colored people, indigenous people and even of members of a particular religion or political party. It would therefore seem that the element to be defined is motivation, and we might be referring to an aggravating circumstance in a case of homicide when it is committed on grounds of a characteristic of the victim that may include sex, sexual orientation, religion, race, etc. The difficulty resides in the fact that on many occasions, the motivation is unclear, even for the aggressors: the rape of a young girl does not appear to be motivated by gender until this becomes evident through an explanation. For this reason, it would perhaps be more effective to define a specific crime requiring it would perhaps be more reasonable to add an inquiry into gender based motivations into the crime of murder, and harsher penalties for all hate-based crimes.

State Responsibility for Femicide

In the year 2003, a group of regional non-governmental organizations (NGOs) requested an audience before the Inter-American Commission on Human Rights to report the situation of violence against women in the region, in particular the increase of sex-motivated murder of women.[18] The attending organizations form part of a transnational network that pressures States through the system of the United Nations, the Organization of American States (OAS), and of international human rights organizations such as Amnesty International. The objective is the goal is to compel governments into taking specific actions to investigate and punish these crimes, as well as to compensate the surviving families. The Mexican government, for instance, has had a positive response to this campaign, admitting its responsibility and incorporating new institutions and policies. These measures, however, have not succeeded in modifying the situation of violence. At the same time, Mexico alleges that this is a structural phenomenon not caused by the State and that change in this regard depends on a long-term action that is not its exclusive responsibility.

6.1.3 Rape as Torture. Jurisprudential Evolution of Human Rights Law

Humanitarian international law, and specifically the Geneva Convention, insofar as it regulates the treatment of civilians and combatants in times of war, established as of 1949 that sexual violence was an act that violated the Convention when it was committed against a protected person (captured civilians and combatants).

[18] Participant organizations: Comisión Mexicana de Defensa y Promoción de los Derechos Humanos, A.C. (CMDPDH); Comité de América Latina y el Caribe para la Defensa de los Derechos de la Mujer (CLADEM); Federación Internacional de Derechos Humanos (FIDH); Centro por la Justicia y el Derecho Internacional (CEJIL); Fundación Kuña Aty, Paraguay; Estudio para la Defensa y los derechos de la Mujer (DEMUS), Peru; Católicas por el Derecho a Decidir, Mexico; Grupo de Mujeres de San Cristóbal de las Casas, A.C. (COLEM), Mexico; Centro de Promoción de la Mujer Gregoria Apaza, Bolivia; Red Nacional de Trabajadoras/es de la Información y Comunicación (RED ADA), Bolivia; Centro para la Acción Legal en Derechos Humanos (CALDH), Guatemala; Sisma Mujer, Colombia; Red de la No violencia contra las Mujeres de Guatemala and Washington, Office on Latin America (WOLA).

However, international human rights law did not establish until the mid 1990s that sexual violence perpetrated by a State agent in the exercise of his/her duties was a State responsibility. In this respect, the advances achieved by the International Courts of Rwanda and Yugoslavia and the creation of the International Criminal Court are considered milestones.

The slow evolution of international law is difficult to explain. It is evident that at least the sexual violence against detained civilians was a daily occurrence in the repressive regimes that inter-American law on human rights condemned in the 1970s and 1980s. However, sexual violence was not considered part of the torture but rather, of the individual whim of the agent. This point of view corresponds, perhaps, to the same factors that conceal sexual violence in national legislations. Additionally, it corresponds to the myth that a State agent practices rape in his capacity as an individual pursuing gratification and not as a State agent engaged in a campaign of violent repression.

This period changed after the Report of the Inter-American Commission on Human Rights (IACHR) on the Raquel Martín de Mejía v. Peru case. The IACHR clearly established that sexual violence is just another method of torture and not an isolated incident. It also made it possible to presume, in conjunction with the ruling of the Inter-American Court on Human Rights in the Velásquez Rodríguez case, that there might be State responsibility for sexual violence suffered at the hands of undetermined persons, for example, paramilitary, guerrillas or bands of criminals, when the State does not fulfill its duty to investigate and sanction this crime. This possibility, however, leads to reflect on the limits that separate rape as torture and rape as an offense in national laws.

Inter-American Commission of Human Rights[19]
Raquel Martín de Mejía v. Peru
March 1, 1996

Main Legal Issue:
If a state agent commits an act of sexual violence in situations of state repression, is the responsibility on the State or only the individual?

Facts:
Dr. Fernando Mejía Egocheaga and his wife, Mrs. Raquel Martín de Mejia were living in Oxapampa, in the Department of Pasco, at the time the events. Dr. Mejía was a lawyer, journalist and political activist. At the time of his death, he was President of the Oxapampa Bar Association and also Chairman of the Provincial Committee of Izquierda Unida (United Left), a Peruvian political party. He was also a member of the Peruvian Journalists' Association and worked as a journalist on the paper "Campanaria Oxapampa," which he had founded and of which he was editor. Mrs. Mejía was a teacher and worked as principal of a school for the handicapped in Oxapampa.

[19] Raquel Martí de Mejía v. Perú, Case 10.970, Inter-Am. Comm'n. H.R., Report No. 5/96, OEA/Ser.L/V/II.91 Doc. 7 at 157 (1996).

In June 1989 some soldiers were killed by Sendero Luminoso (Shining Path) terrorists in Posuzo, a town not far from Oxapampa. A few days afterwards, about 100 military personnel were helicoptered into Oxapampa to conduct counterinsurgency operations in the region. When Dr. Mejía was detained, one of the soldiers remained in the doctor's home and raped Mrs. Mejía on two occasions. He threatened to detain her like they had done with her husband, if she resisted.

Conclusions of the Commission:
The Commission, having established that the three elements of the definition of torture are present in the case under consideration, concludes that the Peruvian State is responsible for violation of Article 5 of the American Convention.

Extracts:
Considerations on the substance of the case
Raquel Mejía informed the Commission that when, on June 20, 1989, she filed her declaration with the Oxapampa police concerning the abduction and subsequent homicide of her husband, she did not report the sexual abuse to which she had been subjected because "[I was] fearful that the violations committed against my person would have caused me to be ostracized and exposed me to greater danger or physical harm...."

[...]

The Commission observes that the reasons given by the petitioner for not submitting a petition in the domestic courts are supported by different documents published by intergovernmental bodies and nongovernmental organizations which expressly note that women who have been victims of sexual abuse by members of the security forces or police have no means open to them for obtaining a remedy for the violations of their rights.

[...]

[T]he proofs submitted demonstrate that the police and armed forces protect those responsible for these violations and award promotions in their careers, implicitly tolerating the commission of these crimes.

<u>Questions raised</u>
[T]he Commission must establish whether the sexual abuses to which Raquel Mejía was subjected constitute violation of the rights to humane treatment (Article 5) and to privacy (Article 11), in connection with the obligation set forth in Article 1(1). [...]

<u>Analysis</u>
The repeated sexual abuse to which Raquel Mejía was subject to constitutes a violation of Article 5 and Article 11 of the American Convention on Human Rights.

Current international law establishes that sexual abuse committed by members of security forces, whether as a result of a deliberate practice promoted by the State or as a result of failure by the State to prevent the occurrence of this crime, constitutes a violation of the victims' human rights, especially the right to physical and mental integrity.

[...]

In the context of international humanitarian law, Article 27[32] of the Fourth Geneva Convention of 1949 concerning the protection due to civilians in times of war explicitly prohibits sexual abuse. Article 147[34] of that Convention, which lists acts considered as "serious offenses" or "war crimes" includes rape in that it constitutes "torture or inhuman treatment." The International Committee of the Red Cross (ICRC) has declared that the "serious offense" of "deliberately causing great suffering or seriously harming physical integrity or health" includes sexual abuse.

Moreover, Article 76 of Additional Protocol I to the 1949 Geneva Conventions expressly prohibits rape or other types of sexual abuse. As established in the Fourth Convention and Protocol I, any act of rape committed individually constitutes a war crime.

In the case of non-international conflicts, both Article 3, common to the four Geneva Conventions, and Article 4(2) of Protocol II, as an addition to the Conventions, include the prohibition against rape and other sexual abuse insofar as they are the outcome of harm deliberately influenced on a person. The ICRC has stated that the prohibition laid down in Protocol II reaffirms and complements the common Article 3 since it was necessary to strengthen the protection of women, who can be victims of rape, forced prostitution or other types of abuse.

[...]

The letter of the Convention does not specify what is to be understood by torture. However, in the inter-American sphere, acts constituting torture are established in the Inter-American Convention to Prevent and Punish Torture, which states:

> [T]orture will be understood to be any act performed intentionally by which physical and mental pain or suffering is inflicted on a person for purposes of criminal investigation, as a means of intimidation, as a personal punishment, as a preventive measure, as a penalty or for any other purpose. Torture will also be understood to be application to a person of methods designed to efface the victim's personality or to diminish his physical or mental capacity, even if they do not cause physical pain or mental anguish.

Accordingly, for torture to exist three elements have to be combined:

1. it must be an intentional act through which physical and mental pain and suffering is inflicted on a person;
2. it must be committed with a purpose;
3. it must be committed by a public official or by a private person acting at the instigation of the former.

Regarding the first element, the Commission considers that rape is a physical and mental abuse that is perpetrated as a result of an act of violence. The definition of rape contained in Article 170 of the Peruvian Criminal Code confirms this by using the phrasing "[h]e who, with violence or serious threat, obliges a person to practice the sex act..." The Special Rapporteur against Torture has noted that sexual abuse is one of the various methods of physical torture. Moreover, rape is considered to be a method of psychological torture because its objective, in many cases, is not just to humiliate the victim but also her family or community. In this connection, the above-mentioned Special Rapporteur has stated that, particularly in Peru, "...rape would appear to be a weapon used to punish, intimidate and humiliate."[...]

[...]

The second element establishes that for an act to be torture it must have been committed intentionally, i.e. to produce a certain result in the victim. The Inter-American Convention to Prevent and Punish Torture includes, among other purposes, personal punishment, and intimidation.

Raquel Mejía was raped with the aim of punishing her personally and intimidating her. According to her testimony, the man who raped her told her that she, too, was wanted as a subversive, like her husband. He also told her that her name was on a list of persons connected with terrorism and, finally, warned her that her friendship with a former official in the previous government would not serve to protect her. On the second occasion, before leaving, he threatened to come back and rape her again. Raquel Mejía felt terrorized not only for her own safety but also for that of her daughter who was sleeping in another room and for the life of her husband.

The third requirement of the definition of torture is that the act must have been perpetrated by a public official or by a private individual at the instigation of the former. As concluded in the foregoing, the man who raped Raquel Mejía was member of the security forces who had himself accompanied by a large group of soldiers.

[...]

International Criminal Court
Rules of Procedure and Evidence
Chapter 4, Section I, Evidence[20]
Provisions relating to various stages of the proceedings

Rule 63- General provisions relating to evidence

1. The rules of evidence set forth in this chapter, together with article 69, shall apply in proceedings before all Chambers.
2. A Chamber shall have the authority, in accordance with the discretion described in article 64, paragraph 9, to assess freely all evidence submitted in order to determine its relevance or admissibility in accordance with article 69.
3. A Chamber shall rule on an application of a party or on its own motion, made under article 64, subparagraph 9 (a), concerning admissibility when it is based on the grounds set out in article 69, paragraph 7.
4. Without prejudice to article 66, paragraph 3, a Chamber shall not impose a legal requirement that corroboration is required in order to prove any crime within the jurisdiction of the Court, in particular, crimes of sexual violence.
5. The Chambers shall not apply national laws governing evidence, other than in accordance with article 21.

[20] International Criminal Court, Rules of Procedure and Evidence, U.N. Doc. PCNICC/2000/1/Add.1 (2000).

Rule 72- In camera procedure to consider relevance or admissibility of evidence

1. Where there is an intention to introduce or elicit, including by means of the questioning of a victim or witness, evidence that the victim consented to an alleged crime of sexual violence, or evidence of the words, conduct, silence or lack of resistance of a victim or witness as referred to in principles (a) through (d) of rule 70, notification shall be provided to the Court which shall describe the substance of the evidence intended to be introduced or elicited and the relevance of the evidence to the issues in the case.
2. In deciding whether the evidence referred to in sub-rule 1 is relevant or admissible, a Chamber shall hear in camera the views of the Prosecutor, the defense, the witness and the victim or his or her legal representative, if any, and shall take into account whether that evidence has a sufficient degree of probative value to an issue in the case and the prejudice that such evidence may cause, in accordance with article 69, paragraph 4. For this purpose, the Chamber shall have regard to article 21, paragraph 3, and articles 67 and 68, and shall be guided by principles (a) to (d) of rule 70, especially with respect to the proposed questioning of a victim.

Truth and Reconciliation Commission of Peru (TRC)
Thematic Public Audience on Anti-terrorist Legislation and Violation of Due Process
Case N. 3: Maria Magdalena Monteza Benavides[21]

Facts:
María Magdalena Monteza Benavides was detained by members of the Intelligence Department of the Special Forces of the Peruvian Army. She was raped on two occasions while she was held incommunicado. She was threatened with greater reprisals if she reported the tortures and the rape. As a result of the rapes, she became pregnant and gave birth to a baby girl. No criminal proceedings were ever instituted with respect to the rapes.

Commission's Ruling:
The TRC is not a deciding body.

Extracts:
[…]
Her arrest was included in the actions initiated by the Armed Forces to detect the existence and utilization of illegal explosives, due to the increase of terrorist actions.
[…]

When Magdalena was arrested, her head was covered with a blanket, and she was placed in a private vehicle headed for an unknown destination. After an approximate two-hour drive, still with her head covered, she was forced to descend from the

[21] Peru, Final Report of the Truth and Reconciliation Commission, *available at* www.cverdad.org.pe. This case is included to highlight the obstacles that victims face when reporting State agents for rapes.

vehicle and taken to a building where she was locked in a dark room which she later identified as a bathroom. [...] The military did not identify themselves, nor was Magdalena formally informed of the reasons for her arrest. [...] Likewise, the TRC's report concludes that she was held incommunicado during the four days that she remained under military custody. [...]

In the afternoon of the same day, Magdalena was taken from her cell and blindfolded and se to be subject to interrogation. The TRC highlights that Magdalena Monteza was subjected to interrogation without the presence of a prosecutor or a lawyer, by officials who were not legally authorized to investigate a crime of terrorism. [...] According to her testimony, when she refused to admit the charges against her, she was battered and later subjected to sexual abuse by her captors. These same actions were allegedly repeated on the following day.

[...]

[F]our days after her detention, she was handed over to the National Directorate against Terrorism (DINCOTE), and she pleaded guilty of the alleged charges against her for fear of the threats of reprisals against her family that she received from the military if she denounced the tortures and rape she had been subjected to.

Magdalena Monteza has declared that she did this "out of fear and shame at the same time, because they were all men" [...] During the course of her trial for terrorism before Criminal Court 14 in Lima, María Magdalena Monteza Benavides reported having been subjected to physical and psychological torture, including rape, by members of the Peruvian army.

She made this same complaint to the director of the Chorrillos Prison, where she was held on charges for the crime of terrorism. The director informed the Ministry of Public Prosecution, which initiated an investigation of which the 44th Provincial Criminal Prosecutor's Office was in charge. This Prosecutor's Office ruled that it had been able to establish that the crime reported had indeed been committed, since the corresponding Medical Report corroborated that "the prisoner filing the complaint is pregnant and, that as a result of these acts, has conceived a child...." However, in spite of this, it ordered the complaint to be shelved provisionally, since "it was not possible to fully identify the suspects in this crime [...] one of the elements of procedural due process, namely, the individualization of the author or authors of the crime committed, is lacking ...." Until the culmination of the TRC's investigation, the Public Ministry had not carried out any additional investigation with a view to finding out the identity of the alleged perpetrators.

Parallel to this investigation, the military also held an inquiry into these events, in charge of the Prosecutor of the Permanent Court Martial of the Army's Second Judicial Zone. Since the crime of rape is not covered by the Military Justice Code, the military tribunal considered that the military personnel involved in the event had overstepped the limits of their functions, for which reason an investigation was initiated on grounds of the alleged perpetration of the military offense of abuse of authority. The Examining Judge issued his Final Report, in which he held "that there is no proven criminal responsibility of military personnel of the Special Forces Division ...," basing his decision on the fact that the Forensic Expert's Report N° 11605/92 showed no results related to the reported rape. The Permanent Court

Martial of the Army's Second Judicial Zone dismissed the case and ordered that it be submitted to the Supreme Council of Military Justice, which finally upheld this ruling on February 26, 1997. One of the central factors for denying that rape had been committed was the results of the different medical exams performed on Magdalena Monteza, which indicated the presence of long-dating lesions and tears.

Inter-American Court of Human Rights
Velásquez Rodríguez v. Honduras[22]
July 29, 1988

Main Legal Issue:
Do human right violations committed by private individuals involve State responsibility?

Facts:
Angel Manfredo Velásquez Rodríguez, a student at the National Autonomous University of Honduras, "was violently detained without a warrant for his arrest by members of the National Office of Investigations (DNI) and G-2 of the Armed Forces of Honduras." According to the petitioners, several eyewitnesses reported that Manfredo Velasquez and others were detained and ... "accused of alleged political crimes and subjected to harsh interrogation and cruel torture." The petition added that on September 17, 1981, Manfredo Velásquez was moved to the First Infantry Battalion, where the interrogation continued, but that the police and security forces denied that he had been detained.

Court Ruling:
Honduras has violated, in the case of Angel Manfredo Velásquez Rodríguez, its obligations to respect and to ensure the right to personal liberty set forth in Article 7 of the Convention, read in conjunction with Article 1(1) thereof. Honduras is hereby required to pay fair compensation to the next-of-kin of the victim.

Extracts:
[...]

166. The second obligation of the States Parties is to "ensure" the free and full exercise of the rights recognized by the Convention to every person subject to its jurisdiction. This obligation implies the duty of the States Parties to organize the governmental apparatus and, in general, all the structures through which public power is exercised, so that they are capable of juridically ensuring the free and full enjoyment of human rights. As a consequence of this obligation, the States must prevent, investigate and punish any violation of the rights recognized by the Convention and, moreover, if possible attempt to restore the right violated and provide compensation as warranted for damages resulting from the violation.

[...]

[22] Velásquez Rodríguez v. Honduras, Judgment, Inter-Am Ct. HR (ser.C) No.4 (July 29, 1988).

172. Thus, in principle, any violation of rights recognized by the Convention carried out by an act of public authority or by persons who use their position of authority is imputable to the State. However, this does not define all the circumstances in which a State is obligated to prevent, investigate and punish human rights violations, nor all the cases in which the State might be found responsible for an infringement of those rights. An illegal act which violates human rights and which is initially not directly imputable to a State (for example, because it is the act of a private person or because the person responsible has not been identified) can lead to international responsibility of the State, not because of the act itself, but because of the lack of due diligence to prevent the violation or to respond to it as required by the Convention.

175. This duty to prevent includes all those means of a legal, political, administrative and cultural nature that promote the protection of human rights and ensure that any violations are considered and treated as illegal acts, which, as such, may lead to the punishment of those responsible and the obligation to indemnify the victims for damages. It is not possible to make a detailed list of all such measures, since they vary with the law and the conditions of each State Party. Of course, while the State is obligated to prevent human rights abuses, the existence of a particular violation does not, in itself, prove the failure to take preventive measures. On the other hand, subjecting a person to official, repressive bodies that practice torture and assassination with impunity is itself a breach of the duty to prevent violations of the rights to life and physical integrity of the person, even if that particular person is not tortured or assassinated, or if those facts cannot be proven in a concrete case. [...]

6.1.3.1 Matters for Debate

Definition of Rape as Torture

In the Raquel Martín de Mejía v. Peru case, the IACHR clearly establishes that since it is a cause of physical and emotional suffering, sexual abuse of any kind is considered a form of torture when it is perpetrated "by members of the Security Forces, whether as a result of a practice conceived from the State or as a result of State failure to prevent the perpetration of this crime." Additionally, it employs the definition of torture of the Inter-American Convention to Prevent and Punish Torture. According to the Convention, "torture shall be understood to be any act intentionally performed whereby physical or mental pain is inflicted on a person for purposes of criminal investigation, as a means of intimidation, as a personal punishment, as a preventive measure, as a penalty, or for any other purpose."[23]

[23] *See* http://www.oas.org/juridico/english/treaties/a-51.html

Procedure to Gather Evidence in Cases of Rape as Torture

In Mejía case, the Peruvian State did not present arguments or evidence in its defense other than pointing out that the Commission already knew about this matter when it produced its ruling on the forced disappearance, torture, and murder of Fernando Mejía. Since Peru did not submit any evidence, the IACHR, in compliance with its own internal rules of procedure, assumed that the events had occurred. In order to confirm this assumption, the IACHR it resorted to different reports on human rights that corroborated that rape, as a strategy of State repression was a common practice within the Peruvian context of that time.

In another case referred to the Inter-American Court of Human Rights, Loayza Tamayo v. Peru,[24] the victim reported that during her illegal detention she was subjected to different forms of torture, and accused of being a member of Shining Path.[25] Repeated rape and sexual abuse perpetrated by her captors, all members of State security organisms, were included among the unlawful acts reported. In this case, the Peruvian State denied the existence of rape, alleging that there was no proof of it, since the victim had not reported it previously and a legal medical examination had been performed on her which did not provide any information regarding concordant lesions. In the ruling ordering Maria Elena Loayza's release from prison, the Inter-American Court concluded that rape had not been proven:

> Although the Commission contended in its application that the victim was raped during her detention, after examination of the file and, given the nature of this fact, the accusation could not be substantiated. However, the other facts alleged, such as incommunicado detention, being exhibited through the media wearing a degrading garment, solitary confinement in a tiny cell with no natural light, blows and maltreatment, including total immersion in water, intimidation with threats of further violence, a restrictive visiting schedule (supra, para. 46 c., d., e., k. and l.), all constitute forms of cruel, inhuman or degrading treatment in the terms of Article 5(2) of the American Convention. A study of the arguments and evidence proffered shows grave and convergent acts that were not refuted by the State and give reason to believe that cruel, inhuman and degrading treatment was meted out in the instant case of Ms. María Elena Loayza-Tamayo, in violation of her right to humane treatment enshrined in Article 5 of the American Convention[26]

Responsibility of the State for the Actions of Private Individuals and Its Application to Rape as Torture

In the above-examined cases, there is no doubt that rape perpetrated by State agents existed. However, it is not always possible to clearly establish this fact in the contexts of State repression in which both paramilitary groups and guerrilla groups in turn utilize these practices, act. Nevertheless, there is the precedent of State respon-

[24] Loayza Tamayo v. Peru, Merits, Inter-Am. Ct. H.R. (ser. C) No. 33 (Sept. 17, 1997).

[25] *Id.*

[26] *Id.*

sibility for actions carried out by groups outside the law, i.e., the Velásquez Rodríguez case. The responsibility of the State is not only that of not violating rights—respect—, but also that of adopting effective measures for the real enjoyment and exercise of those rights—guaranteeing them, especially those of investigating and punishing the violation of rights by private individuals.

6.2 The Difficult Characterization or Definition of Crimes of Violence Against Women

According to criminal dogma, the adequate characterization or definition of a conduct as criminal presents one of the great challenges of the legislative technique. The descriptive elements of a crime must make it possible to clearly identify when there is criminal responsibility. They must be objective enough to minimize discretion in interpretation. This enacts "the rule of law not of men". A principle of modern criminal law, contemplates that criminal responsibility must have as its central element the intention to commit the criminal conduct; that is, willful misconduct.

The importance of this exception to objective responsibility in criminal matters has repercussions on feminist aspiration of incorporating the feminine experience in criminal law norms. Since violence against women is a common case, rooted in a millenary culture that condones it, it turns out to be that "the intention" of the aggressor is to exercise some prerogatives that, in his opinion, he is entitled to. In his conscience, his intention is not to harm but to demand rights, which may lead to qualify his conduct as guilty rather as denoting willful misconduct. For this reason, it is very difficult to have criminal law punish it without incurring precisely in the classification of conducts as involving objective responsibility.

An example: a person pushes another in a fit of rage, and as a result of the fall, his/her arm is broken. In traditional terms, the offense consists in pushing the other with anger, causing a repairable injury. This is certainly the way that the aggressor and the criminal system see it. However, when the incident occurs in the framework of an affective relationship, the impact on the victim is very different from that produced when it occurs between strangers. The battered person stays frightened by their partner, and if she remains in the relationship, which is common, this fear gradually places her in a subordinate position in which she accepts mistreatment and ends up considering that she deserves them. The aggressor, imbued with a chauvinist culture in which this effect is not uncommon, judges the incident from the same perspective he would see a brawl: at a given moment, he lost control and caused a repairable injury. It is probable that he does not relate the incident to the constant humiliations and demands posed to his partner. Or the aggressor, considers that she, too, has her share of responsibility by not adequately fulfilling the corresponding social role: being a bad cook, refusing to have sex, not raising the children or doing the housework the way he likes it.

Let us therefore go back to the elements of a criminal type. The dogma demands that there be malice, and that the incident be enshrined within a classified conduct—that the aggressor should intend to break the arm or anticipate that such a thing would happen. The aggressor excuses himself alleging that it was not his intention to do what he did. For this reason, the point of view of criminal law ends up being the same as the aggressor's; what happened was not serious. It's a matter as trivial as if it had occurred in a street brawl.

What can be done for criminal law to evaluate the event, from the victim's point of view, without changing the structure of criminal law and turning it to objective responsibility, leaving the aggressor's intention aside?

Below are two concrete cases in which traditional dogma renders the protection of women difficult. The first involves consent in rape. From a traditional perspective, rape is defined as sexual penetration, through the use of physical force or the threat of violence. Criminal dogma interprets it from the point of view of the defendant: was it reasonable to suppose that this person knew that the sexual intercourse was the product of the use of force or the threat of violence?

The second case is one of the self-defense of a battered woman. If in the course of an episode of abuse, or in the interval between episodes of abuse, the woman kills her aggressor, generally speaking, does not meet the requisites of exceptionality that define self-defense: she had no other alternative—from a masculine point of view. For criminal law, this implies that any reasonable person, under those circumstances, would think she has no other alternative but to defend herself violently; except that criminal law's notion of a reasonable person is a masculine one, and it does not include the perception of a person who has, for years, been ill-treated and pursued by the aggressor.

Therefore, penal reforms are faced with much greater difficulties than the smaller themes introduced in certain articles and subsections. They imply confronting a juridical tradition which, almost since its conception as modern law, has excluded women both from the roles of aggressor and victim, and consequently, has a modus operandi, a series of principles, of legislative techniques, a manner of understanding rights and a prototype of reasonable human being that does not fit with the situation of women, or does so with difficulty.

6.2.1 Consent of the Rape Victim

The classification of the crime of rape depends on the absence of consent, and is defined precisely as non-consented sexual relationships. The question of consent is, therefore, the centerpiece of the case when the crime is doubtful, which occurs if there is no additional evidence to support the victim's allegation. This happens very frequently because of the difficulty to prove the use of physical force in a rape, causing only the prosecution of cases, which in addition to lack of consent, there is severe physical violence and a medical examination to corroborate it. If the force was of a moral nature, or if it did not leave physical injury, then the defense alleges that there was consent even though the victim denies it. The penal system has tended to trust the word of the aggressor and doubt the victim's.

But, the sexism of the penal system goes beyond calling the victim's story into question. Historically, the norms on sexual crimes have reflected the dominant values regarding women and sexuality, both in their classification and penalization. Consequently, coitus was privileged as the only form of rape; the victim could only be a woman, and in many cases she was even defined as a virgin or an "honest" woman. The penalties were lenient, and in certain cases the law induced an agreement between the victim and the aggressor, or even considered that the subsequent marriage of the victim with her aggressor or one of the aggressors exempted the penalty. In general, there was a tendency to presume consent in these cases and not in other crimes, in which the fact that the victim alleged that she had not consented was usually sufficient proof of the absence of consent.

In the 1990s, several women's groups and international feminist networks promoted a series of reforms of the criminal code and the code of criminal procedure to abolish, totally or partially, discriminatory provisions for sexual crimes, replacing them with norms in which the penalties are more severe and discrimination against women has been reduced or eliminated. The cumulative effect of these reforms called into question the traditional implicit assumption of consent.

However, legal reforms do not result in an immediate change in the juridical culture of law operators nor in the population's conscience of rights. This culture is often reflected in technical matters applied at the discretion of a judicial official, such as the gathering and evaluation of evidence, dosimetry of penalty, conciliation audiences, and even the decision as to whether or not to initiate an investigation. The Chilean case examined below, is a good example of the hopeful transition in the dogma: for the majority, the absence of consent is clear despite there being a marital relationship, while the dissenting opinion reflects the old position.

Fourth Court of Oral Criminal Proceedings of Santiago de Chile
G.T.C. C/O.M.L.S. RUC: 0500289837–5 RIT: 17–2000
Santiago, April 25, 2006

Main Legal Issue:

Is there consent when the wife agrees to having sexual intercourse for fear of greater sexual violence?

Facts:

In a context of marital violence, the husband becomes aggressive and his wife tries to calm him down by kissing him. The husband forces her to have vaginal sexual intercourse, threatening her with anal sex if she refuses. She begs him to stop.

Court Ruling:

The facts constitute a sexual aggression that can be defined primordially as an act of violence in which sex is the aggressor's instrument, but the motivation is the desire to humiliate, control and dominate his victim.

Extracts:

[…]

[T]he psychologist […] explains that in a context of chronic marital violence, the reported sexual aggression is described as "the most serious" but not the only one. With regard to the existence of permanent marital violence exercised by the spouse, Mrs. Guillermina presents characteristics consistent with the psychological and emotional distress experienced by women who live in this situation, and in the specific case of the plaintiff, the professional discards the existence of some alteration in the judgment of reality… Said aggression constitutes an aggravation of the situation of chronic violence and it acquires the value of being an event that stands out from the norm of the plaintiff's life experiences, and that leads her to report the act. This concrete sexual abuse meant, in practice, threats which the plaintiff believed to be real and evident, in view of her experience of chronic violence, such as her husband saying to her "now I am going to be very mean," threatening to harm her or their children, while physical coercion was manifest by holding her hands tightly […]

This intimidation is identified […] with the "acts of moral violence" through which the victim is informed of the imminent reality of the harm she will be exposed to if she does not agree to the aggressor's requirement, inducing in her a state of "psychological commotion" that may have its origin either in a previous situation in which the aggressor simply takes advantage, in the aggressor's sole presence, in his physical appearance or precedents of his known to the victim, as well as in humiliating conducts that the latter has been previously subjected to by the same aggressor. Likewise, in order to determine whether or not this element is present, it is essential to take into consideration the personal circumstances of the aggressor and the victim; in particular, the degree of impressionability of the latter. In other words, the objective magnitude of the stimulus that has aroused the fear or intimidation of the passive subject is not as important as her capacity to react to it.

[…]

Dissenting Opinion of Magistrate Mauricio Olave Astorga

The dissenting opinion establishes that in the case of a relationship between spouses, the resistance to the relationship must be put forth in completely explicit terms, in such a way that the other spouse has no doubts regarding the negative to grant sexual access. The Magistrate was in favor of absolving the defendant of all charges against him, in both the criminal and civil cases.

[…]

"What is being judged is not the history of aggressions recounted by the victim and corroborated by the rest of the evidence submitted during the hearing. What must be determined is whether the vaginal sexual intercourse that took place on the day alleged was actually perpetrated through the use of force or intimidation.

[…]

The victim of the crime expressed that first, and in the context of a discussion with her husband, she mounted herself on top of him and started to kiss him on the mouth to calm him down, adding that she tried to perform oral sex on him, which the plaintiff rejected, forthwith to place himself on top of her and penetrate her holding her wrists, while at the same time telling her he would penetrate her in every way, which she did not want, and therefore, she asked him, in an altered state, to stop and to end the vaginal intercourse quickly. To this narration must be added the replies to the questions posed by the judges comprising this court aimed at clarifying the matter, in which the plaintiff stated that her fear was being subject to anal intercourse, which ultimately did not happen.

In view of the situation, the arguments of the defense cannot be discarded *a priori*, in terms of what happened, which was exclusively a sexual marital intercourse, because, as the defense proposes, this involves a relationship between spouses, any resistance to the relationship must be completely explicit, in such a way that the other spouse have no doubt as to the refusal to have intercourse; this with the aim of avoiding that the actor be confused with the alleged plaintiff's volatile attitude ....

[...]

[W]ith regard to the alleged violence exerted upon the plaintiff, it must be stated that all normal sexual activity implies the use of a certain level of force, and therefore the existence of this element must be discarded, especially since the expert of the Forensic and Medical Service, who diligently examined the plaintiff on the day following the reported abuse, manifested that her body showed no signs of violence, in particular her wrists, which the plaintiff mentions as having been held tightly by her spouse. [...]"

Colombian Constitutional Court
T-453 of 2005
May 2, 2005

Main Legal Issue:
Is the admission of prior sexual or social behavior of a victim admissible as a reasonable measure and necessary and proportionate mechanism to guarantee the defendant's defense?

Facts:
The plaintiff, Sandra Liliana Orejarena, petitioned for a writ for protection of her constitutional rights against the Criminal Court of the Seventh Circuit of Bucaramanga, for violating article 235 of the Criminal Procedures Code, when it ordered and examined evidence requested by the Prosecutor General's Office and the defense in a trial in which she is a rape victim. The evidence requested included documents aimed at investigating her behavior and summoning several witnesses to testify about her life when she was a student, her romantic relationships, and other aspects of her private life. The plaintiff considers this evidence as injurious to her rights to equal treatment, human dignity, and privacy, and she requests an order to suspend the examination of this evidence and to prevent evidence of this type that has already been examined from having probative value.

Court Ruling:
The Court orders some evidence to be excluded from this trial. Victims of sex crimes have a constitutional right to protection of their privacy against the examination of

evidence that implies an unreasonable intrusion, unnecessary and disproportionate, into their private lives. Such an intrusion occurs when there are indiscriminate inquiries into the victim's sexual or social conduct prior or subsequent to the events under investigation.

Extracts:

[…]

Legal issues

For the petitioner, the admission of testimony from relatives and acquaintances in order to examine her personal life infringes her rights to dignity and privacy, given that such evidence does not in any way contribute to arriving at the truth, but rather transforms the criminal trial into a trial whose purpose is to judge the victim. In addition, she points out that admitting evidence regarding matters about which numerous probative items already exist that are scientific in nature, in addition to the admission of testimony from third parties who are not aware of what took place on the day of the events, is inconsistent with her right to an effective judicial remedy, given that it unnecessarily prolongs the judicial proceedings.

For its part, the defendant court, points out that in compliance with its essential investigative duties, it must investigate both that which favors the accused and that which is harmful to him, and so the judge, in order to decide the case, must obtain and examine all evidence that can lead to certainty with regard to the criminal defendant's illicit conduct and responsibility, which does not infringe the plaintiff's rights.

[…]

The Court's order to exclude certain evidence is based on two arguments: first, the decision is grounded on the special protection that, according to the guidelines of international organizations, especially the U.N., is due to crime victims, particularly victims of sex crimes, in order to safeguard their rights to physical, psychological and moral integrity, and to dignity, honor and privacy. Second, the Court has analyzed the conditions of the particular case to determine whether the violation of the right to privacy that the examination of this evidence would cause is reasonable, proportional and vital to guarantee the defense of the accused. It has performed a detailed study of each item of evidence requested and concluded that there is a group of items that should be excluded because, due to both the manner in which they were requested and their contents, they were intended to raise questions about the victim's moral character based on her conduct prior to and following the events in different relationships and with individuals other than the accused.

The rights of sex crime victims in international law, comparative law, and national law

Since the middle of the twentieth century, there has been a tendency to enshrine broad protections to the rights of crime victims, exceeding the traditional vision restricted to financial compensation for human rights violations. This broad protection, which acknowledges for crime victims the rights to truth, justice and redress, their intrinsic dignity, and the equal and inalienable rights of all human beings, has developed in a unique way in the case of the rights of sex crime victims.

Beginning in the 1980—and based on international instruments that establish, among other rights, the right to physical, psychological, and moral integrity, to dignity, to honor and to privacy, as well as access to justice—the American, European, and United Nations systems issued principles with the purpose of reconciling the fundamental rights of due process and a defense to persons investigated and accused, with the rights of victims within the criminal suit. Some of these guidelines, which emphasize respect for victims' dignity, have focused particularly on the protection and guarantee of the rights of sex crime victims, with the understanding that this type of event acutely affects individuals' physical and psychological integrity, as well as their dignity as human beings, which can be deeply affected if the criminal trial is allowed to lead to a renewed victimization. [...]

[...]

Indeed, some international instruments that Colombia is a part of, have tackled the subject of protection of victims of sexual violence within criminal proceedings, and have acknowledged the obligation on the part of authorities to treat victims with dignity and respect, and to adopt measures for decreasing the risk of double victimization that could arise during the examination of evidence or during other legal investigations, or when managing information about the events in the case and victims' identities.

The International Criminal Court's statutes explicitly protect the rights of victims to present observations regarding the Court's competence or the lawsuit's admissibility, the right to make a complete presentation of the facts in the lawsuit in the interest of justice, to be treated with dignity, to have their safety and privacy protected, to have their opinions and observations taken into account, to be materially compensated and to appeal certain decisions that affect their interests. In addition, its Rules Regarding Procedures and Evidence of the International Criminal Court, adopted on September 9, 2002, by the General Assembly of the Member States of the Rome Statute, enshrine specific standards regarding evidence as it related to sexual violence.

[...]

Some of these recommendations for protecting sex crime victims' privacy and dignity have been applied by the Inter-American Human Rights Commission ... for example, in case No. 12.350 against Bolivia, the Commission protected the privacy of the victim and petitioner by using a fictitious name, keeping in mind the nature of the violations and their possible negative effect on the victim's private life. Another example is found in case No. 11.565 against Mexico, where the Commission declared the case admissible despite the fact that there were still internal recourses available. The Commission declared that it was not possible to exhaust the internal mechanisms for protecting victims, given that the attorney general authorized to hear the case was the same one before which the victims had refused to undergo an additional gynecological exam because they considered this a form of psychological torture.

[...]

In comparative law, various countries have adopted measures to protect the privacy and dignity of victims of sexual aggression. In the United States, for example, ... "Rape Shield Laws" [...] have been adopted with the purpose of preventing evidence from being obtained or admitted that unnecessarily impacts on the victim's right to privacy or that inflicts disproportionate harm, as a strategy for demonstrating the victim's consent, with the understanding that doing so would subject her to a process that is almost as degrading as the rape itself. [S]uch information has been considered irrelevant for demonstrating the victim's lack of credibility or for proving consent, and therefore such evidence should be excluded except when the accused is able to demonstrate the specific and direct, as opposed to general and incidental, relevance of the evidence, or can demonstrate that excluding the evidence would constitute a violation of his right to a defense.

[...]

In general, the admission and examination of evidence in criminal proceedings is independent from the rational evaluation, made by the official responsible for the criminal investigation, on the potential of the evidence to shed light on the events and on the culpability of the parties involved. Notwithstanding, this discretional exercise must occur within the framework of the Constitution's due process principles of the presumption of innocence and the impartiality of the right to a defense, and the principles of respect for victims' dignity, integrity and privacy. The truth shall not be investigated at any price, but rather while protecting the fundamental rights of all parties who are involved in the proceedings. Hence there is a close relationship between procedural law and constitutional law.

[...]

Even though within the scope of criminal law, questions regarding the illegality of evidence are most often associated with violations of the rights of the accused, such questions can also arise with regard to violations of the victim's rights. The numerous goals of criminal proceedings and the need to ensure that justice is administered and the rights of crime victims protected does not preclude the possibility that the plaintiff may object to the rendering and examination of evidence that violates the principles of due process or her fundamental rights, in particular her right to privacy.

[...]

In this case, it is necessary to determine whether the introduction of evidence relative to the earlier sexual or social conduct of a sex crime victim is reasonable and proportional as a mechanism for guaranteeing the defense of the accused. An evaluation of the limits of the right to privacy in this context must be done in four steps. First, the goal must be analyzed to determine whether it is vital for the defense; second, it is necessary to examine whether the means of reaching the goal is legitimate; and third, it is necessary to study the relationship between the means and the end, applying a necessity test. Then, if it appears reasonable after these steps have been taken, a proportionality test, in the strictest sense, shall be applied to determine whether the degree to which the right to privacy will be affected is disproportionate.

The thoroughness of the reasonability test depends on the constitutional relevance of the values in play. In this case,, given that it pertains to a conflict between the right of the accused to a defense and the victim's right to privacy, in order to allow an examination of the victim's social and sexual conduct prior to the events in question, the goal that justifies an intrusion of this dimension into the victim's private life must be vital, ... reasonable to limit the sex crime victim's constitutional right to privacy.

In principle, such an examination would be appropriate only if (i) the purpose of the investigation is to demonstrate that the person who performed the illegal act is someone else and not the accused; (ii) or if preventing said investigation would have seriously infringe on the accused party's right to a defense, for example, because an examination of the previous common private life of the victim and the accused would allow a demonstration of consent. Therefore, if the purpose of the intrusion into the victim's private life is only to deduce alleged consent based on inferences drawn from previous or subsequent private relationships other than the relationship under investigation, such an intrusion cannot be considered imperative and, therefore, it should be rejected. What is constitutionally admissible is an investigation into circumstances surrounding the sexual act to which the case pertains. Therefore, by virtue of constitutional law, intimate experiences that are separate from the act under investigation are prima facie protected against irrational and disproportionate interventions.

With regard to the means chosen, it is important to ensure that said means are not prohibited by the applicable body of law.

The third step of the reasonability test consists of establishing whether the means are necessary for achieving the proposed end. In fact, it does not suffice that the end sought is imperative and that the means are not prohibited. In order to constitutionally restrict fundamental rights such as those that are in play, the means must be necessary for achieving the end. Therefore, if the evidence of the victim's consent can be obtained without invading the victim's privacy, or by means of a restrictions that would be less injurious than those requested, the requested evidence becomes unnecessary and should not be examined. Likewise, a general investigation into the victim's life, one that is not related to the specific events or directly related to the case under investigation, or is vague with regard to time, turns out to be disproportionate, given that there is not a clear means-to-end relationship that would justify its examination.

Finally, given that in these cases there is an invasion of the person's private life after she has been victim to acts that violated her dignity and autonomy, it is necessary to analyze whether there is strict compliance with standards of proportionality. That is, the degree to which privacy is affected, on the one hand, and the degree of effectiveness with regard to the right to a defense, on the other, shall be studied in order to determine whether disproportion has occurred in breach of the victim's right to privacy.

If the requested evidence relative to the victim's private life does not meet these criteria, and examination of this evidence is ordered, this constitutes a violation of the victim's rights to privacy and due process, given that the aim of the criminal investigation is no longer to seek the truth and administer justice, but rather it is transformed so that what is on trial is the victim's conduct, denying her of her dignity and reinforcing an implicit prejudice regarding the victim's personal and moral characteristics as a justification of the rape. When the criminal investigation takes on these characteristics, the search for the truth becomes only formal, abandoning the original purpose of the criminal case, and is therefore in violation of the victim's rights and, therefore, of due process.

From the above, we draw the conclusion that sex crime victims have a constitutional right to have their privacy protected against the examination of evidence that constitutes an unreasonable, unnecessary, and disproportionate intrusion into their private life, something that occurs when the victim's sexual or social conduct prior or subsequent to the events under investigation is indiscriminately investigated. Such a circumstance renders the requested or obtained evidence constitutionally inadmissible and subject to exclusion by both the Constitution and the government.

[...]

The Court finds that in the case under examination it is possible to distinguish between two types of evidence based on the purposes for which they were admitted and examined. The first category of evidence has the purpose of shedding light on the events under investigation and the responsibility of the accused. This category includes the tests performed on the victim by the Institute of Legal Medicine to determine whether there was carnal access and whether there was evidence of chemical substances in her body; it also includes statements by witnesses who saw the accused and the victim together on the day when the events occurred and statements by persons who attended to the victim in the first hours following the events, among others. The second category of evidence delves into the victim's private life prior to and subsequent to the events. The majority of the evidence that the petitioner is challenging as being in violation of her rights belongs to this second group.

[...]

This type of evidence does not shed light on the events under investigation, but rather its purpose is to raise doubts about the victim's character based on her conduct in different relationships with individuals other than the accused prior or subsequent to the events. This evidence is not vital for the defense... Such evidence constitutes a serious restriction on the victim's right to privacy that is unreasonable and disproportionate and distorts the purpose of the criminal investigation.

[...]

In conclusion, the Judge of the Criminal Court of the Seventh Circuit violated the victim's rights to privacy and due process upon admitting, examining, and failing to exclude evidence whose purpose was to delve into the victim's sexual conduct prior to the events under investigation, without the restriction of her right to privacy bring reasonable and proportionate. Thus, the criminal proceedings veered away from their original purposes—to administer justice and to arrive at the truth—and were transformed into a mechanism for the reproduction of social prejudices against female victims for behavior that could give rise to crimes in sexual contexts.

[...]

6.2.1.1 Matters for Debate

Consent and Physical Resistance

One of the common problems that judges must face in the appreciation of evidence is the evaluation of the forensic medical report when there are no physical lesions or when these are minimal. Such is the case of the Chilean marital rape case; the dissenting opinion adopts the traditional stance that assumes that the absence of injuries leads immediately to doubt the existence of the use of force, and consequently, the absence of consent. This is especially so because the defendant alleged that the sexual relationship was agreed upon, and the case apparently depended on the credibility of the victim's report.

Conjugal Duties

The issue of marital rape also faces a traditional conception according to which the wife cannot refuse her husband sexual access, for it forms part of her "marital duties." Essentially, the marital duty is the duty of the couple to satisfy their mutual sexual needs, and lack of compliance appears in civil legislation as grounds for divorce. While the legal definition does not imply the loss of sexual freedom as a result of marriage, the term has traditionally been used to signify that the wife must subject herself to the sexual relation even when it is unwanted. This corresponds to the patriarchal notion that the husband is the owner of the wife's body, in exchange for providing sustenance, her body is at his disposal at will. This idea also sustains the ancient belief in exoneration from the crime of sexual assault if the perpetrator later marries his victim, with the assumption that between married persons there can be no rape.

However, the definition of rape in penal law does not make any distinctions between persons who are or are not married, since the element that constitutes the crime is lack of consent or the use of force. This has not sufficed, however, to clarify that rape may involve unwed or married couples, and for this reason the feminist movement has promoted reforms that expressly include marital rape as a type of rape, or that include it as an aggravating factor in the case of sexual crimes.

The Constitutional Court of Colombia provides another example of this feminist type of reasoning when, in 1997, it ruled unconstitutional a norm that assigned a smaller penalty to marital rape than to the other types of rape. The Court considered that:

> The sexual freedom of the spouse cannot be considered diminished because of marriage, for otherwise one would be in the presence of a form of bondage, prohibited by the Constitution. Civil duties are created through marriage, but do not deprive one of personal autonomy. Consequently, the assailant's conduct is as unjust when sexual violence is exercised on his spouse as when the victim is another individual. The legal right protected by the punishment of crimes of access and sexual violence, is sexual freedom and the dignity of the persons; such legal rights cannot be considered to be diminished by the existence of matrimony or simply, previous sexual knowledge.[27]

[27] Colombia, Constitutional Court Ruling C-285/97.

The Victim's Past Sexual History as Proof of Consent

In the absence of conclusive physical evidence that the sexual relation was forced, the courts must resort to other types of proofs and evidence evaluation, and the same applies to the lawyers representing the parties. One of the most significant debates on this issue has been in relation to the importance assigned to the victim's sexual past to determine whether or not there was consent. In the past few decades, even before the reforms to the penal codes were implemented, some Latin American Supreme Courts insisted that the evidence related to the victim's sexual past was not relevant. In several rulings, lower courts, which continue to request and admit this type of evidence, are warned that this kind of evidence is immaterial and irrelevant to determine the existence or non-existence of a crime, or the defendant's innocence or guilt. Recently, the Constitutional Court of Colombia went even further holding that the evidence related to past sexual history infringed upon the right to privacy. The Colombian case reviewed above, dealt with woman who alleged she had been raped by an acquaintance after the latter had drugged her in a bar. The defense wanted to present as evidence that the victim had sexual relations with her previous boyfriend. The Court established that the evidence regarding the victim's sexual past was *prima facie* inadmissible.

6.2.2 Violence as Criterion to Evaluate Self-Defense[28]

Latin American dogma and legislation, in relation to the justification of self-defense, show, despite their pretended scientism, an important evaluative burden.[29] Self-defense justifies a criminal conduct based on the existence of objective criteria that prove that the person acted in self-defense or in defense of his or her rights. Except for some details of legislative and systematic techniques, the penal codes of Argentina, Chile and Peru require the following objective presumptions to have self-defense justified: (a) an illegitimate aggression; (b) the rational need for the means employed to prevent or repel it; (c) the lack of sufficient provocation on the part of the person who defends him/herself. The Colombian Penal Code stipulates a legal requisite for aggression—that by law must be unjust, present and imminent—establishing that the defense must be proportionate to the threat, and omitting any reference to the lack of sufficient provocation. On the other hand, the Penal Code for Mexico's Federal District establishes, with regard to aggression, that apart from being present and imminent, it must also be real and unlawful, and with regard to the provocation, that it must be sufficiently malicious and immediate.

[28] This section was written by Julieta Di Corleto, Professor at the University of Buenos Aires Law School.

[29] *See* Carlos Santiago Nino, *Consideraciones sobre la dogmática jurídica (con referencia particular a la dogmática penal)*, Instituto de Investigaciones Jurídicas de la UNAM, México, 1989, p. 85, 103.

This categorization, in some way, favors the interference of discriminatory criteria regarding women who defend themselves from the domestic violence exerted by their partners. With regard to the first requisite, aggression, none of the codes particularize the assumption of the defense of women assaulted in the intra-family ambit, nor do they mention the psychological aspects, in addition to the physical ones, that are included in the form of control that characterizes domestic violence. In general, the dogma follows the same path as that of the legislator: the impact of violence sustained over time, is overlooked and its existence is treated as a minor issue deprived of context. Thus, for instance, the law perceives in the same way the woman who attacks the person who assaults her regularly at a moment when the assailant is vulnerable, for example, when he sleeps, and the person who attacks any other member of his/her family when they sleep.

In relation to the requisites of "imminence" or "current presence" of aggression explicitly required by some of the analyzed codes and invariably demanded by classical criminal literature, have been understood to not coincide with the beginning of the attempt and the formal consummation of the crime, but that they cover the period ranging from the preparatory acts immediately preceding the beginning of its commission to the material end of the aggression. In any case, the concepts of "imminence" or "current presence" allude to isolated conducts, so the defense must respond to an imminent attack and not the situation that starts the periodic recurring assaults.

A third element that renders the application of justification in the case of battered women difficult is that jurists often assert that imminence and the need for a defense must be judged in accordance with objective criteria, more specifically, in accordance with the judgment of a third-party sensible observer.[30] The way in which women personally experience constant harassment and the repercussions it has on their rational evaluation is completely unintelligible for somebody who does not suffer this kind of violence. That is to say, if the "sensible observer" is not familiar with the concrete circumstances, he/she is not capable of recognizing the imminence and the need for a defense.

Ignorance of the abused woman's point of view also leads to denying the possibility of an error in the interpretation of the objective circumstances of the cause of justification, for example, in the case of the woman who mistakenly attacks thinking that her abuser was going to rape her once again. Although there is consensus in the dogma regarding the systematic classification of self-defense as a cause of justification which excludes penal injustice, there is no agreement regarding the effects of a mistake. Gender prejudice may lead to deny the existence of self-defense on grounds of an error in the evaluation of danger, and seek, in the best of cases, some grounds for exemption from liability or some extenuating circumstance. The concrete effects on the length of the penalty are markedly different.

The last requisite of self-defense is a negative one: lack of sufficient provocation. This is defined as the previous conduct of the person that defends him/herself, which determines the aggression, and which loses juridical value as "sufficient" when it is

---

[30] Claus Roxin, *Derecho Penal, Parte General*, Civitas, Madrid, 1997, p. 631.

predictable. Once again, the lack of understanding of the situation of the abused woman leads to an unfavorable judgment in the interpretation of what constitutes sufficient provocation.

The case of a battered woman who murdered her husband at a moment when he was vulnerable will be examined below. Although she was ultimately convicted, the Court of First Instance accepted the self-defense argument.

Court of Oral Criminal Proceedings N° 3 of Mar del Plata
"G. B. on aggravated homicide"
September 21, 2005

Main Legal Issue:
Does the imminence of the aggression necessary for self-defense exist if the victim momentarily ceased the aggression and was in a vulnerable position?

Facts:
A.J. has battered his wife, G.B. for many years. She attempted in vain to separate. One day he went to the house with a gun, beat her, and dragged her to the bedroom to force her, to have sexual intercourse. When A.J. was off-guard for a moment, G.B. took the gun and murdered him.

Court Ruling:
The Court finds that this case meets the requirements the law demands to plead self-defense. The Court holds that the beatings and threats suffered before the act generated great fear. That state of terror altered her capacity to evaluate and limited her possibilities to act.

Extracts:
[…]
Are there any grounds for exemption from penal liability?

[…]

The issue is whether the defendant's action can pass through the sieve of the rational need for the means employed to prevent or repel the aggression […]; in particular, it is a question of determining whether the current presence or imminence of the aggression existed at the moment when two bullets were shot into A.J.'s head […] It is our duty to evaluate these defense actions through an "ex ante" perspective and not "ex post"; that is, one must place oneself in the situation of the person who defends themselves at the moment of the action […]. I consider that A.J. had ceased beating G.B. because, like she said in the course of this hearing, she began to undress in order to have sexual intercourse as he wished. […] But what we must ask ourselves is what would have happened if the woman refused to meet A.J.'s wishes; the battery would most certainly have continued. The prosecutor weighed the circumstances against G.B. because she did not escape from the place. Beyond the limited options proper to the situation of strong emotional commotion the defendant went through, escaping was not something that guaranteed her liberation; […] the defendant was in real danger. There was a manifest threat on the part of A.J. that rendered the danger and G.B's life-risk situation imminent: if she did not consent to the sexual relation, the assault would continue […].

But to this objective situation of imminent danger to the life of life of the defendant, we must add a subjective one, also presented in the hearing. The beating and the threats suffered before the act generated great fear in the defendant, as reported by the psychiatry expert from this Judicial Department. This situation of terror affected her capacity to evaluate and restricted her possibilities to act; according to the expert, she experienced the situation with great fear. Therefore, I understand that the requisites demanded by the law to plead legitimate defense are present in this case. [...].

2nd Chamber of the Criminal and Correctional Court of Appeals
Mar del Plata Judicial Department
C.D. homicide committed in heat of passion
June 23, 1995

Main Legal Issue:
Can criminal liability be imputed to the defendant, who at the moment of committing the act, was in a state of severe emotional agitation?

Facts:
C.D. repeatedly hit her husband's face, who was asleep, with an iron rod fifty-centimeters long and fourteen millimeters in diameter, which resulted in multiple fractures of the bones in his face and skull, and eventual death.

Court Ruling:
The Court acquits the defendant because she was in a state of severe emotional agitation.

Extracts:
[...]
Are there any grounds for exemption of liability?

[...]

In the present lawsuit, the sole question is the existence or inexistence of the defendant's criminal responsibility. As is well known, each of the analytical strata of the concept of crime demands a certain psychic capacity. [...] In my opinion, C.D. had serious difficulties to understand the unjust nature of the deed she embarked on and that, to make things worse, she could not adapt her behavior to this defective understanding. The profuse experts' evidence presented in these proceedings makes it possible to state, without a doubt, that the psyche of the accused was, during the emergency, frankly limited by a "state of severe emotional agitation" [...]. But that severe state of confusion is a subordinate element of the capacity to understand the criminality of the act, that is, of the first basis for the appraisal of guilt. With that diminished psychic capacity the accused carried out an action that the experts in psychology characterized as an "impulsive and uncontrolled conduct" resulting from the "host of frustrations, indignation and anguish," which in the given situation determined that C.D. "was no longer capable of controlling her emotions, and her capacity to reflect and connect to the external medium, already scarce, was insufficient to contain the state of confusion and disorganization which anguishing feelings, and fundamentally fear, generated within her, in such a way that the deed was a form of impulsive outlet or expression…" I have wondered time and again whether it may be stated that the act imputed to C.D. is one that constitutes an unjust finding of guilt, whether it is one that reveals that its author has performed it to go against the law, when it was possible and necessary to avoid it. I have wondered whether that demerit of performing a choice that goes against the norms has been the product of the deliberation and freedom of the accused. I have wondered whether, as the doctrine demands, C.D. had different alternatives among which she chose homicide. I have wondered whether at any time the idea of killing T.B. was incorporated in her psyche. All the answers have been negative. […].

[I] consider the mental disorder C.D. suffered at the moment of the act, a morbid mental condition conducive to a disturbance of the mental faculties. This is because, as it has already been said, her behavior was frankly abnormal and showed deficits in terms of the neurological, psychiatric and psychological parameters reviewed above. This notion of abnormality, of rupture of the vital antecedent of the accused, fully fits the concept of "morbid" to which the law alludes […].

In accordance with the result of the voting […] the Court rules the acquittal of the accused, C.D. […].

First Penal Chamber, Court of Cassation
Buenos Aires Province
February 18, 2009

Main Legal Issue:
Does the history of violence against a woman constitute precedent in order to plead self-defense?

Facts:
The defense attorney A. I. D. submitted before the Court an extraordinary appeal on points of law against the ruling issued by the Criminal Court N. 4 of San Martín, which sentenced her to 10 years and 8 months of imprisonment for considering her criminally liable for the crime of homicide aggravated by family ties.

Court Ruling:
The Court acquitted the accused and established that the historical violence committed against her configured a right to safeguard her physical integrity.

Extracts:
[…]
To discard the presence of a legitimate defense, the *a quo* has stated: "analyzing the mechanics of the production of the fact, it cannot be verified that the accused has been in such real and imminent danger as to justify her actions. In fact, the discussion initiated in the marital bedroom was just one more that the accused unfortunately had had to put up with for many years. In my opinion there was not a plus that may have enhanced the danger for the accused beyond that of her physical integrity without other legal rights being affected."

This corresponds to a view of the situation that has normalized a woman's beating at the hands of a man ("it was just another discussion"). This "normality" is taken into account to point out that there was not "a serious, real and imminent danger."

This, which has not been explained in the ruling, may signify that there was no danger of death, which exceeds the ground for justification that only requires that the aggression be illegitimate and not sufficiently provoked. But the matter is, contingently, when and why might an assault resulting in death be discarded? The bedroom, where the end to this story of recurring beatings is unleashed, was on the second floor, and there is a record of the woman's falling down the stairs that resulted in her hospitalization for reasons of a ruptured vein.

What must one wait for, in a case like the present one, to carry out a permission to safeguard physical integrity, leaving aside the devastated psychic integrity? The discourse of the accused clearly reflects an ongoing aggression of unpredictable consequences (standing on the bed to jump on top of her, corroborated by the bullet's trajectory) and nothing in the ruling makes it possible to assert that the accused has lied in the least in the chronicle of this life resembling the Stations of the Cross.

The entrenchment of reasons like this one to sustain that the accused should have waited stoically for the wretched aggression of one who knows he is stronger from brute force—the right of beasts—is horrific, and it nourishes the persistence of leniency in the political consideration, in the judicial case, of gender violence.

[…]

Once again, what the *a quo* expected was resignation and the hope that this time it would not be more serious than usual.

From the dogmatic approach, there is recourse to an archaeological paradigm connected to "bad" criminal intent, distinguishing between what would be a defensive intention from the willful misconduct in a case of homicide, denying the former and affirming the latter. When one assumes a defensive attitude (imagine the one demanded by the *a quo*), one wants to neutralize the aggressor, that in the terms of the law is, although referred to alleged defenses, implies legitimizing it, "whatever the damage caused to the aggressor." In the modern doctrine, willful misconduct is a weighted datum that reveals the subject's intention and that—if it occurs in the context of a legitimate defense—implies wounding or killing to avert danger.

The rational need for the chosen means is, as always, a piece of information to be assessed contingently, and this is when having maintained that the beatings were normal and that there was no other alternative but to try to run away assuming the risk of being chased even down some stairs, backfires against the *a quo*.

The analysis of the case in the *hic et nunc* [here and now] entirely reproduces the legal requisites to make the use of deadly force permissible: through illegitimate and unprovoked aggression (neither sufficiently nor non-sufficiently), a constant in the case of batterers, and the chosen means—a low-caliber gun aimed at the belly—appears as necessary (she cannot be required to assume the risk of fleeing downstairs from the second floor in the midst of an ongoing assault) and rational, because only due to the trajectory of the bullet—a component based on randomness—was the shot lethal.

[…]

I am in favor of my colleagues granting the cassation appeal and the acquittal of the accused on grounds of legitimate self-defense. I vote in the affirmative.

6.2.2.1 Matters for Debate

The Scope of the Right to Self-Defense

Prejudices or false beliefs, in general, are accepted as if they were common sense postulates. In matters of violence, one of those false beliefs sustains that women who are battered by their partners enjoy the beatings. The explanation for reaching this assertion is that if they did not like to be battered, those women would abandon their homes.[31] In most cases, the women remain in their homes due to economic and emotional dependence, fear, depression, lack of self-esteem, and believe that their partners' promises to change will become a reality. The woman who is a victim of violence does not experience pleasure in her beatings, nor does she feel capable of confronting violence. The main factors in her decision not to leave are lack of resources, lack of strength, and fundamentally, fear.[32]

On the other hand, women who decide to leave their partners are the ones who face a greater risk of being murdered or seriously injured. The moment of the separation has been studied as the most dangerous period in an abusive relationship and it has been established that it can last up to 2 years following the termination of the relationship.[33] For this reason, the adequate understanding of the phenomenon of violence should never lead to impose on battered women the duty to abandon their homes. On the other hand, from the point of view of criminal law, at the precise moment when an aggression is taking place, this duty requirement could only be imposed in cases in which said aggression could be avoided in a complete and safe way.

However, some manuals and treatises on criminal law teach that the scope of self-defense is limited by the existence of special duties between the actors. The criminal doctrine has been in charge of limiting self-defense in the marriage context. With the argument of the so-called "institutional responsibilities," they have constructed the demand for heroic behaviors. In this respect, the indication is that only when it is effective for self-defense should the victim make an attempt on the aggressor's life, if this is not the case, the victim must avoid the aggression or resort to less dangerous defensive means, even running the risk of sustaining lesser harm. On this issue, Enrique Bacigalupo postulates that "the right to necessary defense is excluded in cases of close personal relationships (parents-children; spouses; life in common, etc.). This means that in such cases one must resort, above all, to the less violent means, even though this is unsafe."[34] To justify his proposal, he utilizes the following example: "the husband has no right to kill his wife to prevent her from

---

[31] Jorge Corsi, "Una mirada abarcativa sobre el problema de la violencia familiar" in Jorge Corsi (comp.), *Violencia familiar. Una mirada interdisciplinaria sobre un grave problema social*, Editorial Paidós, Buenos Aires, 2004, p. 37.

[32] Julieta Di Corleto, "Mujeres que matan. Legítima defensa en el caso de las mujeres golpeadas", in Revista de Derecho Penal y Procesal Penal, N 5, Lexis Nexis, Buenos Aires, 2006, pp. 853–870.

[33] Leonore Walker, "Battered Women Syndrome and Self Defense", *Notre Dame J.L. Ethics & Pub. Pol.*, no. 6, 1992 and Elizabeth Schneider, *Battered Women & Feminist Lawmaking*, Yale University Press, New Haven, 2000.

[34] Enrique Bacigalupo, *Derecho penal. Parte General*, Editorial Hammurabi, Buenos Aires, 1987, p. 230.

slapping him."[35] For his part, Günther Jakobs maintains, "in these relationships of guarantees, there exists a higher obligation to sacrifice oneself—as compared to the obligation due to just any person."[36] With an apparently more flexible criterion, Roxin reasons that the duty of consideration is extinguished if the aggression entails serious injuries or there is continuous ill treatment: "A woman who is battered almost on a daily basis by her husband for *insignificant motives* no longer owes him the solidarity from which he has already disassociated himself a much earlier; that is why she can defend herself with a firearm and she is not obligated to abandon the house instead of defending herself…"[37]

The Imminence or Presence of the Aggression

As discussed in the introduction, the doctrine in matters of self-defense, establishes that one of its basic requirements consists in establishing whether the aggression is sufficiently immediate to authorize a response. The condition of imminence or current of the aggression serves to determine what the right moment to support a defense. In this regard it has been established that the assault must be present, that is, imminent or even ongoing. Consequently, the defensive response could only begin at the very last moment, when possibilities of success still exist, and only at that moment can the risk of being unnecessary be discarded.[38] This requirement is important in order to distinguish a case of self-defense from an alleged defense in the face of future or already repelled assaults. Therefore, underlying this temporal element is the consideration that this defense is necessary, and in turn, the subsidiarity of the incitement. Hence, the aggressors can consider that, in the absence of current and imminent aggression, the person pretending to engage in defense should require the help of the authorities.

The Inclusion of Expert Testimony: The Assessment of the Imminence or Temporal Proximity of the Aggression

One of the issues to be analyzed in the cases of women brought to trial for acting in defense of their husbands is the one related to the background of violence. The adequate presentation and treatment of the record of violence that preceded the defensive conduct can be essential to evaluate the woman's behavior. Its analysis may be necessary to understand the level of danger to which the woman is exposed and also to evaluate her perception of the threat and reaction in view of that threat.

---

[35] *Id.* p. 230.

[36] Günther Jakobs, *Derecho Penal. Parte General. Fundamentos y teoría de la imputación*, traducción de Joaquín Cuello Contreras and José Luis Serrano González de Murillo, Editorial Marcial Pons, Madrid, 1997, pp. 488–489.

[37] Claus Roxin, *op.cit.* p. 652.

[38] Günter Stratenwerth, *Derecho Penal. Parte General I. El hecho punible*, Editorial Hammurabi, Buenos Aires, 2005, pp. 230–231.

The adequate study of the perception of risk has concrete effects for the resolution of the case: appreciation of the danger refers precisely to the knowledge of the objective concurrence of the justification element.

In the context of criminal processes against women who defend themselves from their husband's aggressions, it is possible to resort to an expert—ideally, a psychologist specializing in issues of violence against women—who can explain why the prior beatings a woman endures put her in a high-risk situation and in a special position to predict or fear the magnitude of the violence that can be unleashed. This kind of expert report can be conclusive to evaluate the rationality of the woman's perception of the danger she was facing.

In some cases, the experience of battered women has been explained through the characterization of "the battered woman syndrome," a concept that evaluates the psychological changes generated by the exposure to constant violence. Lenore Walker originally presented this concept in her 1979 book, *Battered Woman Syndrome*, in which she established that the investigations on the battered woman syndrome indicated that, in general, those who suffer situations of abuse and violence respond in a similar way. According to Walker's more in-depth research in subsequent publications,[39] battered woman syndrome is a sub-category of post-traumatic stress disorder. Among its manifestations, three categories of symptoms stand out, which determine if a person who has undergone traumatic situations has developed this syndrome: cognitive disorders, high levels of anxiety and avoidance symptoms.

Cognitive disturbances comprise memory disorders, including intrusive memories which may serve to reconstruct or deny, minimize or repress the incidents of violence. Women who have been subjected to violence also have difficulties concentrating and tend to confuse the episodes of abuse. If they are confronted with a new situation of violence, they can have flashbacks that lead them to re-experience previous situations of abuse and to reinforce and increase their perception of danger.[40] The development of a sense of hypervigilance allowing the identification of any potential danger and recognizing, in signs that may be insignificant to third parties, the possibility of a new outburst of violence, reveals the high levels of anxiety. This leads to nervous behavior, which may be evidenced through panic attacks and phobias or in eating or sleeping disorders. Another manifestation of the high levels of anxiety is compulsive and repetitive behavior, particularly in cases in which the woman believes she is the only one who can modify her partner's behavior.[41] Lastly, avoidance symptoms include depression, denial and minimization, all of them techniques to avoid facing the situation to which these women are exposed. As time goes by, and because of the control exerted by their partners, battered women isolate themselves from their containing environments and lose interest in activities they once enjoyed.[42]

---

[39] L. Walker, *op.cit.* pp. 327–328.

[40] *Id.*

[41] *Id.*

[42] *Id.*

While the ruling in the case "G.B. on homicide" made no reference to battered woman syndrome, it did take into consideration the reports of experts. On the one hand, they explained the consequences of the previous history of violence to which G.B. had been subjected, and on the other, the great feeling of fear she had experienced when the response to A.J.'s aggression was unleashed.

6.3 The Restriction of Women's Autonomy Through the Legal Protection Against Violence

Legislation pretending to protect women who are victims of violence must reconcile protection and respect for the victim's autonomy, and this conciliation poses a series of problems which are, perhaps, the logical result of each and every emancipatory pretension when the cultural and psychological dimension of domination is taken into account. Undoubtedly, even in the cruelest circumstances of bondage and oppression, there are individuals who share with their oppressors the logic of their oppression, and this happens, more often, in ambiguous circumstances that combine, for instance, ill treatment, abuse, and affective and family ties. In this respect, the State's intervention, that has its own logic and dynamics, may affect the freedom of the women who wish to determine their relationships in compliance with their own criteria.

Another problem is the relationship between the feminists who advocate for the reform and the women who would benefit from said reforms. Usually, between the groups that feminists hope to interpret, there are abysses of class, beliefs, social realities and life experiences. In many cases, bridges of solidarity are built over those abysses, but the differences remain and can result in the imposition of a particular way of viewing life—professional, middle-class, feminist—, thus also limiting the autonomy of women.

Lastly, that the State has its own logic and dynamics that is usually authoritative, impersonal and bureaucratic, particularly in the judicial branch, and with all the more reason, in the criminal branch, must be kept in mind. In the process of judicialization and state intervention, women lose autonomy, because they cease to be in charge of directing their own affairs, and are left in the hands of the State authority. This is even more serious in the case of persons from marginal sectors, whose relationship with the State fluctuates between paternalism, social control, and coercion on the part of the police force, for example, in the case of homeless people, prostitutes, inhabitants of illegal settlements, etc.

This last section will deal with different manifestations of the conflict between women's autonomy, State interests, and to a lesser extent, the feminist agenda. Cases and reforms are introduced to delve further into intra-family violence, and prostitution as form of slavery. First, we consider conciliation in matters of violence within the family, where the woman seeks State intervention to end the violence, sometimes without this implying the severing of the bond with the aggressor. She therefore seeks in the State a sort of paternal figure that may control her partner's abuse and facilitate the solution of the conflict. This is not necessarily the interest of the State, which envisages the problem as a minor issue, and needs to operate efficiently and investing the least possible amount of resources. Conciliation appears as an attractive figure in that it is efficient and quick. The models utilized, however, are not usually effective to reach genuine agreements, not to mention follow up and control. Besides, from the feminist stance, leaving women to their fate in supposed conciliation appointment with their aggressors constitutes an unacceptable violation of their rights, especially of their right to obtain justice and protection from the State. However, in principle this vision coincides with the interests of battered women: in individual cases in which the woman wishes to maintain the bond with the aggressor, conciliation appears to be an attractive option.

The second theme in this section examines human trafficking, in which there are other kinds of tensions between autonomy and protection that are also considerably complex. On the one hand, feminists have a legitimate concern for the horrendous situations of exploitation of many trafficked women, a concern that is in a curious synergy with the wish of developed countries to close their borders to immigrants from poor countries. For their part, what many poor women want is to liberate themselves from poverty by migrating to rich countries, and they are ready to run risks in order to do so. In this project, the State, and occasionally its feminist allies, may appear accepting one more form of immigration control.

6.3.1 Conciliation in Cases of Intra-family Violence

The feminist reforms of the 1990s coincided with the attempt to emphasize the positive approach to human rights, expedite the administration of justice, make labor contracts more flexible, and open domestic markets to foreign products and investment. Thus, the laws that regulate state intervention in cases of violence against women coincide, among others, with the reforms aimed at creating the so-called mechanisms for conflict resolution. As a result of this coexistence, conciliation or mediation are incorporated in the alternatives of State response to violence against women or intra-family violence in many instances as part of the same modernizing package.

Conciliation in the context of intra-family violence is enshrined in three different types of legislation. First, the laws that regulate state intervention in cases of violence against women, allowing or requiring the parties to attend a conciliation appointment mediated by a judge or a psychologist. Secondly, some regional legislation considers the requirement of conciliation hearings in order to continue investigations before trial for low penalty offenses, such as intra-family violence, failure to provide child support, and personal injuries. Lastly, the conciliation appointment is compulsory in family law proceedings, including divorces and separations, as well as proceedings involving the custody of minors.

As a result, battered women who resort to the justice system whether in search of a protective order, punishment on the part of criminal law, a divorce, child support or custody in the ambit of common or family law, must go through a conciliation hearing, very often mediated by the same official who, in the case of not reaching an agreement, will be responsible for deciding the case.

Critiques of this system are numerous and may be grouped in two categories: critiques of conciliation as a form of denial of justice, and critiques of conciliation for being a practice that ignores the imbalance of power between the parties. Those who consider that conciliation is a form of denial of justice have verified that women seek in vain protection and justice from the State. From this point of view, it is unacceptable that when requesting State protection, battered women end up forced to reach an agreement with their long-time aggressors. Conciliation critics therefore consider that this is just one more way of ignoring and perpetuating marital violence, and that it constitutes a serious violation of the rights to dignity, to life, health, access to justice, and especially, to a life free from violence.

The second type of critique perceives conciliation as a practice that underestimates the imbalance of power between the parties. This outlook presents an important challenge to alternative means for conflict resolution. There is a profuse bibliography on battered woman syndrome, a phenomenon that explains, for example, the emotional disorders that the victims suffer: constant fear and anguish, a feeling of helplessness, low self-esteem, apathy and passiveness, resignation, suicidal tendencies, depression, as well as diverse psychosomatic disorders. Besides, it is a known fact that ill treatment occurs in cycles of aggression–contrition–reconciliation–tension building–aggression, which makes it difficult for women to end the relationship. Studies have also been carried out on the culture of abuse that emerges in couples and how it contributes to women accepting the terms of their domination, of which physical abuse is barely a part of a much larger picture of domination and control that renders women incapable of defending or demanding their autonomy.[43] Under these circumstances, it is not very reasonable to expect women to reach convenient or just agreements with their aggressors.

However, this perception clashes with the daily experience of the operators of the norm, who observe that while some women seek this alternative with the clear notion that they want help to sever the bond with the aggressor, many others only seek to moderate violence without renouncing to the relationship, even accepting the terms of dominance and control that characterize it. With the aggravating factor that the dominant culture in the region justifies many of the behaviors associated to abuse, the woman views it as normal, or even correct; for instance, jealousy, possessiveness, the woman's responsibility for the affective welfare of the members of the family, the role of the housewife, and men's decision-making in matters regarding money. Moreover, one cannot forget that it is not only the aggressor who is imbued by the dominant culture, but also the victim and the judicial official.

In the face of these critiques, the inevitable question is: What are the alternatives to conciliation? Undoubtedly, not all cases of violence must or can be processed through the criminal system, whose competence is, anyway, called into question, as

---

[43] Judith Lewis Hermann M.D., *Trauma and Recovery: The Aftermath of Violence From Domestic Abuse to Political Terror*, Basic Books, New York (new ed.) 1997 and L. Walker, *op.cit.*

has already been argued in the first part of this chapter. On the other hand, protective measures require abundant resources and a police apparatus committed to their implementation, which is not the case in the region.

Lastly, the dissolution of the bond through the intervention of a policing system creates another series of problems such as revenge, the loss of a source of income, and the negotiation of custody and child support for the common children. For this reason, it is necessary to maintain a reflective attitude with respect to the search for alternatives, taking into account the advantages and disadvantages of conciliation.[44]

Below are two cases that challenge the idea that the State can allow or encourage conciliation hearings without assuring that they effectively defend human rights. In 2005, a claim was presented to the Colombian Constitutional Court, challenging the constitutionality of conciliation as part of the State response to intra-family violence and in particular, the competence of the equity conciliators to act in these matters. The Court ignored the concrete circumstances of violence and the reasons why in other places conciliation is banned in the presence of violence, and it stated instead, in an abstract manner, that "in the case of intra-family violence, ill treatment or abuse, there can be no objections if the response of the State apparatus consists in fostering the application of alternate and complementary, non-repressive formulas, like the one provided for in the accused norm." Additionally, it attributed conciliation the "superior objectives of the integral protection of the family and, likewise, the participation of the community in the problems that affect its members." The ruling is, therefore, a clear example of the way in which the traditional dogma ignores women's experience, on the one hand, and reproduces and perpetuates conservative values, on the other.

Through the Colombian case, we see that there is no reference to the vulnerability of the battered woman at conciliation hearings. As for the second case in the Inter-American Commission of Human Rights, the mentioned attitude is reflected particularly in the notion of the defense of the family, whose implicit corollary is that the family has rights, and that these rights may demand the sacrifice of women as individuals.

Constitutional Court of Colombia
Ruling C-059 of 2005

Main Legal Issues:

Is a norm that authorizes conciliation as a State response to intra-family violence constitutional? Can equity conciliators, who do not require knowledge of the law, summoned to act as neutral third parties in minor matters be apt to decide cases of intra-family violence?

---

[44] *See* Julieta Lemaitre "Justicia Injusta: una crítica feminista a la conciliación en violencia conyugal" in *Revista de Derecho Privado*, Universidad de los Andes, Bogotá, January 2002.

Facts:
Paragraph 1 of Article 1 of Law 575/2000, which authorizes any person who, in the context of the family, be a victim of violence, abuse or aggression, to appear before the Justice of the Peace or Equity Conciliator, with the aim of obtaining, through their mediation, the cessation of violence, abuse or aggression or its avoidance if it were imminent, without prejudice to any pertinent criminal charges, or to the competence of the Family Commissars or the Municipal Court Judges (Civil division) and municipal civil and criminal judges to apply a protective measure in cases of intra-family violence, is challenged.

Court Ruling:
In episodes of intra-family violence, ill treatment or abuse, the response of the State apparatus may consist in the application of alternate, complementary, and non-repressive formulas, aimed at achieving an integral protection of the family.

Extracts:
According to the plaintiff, the norm is unconstitutional because the justices of the peace and the equity conciliators are not constitutionally entitled to hear cases of intra-family violence, but only cases involving minor conflicts that due to their essential nature do not require the intervention of officials with a background in juridical science. In this respect, he concludes that the measure in question is ineffective to combat the mentioned phenomenon and for this reason, it should be removed from the regulations.

The Court holds that the charges will not prevail for the following reasons:
It has been established that, as regards the justices of the peace, the members of the Constituent Assembly conferred on the legislator a wide margin of configuration regarding the regulation of that institution. In this respect, it is therefore clear that the mandate contained in the precept under analysis is none other than the expression of this configuration faculty constitutionally granted to the legislator in relation to the justices of the peace.

This same doctrine can also be extended to encompass the equity conciliators for, as in the case of the justices of the peace, the Constitution provides that private persons may be transitorily invested with the function of administering justice, under the terms determined by the law, corresponding to the legislator all matters related to their implementation and to the assignment of competence, without any other limit than the one imposed by the Constitution itself. In such a way that if the justices of the peace and the equity conciliators are constitutionally entitled to administer justice, there can be no objections to the legislator's assigning them competence to hear cases of intra-family violence under the terms provided in the contested norm, that is, as mediators.

[...]

It is worth remembering that, with respect to violence against women, contrary to what has been asserted by the actor, the international instruments do not require from the Colombian State solely repressive responses, for as has been noted before, in the Inter-American Convention on the Prevention, Punishment and Eradication of Violence against Women, subscribed in the city of Belem do Para, Brazil, on June 9, 1994, approved by Law 248 of December 29, 1995, it was provided as duty of the States, among others, to "include in their domestic legislation penal, civil, administrative and any other type of provisions that may be needed to prevent, punish and eradicate violence against women and to adopt appropriate administrative measures where necessary" (art.7 letter c).

[...]

In this respect, the Court deems that such provision equally conforms to the constitutional postulates regarding the protection of the family and its members, since the aggressor's reluctant conduct or his intransigent position concerning conciliation cannot constitute an obstacle to the action of justice, preventing the adoption of protective measures. If this were not so, the defenselessness of the victims of intra-family violence would be propitiated, leaving them exposed to having to endure a continuous harm or to this harm being inflicted when it were predictable. For this reason, the legislator rightly provided that if the alleged aggressor should not attend the hearing or no agreement is reached between the parties, the victim will be oriented as to what authority she can resort to in order to request a protective measure, and it will proceed ex-officio, sending the customary required documentation.

[...]

In conclusion, from the constitutional perspective, and in cases of intra-family violence, ill treatment or abuse, there can be no objections to the response of the State apparatus consisting in promoting the application of alternate and complementary non-repressive formulas such as the ones provided by the challenged norm, with the aim of achieving the superior objectives of integral protection of the family and the participation of the community members in the problem that affect them.

Based on the forgoing, the Court declares the challenged norm enforceable.

Inter-American Commission of Human Rights
Maria Da Penha Maia Fernandes v. Brasil[45]
April 16, 2001

Main Legal Issue:
Is the Brazilian state internationally responsible for impunity in domestic violence cases?

Facts:
8. The petition states that on May 29, 1983, Mrs. María da Penha Maia Fernandes, a pharmacist, was the victim of attempted murder by her then husband, Marco Antônio Heredia Viveiros, an economist, at her home in Fortaleza, Ceará State. He shot her while she was asleep, bringing to a climax a series of acts of aggression carried out over the course of their married life. As a result of this aggression of her spouse, Mrs. Fernandes sustained serious injuries, had to undergo numerous operations, and suffered irreversible paraplegia and other physical and psychological trauma.

[45] Maria da Penha v. Brazil, Case 12.051, Inter-Am. Comm'n H.R., Report No. 54/01, OEA/Ser.L/V/II.111 Doc. 20 rev. ¶ 704 (2000).

9. The petitioners state that Mr. Heredia Viveiros was an aggressive and violent person, and that he would assault his wife and three daughters during his marriage. According to the victim, the situation became unbearable but she was too afraid to take steps to obtain a separation. They maintain that the husband tried to cover up the attack by reporting it as an attempted robbery and the work of thieves who had fled. Two weeks after Mrs. Fernandes returned from the hospital and was recovering from the attempt on her life on May 29, 1983, Mr. Heredia Viveiros again attempted to kill her by allegedly trying to electrocute her while she was bathing. At that point, she decided to seek a legal separation from him. [...]

19. The petitioners maintain that as of the date of the petition, the Brazilian justice system had dragged its feet for more than 15 years without handing down a final ruling against the ex-husband of Mrs. Fernandes, who has been free during that entire period, despite the serious nature of the charges, the mountain of evidence against him, and the serious nature of the crime committed against Mrs. Fernandes. The judicial system of Ceará and the Brazilian State have thus been ineffective, as seen in their failure to conduct proceedings in a prompt and efficient manner, thereby creating a great risk of impunity, since punishment in this case will be barred by the statute of limitations twenty years after the occurrence of these events, a date that is approaching. They maintain that the primary aim of the Brazilian State ought to have been to ensure compensation for the suffering of Maria da Penha, by guaranteeing her a fair trial within a reasonable time.

Conclusions of the Commission:

60. [...]

2. Based on the facts, which have not been disputed, and the foregoing analysis, the Federative Republic of Brazil is responsible for violation of the right to a fair trial and judicial protection, guaranteed in Articles 8 and 25 of the American Convention, in accordance with the general obligation to respect and guarantee rights set forth in Article 1(1) of this instrument, because of the unwarranted delay and negligent processing of this case of domestic violence in Brazil.

3. The State has adopted a number of measures intended to reduce the scope of domestic violence and tolerance by the State thereof, although these measures have not yet had a significant impact on the pattern of State tolerance of violence against women, in particular as a result of ineffective police and judicial action in Brazil.

4. The State has violated the rights of Mrs. Fernandes and failed to carry out its duty assumed under Article 7 of the Convention of Belém do Pará and Articles 8 and 25 of the American Convention; both in relation to Article 1(1) of the Convention, as a result of its own failure to act and tolerance of the violence inflicted.

Extracts:

A. Right to Justice (Article XVIII of the Declaration); and to a Fair Trial (Article 8) and Judicial Protection (Article 25), in relation to the Obligation to Respect and Guarantee Rights (Article 1(1)) of the Convention.

[...]

38. More than 17 years have elapsed since the launching of the investigation into the attack on the victim Maria da Penha Maia Fernandes and to date, based on the information received, the case against the accused remains open, a final ruling has not been handed down, and remedies have not been provided for the consequences of the attempted murderer of Mrs. Fernandes. The Inter-American Court of Human Rights has stated that the term "reasonable time" established in Article 8(1) of the Convention is not a concept that can be defined easily and has referred to the decisions of the European Court of Human Rights for guidance in this regard. These decisions state that the following elements must be evaluated in determining whether the time within which proceedings take place is reasonable: the complexity of the case, the procedural activity of the interested party, and the conduct of the judicial authorities.

[...]

44. In this case, the Brazilian courts have failed to hand down a final ruling after seventeen years and this delay is leading to the distinct possibility of definitive impunity because of barring of the offense by the statute of limitations, thereby precluding receipt of compensation which, in any event, would be very late. The Commission holds the view that the domestic judicial decisions in this case reveal inefficiency, negligence, and failure to act on the part of the Brazilian judicial authorities and unjustified delay in the prosecution of the accused. These decisions are standing in the way of punishment of the accused and are raising the specter of impunity and failure to compensate the victim as a result of barring of the offense by the statute of limitations. They demonstrate that the State has not been capable of organizing its entities in a manner that guarantees those rights. As a whole, this situation represents a separate violation of Articles 8 and 25 of the American Convention on Human Rights in relation to Article 1(1) thereof and the corresponding Articles of the Declaration.

B. Equality before the Law (Article 24 of the Convention) and Articles II and XVIII of the Declaration

[...]

47. Compared to men, women are the victims of domestic violence in disproportionate numbers. A study done by the National Movement for Human Rights in Brazil compares the incidence of domestic violence against women and men and shows that in terms of murders, women are 30 times more likely to be killed by their husbands than husbands by their wives. In its special report on Brazil in 1997, the Commission found that there was clear discrimination against women who were attacked, resulting from the inefficiency of the Brazilian judicial system and inadequate application of national and international rules, including those arising from the case law of the Brazilian Supreme Court.

[...]

55. The impunity that the ex-husband of Mrs. Fernandes has enjoyed and continues to enjoy is at odds with the international commitment voluntarily assumed by the State when it ratified the Convention of Belém do Pará. The failure to prosecute and

convict the perpetrator under these circumstances is an indication that the State condones the violence suffered by Maria da Penha, and this failure by the Brazilian courts to take action is exacerbating the direct consequences of the aggression by her ex-husband. Furthermore, as has been demonstrated earlier, that tolerance by the State organs is not limited to this case; rather, it is a pattern. The condoning of this situation by the entire system only serves to perpetuate the psychological, social, and historical roots and factors that sustain and encourage violence against women

56. Given the fact that the violence suffered by Maria da Penha is part of a general pattern of negligence and lack of effective action by the State in prosecuting and convicting aggressors, it is the view of the Commission that this case involves not only failure to fulfill the obligation with respect to prosecute and convict, but also the obligation to prevent these degrading practices. That general and discriminatory judicial ineffectiveness also creates a climate that is conducive to domestic violence, since society sees no evidence of willingness by the State, as the representative of the society, to take effective action to sanction such acts.

6.3.2 Human Trafficking

The reforms of the late 1990s and the first decade of 2000 also renovated the definition of crimes related to the exploitation of prostitution. The changes, especially as of 2000, are a result of both the activism of feminist groups and of the pressure exerted by the U.S. in order that the countries in the region suppress human trafficking.

Generally, the theoretical framework used for the trafficking of women is the same as that of prostitution, and both phenomena are often associated, considering that a large proportion of trafficked women are trafficked to be used as prostitutes. They are even usually defined in the same section of the Penal Code. In the region, feminist reforms have focused on there being a more severe punishment for crimes related to prostitution, including in many cases pornography, sexual tourism, and human trafficking.

The form of punishment is the object of a long debate on the status of prostitution for feminism. The debate covers two aspects: first, what is prostitution, and second, what must States do in this respect. At one end of the spectrum of possible stances, there are those who envisage prostitution essentially as a form of exploitation and humiliation of women, and they consider it must be banned, while simultaneously protecting and rehabilitating the prostitutes. On the other end are those who consider that prostitution is a kind of work and that only the different forms of exploitation must be eliminated, providing prostitutes with the protection that the State affords to other crafts and occupations. Thus, for instance, the requests include access to affiliation to social security, the elimination of police raids and policing control, legalization of the occupation and repression of sexual bondage. The stance of legal reforms is an intermediary one according to which many activities related to prostitution, such as running brothels, are punished, but not the act itself.

The consent and autonomy of prostitutes is central to this debate, which extends to the conceptualization of human traffic. It is clear that in terms of human rights, prostitution, like human traffic, act in violation if they infringe upon human freedom. The question is, however, what notion of human freedom must be applied. While it is clear that in the cases where there is brute force there is no discussion, there is discussion in those in which the decision to engage in prostitution is the product of a series of unfortunate circumstances. Should there be a more strict examination of freedom than the one that is practiced when considering human freedom in general, for example, the freedom to choose a job or a couple, or should it not? These latter decisions may also be the fruit of unfortunate circumstances, and yet the State does not protect us from them.

The problem of consent and the definition of human trafficking is studied in this section, showing some arguments on consent in prostitution that may be applicable.

Commission on Human Rights
Fifty-sixth Session
Integration of the Human Rights of Women and the Gender Perspective[46]

I. Introduction

A. The purview of the report—from voluntary migration to trafficking in women: the continuum of women's movement and the human rights violations perpetrated during the course of that movement

1. Trafficking in persons must be viewed within the context of international and national movements and migrations that increasingly are being undertaken owing to economic globalization, the feminization of migration, armed conflict, the break-down or reconfiguration of the State, and the transformation of political boundaries. The Special Rapporteur highlights the fact that trafficking in women is one component of a larger phenomenon of trafficking in persons, including both male and female adults and children. Nonetheless, she would like to highlight the woman-specific character of many violations of human rights committed during the course of trafficking. She calls on Governments to respond to such violations of human rights through policies based on gender-awareness.

[…]

3. Women move and are moved, with and without their consent, for a myriad of reasons. Trafficking in women must be understood to exist within a continuum of women's movement and migrations. The Special Rapporteur is of the firm belief that women and all other persons must enjoy freedom of movement. Trafficking in women, as the Special Rapporteur defines and understands it, is a particularly violent form of movement, which has to be prohibited. Nevertheless, the Special Rapporteur is of the opinion that trafficking must be considered in the broader

[46] Special Rapporteur on the Violence Against Women, Its Causes and Consequences, *Rep. on Trafficking in Women, Women's Migration and Violence Against Women*, Comm'n Hum. Rts, E/CN.4/2000/68, (Feb. 29, 2000) (by Radhika Coomaraswamy).

context of violations that are committed against women in the course of their movement and migrations. While the experience of being trafficked may affect the level or degree of marginalization or violations that are perpetrated against women, trafficking is not the sole determinant of whether women's human rights are violated in the course of their national and international movements. Movement and migration, coupled with Governments' reactions to and attempts to restrict such movements through immigration and emigration policies, and the exploitation of such attempts by traffickers, place women in situations in which they are unprotected or only marginally protected by law. As such, women who attempt to exercise their freedom of movement are often placed in vulnerable positions vis-à-vis the protection of their human rights.

4. Overt forms of violence, including, but not limited to rape, torture, arbitrary execution, deprivation of liberty, forced labour and forced marriage, are perpetrated against women who seek to exercise their freedom of movement. Additionally, the discriminatory policies and practices of Governments, particularly those that seek to curb women's movement, help to create a climate in which such violations are officially tolerated, if not encouraged or in some cases perpetrated by State actors. The Special Rapporteur is concerned that, in some cases, Governments, in their attempts to respond effectively to growing international concern about trafficking, may misconstrue the needs of victims and, in so doing, institute policies and practices that further undermine the rights of women, especially the freedom of movement and the right to earn a living. It is for this reason that the Special Rapporteur believes that trafficking must be appropriately situated in its global context of movement and migrations and the feminization of such movement and migrations. As such, and with special emphasis on trafficking, it is the violations of women's human rights committed in the course of women's movements that this report seeks to highlight [...]

C. The definition of trafficking

12. Trafficking is a dynamic concept, the parameters of which are constantly changing to respond to changing economic, social and political conditions. Although the purposes for which women are trafficked change and the ways in which women are trafficked the countries from which and to which they are trafficked change, the constituent elements remain constant. At the core of any definition of trafficking must be the recognition that trafficking is never consensual. It is the non consensual nature of trafficking that distinguishes it from other forms of migration. The lack of informed consent must not be confused with the illegality of certain forms of migration. While all trafficking is, or should be, illegal, all illegal migration is not trafficking. It is important to refrain from telescoping together the concepts of trafficking and illegal migration. At the heart of this distinction is the issue of consent.

[...]

16. Although numerous separate abuses are committed during the course of trafficking, which themselves violate both national and international law, it is the

combination of the coerced transport and the coerced end practice that makes trafficking a distinct violation from its component parts. Without this linkage, trafficking would be legally indistinguishable from the individual activities of smuggling and forced labour or slavery like practices, when in fact trafficking does differ substantively from its component parts. The transport of trafficked persons is inextricably linked to the end purpose of trafficking. Recruitment and transport in the trafficking context is undertaken with the intent to subject the victim of the coerced transport to additional violations in the form of forced labour or slavery like practices. [...]

III. Violations Perpetrated Against Women in the Course of Movement

B. Discriminatory practices that cause or contribute to violence: restrictions on mobility, nationality laws, equal protection, labour rights, etc.
[...]

43. On the issue of trafficking, Governments overwhelmingly adopt a law and order approach, with an accompanying strong anti-immigration policy. Such an approach is often at odds with the protection of human rights. Further, while many government policies may be inspired by benevolent intentions, they often serve to either create or exacerbate existing situations that cause or contribute to trafficking in women. Policies and practices that either overtly discriminate against women or that sanction or encourage discrimination against women tend to increase women's chances of being trafficked.

44. Despite the fact that trafficked women, and more generally undocumented migrant women, are often the victims of crime, they are often perceived and treated as criminals in countries of destination. The media, often encouraged by the official anti-immigration policies of the State, create and propagate the image of the immigrant as criminal. Such perceptions are caused by the intersection of racism and xenophobia, which is increasingly found implicit in the official policies of highly industrialized States. Such stereotyping serves to marginalize and increase the vulnerability of undocumented immigrants. Further, in addition to all the risks that their male compatriots shoulder, female migrants face threats to their bodily integrity because of the ever present, added risk of sexual abuse by the smugglers, male migrants and even police and immigration officials. Even if they are victimized, however, these undocumented migrants continue to be classified as criminals because of their immigration status and attendant offences which they may have committed.

VI. The Impact of Immigration Laws And Policies on Trafficking and Migration
[...]

61. The Special Rapporteur is concerned by the apparent link between protectionist, anti immigration policies and the phenomenon of trafficking. Restrictive and exclusionary immigration policies, when combined with the destabilizing effects of conflict, globalization and neo-liberal development strategies which result in increasing outflows of legal and illegal migrant labour, serve as important causative

factors in the persistence and prevalence of trafficking. Anti-immigration policies aid and abet traffickers. Documentation shows that inflexible policies of exclusion, which are enforced through severe punishments of a penal nature and deportation for their breach, feed directly into the hands of traffickers. The availability of legal migrant work, which is subject to government regulation and scrutiny, reduces the reliance on third parties of those who seek to migrate for work. Trafficking economies—which arise out of a combination of supply, demand and illegality—are less likely to develop in situations in which opportunities exist for legal migrant work. Increasingly, highly industrialized countries such as those in Europe, North America and Asia have placed restrictions on legal, long-term immigration. Strong anti-immigration regimes are increasingly typical in these countries and are justified by Governments as a component of a rational policy of protectionism and deterrence arising out of economic imperatives. For example, since the end of the Cold War and the establishment of democratic rule in Eastern Europe, Western Europe has responded by tightening its external borders. European migrations from East to West are seen as both a threat to domestic security and to European unity. As a consequence, restrictions on immigration have increased, and with them, trafficking has reportedly increased

Sex Workers Manifesto
Calcutta, 1997[47]

Extracts:

[...] Like many other occupations, sex work is also an occupation, and it is probably one of the "oldest profession" in the world because it meets an important social demand. But the term "prostitute" is rarely used to refer to an occupational group who earn their livelihood through providing sexual services, rather it is deployed as a descriptive term denoting a homogenized category, usually of women, who poses threats to public health, sexual morality, social stability and civic order. Within this discursive boundary we systematically find ourselves to be targets of moralizing impulses of dominant social groups, through missions of cleansing and sanitizing, both materially and symbolically. If and when we figure in political or developmental agenda, we are enmeshed in discursive practices and practical projects which aim to rescue, rehabilitate, improve, "discipline, control or police us. Charity organizations are prone to rescue us and put us in 'safe' homes, developmental organizations are likely to 'rehabilitate' us through meager income generation activities, and the police seem bent upon to regularly raid our quarters in the name of controlling 'immoral' trafficking."

[...] Even when we are inscribed less negatively or even sympathetically within dominant discourses we are not exempt from stigmatization or social exclusion. As powerless, abused victims with no resources, we are seen as objects of pity. Otherwise we appear as self-sacrificing and nurturing supporting cast of characters in popular literature and cinema, ceaselessly ready to give up our hard earned income,

[47] http://www.bayswan.org/manifest.html

our clients, our 'sinful' ways and finally our lives to ensure the well-being of the hero or the society he represents. In either case we are refused enfranchisement as legitimate citizens or workers, and are banished to the margins of society and history.

The kind of oppression that can be meted out to a sex worker can never be perpetrated against a regular worker. The justification given is that sex work is not real work—it is morally sinful. As prostitution is kept hidden behind the facade of sexual morality and social order, unlike other professions there is no legitimacy or scope for any discussion about the demands and needs of the workers of the sex industry.

People who are interested in our welfare, and many are genuinely concerned, often can not think beyond rehabilitating us or abolishing prostitution altogether. However, we know that in reality it is perhaps impossible to "rehabilitate" a sex worker because the society never allows to erase our identity as prostitutes. Is rehabilitation feasible or even desirable?

In a country where unemployment is in such gigantic proportions, where does the compulsion of displacing millions of women and men who are already engaged in an income earning occupation which supports themselves and their extended families, come from? If other workers in similarly exploitative occupations can work within the structures of their profession to improve their working conditions, why can not sex workers remain in the sex industry and demand a better deal in their life and work?

[…]

Protocol to Prevent, Suppress and Punish Trafficking Persons, Especially Women and Children, Supplementing the United Nations Convention Against Transnational Organized Crime[48]

Article 3

Use of terms for the purposes of this Protocol:

(a) "Trafficking in persons" shall mean the recruitment, transportation, transfer, harbouring or receipt of persons, by means of the threat or use of force or other forms of coercion, of abduction, of fraud, of deception, of the abuse of power or of a position of vulnerability or of the giving or receiving of payments or benefits to achieve the consent of a person having control over another person, for the purpose of exploitation. Exploitation shall include, at a minimum, the exploitation of the prostitution of others or other forms of sexual exploitation, forced labour or services, slavery or practices similar to slavery, servitude or the removal of organs;

(b) The consent of a victim of trafficking in persons to the intended exploitation set forth in subparagraph (a) of this article shall be irrelevant where any of the means set forth in subparagraph (a) have been used;

---

[48] Protocol to Prevent, Suppress and Punish Trafficking in Persons, Especially Women and Children, Supplementing the United Nations Convention Against Transnational Organized Crime, G.A. Res. 25, annex II, U.N. GAOR, 55th Sess., Supp. No. 49, at 60, U.N. Doc. A/55/49 (Vol. I) (2001), entered into force Dec. 25, 2003.

(c) The recruitment, transportation, transfer, harbouring or receipt of a child for the purpose of exploitation shall be considered "trafficking in persons" even if this does not involve any of the means set forth in subparagraph (a) of this article;
(d) "Child" shall mean any person under eighteen years of age.

6.3.2.1 Matters for Debate

What is the best way to address prostitution and human trafficking through the law? These discussions are framed in a global context where the interest in the protection of human rights, especially those of women, intersect with the interest of developed countries in stemming the flow of illegal immigrants. For example, the U.S. is exerting considerable pressure in the region for countries to adopt legislations complying with the Protocol to Prevent, Suppress and Punish Trafficking in Persons, Especially Women and Children, and to also vigorously attack human trafficking. U.S. legislation establishes a series of mechanisms to control the actions of other countries in this issue. Thus, in its report on human rights the State Department must include reports on the situation of the actions taken by the other countries to combat the trafficking of persons, and it establishes the mechanisms to assess these actions. When a country does not satisfactorily comply with the demanded requirements, it risks losing U.S. assistance, and even being subject to economic sanctions. This policy has an impact on the legislation in the region and endows it with a particular character.

Chapter 7
Families Beyond Heteronormativity

Juan Marco Vaggione

Family policy is currently characterized by an antagonism between two main sectors that, while articulate different alliances and discourses, respond to opposing definitions of sexuality. Although heterogeneous, these sectors construct the legality and legitimacy of LGBTQ persons and couples differently in the framework of family relationships. This antagonism is, to a large extent, a confrontation on the recognition—legal and social—that must be given to family arrangements outside of the traditional definition of family. One of the central conflicts of contemporary policies, at the national and international levels, occurs between those who defend the family as a unique social institution based, essentially on heterosexuality, and those who break with this pattern and maintain that the family must be recognized as a multiple and diverse reality. LGBTQ persons and couples are a part of this diversity.

In Latin America, the Catholic Church hierarchy and its allies stand out among those who defend a unique conception of family. For the Church, presenting the defense of family is a form of defending Latin American culture that is being threatened by the demands of feminist movements and movements in favor of sexual diversity. This defense is carried out in complex and diverse ways, which have rendered the theoretical framework that explains the religious phenomenon obsolete. On the one hand, the Catholic Church hierarchy is still the main political opponent to passing laws and the articulation of public policies favorable to sexual and reproductive rights. The high degree of legitimacy of the Church and its representatives added to the low legitimacy of politicians in the region, are factors limiting the autonomy of government representatives and legislators who, in exchange for defending the religious conception of family, resort to the Catholic hierarchy in

J.M. Vaggione (✉)
National University of Córdoba/CONICET, Arturo M. Bas 112, Cordoba, Argentina
e-mail: juanvaggione@yahoo.com

C. Motta and M. Sáez (eds.), *Gender and Sexuality in Latin America - Cases and Decisions*, Ius Gentium: Comparative Perspectives on Law and Justice 24,
DOI 10.1007/978-94-007-6199-5_7, © Springer Science+Business Media Dordrecht 2013

search of support. On the other hand, in addition to the fragile institutional separation of State and Church in most Latin American countries, there is the large impact of the Church as a political stakeholder in the region in delimiting the public agenda and influencing government decision-making. The lobbying of legislators and judges by representatives of the Catholic Church significantly curbs changes in the legal system and in the jurisprudence, which institutionalize the conception of the traditional family.

But institutionalization of a unique family model is also sustained by the influence of stakeholders and the religious discourse over the general population. The unique family model not only maintains the legal political power of the hierarchy, but also the construction of a cultural matrix sustained by Catholicism, and the influence it has on the moral and legal constructions of the people. Religiousness is still the variable that best predicts the attitude of the population toward sexual and reproductive rights. The closer people are to and the more identified they are with religion—particularly with those religions which, like Catholicism, defend a traditional conception—, the greater their resistance to recognize sexual and reproductive rights. The most noteworthy case is that of an important group of NGO's known as pro-life or pro-family,[1] formed by citizens who, identified with the Catholic doctrine, defend restrictive legislation on gender and sexuality currently in force in the region. The influence of religion on legislators and judges is also evident, since for many, religious beliefs continue to be a crucial aspect at the time of making decisions on legal regulation of sexuality, without necessarily receiving any external pressure from the Church hierarchy.[2] The way in which religion and morality often overlap, and the historical influence of the Church on Latin American culture, also constitute barriers to the reform of the legal system that is called for in pluralist societies.

In recent decades, however, the family as a symbolic order has started to be redefined on the basis of the growing presence of feminist movements and those in favor of sexual diversity, among other factors, exerting pressure on the State and the political society to change the current legal systems. The aim of these movements is to de-institutionalize the traditional definition that considers the union of a man and a woman as the legal and legitimate family, whose main objective is reproduction. Even though this definition continues to prevail, its hegemonic construction has been interrupted, allowing for the understanding of the family as a plural order. On the one hand, the existence of several types of family arrangements that are outside of the narrow conception that the traditional position defends, particularly, one-parent

---

[1] *See* Micahel W. Cuneo, *The Smoke of Satan*, Oxford University Press, New York, 1997 and Mary Jo Appleby y R. Scout Weaver, eds., in *Being Right: Conservative Catholics in America*, Indiana University Press, Bloomington, 1995.

[2] *See* Juan Marco Vaggione "Dios y la Ley. Las Influencias Religiosas en el Derecho" *Anuario VIII del Centro de Investigaciones Jurídicas y Sociales,* Editorial Lerner, Buenos Aires, Noviembre 2005; Rosa María Rodrigues de Oliveira "Isto é contra a natureza… uma observação de acórdãos judiciais e entrevistas com magistrados sobre conjugalidades homoeróticas em três estados brasileiros", en Anna Paula Uziel, Luiz Mello, Miriam Pillar Grossi, eds., *Conjugalidades, parentalidades e Identidades Lésbicas, Gays e Travestis,* Garamond, Rio de Janeiro, 2007.

homes of women have become demographically visible. On the other hand, the traditional conception as universal and natural has also been criticized because it has been proved the result of a specific history and of responding to certain power relations. The denaturizing of the traditional conception, through existing social diversity or through the historic perspective of its existence, allows opening the space for acceptance of pluralism as a component of family arrangements.

Feminist movements and movements in favor of sexual diversity criticize the traditional/natural conception of family because it masks dominance regimes. First, it is characterized for being patriarchal: men are placed in a situation of privilege in relation to women. The division of roles within the family that relegates women to domestic tasks, the private sphere, and reproduction, is a form of dominance that has been denounced by feminism for decades. Secondly, the traditional conception of family is heteronormative: heterosexuality is formed in the norm from which moral and legal barriers are regulated. Only heterosexual couples are considered an affective arrangement that the State and society may recognize as a legitimate nucleus of contemporary families. LGBTQ persons are found in the margins of the definition of family and are "tolerated" only if they maintain their family bonds in invisibility and illegality.

A common element of patriarchy and heteronormativity as systems of dominance, that also characterizes the traditional definition of family, is the understanding of sexuality as a mainly reproductive function. The Catholic Church has been, and still is, an important stakeholder sustaining that the morality and legality of sexuality are grounded on reproduction—its essential end. In this philosophy, women are defined by their breeding capacity and are consequently "subjected" to the regulations and interest of the State, society and men. Same-sex couples are viewed as the denial of reproductive capacity, and therefore the denial of family and marriage as defined in the traditional way. The strong link between sexuality and reproduction entails the exclusion of women and of LGBTQ persons and couples.

7.1 LGBTQ Persons in Families

In the last few years, the movement in favor of sexual diversity has become a fundamental political stakeholder in the quest for de-institutionalization of the traditional family at a legal and cultural level. In particular, the movement has been successful in making visible the presence of LGBTQ persons as part of contemporary families, and beginning a discussion on the issue. As couples, parents, or children, LGBTQ persons defy the religious, moral, and legal constructions of the family currently in force. What is being challenged, in particular, is a system of heteronormative dominance and heterosexuality as an essential requisite for the makeup of couples and procreation. Marriage does not require opposite-sex couples, nor does paternity/maternity necessarily require heterosexuality. By defending these two aspects, the basic assumptions that ground the traditional family and which have ruled in a hegemonic way in Latin America for years, are blown to pieces. After decades of activism, a gradual change in the international legislation and jurisprudence is being achieved, increasing the chances to incorporate the legality and legitimacy of family definitions that go beyond heteronormativity. Important changes are occurring in legal systems that regulate family relationships in different countries of the world. Alongside the growing legitimacy of sexual diversity, LGBTQ persons are being conferred more legality as part of family relationships; in turn, the ways that family is legally made up begins to be redefined.

However, there is great tension within the movement in favor of sexual diversity, concerning the way of overcoming marginalization of LGBTQ persons in the family regulatory framework. This tension is the result of the movement's significant heterogeneity, both in terms of stakeholders and of the political strategies that are favored. At the stakeholder level, the movement comprises an open list in which, among other persons, lesbians, gays, bisexuals, transvestites, transsexuals, and transgender individuals are distinguished. Although all these share a regime of exclusion and discrimination that deprives them, at least partially, of recognition and rights, each one of them has its own specificities and demands that are not always easy to reconcile. For example, the situation of gays and lesbians cannot be equaled, since even though both are marginalized because of their sexuality, lesbians additionally suffer patriarchal oppression as a system of domination. Transgendered persons, who identify with a sex/gender different from the one assigned to him/her at birth, not only question the dominant conceptions of sexuality, but also checkmate the binary system of sexual difference (man/woman).[3] Finally, this heterogeneity requires taking into account its intersection with other dimensions such as class, race, and handicaps, generating different situations.

Of course, this stakeholder heterogeneity also has political consequences at the time of setting priorities among demands. As analyzed below, one of the main requirements of the movement in favor of sexual diversity is the acceptance of same-sex marriage. Irrespective of the critical analysis that may be made of this demand, the incorporation of same-sex couples to the marriage institution has little to do with the issues that, with regard to that institution, are faced, for example by transgendered persons, who are denied basic civil rights, such as the right to a name, to move freely or to dignified work.[4] "Homosexual marriage" should not be what permits them to formalize their relationship, if they so desired, but rather the fact that they be recognized a gender identity different from the one assigned to them at birth, without having to necessarily undergo sex-change surgery to attain the characteristics of the other sex.[5] Although there is some available jurisprudence recognizing

---

[3] Maffía, Diana (comp), *Sexualidades migrantes. Género y transgénero*, Buenos Aires, Feminaria editora, 2003; Fernández, Josefina, *Cuerpos desobedientes. Travestismo e identidad de género*, Edhasa, Buenos Aires, 2004.

[4] Berkins, Lohana and Fernandez, Josefina. *La gesta del nombre propio. Informe sobre la situación de la comunidad travesti en la Argentina*, Ediciones Madres de Plaza de Mayo, Buenos Aires, 2005.

[5] *See* Mauro Cabral and Paula Viturro, "Transsexual Citizenship in Contemporary Argentina", in P. Currah, R. Juang and S. Minter Price (eds.), *Transgender Rights*, Minnesota University Press, 2006.

the validity of marriage of transsexuals, generally speaking, there still exist strong barriers; barriers different from those that are targeted to change through the legitimization of marriage between persons of the same sex. The heterogeneity proper of the movement in favor of sexual diversity should not be rendered invisible (or depoliticized) by prioritizing certain demands which characterize only some sectors.

Beyond heterogeneity at the stakeholder level, although strongly linked to it, there is an ideological tension in the way of defining and analyzing the system of domination on sexuality as well as the political strategies that should be implemented to overcome them. From an initial position, based particularly on discourses of rights, the main argument is to achieve a fairer society based on including sexual minorities and claiming the principle of equality among citizens. The oppression to which LGBTQ persons and couples are subject to requires political strategies that can be defined as assimilation, strategies that allow for the modification of legal systems currently in force, incorporating these individuals as legitimate subjects of the law. Thus, diverse issues of public law such as social security, pensions, retirement funds, the principles of immigration, or private law matters such as inheritance rights and child support are gradually being amended to incorporate the specific situation of same-sex couples.

The preferred strategy is to politically treat sexual minorities as subjects of law, denouncing the discrimination that gays and lesbians suffer in the legal systems currently in force. The political function of the movement in favor of sexual diversity consists in putting pressure on the State and on the political society to achieve legal reforms that protect the groups that have been excluded on account of sexuality. To this end, legislative bills and legal reforms are proposed and members of the legislative and judicial powers are lobbied to amend existing regulations. As analyzed in detail in this chapter, the discourse on rights holds an important place in the movement in favor of sexual diversity, and he recognition of same-sex couples and the defense of LGBTQ persons as fathers and mothers has made significant progress.

From the perspective of a more transgressor policy, associated to the *queer* theory, the movement in favor of sexual diversity should not be so oriented at obtaining rights that permit the inclusion of LGBTQ persons within the prevailing definitions of family but, it should rather focus on causing these definitions to blow up (*queering*). The *queer* theory questions the idea of a "normal" sexuality, since such theory "legitimize and privilege heterosexuality and heterosexual relationships as fundamental and 'natural' within society."[6] This position implies reviewing how "sexuality, gender, race, and class oppression and privilege come together in the dominant vision of family in our society"[7] in contemporary societies. An approach concerned merely with the subject of rights does not challenge power, and would

---

6 Cathy J. Cohen, "Punks, Bulldaggers, and Welfare Queen: The Radical Potential of Queer Politics?", in E. Patrick Johnson y Mae G. Henderson, eds., *Black Queer Studies,* Duke University Press, Durham, 2005.

7 Valerie Lehr, Queer Family Values: Debunking the Myth of the Nuclear Family, Temple University Press, 1999, p. 10.

only make it possible for some sectors of sexual minorities—those economically better off—to enjoy such privileges while running the risk of reinforcing marginalization of other sectors. Liberation of LGBTQ persons lies in the possibility of de-constructing the normalization policies linked to essentializing identities, which represents a risk in those positions that uncritically privilege enacting civil rights legislation.

The *queer* theory calls for a more radical policy, a policy of transgression. Instead of claiming for incorporation into a heterosexual matrix of rights, the matrix itself should be changed to reflect the way in which heterosexuality is constructed as privileged. What must be achieved is a break with the naturalization/normalization of certain sexual and gender identities and to this end, it is indispensable to de-construct the ways in which sexuality has become institutionalized. The political strategy of this position with regard to the law is different. The different institutions that regulate the family, such as marriage, must be de-constructed instead of incorporating LGBTQ persons. In particular, denouncing the way in which these institutions strengthen heteronormativity and support "mandatory heterosexuality." The "assimilationist" theory strengthens the structural system of domination through the "normalization of the homosexual subject." While this normalization permits access to previously denied rights, at the same time it inscribes an ideal of respectability which establishes a difference between 'good' homosexuals and those who are 'bad' and not respectable; the latter should be excluded from the discourses on citizenship.[8] Law is one of the constructors and sustainers of heteronormativity as a system of domination: the legal discourse is an important place from which sexuality is regulated and the division between homo and hetero is sustained.[9] The essentialism, which generally goes side by side with the claim for rights for gays and lesbians, does not succeed in challenging the system of domination, since it runs the risk of falling into trends of normalization of the liberal legal discourse.[10] More than an emphasis on legal reforms, the *queer* theory privileges the political dimension that will enable them to denounce and overcome the existing dominance regime, particularly and foremost, through the deconstruction of heterosexuality.

Tension generated by an heterogeneity of stakeholders and by the different constructions of diagnoses and strategies is, in a certain way, irreducible, and beyond the position adopted, it is a constitutive element of the policies on sexuality in contemporary societies. A majority of LGBTQ persons need the law to recognize and protect their family arrangements on an equal level with heterosexual unions. However, in reality these kinds of demands run the risk of reinforcing family as an institution of social control; expanding its definition and incorporating, at least partially, "new" subjects (generally gays and lesbians) at the expense of reinforcing the

---

[8] *See* Carl F. Stychin, *Law's Desire: Sexuality and the Limits of Justice*, Routledge, New York, 1995.

[9] *Id.*

[10] *See* Lise Gotell, "*Queering* Law: Not by Vriend", *Canadian Journal of Law and Society*, Vol. 17, No. 1, 2002.

exclusion of others (transsexual, transgender and travestites). The law is a significant producer of subjectivities and identities and therefore, many of the 'advances' with regard to sexual diversity have an associated cost of institutionalizing strongly essentialized constructions of sexuality that entail the risk of reinforcing heteronormativity as a system of domination. That is, the core ambiguity of the law lies in the fact that while it can be an effective instrument against discrimination and in favor of recognition of sexual minorities (or at least some of them), it may also limit the possibilities of a more substantial change.[11] It is important to remember that the "fight" for new rights needs to be constantly vindicated as a political struggle in which the re-allocation of rights is only strategic, that is, by itself does not produce democratization.

7.2 Overcoming the Heteronormativity of the Judicial Reasoning

Undoubtedly, heteronormativity is still a prevailing system of domination, both at the cultural and legal level. This assemblage of moral, religious, and legal principles has also exerted an influence on the legal rationale so as to strengthen, in this way, heterosexuality as the regulating principle in family relationships. Judges are important stakeholders in the continuity marginalizing LGBTQ individuals. With the argument of defense of minors or of the family as a social institution, judicial decisions contribute, to a large degree, to the institutionalizing of the cultural system that constructs and naturalizes heterosexuality as the only possibility.

It may be that heteronormativity, although still powerful, has ceased to be a hegemonic system. The influence of the movement in favor of sexual diversity at the national and transnational levels has cracked heteronormative hegemony, allowing for the recognition of rights favorable to LGBTQ individuals and couples. This does not imply, of course, that such dominance has been dismantled. On the contrary, it was precisely the rupture of heteronormativity as a hegemonic regime that aroused the reaction of sectors opposed to pluralism. The retrocession of sexual and reproductive rights in the United States, or the strong reaction of Spain when same-sex marriages were allowed, are examples of the fact that sectors opposed to these reforms have re-politicized their position to oppose the demands of feminist movements and movements in favor of sexual diversity.[12] Considering specifically the situation in Latin America, this is a crucial moment. Though the movement in favor of sexual diversity has succeeded in inscribing a critical look on heteronormativity, the virulence of those sectors that defend a traditional family model and sexuality has intensified. On account of this, the

---

[11] L. Gotell, *op.cit.*

[12] *See* Juan Marco Vaggione "Reactive Politicization and Religious Dissidence. The Political Mutations of the Religious", *Social Theory and Practice,* Vol. 31, No. 2, April 2005.

partial successes that have been attained in Latin America in recent years concerning the rights of LGBTQ persons, many of which are analyzed in this section, more than ever require a re-creation of activism, since their validity is the result of a fluctuating balance of political forces.

This change in the validity of heteronormativity has also manifested itself in the judiciary. Although a majority of judges continue to institutionalize the heterosexual privileges, it is important to mention the existence of currents of judicial thought that are beginning to undermine these privileges. The existing jurisprudence in different Latin American countries is dynamic and heterogeneous. Different interpretations and positions construct sexuality in a plural way and thus move away from definitions that exclude sexual diversity. With the breakdown of some prejudices and making the unfair treatment by legal systems to LGBTQ persons visible, some sectors of the judiciary have become important actors in the improvement of sexual and reproductive rights. For this reason, to render visible and politicize the ideological folds of existing jurisprudence on sexuality, showing how judges have gradually recognized rights still resisted by the law to LGBTQ individuals and couples, is fundamental.

Judicialization has shown to be a successful strategy for activism in favor of sexual diversity. Legal reforms respond to the logic of agreements and majorities that are sometimes hard to deal with. The judiciary, instead, is in a position to incorporate and recognize the marginalization to which LGBTQ persons are exposed. In this way, it is increasingly frequent to come across votes of judges who, holding dissident positions, gradually legalize and legitimize sexual diversity as a constituting element of contemporary societies. Jurisprudence gradually endows LGBTQ individuals with diverse rights that blur the traditional boundaries of the law that regulates sexuality in Latin America. Many judicial cases analyzed in this section, have provided an important dynamism to the law.[13]

This next section presents part of the judicial arguments that have interrupted the status of heteronormativity as a hegemonic form. When the role of LGBTQ individuals in family relations is considered, it may be stated that the movement in favor of sexual diversity has managed to interrupt the hegemonic constructions in two specific situations. First , sexual diversity breaks with the traditional definition of couple as the union between a man and a woman and inscribes same-sex couples as a legitimate nucleus of contemporary families. Secondly, the concept of family is re defined based on making LGBTQ persons visible as fathers and mothers, re creating a new link between sexuality and reproduction.

[13] *See* Litardo, Emiliano, "Tensiones y conflictos entre los principales agrupamientos políticos GLTTTBI: Antecedentes y desarrollo" in, Gerlero, Mario (coord.) *Derecho a la Sexualidad*, Buenos Aires, 2009. David Grimberg and Campana, Maximiliano "¿Será Justicia? La cuestión del Matrimonio Igualitario en los Tribunales Cordobeses" in, Sgró Ruata et al., *El Debate sobre Matrimonio Igualitario en Córdoba,* Ferreyra Editor 2011.

7.3 Same-Sex Couples

One of the most politicized demands of the movement in favor of sexual diversity is the request for formal recognition of same-sex couples. Although in an initial stage the main activity was to avoid State intervention in the regulation of sexuality—main argument against the laws on sodomy or against the codes on cohabitation—, later on the movement began to demand that the State regulate and include within the legal system the situation of LGBTQ persons. Among the demands of incorporation, of assimilation, according to some, of the LGBTQ movement, the ability of same-sex couples to marry or to have legal recognition has become a political priority.

The debate on the formal recognition of same-sex couples has been characterized by the existence of positions that can hardly be reconciled. On the one hand, there are those who state that marriage is exclusively heterosexual and that any legal recognition of couples that diverge from this norm implies "denaturalizing" an institution that has been crucial for social order. Within this position, even recognition of same-sex couples without amending the marriage regime implies legitimizing situations which should be left outside State recognition. In the case of Latin America, the Catholic Church and its allied sectors are the main defenders of this position. From the Vatican and from the hierarchies of national churches, the recognition of rights to LGBTQ individuals and couples has turned into a central subject for political intervention.[14]

Another position sustains that restricting the recognition of sentimental arrangements exclusively to heterosexual couples is an injustice that is still present in most contemporary democracies. However, the discussion on gay marriage is a subject that manifests the striking ideological and programmatic differences within the movement in favor of sexual diversity. Recognition of same-sex couples is one of the issues that has propelled the most political actions and theoretical analyses. The different views and strategies on what legal and social change should be favored in order to effectively fight off existing exclusion, are added to the strong antagonism between sectors that are opposed to the recognition of any right to LGBTQ persons and those who mobilize and defend them.

For some, it is the marriage institution itself that should be criticized and overcome. The sectors closest to the *queer* theory oppose the consequences that gay marriage can bring to sexuality policies. To request incorporation in one of the most conservative social institutions is considered a contradiction and a depoliticization of the movement. Besides, such incorporation is only partial, since these types of reforms do not favor the wide diversity of sectors that make up the movement but benefits mainly middle class gays and lesbians. Marriage, according to this tendency,

---

[14] *See* Juan Marco Vaggione "Nuevas formas del activismo religioso. La Iglesia Católica frente al reconocimiento legal de las parejas del mismo sexo", *Orientaciones. Revista de Homosexualidades*. Fundación Triángulo, Madrid, Febrero 2006.

is a social institution conceived to regulate sexuality, and demand that sexual minorities be able to marry is to renounce the potential for social change that the movement in favor of sexual diversity has. To demand that the State incorporate same-sex couples in the marriage institution is somehow a way of conveying more power to the regulatory and control apparatus of the same State.[15]

The movement that rejects vindication of marriage for same-sex couples does not seek legal modifications that may allow for a greater inclusion of LGBTQ persons in heteronormative institutions, but instead seeks a political confrontation that permits eliminating the restraints on sexuality imposed by such institutions,[16] marriage being one of them. The aim must not be to incorporate these groups into marriage, but rather to deconstruct marriage as an institution of social and sexual control; deinstitutionalizing heterosexual marriage and reassigning the different benefits and rights that characterize it, such as social security, on the basis of other categories such as citizenship.[17] The movement in favor of sexual diversity should be more directed at breaking the hegemonic rules that regulate marriage than at achieving inclusion in them.[18]

Although habitually the *queer* theory is more linked to academic circles, those who identify with it also seek to exert an influence on policies and legislation on sexuality. An important contribution is that of constantly shifting the terms of the debate and expanding discussions on what is political as regards sexuality. More specifically, contributions of this theoretical perspective have been fundamental in understanding the definitions of "identity" and "power" that characterized the movement in favor of sexual diversity.

The activism of the movement in favor of sexual diversity in Latin America has turned, to a large extent, to introducing modifications in the legal systems in force, so as to achieve some level of recognition for same-sex couples. For an important sector of the movement, it is a priority to transform legislation currently in force, particularly family law, in order to incorporate equality for same-sex couples. For this sector, a more egalitarian society requires the incorporation of sexual minorities in the existing legal and cultural institutions. Marriage is one of these basic social institutions that is crossed by heteronormativity and that should be modified: the possibility that same-sex couples can marry is form of transformation.

Diverse justifications are used in favor of legal recognition of same-sex couples.[19] In general terms, the argument is that the exclusion of a group of persons from a basic social institution such as marriage, constitutes an illegitimate discrimination

---

[15] *See* Michael Warner, *The Trouble with Normal. Sex, Politics, and the Ethics of Queer Life*, The Free Press, New York, 1999.

[16] Valerie Lehr, *Queer Family Values: Debunking the Myth of the Nuclear Family*, Temple University Press, 1999.

[17] Nancy Fraser, "Rethinking Recognition", *The New Left Review*, May–June, 2000.

[18] Urvashi Vais, Virtual Equality: The Mainstreaming of Gay and Lesbian Liberation, Anchor/Doubleday, Nueva York, 1995.

[19] *See* R. Claire Snyder, *Gay Marriage and Democracy: Equality for All,* Rowman & Littlefield Publishers, Lanham, 2006 and Carlos A. Ball, *The Morality of Gay Rights: An Exploration in Political Philosophy,* Routledge, Nueva York, 2002.

in democratic regimes. Democracy as a system presupposes at least a formal process of making all citizens equal, for which reason the barriers that prevent some individuals, on account of their sexual identity, from exercising certain rights that correspond to all citizens must be lifted. To this general argument, a series of specific matters that bring to the forefront the consequences generated by non recognition of same-sex couples may be added. Due to the lack of legal recognition, members of these types of couples have difficulties in inheritance-related matters, the impossibility of settling in the partner's country of residence—on account of being a foreigner—, visiting rights in hospitals and prisons or leave of absence in at the workplace.

In some countries the movement in favor of sexual diversity has been successful, after decades of activism, in achieving some kind of legal recognition for same-sex couples. In general, there are two ways of incorporating this recognition in comparative law. One of them is the creation of a specific figure without substantially modifying family law: de facto unions, whether they homosexual or heterosexual, are recognized and granted certain rights, while marriage remains an exclusively heterosexual institution. For this reason, it is a more politically viable solution. Although some rights are recognized to same-sex couples upon their formalization as such, they are still excluded from other rights such as inheritance or adoption, which remain reserved to the heterosexual marriage regime. In 1989, Denmark became the first country to formally recognize same-sex couples, awarding them the same rights as those of heterosexual couples. Today, this type of recognition is often implemented through the creation of a registry system in which same-sex couples that expressly manifest their will to do so[20] may register, or through the recognition of certain rights after having cohabited for a period of time established by law, generally 1 or 2 years.[21]

The other form in which legal recognition is granted to same-sex couples implies a more substantial and symbolic modification of the definition of marriage. In some countries, family law is amended and the existence of opposite sex couples as a requirement to enter into marriage is repealed. This type of solution treats homosexual couples equally with heterosexual couples, which implies a much deeper legal and symbolic change than in the previous case. At the juridical level, instead of generating a parallel system of marriage for same-sex couples, family law is amended, repealing the requirement of heterosexuality, which, for many, is an essential

---

[20] Denmark (1989), Israel (1994), Hungry (1996) Hawaii, United States (1997), France (1998), California, United States (1999), Vermont, United States (2000), Germany (2001), Finland (2002), Zurich, Switzerland (2002), Croatia (2003), Luxemburg (2004), Tasmania, Australia (2004), Maine, United States (2004), New Jersey, United States (2004), United Kingdom (November de 2004), Andorra (2005), Río Grande del Sur, Brazil (2005), Connecticut, United States (October de 2005), New Zealand (December 2005), Czech Republic (2006), Colombia (2009), Coahuila de Zaragoza, Mexico City, Mexico (January 2007), Uruguay (November 2007), Ecuador (2008), Liechtenstein (2011), Brazil (2011), Illinois, United States (2011) (*See* http://ilga.org/ilga/en/index.html).

[21] Australia, Hungry (1996), Portugal (2001), New Zeeland (2002) y Croatia (2003). M. B. Dias, *op.cit.*

requisite. In 2001, the Netherlands was the first country to authorize marriage of same-sex couples. This total equality between heterosexual and homosexual marriage is currently in force in nine additional countries: Belgium (2003), Spain (2005), Canada (2005) South Africa (2006), Sweden (2009), Norway (2009), Portugal (2010), Iceland (2010) and Argentina (2010). It is also allowed in Mexico City (2010), and seven states of the United States.[22]

A precedent that had a strong impact in Latin America was the case of Spain, where in 2005, family law was amended, repealing the requirement of opposite sex spouses. Already in the 1990s some Spanish autonomous communities had formalized same-sex couples, but marriage legislation is of the exclusive competence of the Spanish State, so the communities were limited in this aspect. The Socialist Party (PSOE)[23] included the reform of the marriage regime in its electoral platform of 2004 and, once in office, this was one of the first modifications to be implemented, turning Spain into the third country in the world to adopt marriage of same-sex couples. The central focus of the amendment to article 44 of the Civil Code, consisted simply in the addition of a second paragraph. The final draft sustains that: "*Man and woman have the right to engage in marriage in conformity with the provisions of this Code. Marriage shall have the same requirements and effects when both spouses are of the same and of different sex.*" The rest of the changes to the law were changed to expressions containing "husband" and "wife" to "spouses" and of "father" and "mother" to "parents."

Judicial activism is an important strategy to expand legal recognition of same-sex couples, even though it may have varied results. In the United States in 1993, the Supreme Court of Hawaii considered that denying same-sex couples the right to marriage was discriminatory.[24] This judgment produced a strong reaction in that country and led to the adoption in 1996, of the *Defense of Marriage Act* (DOMA), according to which should a state legalize same-sex couples, the remaining states were not obliged to recognize such marriages, which in addition would not receive federal benefits. In South Africa, a different situation occurred; the legislative change equaling same and opposite sex couples in relation to the institution of marriage was propelled from the judiciary. In 2005, the South African Constitutional Court considered that the exclusion of same-sex couples from marriage was unfair, discriminatory, and that it damaged equality of rights. The Court gave the government a period of 12 months to reform family law, which was finally amended in November 2006, recognizing the right of same-sex couples to marry.

In Latin America, the strong influence of the Catholic Church added to the weaken democracy in various countries, is an important cause of the low degree of recognition of sexual and reproductive rights. In any case, in recent years, the movement in favor of sexual diversity has had greater impact, succeeding in including in

---

[22] Massachusetts, Connecticut, Iowa, Vermont, New Hampshire, Washington D.C. and New York (2011).

[23] Partido Socialista Obrero Español (PSOE).

[24] *Baehr v. Lewin*, 852 P.2d 44 (Haw. 1993).

the public agenda the demand for legal recognition of same-sex couples. In the different countries, it is frequent to encounter some LGBTQ group putting pressure to achieve family law reform and the visibility of the situation of same-sex couples. In general terms, it is possible to state that sexual diversity has achieved a greater level of acceptance on the part of the citizens and greater awareness within the political society, which allows to presume a future expansion of rights.

This activism has started to have an impact on the legal systems of the region, awarding recognition to same-sex couples. The first precedent was that of the city of Buenos Aires, Argentina, where at the end of 2002, civil unions were recognized and defined as "…the union freely constituted between two persons regardless of their sex or sexual orientation; (b) who have cohabited in a stable and public relationship of affection for a minimum period of 2 years, except where between the members there are common descendants."[25] This law awarded to civil unions a series of rights and opportunities such as the issuance of social security for the couple, maternity or bereavement leaves, and rights to a pension. All these rights were circumscribed to the jurisdiction of the city of Buenos Aires and were mostly applied to those who worked for the local government, since the reform did not involve family law, which would require approval by the legislative power at the national level. The road opened by the city of Buenos Aires was followed by the Province of Río Negro (2005) also in Argentina; the Brazilian state of Rio Grande do Sul (2004); and the Federal District (2006) and the State of Coahuila (2007), in Mexico.

Two reforms of the past 2 years which recognize *de facto* unions of same-sex couples are also worth highlighting. On the one hand, Ecuador reformed its constitution in 2008, recognizing that "[T]he stable and monogamous union between two persons free of the marriage bond who constitute a *de facto* home, and cohabitate for the period and in the conditions and circumstances provided in the law, shall generate the same rights and obligations awarded to families constituted through marriage." However, the article expressly denies same-sex couples the possibility of adoption. On the other hand, in 2009 Uruguay enacted Law 18.246, which defines the union of concubinage as "the *de facto* situation derived from the life in common of two persons—regardless of their sex, identity, orientation or sexual choice—who maintain a relationship of affection of a sexual nature, of exclusive, singular, stable and permanent temperament …."

Other legal changes in the marriage regime awarding the same status to same-sex and opposite-sex couples have also occurred in the region, although only in exceptional cases for the time being. At the end of 2009, the Legislative Assembly of the Federal District of Mexico amended its civil code and authorized marriage between same-sex couples. Some months later, a similar reform took place in Argentina (2010) when the requirement of opposite sexes for the celebration of marriage was excluded from the Civil Code. In the case of Mexico the reform has an impact in only one state, while in Argentina it extends nationally. Both cases

[25] Ley Unión Civil Nro. 1004, Ciudad Autónoma de Buenos Aires, Argentina.

constitute a pivotal moment with regard to sexual and reproductive rights, since they imply the deinstitutionalization of the requirement of heteronormativity from the marriage regime. They do not only grant legal recognition to same-sex couples but such recognition is bestowed through the institution of marriage, which in the region has been historically associated to a religious sacrament.

Latin American activism has also succeeded in producing an impact on jurisprudence, since there are judgments that recognize some type of legal effect on same-sex couples. Judicialization of cases is, additionally, a strategy of the movement in favor of sexual diversity, since it is a way of expanding the repertoire of rights. The legal gap is, in some cases, filled by the judiciary. More and more frequently, recognized NGO's become part of judicial processes, representing the interests of LGBTQ persons in diverse ways; two examples are Colombia Diversa and the Associação da Parada do Orgulho dos Gays, Lésbicas, Bissexuais e Transgêneros of São Paulo, which filed important lawsuits in Colombia and Brazil respectively. Additionally, in Argentina, in 2007, the LGBT Federation lodged a series of complaints requesting that the requirement of sex complementarily be declared unconstitutional; important precedents for the modification of the marriage regime referred to above. Civil society has an increasingly significant presence in the judicial ambit, in matters related to gender and sexuality, a fact that must be highlighted as an important democratizing force. Whether by means of legal reforms or through judicial cases, same-sex couples are gradually achieving legal recognition in the region, thanks to the activism of the movement in favor of sexual diversity. The legal culture has accompanied the changes in the population's attitude toward LGBT persons—the acceptance is greater.

Several judgments in the region have spoken in favor of same-sex couples, weakening the prevalence of heteronormativity as hegemonic system of domination. In spite of the fact that they do not modify the exclusion of the legal system, these rulings manage to formalize the affective/erotic arrangements of same-sex couples by recognizing them some specific effects. Even though, in general, the effects of these rulings are limited to the specific cases under consideration, they gradually contribute to the construction of a diverging judicial rationale that expands the legal constructions on sexuality; they shape the progressive thinking on sexuality in Latin America. The doctrine and jurisprudence are not homogeneous in matters related with (homo) sexuality. For this reason, it is important to note the existing fractures, and even though the law still generally sustains the privileges of heteronormativity, there are voices of judges that gradually construct a dissident opinion with more space for equality.

The judiciary has recognized, among others, economic, sexual, and migratory rights for same-sex couples. Though this does not disrupt the balance between homo and hetero, it does represent what the legal system denies. Different arguments are utilized to recognize rights to same-sex couples. They tend to be the tow most recurring analogies: on the one hand, existing norms of private law which regulate *de facto* societies, and on the other hand, there are norms that regulate marriage or on de facto heterosexual couples. The former allows recognizing rights, particularly property rights, to same-sex couples, while doing so from outside the law. The latter type of analogy, recognizes the bond of affection when legitimizing same-sex families as an alternative of family.

On the recognition of rights of same-sex couples by the judiciary, some countries stand out and constitute relevant precedents for the region. On the one hand, in recent years, the Colombian Constitutional Court has had a crucial role in expanding the rights of gays and lesbians, by recognizing property rights to same-sex couples (2007), permitting affiliation of same-sex couples to the health system and the pension system (2007), considering the duty/right to child support (2008) or the pension to the survivor (2008).[26] In particular, ruling C-029 of 2009, gave a judgment in favor of recognizing rights and duties of same-sex and opposite sex couples as equivalent (with the exception of marriage and adoption). In Brazil, after diverse judicial precedents, the Supreme Federal Court considered by majority vote that same-sex couples constitute stable unions and have rights similar to those of heterosexual marriages.

Although these two rulings, together with the Mexican Supreme Court of Justice which recognized the constitutionality of the marriage reform in the Federal District, are the most relevant, there are diverse judicial precedents that gradually fissured heteronormativity in several rulings. An example of this is the issuance of visas for permanent residence to the same-sex partner of a national. In Brazil, there are at least three known judicial cases of recognition of permanence visas in recent years.

Another type of situation in which rights have been recognized to same-sex couples is authorization for private visits in prisons. In general, penitentiary systems guarantee the inmates' exercise of their sexuality through authorized of visits from their partners, a right which is generally reserved to marriages and/or heterosexual couples. There have been cases that have expanded these rights to same-sex couples, for example, in Córdoba, Argentina.[27] In his ruling the judge sustained that:

> … the attorney general in an impeccable manner when interprets art. 167 of law 24660 noting that the said article 'guarantees the maintenance of intimate relations of the inmates with their spouse or in the absence of one with the person with whom they maintain a permanent marital life in the form determined by the regulations, in the understanding that the enumeration expressed in the norm is not limitative and consequently it is extendable to persons with a different sex choice or homosexual orientation, highlighting that the only limit to the exercise of a right in the prison ambit is based on the security of the premises, a matter that is not linked to the sexual activity of inmates nor to their sexual choice ….

Following this reasoning, the judge ordered the Penitentiary Service to

> … take the necessary measures aimed at implementing the mode of intimate visits in the homosexual pavilion in equal conditions as established for the rest of the prison population, leaving at its discretion the housing of interns, who are a couple, in separate cells when by applying this measure safeguards the internal order of the pavilion and benefits the general conduct of inmates ….

The greatest advances in judicial recognition of same-sex couples has occurred in matters of economic rights. In 1998 a judge in the province of Mendoza, Argentina, recognized a man who was in a homosexual relationship as a concubine to award

---

[26] C-075/07; C-336/07; C-811/08; C-798/08; T-856/07; T-856/07.

[27] Autos: X y otro. Juzg. Ejec. Penal Córdoba. 17-11-2005.

him social security benefits. Judge Graciela B. Mastracusa marks a difference between the family as a cultural construction and the family as a juridical construction, reaffirming the need to accept the pluralism that characterizes contemporary societies. Thus, the ruling stated the following:

> If the mutual material and affective help in the framework of cohabitation aimed at ensuring the validity of the fundamental rights of each member of the family group is what characterizes family life, from a functional point of view there cannot be, therefore, any difference between a marriage union and a heterosexual or homosexual de facto union…
>
> I consider that in this case there is no chance of excluding the petitioners in question from the characterization of cohabitants that convey to each other an ostensible familial treatment, since any difference originating in equality of sexes would mean a discrimination which is prohibited with respect to the same characterization bestowed on partners of heterosexual couples, given that, as it has been said, the law on social security has not contemplated extending the benefit to the cohabitant on account of the children, but quite on the contrary, with clear abstraction of the existence of the said children…
>
> Therefore, I rule that: Mr. A.A., … and Mr. C.C., … have accredited, in conformity with the proof produced in this case, that they are cohabitants, constituting a sexual couple with the characters of notoriety, singularity and permanence for more than four years, granting one another notorious familiar treatment.

In Argentina, in 1999, a property dispute was settled due to the passing away of one of the members of a homosexual couple, was settled in Argentina. The dispute arose between the surviving member of the couple and the heirs of the dead partner. In her ruling, the judge stated that the dispute can be settled "applying the juridical principles which have allowed to reach a settlement of disputes between de facto heterosexual couples, because differences between homosexual and heterosexual de facto unions that justify an unequal juridical treatment as related to the right to marry, to adopt, access to assisted fertilization and filiation … do not exist in conflicts strictly related to property that may arise upon termination of the union."[28]

Brazil too, has made important advances in case law, where property rights have been recognized to same-sex couples.

The following judicial case is that of the Constitutional Court of Colombia which held, in 2007, that the definition of "*de facto* couples" restricted only to the union between men and women, infringes upon human dignity by discriminating against couples made up of persons of the same sex.[29]

7.3.1 Property Regime of Homosexual Couples. The Policies of Dignity

What are the remedies and the arguments that must be applied to promote the legal changes necessary to democratize societies and improve the situation of LGBTQ persons and couples? In the face of these kinds of questions, diverse answers and

---

[28] Autos: "D., J. A. v. V., V. E. y otro"- Tribunal: C. Civ. y Com. San Isidro, sala 1ª. 22/06/1999.

[29] Ruling C- 075, 2007, Constitutional Court of Colombia.

even opposing views are generated. Not only are there different co-existing ways of defining heteronormativity as a system of domination, but there are also different roads to overcome exclusion. This debate cuts across policies on sexuality, causing a continuous re-formulation of the best strategies for action. That which for some sectors represents a step forward—the incorporation of LGBTQ persons in institutions such as marriage—for others, is a strengthening of heteronormativity as a system of domination.

The injustice to which LGBTQ individuals and couples are subject to is rooted in the social subordination in which a sector of the population is immersed on account of the sexual and gender identity of its members; identities which break with the heteronormative matrix. This injustice is derived from the lack of recognition,[30] which is institutionalized both at a cultural and at a legal level, depriving those citizens of their rights and depreciating their existence. The fight of the movement for sexual diversity is, among other things, a struggle for this recognition which is denied on account of the existence of a specific system of domination that prevents a group of citizens from participating in social life as equals. Following this logic, the exclusion of same-sex couples from marriage laws has been considered an example of this lack of recognition that is institutionalized at the legislative level.

The right to equality, regardless of sexual orientation or gender identity, is in opposition to the existence of legislation that denies certain persons the possibility to legally formalize their relationship as a couple. A strategy used to deinstitutionalize heteronormativity of the legal system is the notion of dignity of the human person. In the face of a system that deprives a sector of the citizenship of certain rights on account of their sexual or gender identity, the discourse on the dignity of persons may be used as a legal argument to demand recognition of rights of LGBTQ persons. Precisely, the modern notion of dignity is the result of the "collapse of social hierarchies, which used to be the bases of honor." In this way, dignity serves as an egalitarian and universal discourse, with its benefits and risks: in their capacity as citizens, people have a dignity that should be respected and protected. A democratic culture implies, then, respect for equal recognition of its members, a recognition that, thanks to the feminist movements and movements in favor of sexual diversity, also involves sexual and gender identity.

Below, is the holding of the Constitutional Court of Colombia in which the concept of "dignity" plays a central role in the discussion of the effects of same-sex couples, presented for an in-depth analysis.

Constitutional Court of Colombia
Holding C-075 of 2007

Main Legal Issue:

Does the property regime established for permanent partners, limited to unions between a man and a woman, infringe upon the respect for human dignity and equal

[30] *See* Nancy Fraser, Justice Interruptus. Critical Reflections on the "Postsocialist Condition", New York, Routledge, 1997.

protection, free development of the personality, and the prohibition of discrimination based on sexual orientation, all fundamental rights enshrined in the Political Constitution?

Facts:
Citizens Marcela Sánchez Buitrago, Luz María Mercado Bernal, Alejandra Azuero Quijano and Daniel Bonilla Maldonado, while filing a public legal action of unconstitutionality, partially challenged articles 1 and 2 of Law 54 of 1990 "which defines de facto marital unions and the property regime between permanent partners," partially amended by Law 979 of 2005.

Court Ruling:
The Court declares the enforceability of Law 54 of 1990, as amended by Law 979 of 2005, on condition that the protection regime contained therein be understood to apply also to homosexual couples.

Extracts:
[...]
In the situation now under consideration by the Court, the law, when regulating the so-called "*de facto marital union*," establishes a property protection regime for members of heterosexual couples, but does not do the same with homosexual couples. In principle, it should be noted that the way in which property protection may be given to those who have decided to form a couple as a permanent and singular life project lies within the ambit of legislative configuration, because there is no unique formula that is mandatory under the Constitution to this effect and the required protection may be obtained in different ways. However, the Court notes that the said ambit of legislative configuration is limited by the Constitution and by respect for the fundamental rights of persons. In this scenario, in the Court's opinion, the absence of protection concerning property for homosexual couples is damaging to the person's dignity, contrary to law, to the free development of the personality, and entails a form of discrimination banned by the Constitution.

[...]

As concerns the person's dignity and the free development of the personality, the Court highlights the relevance that the juridical recognition of economic relations, which on account of the nature of things arise between those who opt for cohabitating as a couple, has in terms of the possibility of carrying out a life project in common under conditions of dignity.

[...]

In the ambit of the problem that must now be resolved by the Court, it is clear that the lack of legal recognition of the reality comprised by homosexual couples infringes upon the dignity of its members because it damages their autonomy and capacity for self-determination when preventing their decision to carry out a common life produce juridical effects on property, which means that, under the civil law regime in force, they remain in a situation of helplessness that they are not capable of facing. There is no reason to justify that homosexual couples be subjected to a regime which is incompatible with the life option they have chosen while exercising the right to free development of the personality, nor is it acceptable that the legislative decision of establishing a regime to regulate the property situation between permanent partners, be indifferent to events of helplessness which may result from it when homosexual couples are involved.

In this way, a minimum protection which is mandated by the Constitution may be identified in this case, because the absence of a legal regime which in matters of property applies specifically to homosexual couples, implies that members of such couples must abide by the provisions of an ordinary civil law regime, which limits their autonomy to self-regulate the patrimonial consequences of their decision to live together as a couple and leaves the property dimension of that decision in a juridical limbo, with potentially damaging consequences in the event of termination of cohabitation. That is to say, the protection deficit alluded to is derived from the existence of an imperative regulation on disposal of property for members of a couple, which does not take into account their own reality; from the impossibility of voluntarily acceding to a regulation regime if it is not through non specific and highly cumbersome procedures, and of the potentially damaging consequences that the above-mentioned circumstances may have for the members of the couple. In other words, the legislative decision of not including homosexual couples in the property regime foreseen for *de facto* marital unions, implies an unjustified restriction to the autonomy of members of such couples and may have damaging effects, not only inasmuch as they hinder the realization of their life project in common, but because it does not provide an appropriate answer to situations of conflict which may arise when cohabitation ceases for any reason.

This absence of legislative provision is also manifest in the second dimension in which, according to case law, the dignity of the person is expressed on account of the consequences that the loss of that to which she/he is entitled may have for a person at the material level concerning the property acquired in a joint manner during a relationship as a couple and that may affect their material conditions of existence. The negative effect on dignity, finally, also emerges in a direct way from the absence of legal recognition of the persons' life options. In this case, this happens because the reality of homosexual couples and their members is not recognized and is invisible to the legal system, given that, in spite of the fact that these persons have acted while exercising an option protected by the Constitution, they are ignored by the legal system at the time of resolving the property conflicts that may arise from such decision.

In the light of the criteria mentioned above and without ignoring the ambit of legislative configuration for the adoption of the modalities of protection that are most appropriate to fulfill the requirements of the different social groups, in a democratic and participatory process, the Court finds that to foresee a legal regime that exclusively provides for the protection of heterosexual couples is contrary to the Constitution and consequently, the enforceability of Law 54 of 1990 as amended by Law 979 of 2005 shall be declared, in the understanding that the protection regime contained therein also applies to homosexual couples.

This means that the homosexual couple that complies with the conditions contained in the law for *de facto* marital unions, that is, the existence of a singular and permanent life community, maintained for a period of time of at least two years, shall have access to the protection regime provided for therein, so that the couple shall be covered by the presumption of community property and its members may, individually or jointly, resort to any of the means provided for in the law to establish such a community whenever they deem it necessary.

Dissenting opinion of Justice Jaime Araujo Rentería
Human dignity and the full recognition of rights

The concept of human dignity, elaborated fundamentally by Emmanuel Kant, alludes to that which is inherent in the human being which makes him such, that is, which turns him into a moral subject; it is that which is priceless, namely, that whose exchange value cannot be predicted inasmuch as it is invaluable, inalienable, it cannot be waived and it allows us to characterize ourselves as human beings with rights. On the other hand, recognition of human dignity must be total and complete, it cannot be half dignified. Along this line of thought, if human dignity is recognized to homosexuals, if they are as worthy of dignity as heterosexuals, all rights must be necessarily recognized to them. The necessary outcome of the recognition of human dignity is the recognition of all rights; this is the classic argumentation of human rights from the time of the liberal Kantian tradition to our days.

For this reason, the fact that homosexual persons are recognized the right to dignity and immediately afterward are denied the recognition of basic rights that are necessary for their development as autonomous, free and equal subjects, such as marriage, adoption, labor rights, pensions, to mention only some, is not easy to understand.

In my opinion, existing jurisprudence … of this Court in relation to the rights of homosexual persons, in the individual ambit, for the development of the personality, human dignity, and equality, become ineffectual and have no real effects, since it does not touch the sphere of the couple, which has direct relation with the essential nucleus of freedom and of free development of the personality, since it is a fundamental aspect that makes the freedom and autonomy of the individual real and effective, through the right to freedom of free sexual options and free choice and development of a life plan or project in the company of the love mate or sex partner.

Therefore, I consider that people cannot be so incoherent and recognize human dignity to homosexuals on the one hand, and on the other, deny them their rights and restrict them. Either recognize that homosexuals have human dignity and are therefore free and equal, and consequently all the rights inherent in this condition are recognized to them in their capacity as human beings endowed with dignity; or the dilatory game of recognizing, a partial dignity that does not imply the necessary recognition of rights and which leads to a logic contradiction, is uncovered.

Consequently, in my view, the central issue at stake in this case is whether the recognition of dignity and therefore of equal rights should be partial or whether full rights should be recognized, in conformity with the idea of human dignity and the principle of equality.

In the debate that arose, for instance, on marriage of homosexual couples, there are difficult matters, but I consider that a clear differentiation should be made between the religious conception of a certain marriage form and the recognition of lay marriage or marriage of homosexual couples with all the legal effects, and for this reason the heterosexual and, in addition, religious marriage cannot be considered superior to the lay homosexual forms. Likewise, the treatment given to *de facto* unions in a State based on the rule of law must be equal, with the same effects and the same juridical consequences.

In summary, I state that in a Constitutional State based on the rule of law the first among all principles is that of human dignity and among all rights the right to equality on a par with the right to freedom. I therefore reiterate my formula that equality of homosexual couples be recognized in all spheres: civil, labor, penal, social benefits, family, migratory, and so on, as a consequence of the recognition of human dignity in these persons.

To present it in a graphic way: I claim that if today we had a group of persons enslaved and chained with 30 chains, and if we take one of the 30 chains off these slaves, they will still be chained by 29 chains, so that they will still remain equally slaves and we have not managed to progress at all. We can even take off 29 chains, but if we leave only one, we keep them enslaved, so that we cannot assume that we have made any progress. In this way, I affirm that the only way of re-establishing liberty and equality of non heterosexual couples is by taking away ALL the 30 chains, so that they are really and truly free and equal.

In conclusion, I argue that the only way to protect the fundamental rights enshrined in the Constitution is to grant ALL the rights and in a complete way, as well as to all persons, without distinctions, in this case, regarding their sexual preferences. I consider that we do not really protect the rights, and we do them no favor, when we protect partially, and halfway, which in my opinion is what happened in the case of this judgment, because they were not awarded all the civil rights and much less the other rights, such as labor rights, pension rights, penal rights, etc.

7.3.1.1 Matters for Debate

This holding of the Colombian Court constitutes a leading case with regard to rights of same-sex couples in Latin America. The holding considers that their exclusion from the property regime established for heterosexual couples is contrary to the Political Constitution. Both the majority and the minority vote propose arguments against the discrimination implied by this exclusion based on the principle of human dignity. The majority's legal reasoning sustains that the exclusion of homosexual couples from certain legal effects infringes upon the principle of human dignity, since it "limits the possibility of these persons of having a life plan and develop freely." The complaint proposed three dimension to defend the right of homosexual couples to a life with dignity based on three dimensions: "… in the first place, the possibility of living as each person wants, without interfering in the orbit of other persons' rights, so that each person may choose the life plan he/she prefers; secondly, the possibility of living well, that is, of having access to certain material conditions of existence, and lastly, the possibility of living without being humiliated, which implies preserving physical and moral integrity."

However, the dissenting opinion pushes the interpretation of the principle of dignity further than has already been done by those sharing the majority vote, sustaining that the partial granting of rights is a partial recognition of the dignity of the human person. It is possible to note, in the dissenting opinion, the limitations and potentialities that general principles like that of dignity of the human person may have in relation to rights of LGBTQ persons.

7.4 Queer Paternities and Maternities

Another way in which sexual diversity challenges the traditional definition of family is by questioning heterosexuality as a rule in the exercise of paternity and maternity. Heteronormativity, as a power structure, is based on the assumption that biological, moral and legal capabilities for being fathers and mothers reside as a rule in heterosexual couples. LGBTQ persons remain outside these bonds and their claim for having equal rights as parents generates adverse reactions.

It may be said that legitimating *queer* paternities and maternities is more problematic than the recognition of same-sex couples. The presence of minors boosts the social prejudice and justifies the State's intervention to avoid and/or restrict the performance of LGBTQ persons as fathers and mothers. Even part of the sectors that are in favor of legally recognizing same-sex couples do not agree, for example, with giving minors in adoption to these couples. Although they accept the decision of LGBTQ persons of living their sexuality, they place obstacles to allowing them to establish, with the same freedom, filiation bonds. This situation is evident in countries that despite having enacted progressive legislation recognizing same-sex couples, limit the right of these to adopt.

If same-sex couples challenge the hegemonic constructions, deepening the separation between sexuality and reproduction, paternity/maternity of LGBTQ persons re-inscribe a link between sexuality and reproduction from dissenting places. Persons and couples whose sexuality is assumed to be non reproductive reproduce. Adoption, artificial insemination, intervention of third parties, previous partners, etc., are some of the forms utilized to re-define reproduction from an "impossible" place. The presence of non-heterosexual men and women with children produces "mothers" and "fathers" where procreative incapacity should reign. These situations are inevitably political, since they contradict the basic principles on which the family as an institution for reproduction rests.

The greater visibility of LGBTQ persons and their demands have also led to a greater presence of their roles as fathers and mothers. Transvestites, transgender persons, lesbians and gays, alone or in couples, mobilize to claim legal and cultural recognition—sometimes only protection—as parents. The existence of *queer* families is not a novelty, and, for decades, in many ways, LGBTQ persons have gradually built alternative affection arrangements in which the presence of children is not surprising. What is novel, however, is the politicization of these arrangements and that they seek incorporation as a legitimate alternative. LGBTQ persons want recognition of their rights as fathers and mothers, an aspiration that involves legal, moral, religious, cultural, and scientific dimensions, among others.

The early 1970s in the United States were a crucial moment in the visibilization and political defense of LGBTQ fathers and mothers. This defense was due largely to the mobilization of lesbians who in the women's movement and in the movement in favor of sexual diversity included the possibility of retaining custody of their biological children once divorced. The first organization by civil society, at least in the United States, to politicize this subject was the *Lesbian Mothers National Defense Fund* (LMNDF), created in 1974 in Seattle, W.A., to deal with legal matters of lesbian mothers.[31] Gradually, the subject of paternity and maternity, and rights associated to them, started to occupy a prominent space among the demands of the movement in favor of sexual diversity.

Also in this decade, journalistic articles discussing the situation of homosexual fathers and mothers started to appear in academic and news media. During those years, in the U.S., the subject started to be discussed in the mass media and academic analyses considering the situation of discrimination affecting mainly women with children began to appear. One of these antecedents is Phyllis Lyon and Del Martin's book *Lesbian/Woman* (1972), which included a chapter on lesbian mothers. Both the journalistic and the academic articles aimed at making visible the existence of these fathers and mothers, as well as the marginality that they were subject to. They also registered, publicly, arguments affirming that there were no differences between their roles as father and mothers of LGBTQ persons or couples as compared to heterosexuals.

During the past few years, both the number of organizations and of researches in favor of recognizing rights of LGBTQ fathers and mothers have increased. Together with the growth and transnationalization of the movement in favor of sexual diversity, the demands to modify the legal barriers that complicate the effective exercise of rights have also been globalized. After decades of activism, the movement has succeeded in progressing considerably in the recognition of *queer* parenthood rights. Several countries have modified their legislations and jurisprudence to take into account, although partially, filiation rights of LGBTQ persons and couples. What some decades ago were invisible situations, now, have turned into a significant political dimension in contemporary democratic societies.

In particular, there are two situations that have received greater attention in terms of legal and judicial regulations on LGBTQ persons: the possibility of adopting minors and the guardianship/custody of children. Even though these situations place

---

[31] *See* Nancy Polikoff "Raising Children: Lesbian and Gay Parents Face the Public and the Courts" in John D'Emilio, William B. Turner, Urvashi Vaid, eds., *Creating Change. Sexuality, public policy, and civil rights,* St. Martin's, New York, 2000. "Pushed by lesbian activists, nondiscrimination in custody determinations became a plank of the Plan of Action adopted at the federally sponsored 1977 National's Conference in Houston and one of the three principal demands of the first national gay rights march, held in Washington, D.C., in 1979. At that March the first national gay father's group, Gay Fathers Coalition, was formed, primarily as a support network and a convener of annual conferences, rather than as a legal advocacy and defense fund as was LMNDF" (308).

diverse elements at stake, it discusses both the subjects of sexuality as a limiting factor, or not, when raising children. Debates that arise in relation to these situations highlight different legal, and extralegal, constructions on sexuality. In the case of adoption, the discussion is about whether LGBTQ persons should be authorized to be fathers and/or mothers, by recognizing them the right to adopt. Instead, in cases of guardianship-custody, one faces the existence of LGBTQ persons who are already fathers and/or mothers; the discussion turns on whether, on account of their sexual identity, their rights, such as the right to exercise child custody, as compared to heterosexuals, should be limited.

7.4.1 Adoption

Whether because of the impossibility to have biological children, or for the election to have them through adoption, adoption is a frequently utilized process. Not only does it make possible for people, who wish to do so, to fulfill themselves as parents, but it also provides minors who cannot be brought up for different reasons by their biological parents with a home. Even though any person or couple can have access to the care and education of minors, formally recognized adoption by the State awards a series of rights and protections, both to the parents and to the minors, which mere custody does not grant. The State establishes requisites to persons or couples interested in adopting, such as minimum age of the adopter, age difference between adopter and adoptee, socio-economic possibilities, and moral values, among others. These requisites are used to guarantee to the minor certain conditions in the home where the said minor shall be placed, as part of the adoption process. In particular, the requisite of moral values opens the way to act in a discretionary manner. Heteronormativity, considers LGBTQ persons as not apt, since adoption is exclusively defined as heterosexual. With the aim of breaking this interpretation, the movement in favor of sexual diversity has included the right of LGBTQ persons to adopt among their demands.

This right has become one of the most controversial subjects; there are religious, moral, medical, psychological, and legal positions that reject the possibility of LGBTQ persons being legally capable of adopting. Adoption has become, for some, a limit that cannot be crossed in the process of recognition of rights to LGBTQ persons. Moral values are, precisely, the requirement utilized to deny LGBTQ persons the right to adopt, because only heterosexual persons are assumed to meet the requirements to become adoptive fathers or mothers. In the face of the gradual recognition of rights in diverse areas, the possibility of recognizing the right of adoption to LGBTQ persons and couples is one of the most resisted matters.

The adverse reactions generated by adoptions from LGBTQ persons not only appears in those sectors that oppose sexual and reproductive rights in general, but also among those that have a broader and more open position in this area. Within the former, the Catholic Church is the main stakeholder, mobilizing diverse resources to avoid adoption by non heterosexuals. In 2003, the Congregation for the Doctrine of the Faith, whose prefect was at that time the current Pope, elaborated a document in which it expressly pronounces itself against adoption by same-sex couples.[32] Adoption of children by homosexuals is pointed out not only as an immoral practice contrary to the Convention on the Rights of the Child, but also as an act of violence toward the minors. This document considers that "the absence of sexual complementarity in these unions creates obstacles in the normal development of children who would be placed in the care of such persons."[33]

The fact that the Church and its allied sectors oppose recognition of sexual rights is not surprising, but the resistance to adoption by LGBTQ persons is also found in sectors that support other types of claims of the movement in favor of sexual diversity. There are sectors that, in spite of accepting formal recognition of same-sex couples, oppose that they be allowed to adopt. In Europe, for example, the population that opposes adoption by LGBTQ persons is more numerous than that against same-sex marriage.[34] For this reason, there are countries where although same-sex couples are legal, they are not authorized to adopt. This is the situation in France, where, same-sex couples were recognized but were expressly denied the possibility of adoption.

When considering the possibility of adoption by LGBTQ persons in a specific way, it is presented under different circumstances. The most resisted situation from the legal point of view, is joint adoption by cohabiting same-sex couples. The legislation generally requires that the persons who adopt jointly be married and, because the marriage regime excludes same-sex couples, for them, adoption is impossible. There are, however, legislations that allow same-sex couples to adopt. The first country to authorize this was the Netherlands in the year 2001, establishing the same requirements for adoption by homosexual and heterosexual couples when the children are of Dutch nationality. In 2002, England followed, permitting adoption by same-sex couples. In 2003, Sweden granted homosexual couples the right to adopt children, but unlike the Netherlands, it permitted adoption of foreign children. In South Africa, in 2002, the Constitutional Court decided that same-sex couples have the right to adopt minors and the laws that prohibit this infringe upon the constitutional principles.[35] The *Civil Union Act,* was enacted in 2006, placing the rights of same-sex couples on legal par with those of heterosexual couples. The case of Spain is significant, considering that it shares with the rest of Latin America the historic presence of the Catholic Church, whose political weight obstructs any reform linked with gender and/or sexuality. However, as previously stated, family law was reformed in 2005, granting equal rights to homo and heterosexual couples, a reform that also comprised the possibility of adoption.

---

[32] Congregation for the Doctrine of Faith "Considerations Regarding Proposals to Give Legal Recognition to Unions Between Homosexual Persons".

[33] *Id.*

[34] "Public Opinion in the European Union" Eurobarometer 66, December 2006, European Commission. http://ec.europa.eu/public_opinion/archives/eb/eb66/eb66_en.pdf

[35] *Du Toit and another v. Minister of Welfare and Population Development and others,* September 10, 2002 (Same-Sex Couple Adoption).

Another legal assumption that may permit adoption by LGBTQ persons is the possibility known as *second-parent adoption* or adoption of the son/daughter of the homosexual cohabitant. There is a group of countries that permit the homosexual partner of a person who has a biological child, or even an adopted one, to in turn adopt that same minor. Denmark, Germany, Iceland, and Norway are some of the countries that recognize this legal possibility. In the U.S., several states expressly authorize *second-parent adoption*: California, Connecticut, Massachusetts, New York, and Washington D.C., among others.

Finally, the other assumption of adoption is when it is carried out by an individual LGBTQ person. In general, legal systems do not expressly exclude LGBTQ persons from adopting individually, for which reason it is a more widespread possibility than those mentioned above. However, in many countries this is a possibility because the sexual identity of the individual is invisible. If identity is expressed outwardly, the request for adoption may be rejected based on the child's best interest. A case that illustrates this is "Fretté v. France,"[36] in which the European Court of Human Rights, in a divided ruling, held that the dismissal on account of his homosexuality of Philippe Fretté's application to become an adoptive father was reasonable, objective and non discriminatory.[37]

In Latin America, joint adoption by same-sex couples has occurred exceptionally. In Uruguay in 2009 and in Argentina in 2010, legal reforms authorized adoption by same-sex couples. The former, due to enactment of an adoption law, while the latter, through the reform of the abovementioned marriage regime. If LGBTQ persons have the possibility to adopt, it is because the manifest unexpressed prohibition, or because heterosexuality is not a specific requisite, allows for adoption as an individual, not a couple.

However, the region's jurisprudence shows some progress. In Brazil, a resounding case was the authorization, in 2002, by Rio de Janeiro judge that awarded guardianship of her partner's son to a lesbian woman upon the death of the former. Another noteworthy Brazilian case occurred in 2006, when the adoption of a minor was granted to a male couple. The girl was first adopted by one of the two men and later, the request for adoption was extended to his partner. Finally, the most important Brazilian resolution was issued in 2010, when the Supreme Court of Justice of Brazil recognized the right to adoption by same-sex couples. These cases represent important landmarks with regard to the reformulation of the rules that regulate adoption and also to the way in which the family is built in contemporary societies. Though they respond to the concrete situations that originated these decisions, these are legal processes that gradually fracture the hegemonic judicial rationale that denies same-sex couples the possibility to adopt.

The situation of transsexuals is much more precarious than that of the rest of the collective of sexual diversity. As previously stated, transsexuals have no guarantees on their basic rights of citizenship and their legal situation is, in general, much more

[36] Fretté v. France (36515/97), European Court of Human Rights.

[37] *Id.*

infringed upon. In the case of transvestites, for example, the police and social violence to which they are subject to, because of their gender expression, has been profusely documented.[38] Although exceptionally and temporarily, there have been some advances in case law regarding the potential of adoption by transvestites. For example, in 2003, the National Childhood Trust of Costa Rica granted Mairena, a transvestite, "provisional guardianship" of a 9-year-old boy whom she had looked after since he was a baby. Provisional guardianship is the first step to obtain legal adoption. The Trust considered that Mairena "… had provided food, care, protection, surveillance, child-raising, education, assistance, recreation, health care, clothing, housing, affection and had satisfied other needs that, today, are rights, assuming the role of a good family father." In 2006, a judge of the juvenile court of Río Cuarto, Argentina, awarded provisional custody of two minors to a transvestite, though clarifying that this did not imply the initiation of an adoption process. During a journalistic interview, the magistrate stated that his main fear was that the custody provoke rejection among the neighbors and alter the calm environment that small children need, but the opposite happened: "I was expecting a blow on account of prejudice, but people ended up expressing their support."[39] Finally, in 2010, definite custody was confirmed, and the transvestite was able to initiate the adoption procedure.[40]

But undoubtedly, heteronormativity continues to be a central structure at the time of deciding if LGBTQ persons meet the requirements to adopt minors. Faced with the advances of the movement in favor of sexual diversity, the judicial heteronormative rationale has become more sophisticated, and even though LGBTQ persons are still being excluded based on evidently homophobic justifications—essential incompatibility between homosexuality and being a father or a mother—, it is not uncommon that they be excluded due to another series of motivations. The growing awareness, in terms of non discrimination or tolerance, which has been achieved through activism, does not necessarily imply a more plural judicial rationale that will confer legality to LGBTQ persons as adopting individuals. In diverse judicial cases sexuality is not utilized as the main argument, to justify rejecting adoption by LGBTQ persons.

For example, in 1995, in the Constitutional Court of Colombia, plaintiff, José Gerardo Córdoba, alleged that his homosexuality was the sole factor that the Colombian Institute for Family Welfare (I.C.B.F. Spanish acronym) took into account to declare the girl was in danger and award her custody to third parties.[41] The Court sustained, however, that "it is evident that the I.C.B.F. had sufficient objective reasons to dictate the measures of protection that it considered necessary in favor of the

---

[38] Lohana Berkins and Josefina Fernandez. *La gesta del nombre propio. Informe sobre la situación de la comunidad travesti en la Argentina*. Ediciones Madres de Plaza de Mayo, Buenos Aires, 2005.

[39] *El Puntal Río Cuarto*, Córdoba, Argentina. Aug. 4, 2007 www.diariopuntal.com.ar/imprimir_noticia.php?id=5067

[40] *See* http://www.lavoz.com.ar/content/otorgan-guarda-definitiva-de-dos-ninos-una-travesti-en-rio-cuarto-0

[41] Constitutional Court of Colombia, Ruling T-290 of 1995.

minor xx, and that its ruling was not arbitrary, nor was it due to a prejudice of its officials with respect to Mr. Córdoba's sexuality."[42] The objective reasons cited had to do with the size of the house, its location, and the drunkenness of the "plaintiff's friend or partner." Nevertheless, what is particularly noteworthy about this judgment is the ruling's explanation, which evidences the complex role that sexuality plays in the judicial rationale and, at the same time, stating in a dissident manner, that homosexuality cannot be the reason to prevent a person from adopting.

It may be said that in the ruling's explanation, Justice Carlos Gaviria Díaz provided proof of the Court's implicit heteronormative rationale. In spite of the fact that the decision was based on a series of motivations which are not related with sexual identity, one version of the judgment expressly stated that "denying a person the possibility of adopting or caring for a child, for the sole reason of the person being a homosexual, would certainly constitute a discriminatory act infringing on the principles that inspire our Constitution." However, some of the justices decided to exclude this clarification, which did not eventually form part of the final ruling. For this reason, Justice Gaviria Díaz decided to clearly state his position on the ruling's explanation:

> The undersigned deems it necessary to make explicit, with all clarity, that these words synthesize his thought on the matter in an unequivocal way. Homosexuality is not in itself a moral burden, for a person's honest or deviant behavior has nothing to do with their sexual preferences.
>
> In the referred case, the plaintiff lodges a complaint against the resolution of Family Welfare, precisely because he felt discriminated on account of his homosexuality. I think that it was the Court's duty not only to expose the reasons of another kind justifying the decision, but to record, without the slightest hesitation, that the ethical behavior of a person has nothing to do with their romantic preferences, and that it is this behavior and not these latter preferences that should be evaluated at the time of deciding whether an adult is or is not competent to educate a child.

In subjects related to sexuality the dissidences, clarifications, and provisos are important instruments. It is very common to find that the most favorable elaborations in favor of LGBTQ persons have given expression to them. These dissidences, even though they may not form part of the majority decision, push the limits of the interpretations beyond what has been agreed, contributing important lines of judicial rationale that remain blurred in the transcendence of the majority vote. The following cases are clear examples of how the progressive judicial rationale is gradually incorporated into minority votes.

7.4.1.1 The Policies of Naturalization of the Family

A fundamental dimension that is disputed at the moment of discussing the rights of adoption by LGBTQ persons and couples, is the definition of family. What are the

---

[42] Id.

bonds that the State must legitimize and protect as a part of family arrangements? Different answers to this question characterize most debates, alliances and conflicts in contemporary democracies. As correctly pointed out by Isabel Jaramillo, "the place occupied by the family in contemporary political thought is the result of an intense battle, rooted in the nineteenth century, between liberals, socialists, and conservatives, around how to administer in the best possible way the needs regarding the regulation of sexuality, population control, and economic survival."[43] Currently, a central line of antagonism arises between those who defend the family as the only reality versus those who consider that there is a pluralism that must be recognized. Pluralism that is not only the factual co-existence of different family arrangements but, mainly, that these arrangements deserve equal legality and legitimacy.

The discussion on the rights of LGBTQ persons as fathers and mothers is part of the debate on families in contemporary societies. Both sides of this debate articulate different definitions of the family that bring forth arguments supporting opposite positions concerning LGBTQ persons. For one sector, recognizing rights is a direct attack on the family as a basic social institution. Filiation is essentially a bond of heterosexuals, and to grant equality of rights to LGBTQ persons is to break the symbolic and social order on which the family rests. For the opposing sector the family is, a historic and cultural construction. Legitimating LGBTQ persons as fathers or mothers is simply recognition of the plural and diverse nature of family arrangements in contemporary societies. The demand for these rights is a demand for a fairer and more democratic society.

The judicial power is an important stakeholder in this dispute, because judges have the authority to "legitimize" one definition of family or another, and therefore, to recognize, or not the rights of LGBTQ persons. Judges impose identities that have symbolic and practical consequences. The type of family recognized by law has a legitimacy that sets it up as the rule against which other family arrangements are measured. Deciding that homosexuality is limiting to the exercise of paternity or maternity not only has consequences at a symbolic level, reinforcing the heteronormativity, but it has also practical consequences on the persons whose concrete exercise of certain rights is limited.

The case summaries presented below reflect the different and often opposing ways in which, from the judicial rationale, the family is defined to justify different solutions regarding the rights of LGBTQ persons. Both are rulings of the Constitutional Court of Colombia; one debates the ways of defining the family in a case directly related to adoption, while the second judgment is related to equality of treatment in heterosexual and same-sex couples. To a large extent, the debate on the rights of same-sex couples is a debate on the ways of defining the family where the cultural, religious and legal dimensions intersect.

---

[43] Isabel Jaramillo, *Familia* [Family], *in* Cristina Motta & Macarena Sáez, La Mirada de los Jueces 267 (Siglo de Hombres eds., 2008).

Constitutional Court of Colombia
Ruling C-814 of 2001

Main Legal Issue:
Do the expressions "moral values" and "the couple formed by the man and the woman" established as requisites for adoption infringe upon the Constitution, and constitute discriminatory expressions of the homosexual condition?

Facts:
Luis Eduardo Montoya lodged a complaint in the Constitutional Court claiming the unconstitutionality of the expression "moral" contained in article 89 and numeral 2 of article 90 of Decree 2737 of 1989, on grounds that they infringe on the Fundamental Chart.

Court Ruling:
The Court declares the word "moral" and the expression "the couple formed by a man and a woman capable of proving an uninterrupted cohabitation of at least three (3) years" enforceable.

Extracts:
[…]
[W]hat should be determined in the present case is if the *de facto* hypothesis regulated by the challenged norm, that is, the joint adoption by heterosexual couples who have freely cohabited for at least three years, is identical to that of homosexual couples who have cohabited in the same situation for that same period of time, so that the legislator should have given equal treatment to both situations, granting in both events the authorization to adopt jointly.

In the Court's opinion, the identity of hypotheses that imposes on the legislator the obligation to grant identical juridical treatment is not manifest, if it is taken in to account that adoption is in the first place a way of satisfying the prevalent right of a minor to have a family, and that the family that the Constitution protects is the heterosexual and monogamous one, as has been said. From this point of view, the legislator is not indifferent to the type of family within which he is authorizing the minor to be inserted, since it is his obligation to provide the child with the family which responds to the concept admitted by the superior norms. Therefore, not only did he not incur in a discriminatory omission, but it was not possible for Congress to authorize the adoption by homosexuals, since the conception of family in the Constitution does not correspond to the life in common originating from this type of cohabitation, and the relationships derived from the adoption.

As a matter of fact, the provision that calls the Court's attention only pretends to protect the constitutional family, granting it the right to constitute itself grounded upon adoption. It does not discriminate homosexual couples, nor any other form of cohabitation or affective union that could be called a family, but not one protected by article 42 of the Constitution. For this reason it cannot be considered discriminatory, but properly speaking, protectionist of the superior notion of family union.

With that being said, it is in conformity with the Constitution that the legislator limits the freedom of the judge to grant adoption, pointing out that the authorization for adopting may only be granted to those who intend to form the family that the members of the Constituent Assembly wished to protect. This and none other is the child's best interest, within the axiology determined by the superior norms.

[...]

Evidently, this presents a conflict between the right to equality and free development of the personality of homosexuals or of other persons, who cohabit in affective unions that do not constitute a family in light of the constitution and who wish to adopt, and the right of the minor to form part of a family protected by the Constitution and not of any other. Nevertheless, the Constitution resolves this tension among rights, which, in article 44, peremptorily notes the prevalence of children's rights over the rest. This being the case, it may be said that the alluded restriction arises from the superior norms themselves, and that the partially challenged provision is limited to reflect the constitutional solution.

Dissenting opinion to Ruling C-814 of 2001

First, those of us who issued a dissenting vote consider that the Constitution does not only protect the heterosexual monogamous family, as expressed in the judgment. Second, we will show why the legal restrictions, general and abstract, of limiting joint adoption to heterosexual couples does not satisfy the child's best interest, is discriminatory, ignores the right to personal autonomy and infringes upon the principles of human dignity and pluralism.

[...] In our opinion, when the majority of the justices of the Chamber resolved that a norm that only allows heterosexual couples to adopt jointly is not contrary to the Political Constitution of 1991, before analyzing the case in depth, they were concerned with imposing on the whole Colombian society a conception of monogamous and heterosexual family which according to them, is the one contemplated and defended by the Constitution. Therefore, the judgment itself notes that the said norm "cannot be considered discriminatory, but rather, properly speaking, protectionist of the superior notion of family union."

How could the Chamber omit that in the clause which precisely regulates the subject of the decision to have children, the mention of "the couple" has no limitation whatsoever? The morn makes no distinction, it does not require that the couple be heterosexual.

[...]

It is then clear that the superior interest of the minor is not an abstract entelechy that may be defined outside all context and particular situation, as the Court pretended to, when saying that the interest of every minor is to belong to a monogamous and heterosexual family. The minor's interest is only appreciable on a case-by-case basis. Of course, there are things that, previously and without any consideration of real cases, may be considered beneficial for every boy and girl, but the principle of the child's best interest involve evaluating and weighting concrete and possible situations.

[...]

The argumentative strategy of the Court consists in saying that only the heterosexual couple gives origin to a family. In that respect it is not susceptible of being compared with a homosexual couple and therefore, any unequal treatment with regard to any other type of relationship that for not being monogamous and heterosexual is not family, is justified. Thus, no unequal treatment, however arbitrary it may seem, constitutes discrimination.... Once again .... we must say that this position denotes a great lack of sensitivity with regard to the subject of equality.

In our opinion, ... it is not admissible to say that a person is not being discriminated for the simple fact that he/she is allowed to exist, even when the person is deprived of a high percentage of the constitutional guarantees. This does not only go against the original function of equality, which consisted of avoiding discrimination and exclusion by juridical imposition, but it is also contrary to the text of article 13, understood even in its most formalist sense: "all persons are born equal before the law, and shall enjoy equal rights." In this judgment, the founding principles of freedom, equality and dignity are subordinated to an excluding conception of family.

The judgment with which we respectfully dissent ignores, in this case, a fundamental constitutional right that in various memorable rulings this entity had protected: the right to personal autonomy. The Court, today, is imposing a model of couple relationship to all Colombians: the monogamous and heterosexual one. And it is saying to homosexuals: be as you wish, it's up to "you," but do not relate to each other, do not create solid and stable affection bonds, do not build significant lives in common, and do not pretend to exercise the rights that the text of the Constitution recognizes to all persons as equally dignified subjects.

We do not share that vision that annuls the right to personal autonomy. It is absolutely individualistic, to the point of only recognizing that one individual, isolated, can be homosexual and not be sanctioned, on one condition: that he/she does not freely express his/her sexual orientation in a responsible manner with the aim of forming a stable couple that aspires to adopt a son.

Constitutional Court of Colombia Ruling C-029 of 2009

Main Legal Issue:

Do the benefits and impositions for heterosexual couples infringe on the principle of equal treatment for those formed by same sex persons?

Court Ruling:

According to constitutional case law, inasmuch as there are clear differences between homosexual and heterosexual couples, there is no constitutional imperative to give an equal treatment to both. This implies that to construct a claim for infringement of the principle of equality it is necessary to establish that, in each actual case, the situation of both types of couples is comparable, as a postulation that permits to enter the stage of determining if the difference in treatment is discriminatory.

Extracts:

[...]

To begin, the Court observes that, despite the fact that between the challenged expressions in different provisions there are those of "*family*," "*related to family*," or "*family group*," the plaintiffs do not file claims specifically oriented to question the concept of family provided in the law, nor the scope of this concept according to case law, for which reason the Court shall refrain from making a substantive judgment in relation to such expressions, without prejudice of the possibility of integrating the normative unity whenever the constitutional defect pointed out by the plaintiffs originates in an integral consideration of the provision that contains the aforementioned expressions.

[...]

[N]ot every difference in treatment between heterosexual and homosexual couples can be considered discriminatory *per se*, nor be considered grounded on the sexual orientation of persons, inasmuch as they may arise from the differences that exist between some couples and others.

In particular, the mandate of the family's integral protection and the definition of this institution as a fundamental nucleus of society, may give rise to legislative provisions that attend to this particular reality, and that insofar as they are oriented to the protection of this essential nucleus of society as a response to a constitutional imperative, cannot be considered discriminatory for not including situations that do not fit in the constitutional concept of family.

However, it is necessary to bear in mind that according to constitutional case law, the couple, as a life project in common that has a vocation or permanence and implies reciprocal assistance and solidarity among its members, enjoys constitutional protection, whether they be heterosexual or homosexual. In this context, the difference of treatment for couples in comparable situations may give rise to equality problems and in the same way, the absence of legal provisions for same-sex couples with regard to advantages or benefits that are applicable to heterosexual couples, may originate a protection deficit contrary to the Constitution, inasmuch as it ignores a superior imperative according to which, in certain circumstances, the legal system must contemplate a minimum of protection for certain subjects, minimum without which principles and superior rights such as the person's dignity, free development of the personality or solidarity may be compromised.

Explanation of Justice Jaime Araujo Rentería's Vote

Article 42 referring to the family, states the diverse paths, or ways that lead to the family, so that there is not in our legal system a unique road leading to the family organization but there rather paths and different classes of family in our constitutional system.

Marriage is barely one of the roads that lead to the family, and in our legal system it can only be celebrated between a man and a woman. In this sense, same-sex marriages are excluded. However, the fact that this is a road to family does not imply that it is the only one, since there are other pathways based on the establishment of natural or juridical bonds.

[...]

It is in this sense that the Constitution contains various distinctions, grammatically expressed by the expression "or." The members of the Constituent Assembly made reference twice to "will," to refer to two kinds of family: in one case to the will, free decision, of a man and a woman, who form a family through marriage and, in the other, by the responsible will of two persons to form it, without requiring that it involve a man and a woman, which also covers families of same-sex couples, or of opposite sexes, but who have not yet entered into marriage.

In summary, the restrictive interpretation of the constitutional norm contained in article 42 is erroneously interpreted in the sense that the family is always composed of or based on a man and a woman. This way of forming the family is only requested for marriage, but is not needed for the other types of family that are equally protected by our Constitution.

As a consequence of the above, I have stated that the constitutional protection of all the rights granted to the family as concerns marriage, adoption, social security, inheritance, as in all other matters and juridical ambits must be granted not only to families formed by the marriage of men and women, to whom the constitutional State based on the Rule of Law cannot grant a special treatment but an egalitarian one, but also to *de facto* marital unions, either of the same or of different sex.

7.4.1.2 Matters for Debate

The judgments of the Constitutional Court of Colombia incorporate the possibility of adoption of minors by same-sex couples in the debate on what kind of family(s) the modern state must legally protect. This discussion is one of the dimensions of contemporary politics at the national and transnational levels where cultural, religious, and legal aspects interweave. For some, the growing legitimacy of diverse sexual identities intensifies the need to defend the family as an essentially heterosexual institution. From this position, if discrimination of LGBTQ persons should be avoided, the family must stand up as the moral and legal limit to the advance of sexual rights. In the case of adoption, the child's interest is considered in tension with the possibility of forming same-sex couples, since these are placed on the margins of the law. Instead, for others, the family is a plural reality where no arrangement should legally prevail over the other. The concept of family has expanded, so that the law must have enough dynamism to incorporate this diversity. Today, a large part of the debate on this diversity precisely focuses on same-sex couples. Non-discrimination requires legitimization of same-sex couples and their capacity to adopt minors.

7.4.2 Guardianship/Custody

Although the law may prevent LGBTQ persons from adopting formally, the power of the law as an instrument in the face of the biological children of LGBTQ persons is limited, since it cannot avoid reproduction. The presence of biological children takes the discussion of *queer* parenting to another level: the point is not whether people can or cannot have children under their care, but the level of legitimacy and the juridical effects that will be recognized to the filiation bonds of LGBTQ persons. If in the case of adoption, the discussion is on whether or not LGBTQ persons should constitute fathers or mothers; when such persons have biological children the discussion shifts to whether their rights concerning filiation relations should be limited or not.

The mechanisms and motivations that lead LGBTQ persons to have biological children are diverse, but a weighty circumstance is the existence, at some time, of a heterosexual couple. Biographies are multiple and complex, and identities are flexible and changing, for which reason it is not uncommon that persons who identify themselves as gays or lesbians, for example, have had heterosexual couples with whom they may have had biological children. The end of these relationships entails a series of decisions that may imply different levels of controversy, amongst which guardianship/custody of children stands out. In some circumstances the homosexuality of one of the former spouses has been brought before the court, as an argument to judicially limit guardianship/custody. These cases, though low in numbers, have generated an important legal debate on *queer* parenting, since they set in motion a series of juridical, moral, and scientific constructions that connect to broader debates on sexuality, the family and social order in contemporary societies. When the judiciary must decide on the guardianship/custody regime, heteronormativity as a system of power that places LGBTQ persons at a disadvantage comes into play.

When analyzing these types of cases, different solutions are constructed from the doctrine and the case law that place different weight on (homo)sexuality. For one sector, people's sexuality should not be a factor when judging the capabilities as fathers or mothers; limiting rights based on sexual orientation is discriminatory. For another sector, on the other hand, (homo)sexuality constitutes an important factor when considering the right that should be recognized to fathers and mothers. From this position, heterosexuality is the legal, moral, and cultural rule that must govern filiation. The presence of LGBTQ persons as biological fathers and mothers, although unavoidable, must be, instead, regulated and restricted.

The way in which heteronormativity permeates the legal thinking when cases of guardianship/custody are debated is complex. In principle there are three types of heteronormative rationales that, although they share the distrust in the capabilities of LGBTQ persons to be parents, present themselves in diverse manners.[44] First, for some judges the condition of homosexuality is enough to deny and/or limit parents' rights. Homosexuality is presented as a deviation or as an illness; as such, it cannot be considered on a par with heterosexuality. From this, there is an insurmountable contrast between homosexuality and being a good father or mother, for which reason the son will remain under the guardianship/custody of the heterosexual parent whenever this is possible.

Another way that manifests the heteronormative thought of judges is through the authorization of rights to guardianship/custody to homosexual persons *insofar as they prove* that this situation is not damaging. In this way, sexual minorities must prove and show that they will not bring negative consequences to the minors; this requirement does not exist for heterosexuals. Although more sophisticated than the previous reasoning, heterosexuality is still privileged as the rule.

The third modality of heteronormative thinking is more complex and is the one currently used in most judicial cases in the U.S. Termed the "*nexus approach*," it

[44] Amy D. Ronner, *Homophobia and the Law*, American Psychological Association, Washington, DC, 2005, pp. 81–89.

states that even though homosexuality is not in itself damaging—rejecting the first approach—it must be utilized to deny custody when there are proofs—shifting the burden—of potential negative consequences for minors. Although different to the previous rationales, in the nexus approach heterosexuality is still the rule, since it is in the case of non heterosexuals that sexuality is open to the existence of proof to discourage custody. Heterosexual sexuality in itself is not constructed as potentially damaging to the minors; homosexuality, on the other hand, has that potential. This implies that the lives of LGBTQ persons are open to inspection and publicizing that search for elements that advises against custody.

The guardianship/custody of biological children is one of the dimensions of *queer* parenting defended by the movement for sexual diversity. As mentioned before, politicization of these situations, at least in the United States, arose in the 1970s under the impulse of lesbians who required protection of the children they had begotten with former heterosexual couples. Activism advanced notoriously in the visibilization and protection in these circumstances and in general, the majority of judicial rationales began to consider that (homo)sexuality should not be *per se* considered a significant factor when the guardianship/custody regime of gays and lesbians is decided. In any case, there are still judicial decisions in the U.S. that utilize the parents' sexual orientation as a cause to limit the rights of guardianship/custody. For example, the Court of Appeals of Mississippi, in 2001, considered the bisexuality of a mother a reason to award custody to the father; and, the Supreme Court of Alabama, denied custody to a lesbian mother.

In Europe, it is important to mention the Salgueiro da Silva Mouta v. Portugal case,[45] where the right to the guardianship/custody of a biological son was denied to a gay father as a way of defending the traditional family. The judgment stated, "[t]he child must live in a family environment, a traditional Portuguese family, which is certainly not the situation in which the child's father has decided to enter, since he is living with another man as if they were man and wife. It is not our task here to determine whether homosexuality is or is not an illness, or if it is a sexual orientation to persons of the same sex. In both cases it is an abnormality, and children must not grow in the shadows of abnormal situations…."[46] However, it is important to highlight that the European Court imposed sanctions on Portugal for this ruling, establishing that sexual orientation could not be considered a determining factor of responsible paternity or maternity.[47]

In Latin America, there have been some cases of guardianship/custody involving LGBTQ persons that allow the observation of different juridical, moral, and scientific constructions on *queer* parenting in particular, and on sexuality, in general. Although the legal provisions may hinder and prohibit adoption, they cannot impede the biological reproduction of LGBTQ persons. These biological bonds are "inevitably" legal; they exist and they have juridical effects. However, what the norms can

[45] Salgueiro da Silva Mouta v. Portugal, 1999-IX Eur. Ct. H.R. 309.

[46] Salgueiro da Silva Mouta v. Portugal, European Court of Human Rights, March 21, 2000.

[47] *Id.*

achieve from a heteronormative judicial rationale is the restriction of the rights of guardianship/custody based on the non heterosexuality of one of the parents. Using this same argument, that LGBTQ persons are not good parents, their rights related to the exercise of paternity or maternity are limited.

Judgments that protect LGBTQ persons in their roles as fathers and mothers have started to appear in the region. In spite of the fact that judges must choose the "fittest" and "most appropriate" for the guardianship/custody, sexual identity has ceased to be a factor worth taking into account in this decision. An interesting case occurred in Córdoba, Argentina, in 2003.[48] The judge of the case considered that the sexual condition did not constitute *per se* a factor that determined the lack of aptness in the parental function, and that claiming the contrary would be a source of "unacceptable discrimination today."[49]

Although case law has evolved in relation to considering that sexuality is not a relevant dimension to assess the capabilities of fathers and mothers, this is still a controversial issue. The Argentine case is an isolated case; heteronormativity continues to cut across the judicial rationale, placing LGBTQ persons in a suspect class regarding the exercise of their rights.

7.4.2.1 The Child's Best Interest: Protection Policies

How do judges assess the child's best interest when deciding on guardianship/custody by LGBTQ persons? When the traditional family definition goes into a crisis, the moral anxiety focuses on the responsibilities of adults toward children.[50] "The child's best interest" transforms into a political window of intervention by the State that is sometimes based on situations of real danger—abuse, violence, or abandonment—and sometimes channels the phobias and social prejudices of the times—single-parent homes or interracial couples. The recognition of LGBTQ persons in relation to filiation bonds finds itself in this dilemma, real risk or social phobia.

The child's best interest is the most common argument when *queer* parenting is debated. The construction of sexuality and its potential consequences for minors is a central rationale at the time of deciding the rights of LGBTQ persons to guardianship/custody. The discussion on the child's best interest is a way of discussing the competence of LGBTQ persons to be fathers or mothers. Be it at the individual level or as a couple, what is at stake is whether sexual identities that diverge from heterosexuality, are disqualified to carry out the roles of parents in a satisfactory way.

Have children brought up in *queer* homes suffered more harm or encountered greater risks than those raised in heterosexual homes? Legal decisions respond to

[48] Juzgado de Familia, Córdoba L., S. F. y A., C. P., n. 4. 06/08/2003.

[49] *Id.*

[50] *See* Jeffrey Weeks, *Same Sex Intimacies. Families of choice and other life experiments,* Routledge, New York, 2001, p. 157.

this question in two opposing ways. The heteronormative position sustains that *queer* homes, whether single-parent or a couple, bring negative consequences to minors, consequences that justify limiting the rights related to guardianship/custody of LGBTQ persons. Despite being a predominantly moral and religious subject, the debate on the negative consequences for the minors has also turned into a scientific debate. It grants that the absence of a "normal sexuality" model will be occasion for a series of negative psychological consequences.

This type of research follows the line of studies carried out on the consequences of minors in single-parent homes with some studies emphasizing the high instability and divorce rate in homosexual couples. A frequently quoted study affirms that gay couples have 50 % more chances of divorcing than heterosexual couples, while lesbian couples have 167 % more chances.[51] Another type of argument states that gays and lesbians have a higher prevalence of mental illnesses than heterosexuals do, and therefore, adoption by same-sex couples should not be permitted.[52] In the face of the movement in favor of sexual diversity's success in lifting the barriers that excluded homosexuality, particularly the psychological and psychiatric constructions, conservative activism seeks to discredit those researches with the aim of strengthening the system's heteronormativity.

From another position, however, it is stated that sexual identity is not a significant variable at the time of considering the consequences on minors. Concerning "*queer* homes," different kinds of research have been produced to show the capacity of LGBTQ persons and couples to develop as fathers and mothers. The aim of such research is to offset the moral and scientific arguments that state that the minors raised by LGBTQ persons suffer negative consequences as compared to those brought up in heterosexual homes. The diverse research rejects the main motives that claim that the presence of LGBTQ persons and couples is damaging to minors.[53] For instance, that it cannot be concluded that minors brought up in "homosexual homes" have a greater identity and sexual identification problem than those raised in "heterosexual homes." Nor is it found that these minors have psychological sequels or behavioral problems for having been brought up by same-sex couples. Moreover, these minors have not presented problems in their social relationships, such as stigmatization in their environment, and they have "normal" relations with elders and with peers.

This management of scientific information is a political strategy, because it serves to criticize and de-naturalize cultural, legal, and scientific constructions on sexuality. However, its use has also succeeded in making scientific institutions express that there are no substantial differences between same-sex couples and heterosexual couples when exercising the role of parents. Both the American

---

[51] Maggie Gallagher and Joshua Baker, "Demand for Same-Sex Marriage: Evidence from the United States, Canada, and Europe", *MAPP Policy Brief*, Institute for Marriage and Public Policy, Vol. 3, No.1, April 26, 2006.

[52] George Rekers and Mark Kilgus "Studies of Homosexual Parenting: A Critical Review", *Regent University Law Review*, Vol. 14, p. 342 ff.

[53] *See* Cooper, Leslie and Paul Cates. *Too High a Price: The Case Against Restricting Gay Parenting*, American Civil Liberties Union, New York, 2006.

Psychological Association[54] and the American Medical Association,[55] for example, explicitly support adoption and parenting by same-sex couples. This type of research is used by activism in favor of sexual diversity to support legal and public policy reforms which grant rights to LGBTQ persons and couples as fathers and mothers. Thus, it is frequent to find that diverse movements and organizations of the civil society prepare reports compiling these kinds of research for influencing and exerting pressure in public and legislative discussions. Overall, this position sustains that it cannot affirm that hetero and *queer* homes have different consequences for minors. In this way, "the child's best interest" is not opposed to the other rights of LGBTQ persons to be fathers or mothers. Sexuality is a non-fact when considering and evaluating the capabilities and fitness of men and women.

The following case summary illustrates how the dimension "child's best interest" is used in a divergent way in the analysis of homosexuality as limiting of maternity. The case is relevant to this debate because it proposes different interpretations on the minors' interest regarding *queer* parenting and the strong disagreement that exists among judges regarding the consequences that diverse sexual identities have on minors.

Report n° 42/08 Admissibility
Petition 1271–04
Karen Atala and daughters v. Chile
July 23, 2008

Main Legal Issue:
Is a mother's lesbian cohabitation an infringement on the principle of the child's best interest and cause for unsuitability to exercise custody of her minor children?

Facts:
Ricardo Jaime López filed a complaint against Jacqueline Karen Atala Riffo, from whom he had separated, claiming custody of their three minor daughters. He claims that both the personal separation of the couple and the parting from his son and the claim for custody of their daughters, are a consequence of the recognition that Karen Atala had made of her sexual condition, cohabiting in their home with her new partner. The father's claim was rejected because there was no legal cause to prevent her from exercising physical custody of her daughters. The ruling was confirmed on appeal and repealed by the Supreme Court of Chile. The high court decided that the judgment had not taken the child's best interest into account, a principle by which custody of the minors should be awarded to the father, since the mother, by cohabiting with a person of the same sex, placed her daughters in a situation of social stigmatization.

In 2004, Karen Atala entered a claim against the Chilean State at the Inter American Commission of Human Rights (CIDH) that concluded in 2009. The judgment expressed that the State was responsible for discrimination in the judicial

[54] Lesbian and gay parenting: A resource for psychologists. Washington, DC: American Psychological Association, 1995. http://www.apa.org/pi/parent.html

[55] "Policy regarding sexual orientation" de la American Medical Association en http://www.ama-assn.org/ama/pub/category/14754.html

procedure by issuing a series of recommendations that have still not been implemented to the Commission's satisfaction. The CIDH filed a claim at the Inter American Court of Human Rights in 2010.

I. Summary

1. On November 24, 2004, the Inter-American Commission on Human Rights [...] received a petition alleging that the State of Chile is internationally responsible for violations committed by means of a Supreme Court of Justice ruling that revoked from Ms. Karen Atala custody of her three daughters (aged 5, 6, and 10 years). They claim the ruling was grounded exclusively on discriminatory prejudices based on Ms. Atala's sexual orientation. [...]
2. The petitioners hold that the facts violate ... rights recognized by the American Convention on Human Rights [...] The petitioners argue that all domestic remedies were exhausted with the Judgment of the Supreme Court of Justice of Chile which, they allege, permanently, arbitrarily, and in a discriminatory manner revoked Ms. Atala custody of her three minor children because of her sexual orientation.
3. The State, for its part, requests that the petition be declared inadmissible, because the ruling was based on the best interest of the girls and, "according to evidence presented in the trial, on the conduct of the mother, who opted to cohabit with a partner of the same sex, with whom she proposed to raise her daughters, which was deemed inadvisable for the girls' upbringing and a risk to their development in the current context of the Chilean society." The State also reiterates that domestic remedies have not been fully exhausted because under Chilean law Ms. Atala is able to file a new complaint to claim custody of her daughters.
4. Without prejudging the merits of the matter, the IACHR concludes in this report that the petition is admissible under Articles 46 and 47 of the American Convention. [...]

   [...]

III. Positions Of The Parties

A. Position of the petitioners

13. The petitioners argue that several rights of Ms. Karen Atala and her three daughters were arbitrarily and abusively abridged when the Supreme Court of Justice of Chile revoked from Ms. Atala custody of her three daughters based exclusively on discriminatory prejudices by reason of her sexual orientation. They claim that the judgment of the Supreme Court of Justice discriminatorily applied the substantive rules that govern custody matters in Chile, which are founded on the best interests of the child, by making an arbitrary and unwarranted distinction between the ability of heterosexual and homosexual parents to care adequately for their children. The petitioners also alleged due process violations because through the implementation of a disciplinary action (*recurso de queja*), which is a remedy of a purely disciplinary nature, the members of the Supreme Court adopted a final decision on the merits of the case without due regard to the arguments of the parties and without ordering new expert examinations that would provide them with a solid foundation to reconsider the custody decision of the two lower courts.

    [...]

17. On May 2, 2003, the Regular Judge of the Juvenile Court in Villarrica granted provisional custody of the girls to the father at his request … despite his express recognition that there was no evidence to presume grounds for legal incompetence of the mother that warranted a change in the existing custody arrangement. It later fell to the Acting Judge of the Court of First Instance in Villarrica to issue the final ruling. On October 29, 2003, that judge rejected the custody suit because she found that:

    The sexual orientation of the mother does not constitute an impediment to develop a responsible motherhood. … The respondent suffers from no psychiatric pathology that would make her unfit to perform a mother's role.… no concrete evidence has been shown that the presence of the mother's partner in the home is harmful to the well-being of the girls …. [H]aving analyzed the evidence presented, there is no reason to presume the existence of bad or dangerous examples for the morality of the girls …. [T]he court concludes that the girls have not suffered any discrimination to date and what the witnesses for and relatives of the plaintiff express is a fear of possible discrimination in the future. With respect to this point it should be mentioned that this court must base its decision on definite and proven facts in the case and not on mere assumptions or fears …
18. Accordingly, the Tribunal ordered the girls to return to the care of their mother on December 18, 2003. In the interim, however, on November 11, 2003, the father of the children appealed the judgment and sued for an injunction to prevent their removal (*orden de no innovar*), arguing that to implement the judgment would entail a radical and violent change in the current situation of the girls. On November 24, 2003, the Court of Appeals granted the injunction. On March 30, 2004, the Court of Appeals in Temuco unanimously upheld the appealed judgment ….
19. On April 5, 2004, the father of the girls presented a disciplinary action (*recurso de queja*) against the judges of the Court of Appeals in Temuco before the Supreme Court … The father of the girls specifically argued that the decision of the mother to make her sexual orientation public was harmful to the girls' development both mentally and overall, as well as to their social relations. He, therefore, requested that the girls provisionally remain in his care. That request was granted by the Court, which issued an injunction to prevent their removal on April 7, 2004.
20. On May 31, 2004, the Fourth Chamber of the Supreme Court, in a split decision of three votes to two, admitted the disciplinary action and awarded permanent custody to the father. The petitioners say that the judgment of the Supreme Court determined that Ms. Atala had put her interests before those of her daughters when she made the decision to be open about her homosexuality and began to live with a same-sex partner, and that in its decision the Court gave consideration to testimonies that suggested that the girls could become confused about their sexual roles and become the object of social discrimination in the future.

    […]

21. The Court deemed the girls to be in a "situation of risk" that placed them in a "vulnerable position in their social environment, since clearly their unique family environment differs significantly from that of their school companions and acquaintances in the neighborhood where they live, exposing them to ostracism and discrimination, which would also affect their personal development." The minority dissenting judges of the Supreme Court determined, by contrast, that "the opinions contained in the record, both from psychologists and from social workers, infer that the mother's homosexuality does not harm the rights of the girls."
[...]
26. According to the petitioners, the ruling of the Supreme Court is notable for the fact that it centered exclusively on Ms. Karen Atala's sexual orientation, and not on other grounds of legal incapacity to revoke custody of her children, which contravened the principle of equality before the law inasmuch as it constituted a discriminatory application of the substantive rules on custody. The petitioner argues that homosexuality cannot be considered a just cause for declaring her unfit as a mother unless it can be conclusively proven that it harms her daughters, which the Court has not done. According to the petitioners, the Supreme Court reduces the best interests of the girls to living in a traditional, heterosexual, "normally structured" environment.
[...]
32. In regards to the exhaustion of domestic remedies, the petitioners argue that the ruling of the Fourth Chamber of the Chilean Supreme Court exhausted all the domestic judicial remedies that could have been attempted in the suit over the custody of the girls. Ms. Atala alleges that if she sues for custody again she knows that no judge will rule in her favor due to the absence of domestic judicial independence in cases of this type before the Supreme Court of Justice.

B. Position of the State

33. The State requests that the petition be declared inadmissible because the facts described therein do not tend to establish violations of the rights protected by the Convention and that the petitioners have turned to the inter-American system as if it were "a kind of fourth instance," competent to review the decisions of the domestic tribunals issued within their jurisdiction and in accordance with due process guarantees. The State holds that given the subsidiary nature of the organs of the inter-American system, both the Court and the Commission have adopted case law in which they indicate that said organs shall only review domestic judicial decisions when the petition is based on a judgment that violates due process guarantees or appears to violate any other right recognized in the Convention, which has not happened in this case.
34. According to the State, the "lack of foundation in support of the varied allegations addressed in the complainant's extensive petition ought to be clear from the mere reading of the judgment that supposedly perpetrated the violations described." Thus, the State alleges, it is understandable that a person who loses a lawsuit should not agree with a verdict disfavorable to them, but "it is surprising that [this person], when she is a Judge of the Republic vested with the power to hear and adjudicate the disputes of others, should dismiss in the terms contained in the aforementioned

petition a judgment of the highest Tribunal of that Republic and resort to the Inter-American Commission on Human Rights to challenge said ruling."

35. The sentence of the Supreme Court, according to the State, does not violate the rights of the girls. To the contrary, the State alleges that the ruling was based on "the imperative need to protect the best interests of the daughters, threatened, according to the evidence in the case, by the conduct of the mother, who opted to cohabit with a partner of the same sex, with whom she proposed to raise her daughters, which was deemed inadvisable for the girls' upbringing and a risk to their development given the current climate in Chilean society." The State equally advances that "regarding personal care it is not the right of the parents that is relevant, but the right of the children affected." The State specifically argues that "in effect, this is how in this type of matters the best interests of the child are the priority, since this is the guiding principle of national and international law. This issue is not considered by the complainant in the petition, but it motivated the custody decision in favor of the father. The ruling was not based on the sexual orientation of the mother, even though she emphasizes this aspect as part of an overall context of discrimination and unequal treatment."

[...]

39. The State also argues that the award of custody of the girls to their father was not the result of any discrimination prohibited by the American Convention. In the opinion of the State, the decision was not prompted by the homosexuality of Ms. Atala, but by the effect that her cohabitation with another person of the same sex could have on the wellbeing and psychological and emotional development of her daughters. Those were the overriding considerations in the disputed ruling, and not the decision of the petitioner to declare her homosexuality "whose legitimate exercise as a private right was expressly acknowledged by the judgment." The State therefore alleges that was the situation of the girls, "which, at least in the current climate in Chilean society, may be considered peculiar and it deemed it just cause to award custody to the father because the best interests of the girls made it essential."

40. In the hearing before the IACHR, the State also noted that "the judgment of the Supreme Court of Justice focuses on the best interests of the child. In one of its arguments, the Supreme Court mentions that Chile has a conservative cultural environment. For example, divorce only became possible two years ago. If to that one adds the public exposure of the mother's sexual preference, the difficulties that the case was creating for the girls were clear to the State."

[...]

IV. Analysis

A. Competence of the Commission *ratione personae, ratione loci, ratione temporis*, and *ratione materiae*

[...]

45. The Commission is competent *ratione loci* to consider the petition inasmuch as it alleges violations of rights protected under the American Convention which are said to have taken place within the territory of Chile, a state party to said treaty.

[...]

60. [T]he Commission notes that in admitting this petition it does not seek to encroach on the jurisdiction of the domestic judicial authorities to determine child custody matters or to examine any errors of fact and law possibly committed by the domestic courts. The Commission will not determine if the Chilean courts applied Chilean procedural law appropriately or on the assessment of evidence, since such matters are in principle reserved to the domestic courts. The only determination that the Commission will make in the merits stage is whether the decision of the Supreme Court Justice of Chile was issued without regard to due process guarantees and in violation of the rights protected by the American Convention.
61. In the admissibility stage the Commission considers that it is not appropriate to determine whether or not the alleged violations occurred. For the purposes of admissibility, the IACHR should determine whether the arguments advanced in the petition state facts that tend to establish violations of the American Convention, as required under Article 47(b) thereof ….

    […]
63. The Commission finds *prima facie* that the arguments raise questions related with the right to equal protection recognized in Article 24, which correspond to an analysis in the merits stage. The petitioners allege that the Supreme Court Justice of Chile accorded a different treatment to Ms. Atala and her former spouse in its ruling on the custody of their daughters, in which the sexual orientation of Ms. Atala was the decisive factor in granting permanent custody to the father. They claim that the distinction based on Ms. Atala's homosexuality in the custody suit was neither objective nor reasonable and it did not have a legitimate purpose, in contravention of international human rights principles. They also contend that the Court's ruling has a disproportionate and limiting impact on the exercise of rights by homosexual parents, by promoting that they never retain custody of their children due to stereotypical conceptions of their ability to care and create a healthy family environment for them.
64. The Commission also finds that the allegations could constitute violations of the right to privacy and the rights of the family of the victims protected, respectively, by Articles11(2) and 17(1) of the American Convention. The petitioners claim that the State allegedly interfered in an arbitrary and abusive manner in the private and family life of Ms. Karen Atala and her daughters when it revoked custody purely out of discriminatory prejudice based on Ms. Atala's sexual orientation. They also argue that the separation measure adopted by the Supreme Court was neither reasonable nor proportional because it could have adopted other measures that were less invasive on the victims' private and family life.
65. The Inter-American Commission will also examine arguments with respect to Articles 8(1) and 25 of the American Convention in connection with the claims of the petitioners regarding alleged violations of due-process guarantees during the custody trial. The petitioners allege, in particular, that the Supreme Court, through a disciplinary action (*recurso de queja*), which is a remedy of a purely disciplinary nature designed to correct faults or abuses committed in judicial decisions, opened a third judicial instance that does not exist in the Chilean

criminal procedure. The petitioners argue that the Court issued an unjustified decision on the merits of the matter and unduly interfered in the principle of judicial independence.
[...]

V. Conclusions

69. The Inter-American Commission concludes that it is competent to address the merits of this case and that the petition is admissible in accordance with Articles 46 and 47 of the American Convention. Based on the factual and legal arguments exposed above and without prejudging the merits of the matter,

The INTER-AMERICAN COMMISSION ON HUMAN RIGHTS, DECIDES

1. To declare the instant petition admissible with regard to the alleged violation of the rights recognized by Articles 8(1), 11(2), 17(1), 24, and 25 of the American Convention, in connection with Articles 1(1) and 2 thereof, to the detriment of Ms. Karen Atala and her daughters; and the alleged violation of the rights of the child protected by Articles 19 and 17(4), in connection with Article 1(1), with regard to the daughters of Ms. Karen Atala.
2. To declare the instant petition inadmissible as regards to the alleged violation of Articles 5(1) and 11(1) of the American Convention.
[...]

7.4.2.2 Matters for Debate

A central dimension of legal cases in which the rights of LGBTQ persons are dealt with is the one related with proof, and this is especially true in cases in which *queer* parenting is discussed. Be it in matters of adoption or of guardianship/custody, it must be proved that the minors will not suffer damage by being brought up by LGBTQ persons or couples. This reasoning reflects, in various ways, the heteronormative thought, since heterosexuality is constructed as normality in matters of filiation, laying the burden of proof on those who are more distant from this normality. Heterosexuality is presumed innocuous for the minors' well being, while homosexuality has to show, in concrete cases, that it does not entail major risks. Thus, the ruling favorable to the lesbian mother conveys a central argumentative weight on the reports and scientific evidence which confirm the absence of differential risks between "heterosexual homes" and "*queer* homes."

Chapter 8
Prejudice-Based Violence

María Mercedes Gómez

The first part of this chapter will be devoted to defining what we understand, in general, as prejudice-based violence and its potential links with the law. Violence manifests itself in many ways and through many forms of expression: there are verbal violence, violence by omission, social violence and psychological violence. Specifically, we shall deal with violence exerted on individual bodies for being what they are, in our case, bodies that are displayed or perceived as non-normative, for example, non-heterosexual. This form of violence has the particularity of going beyond the individual aspect of the gesture and becoming expressive, acquiring the character of a message, a message that terrifies all those who feel that they participate, or that they can be perceived as participating, in the identifications of the individual body that has been wounded or annihilated. In some contemporary societies, this kind of violence is known, in popular terminology and in some laws, as "hate crimes" because they have been defined and are punishable. The second part will present a general framework concerning the legislation against prejudice-based violence in Latin America, and it will make reference to the reports on the human rights situation of the lesbian, gay, bisexual, transgendered, and queer (LGBTQ)[1] population in Argentina, Chile, Colombia, Mexico, and Peru. Lastly, the third part will focus on an analysis of cases of violence based on sexual prejudice in the region, drawn from articles in the press, court decisions, and reports from social organizations.

[1] The author adds the letter "Q" when including persons who are *queer*, because its political value is rooted in its reference to practices of resistance against the absolute explanation of the social world according to hierarchical binaries, whether of gender, sexual orientation, or race among others.

M.M. Gómez (✉)
University of Los Andes, Bogotá, Colombia
e-mail: mmgomez801@gmail.com

C. Motta and M. Sáez (eds.), *Gender and Sexuality in Latin America - Cases and Decisions*, Ius Gentium: Comparative Perspectives on Law and Justice 24,
DOI 10.1007/978-94-007-6199-5_8, © Springer Science+Business Media Dordrecht 2013

8.1 General Aspects[2]

8.1.1 Violence

I speak of violence not so much to say that violence is often suffered, verbally, physically, derived from humiliation, from over-exposition or invisibility, but above all, because I believe that violence can be organized around its use, its motive, and its ends. For this reason, two concepts of violence are proposed in accordance with their paradoxical functions: the hierarchical and the exclusionary. Hierarchical violence is one that is exercised, and can be lethal, to remind the 'other' of his/her condition of subordination or inferiority, to impart a lesson about the place that the 'other' must occupy. Exclusionary violence, on the other hand, is the one that is exercised to do away with what the other represents, to make him/her disappear.

8.1.2 Prejudice and Sexual Prejudice

The notion of prejudice has a long history. For some philosophers, prejudice is the condition of all knowledge, it has connotations of rapprochement and interest, it is prior to a well-founded judgment but it is a condition of the same.[3] In a more popular usage, however, the imposed definition of prejudice is understood as an attempt of knowledge prior to judgment that presents itself as already justified and well-grounded. Prejudice assumes, so to speak, the obstinacy of a fixation. Sartre, in his magnificent text on the *Portrait of the Antisemite*,[4] or Adorno and his collaborators in the studies on authoritarian personality, point to obstinacy and resistance to difference and/or change[5] as a prominent trait of prejudice. In that same sense, prejudice, can be defined as a "*rationalization*" which, even in psychoanalytic terms, indicates a procedure through which individuals give to themselves and to others, reasons to justify before their social group and before

---

[2] This chapter partially reformulates or reproduces arguments presented in María Mercedes Gómez, "Crímenes de Odio en Estados Unidos. La Distinción Analítica entre Excluir y Discriminar" in *Debate Feminista.* Vol. 15, No. 29, México, 2004, pp. 158–186, "Los usos jerárquicos y excluyentes de la violencia" in L. Cabal y C. Motta (Comp.), *Más allá del derecho*, Bogotá, Siglo del Hombre Editores, 2006, pp. 19–55 and, *On Discrimination and Exclusion: An Approach to Hate Crime Politics.* Ph.D Dissertation, New School for Social Research, New York City (2006).

[3] *See* Hans-Georg Gadamer, *Truth and Method,* Continuum Publishing Group, 1975.

[4] Jean-Paul Sartre, "Portrait of the Anti-Semite" in Bigotry, Prejudice and Hatred (R. Baird & S.E. Rosenbaum eds., 1946), pp. 35–45.

[5] Teodore Adorno, Else Frankel-Brunswick, Daniel J. Levinson Y R. Nevitt Sanford, *The Authoritarian Personality*, New York, Harper, 1950.

themselves, the reaction, generally negative, that they experience towards something or someone.[6] Besides conceiving prejudice as a rationalization, I also assert that prejudice, or prejudices, are always social; they have an echo in groups and for this reason, they are local and site-specific. Each society or group produces or reproduces its particular prejudices. Prejudice does not exist as a solitary action: there is no prejudice without a context to support it, there is no individual prejudice without social complicity.[7]

Similarly, "sexual prejudice," according to social psychologist, Gregory Herek, refers to negative attitudes toward an individual because of her or his sexual orientation. It is used to characterize heterosexuals' negative attitudes toward (a) homosexual behavior; (b) people with a homosexual or bisexual orientation; and (c) communities of gay, lesbian, bisexual and transgender individuals.[8] Another term for this, is "homophobia." Herek favors notion of sexual prejudice over that of "homophobia" because he considers the latter in its more technical sense, as a phobia, that is, as an irrational fear that takes the form of an individual pathology rather than a socially reinforced prejudice.[9] Herek's concern, when speaking of homophobia, in certain cases, has been the cause of erroneous evaluations of violent behaviors. That is to say, if homophobia is an individual pathology, it is isolated and dealt with "in the concrete case" of the disturbed person. Herek and others believe that here lies one of the causes of the invisibility of these practices and of the clumsiness with which they are usually handled both legally and culturally. However, "homophobia" and "sexual prejudice" are used as synonymous; the thought is that the cultural redefining of the word "homophobia" goes beyond its aspect of mere individual psychology and includes the social component proper to prejudices, making an implicit reference to the complicity of the environment in the internalization and externalization of hostility in the perpetrators. Homophobia may in some cases make reference to an "irrational fear," as other prejudices also do. There is a concern about a definition of "homophobia" that emphasizes in an exclusive way the irrational nature of fear and presupposes the occlusion of the objective responsibility of the perpetrator and the social context that facilitates the crime. Such is the case of the "syndrome of homosexual panic," which functions in some criminal systems as an extenuating circumstance in a criminal case.[10]

---

[6] Jean Laplanche and Jean –Bertrand Pontalis, *Diccionario de Psicoanálisis*, Barcelona, Editorial Labor, 1981, p. 349.

[7] Donald Moss, *Hating in the First Person Plural. Psychoanalytic Essays on Racism, Homophia, Misogyny, and Terror*, New York, Other Press, 2003.

[8] Gregory Herek, "The Psychology of Sexual Prejudice" in *Current Directions in Psychological Science*. Vol. 9, No. 1, 1999, pp. 19–22.

[9] *Id.*

[10] *See* Eve Kosofsky Sedgwick, *The Epistemology of the Closet*, Berkeley, University of California Press, 1990, p. 19.

8.1.3 Compulsory Heterosexuality

For the purposes of this chapter, and along with Adrianne Rich and others, compulsory heterosexuality is defined as a political regime[11]; one that emphasizes normative, cultural, and political aspects incompatible with non-normative sexualities. Violence based on homophobia or sexual prejudice is the violent manifestation of a type of hostility that has its source in the fear of losing the "masculine credentials"[12] or credentials of gender conformity. These are considered socially appropriate to move with certain material or symbolic privileges in a world that despises and disempowers individuals and conducts perceived as transgressive of the (hetero)sexual norms.

8.1.4 The Construction of Otherness

Differences are social constructions and not immutable characteristics of individuals or groups. These differences, real or imagined, only acquire consistency because they are assigned a value. The assignment of values[13] to real or imagined difference is, on the one hand, usually the "productive" or "constitutive" act of the emergence of the other who is different from me, and on the other hand, it is the gesture that justifies the aggressions against that 'other' to consolidate the privileges derived from the fact that it is I/we who hold the power to construct them. By assigning values to the 'other', we establish in a relational and binary way a "us" before a "them." The "us" has the creative power, the generator of the hierarchies between the differences. "Us" exists as a cohesive group because we are not—and here is the relational gesture—because we are not "them."[14]

In other words, in societies of compulsory heterosexuality,—with their rights, their cultural, medical, communicational, and political standards—non-normative sexual differences are perceived as foreign in the presence of what Benedict Anderson terms the "imagined community,"[15] that is, what shakes the foundations of the social ideal of homogeneity and cohesion. But despite the social anxiety that differences generate, their production demands, at the same time, that they be permanently confirmed and re-inscribed, for it is only through them that hegemonic groups that hold the power to produce and reproduce them are formed.

---

[11] Adrianne Rich, "Compulsory Heterosexuality and Lesbian Existence." En *The Lesbian and Gay Studies Reader*, edited by H. Abelove, M. Aina Barale, and M. Halperin. New York, Routledge, 1993, p. 227. Judith Butler, *Gender Trouble*, New York, Routledge Press, 1999. Monique Wittig, *The Straight Mind and Other Essays*, Boston, Beacon Press, 1992, p. 28.

[12] See, Gail Mason, "Not Our Kind of Hate Crime", *Law and Critique*. Vol. 12, No. 3, 2001, p. 268.

[13] Albert Memmi, *Dominated Men*. Boston, Beacon Press, 1971, p. 185.

[14] Jacques Derrida, *Of Grammatology*, publ. John Hopkins University Press, 1974.

[15] Benedict Anderson, *Imagined Communities. Reflections on the Origin and Spread of Nationalism*. New York, Verso, 1991.

The production of the other as a threat—that is, the creation of the enemy—has a fundamental role in what David Goldberg calls "homogenized equality."[16] The establishment of an "us" is forced through the affirmation of the norm in "creating" the contrary, a "them." However, this homogeneity—forced and socially constructed—is a source of anxiety due to the fact that the borders between "us" and "them" are porous and weak.[17] These boundaries, because they are fraudulent, require the marking of differences, and this marking is usually violent.

8.1.5 From Prejudice to Violence

In some categories or groups resulting from the creation of differences, the latter are perceived or want to be experimented as rigid, and in others, as more porous and indeterminate. For example, academicians such as Iris M. Young and Kenji Yoshino, among others, have asserted that from legal and cultural perspectives, the characteristics ascribed to race and gender appear or are perceived as visible and immutable. In this sense, the cultural production of racialized or gender subjectivities makes it possible for a white man to believe that he is not, nor is he in any danger of being, a colored woman.[18] On the contrary, sexual orientation has been legal and culturally perceived as invisible and mutable.[19] Individuals perceive or experiment the boundaries between heterosexuality and non-heterosexuality as more flexible than those of race or gender; consequently, the need to mark the differences is more urgent.

Of course this is not absolute; biological, cultural and economic differences are superimposed and configure one another. However, as Young reminds us, "in modern and multicultural societies the 'differences' seem to vanish and with them the certainties regarding the frontiers that permit ascribing values and privileges."[20] Hence why groups in danger of losing racial, (hetero)sexual, gender and class hegemonies, among others, feel it is necessary to re-inscribe the 'other' as different, a re-inscription that runs counter to the practices of social participation and democratization, and heading towards prejudice-based violence.

The use of the notion of "visibility of the differences" helps explain the problem of anxiety in the presence of limits or boundaries and the requirement of violent externalization of the difference, and it operates as an example of the role that the uses of violence play in the production of the 'other' as threat. In differentiated and multicultural societies the 'other' is no longer so different than me, consequently,

---

[16] David Theo Goldberg, *The Racial State.* Malden, Blackwell Publishers Inc. 2002, p. 10.

[17] Iris M. Young, "The Scaling of Bodies and the Politics of Identity" in *Justice and the Politics of Difference*, Princeton, Princeton University Press, 1990, p. 146; Kenji Yoshino, "Covering" in *Yale Law Journal.* Vol. 111, No. 4, January, 2002, p. 771.

[18] *Id.* p. 146.

[19] Yoshino, *op.cit*, p. 771.

[20] Young, *op.cit*, p. 146.

historically privileged individuals and groups have lost clarity with regard to the ways of marking the difference,[21] above all because they believe that if they do not render it evident in some way, they run the risk of losing "the privileges" that accompany their identifications or what they perceive as their identity. If, for example, the boundaries between genders and races are "notorious," otherness appears as visible *a priori* of the violent gesture. The gesture is only a warning so that the 'other' does not dare subvert a social hierarchy established beforehand. Such is the case of domestic violence against women; a hierarchical use of violence.

In the case of violence based on sexual prejudice, in which the differences are less visible, the construction of otherness also occurs *a posteriori*, that is, as a result of the violent gesture. The objective of executing the violent act is to eliminate danger, and in so doing, the perpetrator believes he/she simultaneously *fixates* his/her identity (as heterosexual) and that of his/her victim (as non-heterosexual). This would be an exclusionary use of violence. In both cases the question is the mark in relation to the function of the violent gesture. Of course, in order to acquire a meaning and cause terror, both uses of violence presuppose a previous and prejudiced social order.

In a certain way, the *exclusionary* use of violence results in a paradox: through the violent act, the perpetrator does not only affirm his identity but he also affirms the identity he was trying to suppress. By reaffirming his own identity as different from that of the victim, the perpetrator is also re-inscribing that of the "other," that is, granting it signification and relating it to himself. But it looks as though he achieves an opposite effect to that which was expected: in trying to eliminate a characteristic perceived as "intolerable," he constitutes it. Both types of violence are *exemplary and they follow the logic of terror*, sometimes they occur in a continuum and sometimes they intertwine, depending on the variables in question. However, they have different uses; one pretends to subordinate the difference; the other pretends to annihilate it. And they face us with different prejudices: different ways of instrumentation of violence, different types of resistance to differences;, and a tacit categorization of the more or less tolerable differences as opposed to those entirely undesirable.

8.2 Legislation Against Violence Based on Sexual Prejudice and LGBTQ Persons' Human Rights Situation in Latin America

In Latin America, the discourse against violence based on homophobia is enshrined in the defense of human rights. Therefore, it does not refer exclusively to non-State agents or institutions but above all, to those who hold the exclusive use of force. The majority of the countries that submit annual reports do so on behalf and in defense

[21] *Id.*

of the human rights of the LGBTQ communities. A pertinent question would be if the enshrining of the legal anti-homophobic discourse in the framework of the discourses on human rights is done out of an absence of particular legislation on this type of violence or following a strategic decision to inscribe this type of violence as conducts that infringe upon the fundamental rights enshrined in the political constitutions and in international agreements. In the United States, instead, the LGBTQ groups emphasize on promoting federal and State laws against hate crimes. These laws operate in criminal law parallel to the way in which anti-discrimination laws operate in civil law. This parallel is motive to debate whether in the Latin American contexts, the laws against discrimination, when they exist and include separate sections on physical violence and they protect certain categories, do not run the risk of experiencing problems similar to those of hate crimes in the United States: defining, identifying, and processing the crime.

There is a need for questioning and debating the convenience of implementing laws against hate crimes: in most cases, the criminal systems of countries and international agreements are sufficient tools to hear cases of the fundamental rights enshrined in the constitutions; it appears unnecessary to resort to a new legislation.

This sub-section will feature a compilation of modern legislation against violence based on sexual prejudice in Latin America, beginning with the presentation of the existing legislation and its sources. This is followed by a brief presentation of aspects relevant to this type of violence recorded in the reports on human rights drafted by some of the social LGBT movements in the region.

8.2.1 Legislation[22]

Latin American legislations protecting the rights of the LGBT population fall into two types: anti-discrimination laws and their inclusion of the category of "sexual orientation" or of "gender identity" as spaces for the possible vulnerability of the subjects, and laws that explicitly legislate on violence based on sexual orientation. Yet, in addition to the defense of the LGBT population via laws included in the codes, there are cases in which non-discrimination clauses are incorporated in constitutions, whether they be national, federal or state constitutions. Below are examples of the Latin American countries that have some kind of legislation against violence based on sexual prejudice or gender identity and that include violence in their sub-sections.

[22] The author thanks Julia Alejandra Morales for her assistance in the research of legal cases and legislation. For useful documents dedicated to identifying the state of relevant legislations for LGBTQ communities, see *International Lesbian and Gay Association* (ILGA): *LGBT World Legal Wrap Up Survey*, compiled by Daniel Ottosson, International Lesbian and Gay Association (ILGA), November Edition, 2006. And *World Legal Survey*, Laws Prohibiting Discrimination Based On Sexual Orientation, 2002. www.ilga.org

8.2.1.1 Countries with Laws Against Hate Crimes

Uruguay

Uruguay is the only country in the region that defines specific penalties for hate-based violence, and that protects the categories of sexual orientation and sexual identity. Within its legislative framework, there are two laws that elaborate on the subject: Law N° 17677, Art. 1: Art. 149 bis of August 6 of 2003, "Incitement of hatred, disdain or violence or commission of these acts against certain persons." This law modifies article 149 of 1989 of the Penal Code and establishes a penalty of imprisonment for 3–18 months for those who *incite through any public means*, hate-based violence or disdain, and protects, among others, the categories of sexual orientation and sexual identity. Article 2 of this law replaces article 149 ter of 1989 with article 149 ter of 2003, and it punishes *acts of moral or physical violence* based on hate or disdain with 6–24 months of imprisonment. The categories of sexual orientation and sexual identity are protected through Law No; 17817 of 2004. *Fight against racism, xenophobia, and discrimination* as a sphere of special interest for the State and therefore can legislate on the mechanisms to fight this.

8.2.1.2 Countries with Laws Against Discrimination[23]

Peru

A reform of the Code of Constitutional Procedure, in force since December of 2004, enshrined the right to non-discrimination on grounds of sexual orientation and granting the right to demand non-discrimination via writs of *amparo*. On May 31, 2007, the Peruvian LGBT movement obtained support from all the representatives of the Peruvian Nationalist Party (PNP) to sponsor the bill Non-discrimination on Grounds of Sexual Orientation and Gender Identity. Although a National Human Rights Plan for the defense of LGBT populations exists, activists claim that it has not been implemented to date, and for this reason they have great expectations regarding this legislative initiative which not only includes the protection of sexual orientation but also of sexual identity.

Besides, the Peruvian Constitutional Code of Procedure provides certain spaces for the legal standing of due process. This Code enshrines, via Law 28237 of 2004, in Title III, Chapter I. Article 37, the right to non-discrimination and it includes the category of sexual orientation.

[23] Brazil has a rich legal and social tradition of resistance against violence based on prejudice. I am not studying the situation of Brazil in this piece. For an interesting article on the topic see: Carrara, S, Vianna, A et al. 2001. *Lethal Violence Against Homosexuals in Rio de Janeiro City: General Characteristics*. http://www.clam.org.br/pdf/lethalviolence.pdf

Mexico

In Mexico, there are two documents of significant relevance for determining the categorization of discrimination as a crime. On the one hand, there is the Penal Code for the Federal District, Mexico City, in Article 206, where it is decreed in Title X, Only Chapter, that discrimination will be punished with penalties including both imprisonment and fines or community work. Sexual orientation is viewed as a protected category and any person "who provokes or incites hatred or violence" is punished.

On the other hand, there is a federal law against discrimination: *Federal Law for the Prevention and Elimination of Discrimination* of June 11, 2003. This law provides mechanisms for the effective fight against discrimination in a wide variety of spheres. In Chapter I, General Provisions, Article 4, it incorporates the definition of the concept of discrimination for the purposes of the law, and the "sexual preferences of persons" is one of the categories protected therein.

Chile

An anti-discrimination legislative bill of 2006 that included sexual orientation passed as an enhancing penalties law on July 2012. The killing of a 24 year old self-identified gay man, Daniel Zamudio, at the hands of a neo-nazi group accelerated the legislative process. In Chile, there are no protected categories in the Political Constitution of 1980, where in its Chapter III, Art. 19, Number 2, equality before the law is enshrined and states, "In Chile there are no privileged persons or groups." In spite of this, Chile has instituted a higher age of consent for formalizing relationships between same-sex persons than the one provided for heterosexual relationships.

Costa Rica

Costa Rica is a special case, since its legislation against discrimination is enshrined within the general law on HIV/AIDS (Law N° 7771). Within the framework of this law, in Chapter III, discrimination is defined as a contravention. Penalties range from 20 to 60 days of imprisonment, to fines or disability. And the notion of discrimination is only categorized within the framework of illness as dominant determining factor. In this way, other spaces of violation of the right to non-discrimination can be easily excluded from the application of the law.

Colombia

The Colombian Congress approved in August 2011 a law punishing those guilty of discrimination with 1–3 years in prison. The law makes a crime to discriminate against a person based on race, ethnicity, religion, gender or sexual orientation.

8.2.1.3 Countries with Articles That Legitimate Sexual Orientation as a Category Within the Right to Equality

Argentina

The Constitution of the Autonomous City of Buenos Aires includes the category of sexual orientation under the right to equal dignity and equality before the law. In its First Book, First Title, Article 11, the Constitution guarantees the right to be different and not to be discriminated for reasons of sexual orientation, among others. In addition, Argentina approved, via Decree 1086 of 2005, the document entitled "Towards a National Plan Against Discrimination: Discrimination in Argentina, Diagnosis and Proposals," which made reference to the need for the State to generate preventive measures against homophobic violence. However, Argentina has a federal ban on the participation in the army, of persons who openly express their belonging in the LGBTQ communities and on artificial insemination treatments in the case of single women or same-sex couples.[24]

Bolivia

Bolivia provides, in article 14 of its National Constitution, that sexual orientation is a protected category.

Ecuador

Ecuador provides, in its National Constitution, Chapter 2. Of Civil Rights, Article 23, numeral 3, equality before the law, and it enshrines sexual orientation as a protected category.

Colombia

Besides the recently approved law against discrimination, the recognition of the rights of LGBTQ persons has been achieved especially through writs of *amparo* and rulings of the Constitutional Court. Thus, Article 13 of the Constitution and its constitutional interpretation associate "sexual orientation" to "sex" and several *amparo* rulings contribute to the case law. In addition, there is the following legislation[25]:

- Colombian Penal Code, Article 58. Circumstances of Greater Criminality. The following constitute circumstances of greater criminality, insofar as they have

[24] *LGBT World Legal Wrap Up Survey*, compiled by Daniel Ottosson, International Lesbian and Gay Association (ILGA), November Edition, 2006.

[25] Compilation by Mauricio Albarracín from *Colombia Diversa* in "Balance sobre Violencia por homofobia en Colombia", Universidad de los Andes, Bogotá, April 2007.

not been otherwise provided for: [...] "3. The execution of the criminal conduct is inspired by reasons of intolerance and discrimination based on race, ethnicity, ideology, religion or beliefs, sex or sexual orientation, or some illness or handicap of the victim's."

- Penal Code, Article 268-B: Special aggravating circumstances of the crime of forced disappearances [...] 4. When the conduct is committed, for reasons of their qualities, against the following persons: civil servants, communicators, human rights defenders, candidates for popularly elected positions, trade union, political or religious leaders, against those who have been witnesses of criminal or disciplinary conducts, justices of the peace, or any other person for reasons of their beliefs or political opinions, or for any reason implying some form of discrimination or intolerance.
- The City Council of Medellin adopted, in June of 2006, an agreement leading to the development of "the public policy for the prevention and attention of the sexual violence that affect citizens, mainly women, girls and boys in the city." In this agreement, LGBT persons are included as beneficiaries of the policy.
- The Code of the Police Force of Bogotá established norms that foster respect for the sexual orientation of individuals, and educational campaigns for the tolerance and respect of LGBT persons.[26]

8.2.2 Reports on LGBTQ Human Rights in Argentina, Chile, Colombia, Mexico and Peru[27]

The following is a brief presentation of the Reports on Human Rights submitted by five Latin American countries. All the reports state that statistics on violence based on homophobia may be below the actual level because persons investigating violence, as well as the media, police, and even the families, tend to ignore that these violent acts are motivated by homophobia. The purpose is to familiarize persons with an interest in the subject, with the work of the different organizations and indicate sources for future investigations.

8.2.2.1 Argentina

The report on human rights of the LGBTQ community in Argentina is drafted by the Argentine Homosexual Community (AHC) and produced annually. This report

[26] *See* "Voces Excluidas: legislación y derechos de lesbianas, gays, bisexuales y transgeneristas en Colombia," *Colombia Diversa*, Bogotá, 2005; "Derechos humanos de lesbianas, gays, bisexuales y transgeneristas en Colombia" *Colombia Diversa*, Bogotá, 2005, www.colombiadiversa.org

[27] The information in this section goes until 2006.

documents specific cases of violation of human rights, with a focus on homicides and illegal detentions, as well as advancements in terms of public visualization of these types of actions and legislation for the benefit of the LGBT community. ACH has submitted reports on the situation of this community in Argentina since 1998. The first report contained a historical account of murder cases based on homophobia that occurred since the early 1980s. This report links the 17 murder cases that occurred during the military dictatorship, apart from suggesting the enforced disappearance of 400 LGBTQ persons. The report also recounts 57 cases of murder based on homophobia that took place between the years 1990 and 1998.

In 1999, the report document seven murder cases based on homophobia; four cases in 2000; three cases in 2001; and, five cases in 2002. The different reports document cases drawn from news in the media and explain that there are probably many unreported cases of this type of crime. The reports do not include any special follow up of the judicial situation of each of these cases.[28]

8.2.2.2 Chile

Throughout the past decade, the Movement for Homosexual Integration and Liberation (acronym in Spanish MOVILH) had produced an annual report on the situation of sexual minorities' human rights in Chile. The annual reports, drafted by a varied group of researchers, analyses this situation and follow up on cases in which the rights of LGBTQ communities are infringed. In the report published in February of 2007, a special review is made of the tendencies that the cases of discrimination based on sexual orientation have historically followed since the movement's first report. In the category of cases based on sexual orientation, the reports include data ranging from discrimination episodes in cultural, political and social activities to homicides based on homophobia, making, of course, the pertinent distinction.

In 2002, the report focused primarily on discrimination actions against LGBTQ persons; 48 cases were reported that year, of which five were homicides, two were death threats, and 14 involved violent acts. In 2003, the report made reference to a remarkable increment from the previous year. The number of cases rose to 66, though none were murder cases based on homophobia; 12 were cases of physical violence against LGBTQ persons, four at the hands of State forces and eight at the hands of civilians. In 2004, the cases of violation of human rights of that segment of the population decreased to 46. Of these, two were murder cases based on homophobia, two were cases of violent physical acts perpetrated by civilians, and one was a case of physical action perpetrated by members of State forces. On the other hand, the 2005 report accounted for 58 cases, none of which was a homicide, but nine of which were acts of physical violence, all perpetrated by civilians.

[28] Reports available at www.cha.org.ar

The year 2006 came to a close with a positive balance for the Chilean LGBT community in matters of discrimination with only 49 cases all kinds of discrimination. Of those, 14 were cases of physical violence; two were homicides, one based on homophobia and one on transphobia; and, 12 were cases of physical violence against LGBTQ persons, nine of which were perpetrated by civilians and three by members of the State.

MOVILH, on its part, has achieved remarkable advances in the juridical and social fields, including: the decriminalization of sodomy in 1998; the reopening of the case involving the fire at the Divine discotheque in 2003; the elimination of restrictions for blood donation on the part of gay persons in public blood banks; the triumph of the *OpusGay* newspaper in a lawsuit filed by the Prelature of the Opus Dei in 2004; and the signature by the Chilean Government of a United Nations resolution condemning crimes based on homophobia in 2004.[29]

8.2.2.3 Colombia

The NGO *Colombia Diversa* has championed the defense and the development of LGBTQ persons in Colombia. The organization has presented two reports: *Excluded Voices* (2005), focused on a revision of the Colombian legal system and its relationship with the human rights of those communities, and the first report on *Human Rights of Lesbians, Gays, Bisexuals, and Transgender Persons in Colombia in 2005* (2006), the first of its kind in the country. The latter report makes a special distinction regarding cases of violence: it understands all the manifestations of physical and moral violence against the LGBTQ population based on their sexual orientation or gender identity. The report reviews the acts of violence in three dimensions: homicide, violence based on intolerance, and homophobic violence within the Colombian military forces. It takes as the basis for its investigation of cases, the statistics produced by the National Institute of Legal Medicine and Forensic Science and journalistic documents. However, the document makes clear that the actual figures in these kinds of cases must be higher, since there are no more adequate documentation processes followed.

There are statistics available about homophobic-based homicides only since 2000, compiled by Doctor Andrés Rodríguez, from the Institute of Legal Medicine. Dr. Rodríguez suspects the existence of at least 60 cases of homicides of homosexual men in Bogotá between 2000 and 2005. The report also discloses a higher number of registered cases since then. The majority of these homicides reveal a similar *modus operandi*. The report, however, does not make a revision of specific cases, or at a national level, of the homicides based on homophobia in Colombia. Among the reasons, are that violence based on sexual orientation has not been characterized as a crime, and therefore the competent authorities do not produce specific statistics and the crimes are classified under other categories.

[29] www.movilh.cl

Now, given the country's situation of internal conflict, the report defines violence based on intolerance as "a form of violence exerted by armed groups against a person or groups of persons considered 'problematic' by the perpetrators, or 'unwanted' by society." That is to say, the report highlights the pertinence of reexamining the situation of the LGBTQ community in relation to armed groups, including both well-known actors of the armed conflict and groups of civilians. It analyzes five cases of this kind, pointing out, however, to the absence of relevant statistics.

Lastly, the report makes reference to the cases of violence based on homophobia within the Armed Forces. It analyzes a case of sexual abuse of a soldier for being, supposedly, homosexual, and a case of physical abuse of a soldier for reasons of his sexual orientation. Additionally, *Colombia Diversa* has filed certain appeals concerning these cases. However, they explain that although the Colombian Military Forces do not consider the category of sexual orientation in a special manner in the human rights training its members receive, the Constitution protects the participation of LGBTQ persons in the Armed Forces.[30]

In addition to *Colombia Diversa*'s reports, the *Corporación Promover Ciudadanía* of Bogota, submitted in July of 2006 a survey on the infringement of the right of sexual autonomy in the city. The survey included 440 participants in the gay march in Bogotá. Some of the conclusions show that nearly 25% of those polled have suffered physical violence for reasons of their sexual orientation, and 21% have been subjected to physical violence by the police. Seven out of every ten inhabitants of Bogotá admitted that the sight of shows of affection between same-sex persons "bothers" them.[31]

8.2.2.4 Mexico

The Citizens Commission against Hate Crime because of Homophobia has been in charge of drafting the report on the violation of human rights of the Mexican LGBTQ population. This Commission, the result of the joint work of several Mexican citizens with the NGO *Letra S*, has as its mission, the defense of the human and sexual rights of the LGBTQ population. *Letra S*, focuses on hate crimes based on homophobia. While hate crimes are not legally defined in Mexico, the Commission has decided to call them thus and it even calls them executions; its approach focuses exclusively on the acts that may be inscribed within this category. Since 1998, the Commission has produced reports based on a hemerographic system in order to expose the executions involving members of these communities. In the period between 1998 and 2004, 332 proven executions based on homophobia, and 996 estimated executions based on homophobia have been documented. The reports make it clear that they resort to a hemerographic methodology in order to document the existence of this phenomenon and document the cases with the

[30] Colombian Constitutional Court, Rulings C-507 de 1999; T-097 de 1994, and C-431 de 2004.

[31] "http://www.colombiadiversa.org", www.colombiadiversa.org. For the poll *see* "http://www.promoverciudadanía.com", www.promoverciudadanía.com. For the press note *see* "Una ciudad poco abierta a los gays" in El Tiempo, 19 de noviembre de 2006. "http://www.eltiempo.terra.com", www.eltiempo.terra.com

information available, but above all because the Mexican authorities in charge of criminal investigations, state that only the victims' lawyers and relatives have legal interest in the investigations.

According to the reports, in Mexico an average of 35 proven murders based on homophobia occur every year. This number of cases represents only a sample of the real situation, for there is no clear methodology to document the cases, and therefore many of them go unnoticed both by the authorities and by the victims' relatives, or the social and cultural homophobia inhibits the relatives from fighting to obtain justice. In Mexico, 38 cases of homophobic-based hate crimes were reported in 1995; 42 in 1996; 37 in 1997; 47 in 1998; 26 in 1999; 24 in 2000; 21 in 2001; 40 in 2002; 26 in 2003; and 30 in 2004. The reports categorize the cases according to the year in which they occurred, the city or the state where they occurred, the victim's gender and age, the manner of death and the place where the victim was found. As in other countries of the region, in Mexico, the authorities consider the majority of these cases "crimes of passion," thus preventing the development of a more specific investigation that may recognize the special characteristics of the crimes.[32]

8.2.2.5 Peru

The Homosexual Movement of Lima (Spanish acronym MHOL) produces the report on the human rights of the Peruvian LGBTQ community. The annual report for 2005, "Situation of the human rights of lesbians, transsexuals, gays, and bisexuals of Peru," is concerned with reporting the cases of physical violence against members of the LGBTQ community and reveal the special circumstances that promote discrimination. In the first two chapters of the report, there is a chronicle of the crimes based on homophobia, understanding as homophobic-based crime any type of violation of the human rights of these communities, from verbal violence to homicide, and they even specifically include hate crimes.

The report documents and analyses cases assumed to be hate crimes from a journalistic basis to identify the cases. In the report reference is made to the cases which occurred between 2004 and 2005, observing, like other reports from the region, that the number of cases may be greater for the same reasons because neither the media, nor the legal sphere, nor the victims' families recognize them as acts motivated by homophobia or transphobia.

The report documents the facts concerning the crimes and the legal proceedings of two cases of homicide of transgender persons reported as hate crimes in 2004. In 2005, on the other hand, 14 cases of homophobic-based hate crimes were presented; they have been documented in the report and reference is made, whenever pertinent, to the corresponding legal and investigative advances. The report suggests, however, that for every properly documented case there must be another four cases

[32] *See* http://www.letraese.org.mx/contracrimenes.htm; http://www.ilga.org/news; http://www.cesarsalgado.net/200306/030606.htm

which are not, so that homophobic-based cases of homicide in Peru would actually be around 70. The report includes certain cases of physical violence and discrimination based on homophobia committed against LGBTQ persons, but it does not provide statistical data in this respect.[33]

8.3 Case Analysis

Whereas the legislation against prejudice-based violence in Latin America is relatively scarce, the work of LGBT human rights organizations is meticulous and significant, and so are some jurisprudential debates and judicial decisions that are beginning to clarify perspectives on the issue. Although it is difficult to identify the legal cases addressing homophobic-based violence in the region—regional lack of communication is, partly, the problem for those investigating the matter, a factor that this book attempts to reduce—it is interesting to examine, in the absence of specific laws against violence based on hate, the juridical treatment accorded or not accorded to these conducts when they are referred to diverse or non-normative sexualities. For this reason, we will examine some rulings and also some cases which were not brought before the court but which have been included in the reports of different organizations. For the analysis of the cases, we propose examining three particular problems: the invisibility or camouflage of the homophobic motives involved in the violent gestures; the repeated recourse to extenuating factors such as anger and intense pain and their relation with the "smokescreen" of crimes of passion, and the tensions between the public and private ambits in the presence of the expression of diverse sexualities. Many of the problems we come across include the classification of cases—the distinction between symbolic and instrumental crime—the discretionary application of the law, police abuse, and secondary victimization.

8.3.1 Invisibility

By invisibility we understand not only "that which cannot be seen" but also that which is ignored or camouflaged out of ignorance or with full awareness. The invisibility of prejudice-based violence has been a constant in Latin America. It is not by chance that the first interest of all LGBT organizations is methodologically oriented towards making a diagnosis, towards gathering information to show that the phenomenon exists. The reasons for the mentioned invisibility are multiple and they may be recognized in the difficulty to identify concrete legal cases, partly because they have not been defined, because the police resists their identification, or because the crime is immediately

[33] *See* http://www.mhol.org.pe

categorized as a crime of passion, because of the victims' fear to report the attacks and become exposed to "secondary victimization." But above all, what becomes relevant in the case of invisibility or of excessive visibility is the discretionary use that State agents and juridical operators make of the notion of gender identity or sexual orientation when identifying the cases, when carrying out judicial proceedings, and when sentencing. The cases and rulings below illustrate these tensions. The problem of invisibility is divided into three issues: the role of the police and the prosecutors in the identification of the cases, secondary or double victimization, and the discretionary use of the categories of sexual orientation or gender identity.

8.3.1.1 The Role of the Police and the Public Prosecutors in the Identification of Cases

The informed participation of police and public prosecutors is fundamental because they are the first State organism to have access to the events of a case. Their lack of information or their prejudiced attitude generates resistance to admit the existence of a homophobic component of an incident. This would lead to classifying a murder case without further investigation, for example, as a crime of passion, and thus, base the incident on emotional aspects particular to a couple. Other effects are negligence or shortsightedness in the gathering of the evidence, and consequently, to the reduction or disappearance of evidence of potential homophobic components of the incident. Among the consequences of this situation, we find the difficulty in trying the crimes in an adequate way, and above all, to elaborate a diagnosis of the social situation in the presence of violence based on homophobia. The following article deals with the legal question of how to articulate penal categories that allow a precise identification of violent conduct motivated by sexual prejudice bearing in mind that the motivations frequently combine instrumental and symbolic aspects.

Press article
***El Tiempo*, Bogota, Colombia**
Coincidences in Deaths of Homosexuals in Bogota Lead to Suspicions of the Existence of a Serial Killer
June 10, 2006

Extracts:
This year there have been at least eight cases characterized by a similar pattern: the victims are gay men, over forty years old, with economic stability. Additionally, they are attacked in their residences and their bodies are usually naked. The majority of the homicides have occurred in the locality of Chapinero, and the cause of death is ligature strangulation with other lesions present.

At the Institute of Legal Medicine, medical doctor, Andrés Rodríguez, has devoted himself to studying this situation. His interest originated when, for his graduation project as forensic doctor at the National University, Rodríguez focused on the subject of homicide by mechanical asphyxiation in Bogotá.

When analyzing the cases, he discovered that the great majority of the victims were homosexuals. "It got my attention, and I began to investigate what other things they had in common," he explains.

According to his estimates, over sixty homosexuals since the year 2000 have been murdered. The doctor's conclusions show that there are patterns that repeat themselves: "Strangulation by ligature," Rodríguez specifies, "they employ some element that applies pressure; the most usual in these cases is electrical wire."

As confirmed in the official documents to which he has access because of his forensic work, there are almost always witnesses who declare that they have seen the victims enter their residences with one or two young men. Also, there are traces of alcohol or drug use.

"Theft is usually suggested as criminal motive. But I think that if there is any larceny it is an opportunistic thing, and not the main intention." Andrés Rodríguez has reasons to state this: If it were only a question of theft, why murder them in such a violent way? The victims suffer a number of lesions that exceeds those necessary to finish with their lives. In addition to asphyxia, they are attacked with a knife or receive blows from blunt objects.

The areas of the heart and the neck suffer the greatest number of attacks. "And they have a strong representation of passion," Rodríguez remarks, "What is the reason for all these attacks if the objective were to rob the apartment?"[34]

"Does the repetition of methods lead you to think that the author may be a single person or a band?"

"I cannot state that the same person is responsible for all these homicides, but it is possible that there be a repeat offense. A person or a band may have acted in several cases," the doctor comments.

The death of the owner of The Red Panther

"He does not listen to that, he only likes ballads," Albeiro Zabala told the policemen who waited for someone to finally answer the door of Félix Rodríguez's apartment, on 45th street, past 13th Avenue.

"Something has happened to him. Let's break the door," he insisted.

"And if he is only asleep?"

Zabala persuaded them and they finally forced the door. Félix Rodríguez, the owner of one of the oldest gay bars in Bogota, "The Red Panther," was not asleep. He lay on his bed, naked, and a pillow covered his face. He was dead.

… "He was strangled. He was also hit on the head with a stone that they left there."

"Was he robbed?"

"They took his ring, and it seems they also took some cash he had. Nothing else."

[…]

[34] Personal conversation with Dr. Andrés Rodríguez (February 2007). Notes taken from his presentation: "Homicidios de hombres gay en Bogotá" at the *Seminario Internacional sobre violencia por homofobia*, Universidad de los Andes, Bogotá, April 12, 2007.

Crimes in the closet

[...]

What doctor [Andrés Rodríguez] is most concerned about is the fact that the authorities do not seem to pay enough attention. "It is a vulnerable group, and the fact that they have homosexual conducts does not justify their being killed," Rodríguez states. He has even perceived a biased attitude in some of the investigators. "It is as if they said: They had it coming for living like that."

[...]

Crimes in the closet. This is how the deaths are defined in a document that *Colombia Diversa* is preparing. They are deaths that are shelved because they are not well investigated or because people do not report them for fear of their coming out in the public light. "What we demand from the authorities is that they record this in writing, in order to demonstrate that this is happening," says Marcela Sánchez.[35]

8.3.1.2 Matters for Debate

The motive for the attacks is usually mistaken. If there is larceny, for instance, this can be identified as the motive (instrumental crime) and overlook the homophobic (symbolic) component. What renders larceny as sole motive suspicious, the forensic doctor points out, is the excessive brutality of the crimes. This is a common perception for investigators in different societies. How should the lack of proportion between the motive and the manner of the crime be evaluated?

Doctor Rodríguez comments that that he generally comes across great deficiencies in the gathering of evidence by the police and meets the resistance of a majority of prosecutors to recognize the cases as motivated by sexual prejudice, and he points out the importance of determining a pattern in the incidents, among others: in his investigation he finds similarities in terms of the sector of the city in which the crimes are committed, asphyxia and knife wounds as the cause of death, and the age and economic status of the victims. However, of the 60 cases of homicide possibly motivated by homophobia examined in his laboratory, there are approximately 15 proceedings in the city's prosecution service. Access to the files has not been possible because of the *sub-judice* rule.

In the case of the homicide of Félix Rodríguez, the owner of *The Red Panther*, however, the perpetrator has already been tried and condemned to 17 years and 4 months of imprisonment. The individual resorted to a plea bargaining agreement. In other cases of violence based on sexual prejudice, we could only have access to the first and second instance [lower courts'] rulings through the rights of petition, with delays and paperwork involved in their observance, telephone calls to the clerks of court, long visits to the same, and frustration because a special interest in the proceedings is required in order to have access to the files. It is worth pointing out that this situation is not found in the high courts, where information is systematized and available in a database.

[35]http://eltiempo.terra.com.co/judi/2006-06-11/ARTICULO-WEB-_NOTA_INTERIOR-2941878.html By María Paulina Ortiz.

With regard to the perpetrator, it is worth noting the title of the newspaper article, which alludes to a potential serial killer. Without being able to provide further information regarding this matter, and admitting the possibility that this might indeed be true, we believe it is worth proposing as a "matter for debate" the tendency to think of the perpetrators of this kind of violence as individuals with "mental disorders." It is important to pay attention to the need to take into account the social character of the prejudice and the contexts in which the perpetrators legitimate their violent conduct. That is to say, a society that features homophobic gestures in its cultural manifestations, its legal decisions, its media, its political discourses, and its laws, is constantly producing the context in which violence takes place and in which it articulates its messages. The perpetrators tend to believe that their acts are meant to preserve a world order, that of compulsory heterosexuality, for instance, which appears as natural and necessary and where the non-normative sexualities stand defiantly. In this respect it is important to point out that the agents of violence based on prejudice tend to be common citizens who feel they are being damaged by the differences. There is an urgent need to inquire into these matters in Latin America, and the recommendation is that any initiative should take into account factors such as race, gender, national origin, and age, to examine how these factors intersect with sexual orientation and gender identity.

The recommendation answers the need to clearly determine the motives behind the violent incidents, especially of those which are voluntary and effectively or potentially lethal, so as to identify the factors of prejudice and of greater risk in each society. This generates an interesting debate on the role of the criminal motive. In the dogma, this role, although relevant as a factor entailing a greater penalty, loses weight when it comes to establishing criminal responsibility. This is pointed out by the Criminal Chamber of the Supreme Court of Colombia:

> ... it is to be noted that the law does not require that in order to configure the responsibility in the crime of voluntary homicide, the specific end that is pursued through the conduct of causing a person's death, or the motive for having proceeded in the manner alluded be proved, but only that the action should have been committed voluntarily and with knowledge of its unlawful nature.[36]

If the criminal dogma does not require establishing the motive for the action in order to determine the responsibility and it only requires the willful intent to commit the crime, the socio-juridical importance of inquiring into the motive may be overlooked. Such inquiry is what provides clues regarding the social situation of prejudices, besides helping determine the factor of greater or lesser criminality of the offenses.

Other issues addressed in the press article are discussed in the sections: fear of secondary victimization and the classification of the crimes as crimes of passion.

Secondary Victimization or Double Victimization

Few issues are so problematic for victims of violence based on sexual prejudice as the fear of secondary victimization at the hands of State agents. This is the victim's fear of finding themselves stigmatized, exposed, overwhelmed by the burden of

[36] Case No 11829. Colombian Supreme Court of Justice. April 4, 2002.

proof when they are most vulnerable and urgently require that their rights be guaranteed. Secondary victimization appears with remarkable frequency in cases of rape and in cases of violence against gay men, lesbians and transgender persons, and it follows several patterns. First, is the notion that the victim "was looking for trouble," this means that the perpetrators were "provoked" by the victims, for example, by the way they dressed, by walking on certain streets or at certain hours, or for having certain conduct or practice. Another pattern is the intromission of State agents in the body or the privacy of the victims to gather evidence of the incident, for example, of a rape, and when medical and psychological discourses regarding diverse or non-normative sexualities are used to justify "treatments" aimed at finding a pathology conversion. Below are two examples.

Press Article
***El Tiempo*, Bogota, Colombia**
Crime of Passion Behind the Murder of Cuban University Professor
February 25, 2007

The Police Commander of Bolívar asserts that the murderer entered the house where the event occurred with the consent of the victim, Rolando Pérez, aged 43. "All the evidence we have gathered and the information that has been verified by the Judicial Police… indicate that the motives behind this crime are evidently those of a crime of passion, for this citizen led a disorderly life, was promiscuous, and in his condition as a homosexual, had several partners," Colonel Carlos Mena Bravo stated. The body was found on Saturday morning in an apartment in Torices, the neighborhood where Pérez lived. He had received several blows on the head, apparently delivered with a hammer. He already presented signs of decomposition, for which reason it is presumed that his death occurred between Thursday and Friday. According to the information that Colonel Mena reiterated, the perpetrator entered Pérez's room with the latter's full consent, given that the security was not violated and none of the Cuban citizen's belongings have been lost. As for the aggressor's identity, the officer explained that the police were evaluating "important" data obtained in the course of interviews with people closely related to the victim, "precisely, homosexual partners of his" he specified.

Regional Court of Social and Cultural Rights of Women
Lima, July 15, 2005[37]

Main Legal Issue:
Does the involuntary confinement of a person in a clinic with the aim of subjecting him/her to "treatment" for his/her "rehabilitation" on account of his/her non-heterosexual behaviors infringe upon the rights to equality, to physical integrity, to health, to freedom, to the free development of the personality? Can the mentioned "treatments" constitute cruel, inhuman, and degrading treatment? Is the responsibility of the State compromised by permitting such situations?

[37] This complaint was submitted before the Regional Court of Social and Cultural Rights of Women by Fundacion Causana from Ecuador. All the excerpts are taken from the Tribunal Memoirs.

Facts:
A. was born in Manta, Ecuador and at the age of 24, she relocated to Quito. After finishing her career, she did not wish to return to her parent's house in her home town, and she stayed with her partner. After five years, her family found out that she defined herself as a lesbian, and they made arrangements to have her confined against her will in a private rehabilitation clinic. When she went to the clinic to receive therapy for alcohol abuse, she was informed that her father had decided that she remain there for a while. At first she thought that her alcohol problem was the reason for the intervention. She was confined for four months and a half, and the fundamental cause of the "treatment" was her lesbianism. During her confinement, she suffered physical and psychological tortures, with the complicity of her family and the failure of the State through omission to control these institutions.

Court Ruling:
The Court's verdict recognizes that A. was the object of cruel, inhuman and degrading treatment; she was discriminated against based on her sexual orientation; she was arbitrarily deprived of freedom; and her physical and psychological health were infringed upon. The Court finds liability on the State both for action and for omission.

Extracts of the Complaint:
Acts infringing upon rights
We report before this Court that several lesbian women dependent on their traditional family nuclei have been confined against their will in private clinics in different regions of Ecuador, mainly in the Coast. The referred clinics offer in a discreet and discretionary way, "rehabilitation" therapies or therapies for the "cure of homosexuality;" and they are careful enough not to explain what these therapies are in the contracts that they sign with the patients or with their representatives.

The persons who decide to subject these women to therapy are members of the family who hold the power within it; especially the father or the mother. Confinement generally violates, in the first place, the rights to physical integrity and freedom, because after determining a medical treatment against the will of the women, they are confined in the clinics through the use of physical force. The methods these institutions employ in their treatments continue to infringe upon basic civil rights, and may even configure torture, cruel, inhuman and degrading treatment in the light of international norms currently in force in Ecuador.

The Court must know that the confinement and treatment to which these women are subjected constitutes an infringement upon several civil, social, and cultural rights. The rights to the free development of the personality are violated, and in particular, the right to the free expression of the sexual identity, to equality before the law, and in particular, to equal opportunities among the members of the family.

Finally, the Court needs to know that the responsibility for the violation of rights in this case is shared by those who have committed or have contributed to the commission of the violations, on the one hand; and by the Ecuadorian State, on the other, insofar as it has failed to fulfill, and continues failing to fulfill through omission, its constitutional and supra legal duties of guaranteeing rights, and of prevention, investigation, punishment, and reparation of the violations.

Analysis of the violations
[…]
The violations they have suffered have transcended the threshold of privacy. This threshold exists because their condition of being lesbians, their sexual experiences and practices usually occur in the "private" ambit, and even the violations of rights occur in this ambit. Across this threshold, however, the situation described before the Court does not constitute a singular or exceptional case, but is rather common to many lesbian women.

It is important to report before the Court the way in which, through social practices deeply rooted in the culture, the violation of the rights of lesbians becomes normalized or their capacity to claim the enforceability of these rights is diminished. In this particular case, the patriarchal hierarchy within the family plays a fundamental role, and this is especially true in the case of one of its aspects: the historical control over women's sexuality on the part of the men who hold the power in the family; especially the husband or the father. This element helps to explain the natural way in which the Ecuadorian State incurs in omission in the presence of the flagrant violations in this case.

The control over women's sexuality adopts particularly aggressive forms—forms of explicit violence which on occasions can even configure torture—when a dissident sexual orientation is verified; for example, lesbianism in the case of a daughter born into a conservative family; which is tantamount to verifying that the daughter—in the conception of the mother or the father—"got out of hand."

Likewise, the patriarchal hierarchy is based upon a specific heterosexual order …. [W]ithin this order, the allocation of sex to the private sphere is fundamental. Consequently, the Ecuadorean culture only admits that certain manifestations of (hetero)sexuality, such as marriage, transcend to the public sphere. This usually reduces lesbian practice and identity to concealment in the private sphere, in the family, in the clinics, and in the private and discretionary contract signed between the former and the latter.

It is substantial to point out that when the family or society perceive the threat that lesbian identity may project itself into the public levels, off limits to them, several discourses are activated to reproach this public appearance: that of setting a bad example, that of sin, that of family dishonor, and especially relevant in the case we are reporting, that of the pathologization of lesbian practices and conducts, and even the lesbian identity itself.

At the social level, it is evident that pathologization detracts from lesbians' power, insofar as it de-legitimizes their actions….

In the same way, at the juridical level, the effect of pathology is the restriction or deprivation of the formal capacity to exercise rights. This effect deserves special attention from the Court when it comes to carrying out a critical analysis of the violations of rights suffered by individuals traditionally at the margins of the dominant lifestyles, as is the case of lesbians….

There certainly is no positive norm in force in Ecuador that provides restriction of rights for, or of the capacity to exercise those rights, on the part of lesbian women, as there was, indeed, with respect to prostitutes or to married women in past legislations. However, the extra-juridical imaginary of the pathology manages to reach the juridical sphere, not by way of the validity of discriminatory norms, but through an absence of norms protecting civil liberties, which entails lack of enforceability.

As can be deduced from this Case, neither the third parties directly involved in the violations, nor the State itself (the latter neither in the concrete nor in the general case) legitimize the experience of the young lesbian women: their personal truth, their life project and their demands are invalidated; the assertion made at the top of their lungs that their rights are being infringed upon is subjugated; and their very existence as subjects of rights is delegitimized.

[...] We point out to the Court that the confinement of lesbians in private clinics is a mechanism that serves several ends: it is a mechanism for the intensification of control over the daughters' sexuality; it is a mechanism of delegation of punishment for sexual dissidence, which the family leaves in the hands of the health professionals; and finally, it is a mechanism of subjugation of women, which consists in breaking them physically and undermining them psychologically, through actions which, on occasions, may even configure torture, with the aim of restoring the heterosexual and patriarchal order they have transgressed.

The Court knows, of course, that at present family rights are public and not contractual, thanks to the achievements regarding gender in force in States operating under the rule of law, and included in the Constitution and supra legally. However, it will be able to verify that, in Ecuador, this formal equality of spaces, endowed with constitutional rank, does not succeed in positivizing itself in certain secondary norms. The norms dealing with family rights are particularly exclusive. The legal protection of only one type of family, the heterosexual one, implies vulnerability, not only of the alternative family nuclei, but of the "different" persons who cohabit within traditional nuclei.

Besides, based on the conception that the lesbian sexual identity must not project itself onto the public spheres, health is privatized in the discretionary contracts signed by the clinics and the informants' relatives.... In short, the privatization of the right to health is closely related to the privatization of lesbian sexuality. The content of the law becomes contractual, as do the treatments chosen for the "rehabilitation" (actually, subjugation); contractual treatments that involve—no more, no less—than torture and complex violation of all the rights that have been analyzed.

Finally, it would be convenient for the Court to make a critical analysis of the nature of dependence and the way in which it hinders reporting violations in the case presented. The complaining parties hold the clinics' "professionals," or the State, responsible for the violations they have suffered, but they soften their testimony when it comes to holding their mother, or their father, or their brother in law directly responsible, insofar as they reason that their relatives ultimately "meant well"; they wished to reintegrate them into a "normal" life, with all the privileges that normality implies. There are few who, in these situations of conflict with the family, can or wish to proceed with the rupture and assume its consequences.

8.3.1.3 Matters for Debate

Three registries of secondary victimization have been pointed out, namely, blaming the victim, intromission in the victim's body to gather evidence of the incident, and the influence of medical and psychiatric discourses on juridical discourses to omit or reinforce cruel and humiliating practices on individuals with non-normative sexualities. It is important to ask, on the basis of concrete cases representing these three dimensions, how the contexts of gender-based violence and sexual prejudiced violence exert an influence on the commission of secondary victimization. The following presents specific items for debate concerning the case of the lesbian confined to a psychiatric institution by her family. Perhaps the matter revolves around the regulation of the interdependence of the medical-psychiatric and criminal discourses in order to evaluate and grant the full enjoyment of rights to individuals belonging to sexual minorities, in societies characterized by compulsory heterosexuality and by the disassociation between enshrined constitutional rights and socio-cultural practices, in particular those concerning the family and the private sphere. In these cases, it is worth taking into account the possible similarities and differences in the juridical treatment of the victims when these are gay men, lesbians or transgender persons. That is, how do the contexts of gender-based violence and sexual prejudiced violence influence the commission of secondary victimization?

We must bear in mind that homosexuality was eliminated from the *Diagnostic and Statistical Manual of Mental Disorders* (DSM) of the American Association of Psychiatry (APA) in 1973, and that the World Health Organization (WHO) removed it from its list of mental illnesses in 1990. Those "historical mistakes of science," however, still exert an influence on certain social groups and, together with the recurring resistance of many families to accept, support, or admit the sexual differences of some of their members, they frequently result in obstacles to clearly determine the circumstances of the episodes of violence or they themselves become a source of violence.

The arguments presented by the Fundación Causana, in the case of the Ecuadorian woman, articulate the pathologization of non-normative sexual practices and the desired aims of "conversion" and naturalization of the heterosexual family. The hierarchies that are generated in societies based on compulsory heterosexuality find in the discourses of certain mental institutions and in the State's omission to regulate them, a justification to intervene and co-execute the violation of fundamental rights of its members.

The institutionalization of lesbian women in the mentioned conditions and under the mentioned treatments constitutes torture, cruel, inhuman, and degrading treatment in the light of international norms and treaties in force. But, it is a fact that socio-cultural practices continue to reproduce discrimination and are practiced in the name of the privacy of the family, i.e., "that even the violations of their rights [those of lesbian women] occur in this ambit."[38]

---

[38] *Memoria del Tribunal Regional por los Derechos Económicos, Sociales y Culturales de las Mujeres*, p. 135.

The "treatment or cure" in the clinics is organized around the argument that homosexuality is a deviation, and that the person can be "converted" back to the (heterosexual) norm.[39] This argument is based on the belief that there is "a strict correspondence between biological sex and gender, and between gender roles and sexual conducts and practices."[40] Recall A.'s narration:

> For three days in a row they made me wear a dress of one of the fellow patients who was a sexual worker—an extremely tight-fitting dress, and very short… They made me wear it for three days during therapy, and the therapists said to me: 'these days your fellow male patient's will masturbate in your name seeing you like that'… The therapist incited a male patient to harass me … and he said: 'I can make love to you, you will know what penetration is … if you are with me, I am sure that you will like men.'[41]

Parallel to this illusory correspondence between biological sex, gender, roles, practices and desires, there is also the conception, when it is a question of sex between women that "if they know a man the conversion is guaranteed." This belief, which is really a fantasy, is constructed in the shadow of the privileges derived from the control of sexuality. What sex between women implies to the patriarchal hierarchy, is the presentation of a kind of pleasure that is out of reach for those who have historically controlled the economy of the bodies: the heterosexual alliance. Lesbians, or rather, lesbian desire, is perceived as "stealing the pleasures of heterosexuality"[42] and the statement "you will know what a penetration is" is a way of saying "only men can/know how to penetrate, if you or another like you does it, or if you experience pleasure without it, you are usurping my place and my privileges and then I will not know who I am." This is the reason why lesbian desire blows off the hinges of the regime of compulsory heterosexuality, because it demonstrates the radical fragility of power (masculine-heterosexual) over the bodies. The non-heterosexual male is certainly a threat for this economy, but in the same way that he jeopardizes it because he declines a privilege, he also helps to configure it, for he is the opposite, "the other that defines what I am-not." But the lesbian is, in the words of the French philosopher Monique Wittig, a non-sense. If in the register of compulsory heterosexuality a woman is defined in relation to a man, and being a man is having access to women, "a lesbian," says Wittig, "is not a woman"[43] and, therefore, she threatens an entire order based on the mentioned relationships because she has the power to reveal its contingency. That is the power that destabilizes; that is the power that compulsory heterosexuality does not hesitate in challenging through different means, including torture and cruel and degrading treatment.

---

[39] *See* Yoshino, *op.cit.*

[40] *Memoria del Tribunal Regional por los Derechos Económicos, Sociales Culturales de las Mujeres*, p. 135.

[41] *Id.* pp. 132–133.

[42] G. Mason, "Not our Kind of Hate Crime" *op.cit*, p. 275.

[43] Wittig, *op.cit*, p. 28.

The Discretionary Use of Categories

The discretionary use of the categories of homosexuality, sexual orientation, gender identity, may be used or omitted in legal cases at the discretion of the judges and prosecutors. Case law is not homogeneous, and in some legal cases, operators may emphasize the fact that the sexual orientation of those involved is not relevant to make decisions. However, in cases of violence we are faced, on the one hand, with excesses of visibility, where the non-normative difference becomes the fundamental signifier. This focus is evaluative and it usually adopts the meaning of the specific cultural context in which the incident takes place. On the other hand, we are faced with situations in which the sexual orientation or gender identity components would be pertinent to the explanation and context of violent conduct, yet they can be omitted, camouflaged, or underestimated by the judicial officials. Some cases that illustrate these situations are presented below.

MOVILH-DIVINE Report[44]
The justice that victims deserve

Main Legal Issue:
When it is proven that all the possible steps to clarify the causes and determine the responsibilities in a fire were not exhausted, is the State's responsibility compromised, in its administration of justice?

Facts:
On September 4, 1993, a fire completely destroyed the discotheque *Divine* in Valparaíso, Chile, causing the death of almost twenty people. One of the great doubts that still lingers is whether the fire was the result of an attack based on sexual prejudice or was caused by an electrical system failure, as documented in the official reports.

On March 23, 1994, after only six months of investigation, the magistrate of the Seventh (currently Fifth) Criminal Court of Valparaíso, Jorge Gándara, closed the case without there being any culprits or accused, and without having reached a conclusion as to the causes of the fire. During the years that followed, the Movement for Homosexual Integration and Liberation (Movilh) took several steps and carried out different studies with the objective to reopen the case. On August 29, 2002, Movilh publicly presented the "*Movilh-Divine Report, the Justice that the Victims Deserve*," a text that contributed new evidence that finally led to the reopening of the case.

Extracts:
Although this report, which has the support of Amnesty International, does not establish the actual cause of the fire, it clearly reveals for the first time, based on concrete evidence, that the authorities that were then in office committed serious irregularities ranging from infringements on human rights to the non-elucidation of facts of extreme relevance for the efficient development of the investigation.

---

[44] *Informe MOVILH-DIVINE: la justicia que merecen las víctimas* (August 2002) and *Informe MOVILH-DIVINE II* (2004), www.movilh.cl

The scarce thoroughness regarding every aspect of the evidence attests to the absolute lack of competence and professionalism of the judge of the Seventh Criminal Court of Valparaíso, Jorge Gándara, to reach conclusive results in topics that were easy to clarify, a situation which was all the more important… [since] all the antecedents submitted by human rights organizations or the press of the time regarding irregularities in the case were known in greater detail and with more evidence never before made public by that magistrate. Other data that had never been mentioned, such as the existence of two suspects who were never investigated, will also corroborate the negligence of the judicial and police authorities, while Judge Gándara's continuous questions to the witnesses regarding the sexual orientation of the victims will show his grave discriminatory spirit.

[…]

The main contributions of the "Movilh-Divine Report" evidenced that 1) the courts had not exhausted all the measures to clarify the causes and determine the responsibility for the fire, 2) during the investigation, serious irregularities were committed, for example, the violation of the human rights of witnesses by the police and the judicial authorities, 3) the inexistence of a document accounting for the number and identity of the injured persons and the dead persons, and 4) the absence of penalties against those responsible for the fire, even if it had been caused by failures in the electrical system.

[…]

Infringements upon the human rights of the witnesses and the victims' relatives

A week after the fire, the Movement for Homosexual Integration and Liberation reported via the press that several witnesses had been abused during the interrogation sessions carried out by police officers from the Criminal Investigation Department.

[…]

The permanent intimidation the witnesses were subjected to definitely constitutes a serious obstacle for the efficient compilation and analysis of data concerning the *Divine* case, for the declarant had to focus a large part of their statement on antecedents referring to their private life and sexual orientation, at the explicit demand of the Civil or the Military Police.

That situation is doubly dramatic when considering that in most parts of the file, some of the witnesses are identified by name, age, address, and also sexual orientation, as if that were a relevant datum for the cause. […]

It is telling […] that people's sexual orientation had become in some cases more relevant than the deaths and the causes of the fire, which drew the focus of the investigation away from the truly transcendent issues. That situation even had an adverse effect on the statements issued by the victims' relatives, some of whom, when faced with the possibility of discrimination, fear or shame in case some relative were homosexual, focused on explaining throughout a large part of the investigation that the presence of their brother, son, uncle or nephew at the discotheque did not prove that they were gay. […]

8.3.1.4 Matters for Debate

Secondary victimization due to the influence of prejudices on juridical operators and processes that involve diverse sexualities.
The case of the *Divine* discotheque fire is very complex: it is not possible to assert what the motive behind it was until the courts do so. Consequently, it cannot be categorized as an act of violence based on sexual prejudice. What is worth pointing out are the vicissitudes of the process in which many irregularities, for instance, the judge's decision to close the case without having thoroughly examined the evidence, and the tortures and secondary victimization that the witnesses suffered at the hands of the police, reveal prejudiced conducts and an over-exposure, at the agents discretion, of the witnesses' sexual orientation without its being relevant. Also fundamental for understanding the process is bearing in mind that it was thanks to MOVILH's intervention that the case was reopened and new evidence and officials willing to conduct a rigorous investigation were incorporated. It is for this reason that besides pointing out problems of visibility and over- exposure, violence and abuse against witnesses, and homophobia on the part of the families, this case introduces the question of the relationship between weak social or public movements and a strong administration of justice or a strong public.[45]

Another aspect of the potential problems or discretionary use of or allusion to sexual orientation appears in the case of a homosexual convict who suffers secondary victimization in the lower courts' rulings as shown in the following decisions.

Constitutional Court of Colombia
Ruling T-1096 of 2004

Main Legal Issue:
Does the State, through the National Institute of Penitentiaries and Prisons (INPEC),[46] *fail to protect the rights to life, health, physical and moral integrity, and sexual freedom that have been violated, when it refuses to relocate a detained person to a correctional facility in which he may be provided adequate health services and where he will not be subject to permanent harassment and sexual abuse?*

Facts:
MGJ filed a writ for protection against INPEC, alleging, that his rights to life, health, physical and moral integrity, and sexual freedom were being infringed upon when he was refused a transfer to a correctional facility where he could be provided adequate health services and where he would not be subjected to harassment and permanent sexual abuse. He has been transferred to several penitentiary facilities, and he affirms that in all of them he has suffered persecution and harassment due to his

[45] For this distinction see Nancy Fraser, 1997. "Rethinking the Public Sphere" in *Justice Interruptus. Critical Reflections on the "Postsocialist" Condition*. New York: Routledge.

[46] Instituto Nacional Penitenciariao y Carcelario (INPEC).

sexual orientation. He has filed four writs for protection for the same motive and they have all been denied.

Court Ruling:
The Constitutional Court protects MGJ's fundamental rights to dignity, life, physical integrityl and health, and orders his transfer to a detention center where he may be free from risks and it concludes that INPEC grossly, and in a manifest way, infringes upon such rights if it does not adopt measures to prevent sexual abuse of a person detained in a correctional institution at the hands of other inmates, and above all, if this person belongs to a traditionally discriminated group.

Extracts:
[...]
This Court's jurisprudence has pointed out that *persons who are deprived of their freedom are in a situation of special vulnerability which demands special duties from the State.* It is established that this duty originates in the Constitution, the law, and jurisprudence, as well as in the system of protection of human rights...

[...]

For the Constitutional Court, from "[...] the right to dignity and the concept of the social state of law, the right of prisoners to have access to correctional institutions that guarantee the possibility of reinserting themselves in society is deduced [...]" for which reason "[...] the analysis of the penitentiary system must always revolve around the question about whether this system meets its re-socializing function, which is its main raison d' être. [...]"

[...]

The Constitutional Court has recognized that the affective and sexual dimensions of every human being, the manifestation of the free development of the personality, may be the object of reasonable restrictions, but it cannot be eliminated. [...]

His dignity, like that of the majority of persons deprived of their freedom in Colombia, as this Court has corroborated in the course of the different cases resolved in this respect, has been disregarded in a grave and manifest way; he has been subjected to circumstances of insecurity and risk which might have even compromised his life and health in an irreparable way, had he effectively been infected with AIDS.

The penitentiary authorities have limited themselves to corroborating that the plaintiff had in fact been subjected to some of the offenses and abuses to which he makes reference, and corroborated the institutional incapacity of the penitentiary system, of which they form part, to treat the specific case of a person with the character, behavior, and personality of the plaintiff. The prison authorities have merely transferred him indefinitely to different penitentiary centers without any of these decisions implying a real guarantee for the protection of MGJ's life, health, physical integrity, dignity and sexual freedom, rights to which he is entitled and which are disregarded on a daily basis, as the different penitentiary authorities have admitted throughout the course of the proceedings.

8.3.1.5 Matters for Debate

The previous ruling shows the influence of prejudices on legal decisions when they involve tensions between fundamental rights and socio-cultural practices, and it shows the corrective potentialities of constitutional interpretation. Regarding this ruling, the issue of the rights of citizens deprived of their freedom is worth discussing. In Colombia, and probably in the whole of Latin America, "the unconstitutional state of affairs" in which a large percentage of the inmates live is notorious. This situation is further aggravated when in addition to the violations of their fundamental rights to dignity, to health, to education, to work, to family, and to not being victims of violence, the inmates live in overcrowded spaces without enough guards to protect them, or who have no interest in doing so, and are exposed to corruption and abuse by those who are stronger.

It is a well-known fact that sexual abuse is a common occurrence in prisons and that not only those individuals who recognize themselves as homosexuals are victimized. Any inmate may suffer this abuse without this necessarily coinciding with a homosexual identity of the perpetrator. Sexual practices between same-sex inmates are subordination exercises and not the confirmation of a previous sexual identity. In other words, if being "homosexual" is having sex with a person of the same sex, certainly a polemic assertion, subject to diverse social perceptions and theoretical perspectives, in prison it is the power hierarchies that create the homosexual. An Argentine inmate confirms this view: *"if they sent an inmate whom they did not know"*—he is referring to those for whom he worked—*"he has to fight for his rights, since otherwise he becomes a homosexual and he must cook, sweep the floor, and wash the clothes of the rest of the inmates and get up after the roll is called to do those chores and comply with any demand to have sexual intercourse and brew mate."*[47] (emphasis added). He explained that if they paid, inmates were allowed to "have sex with the wife or the concubine" in a room adjoining the church, and he adds: "you can also buy whatever is necessary to obtain a commutation, that is, you negotiate the swiftness in obtaining certified copy of the Court's judgment and credit for time served," and he ends up saying: "inside this place, everything is negotiable."

Given this landscape, we consider it important to examine the conditions of intense sexual abuse to which individuals who recognize themselves as homosexuals or as transgender are subjected to, for they do not only suffer an inhuman and cruel treatment on the part of other inmates, a fate potentially shared by anyone, homosexual or not, "who falls from favor" in the hierarchic, extortive and corrupt structures that seem to prevail in the prisons. They are also subject to secondary victimization by those who manage the detention centers and have the obligation to protect them. For example, the director of the National Model Prison (Colombia), Lieutenant of the Penitentiary Guard Pedro José Martínez, reported to the

[47] "Ruben Badin y otors v. Provincia de Buenos Aires", Corte Suprema, 19/10/1995, Published; JA 1995-IV-142. Fallos 318, 2002, Lexis No 954063.

Constitutional Court that overcrowded prisons may lead to an increment in violence and justified his assertion in the following way:

> ...the problem [overcrowding] may increment violence; the inmate takes possession of the shared cell and rents it, there is extortion and this generates violence, as does living with a drug addict, a night bird or a *homosexual*. The *abnormal and maladjusted* inmate affects living together and conflicts arise, which result in acts of violence...[48]

[T]he officials' opinions when they deem inmates partially responsible for the abuses are "legally inadmissible." This, however, does not prevent the mentioned behaviors from being common, and there is therefore an urgent need for a special training and greater control over the actions of penitentiary and judicial officials in similar cases.

Tribunal III
Seventh Chamber of Crime of Córdoba
Daniel Esteban Torres as alleged author of aggravated homicide
Córdoba, Argentina, 2011

Main Legal Issue:
Is there a cause and effect relationship between a murder and the sexuality of the victim?

Facts:
A twenty-seven-year-old lesbian woman is murdered by her partner's step-father, after a quarrel, in which they exchanged blows and insults. The man asserted he had acted in self-defense, since the victim had a knife. The prosecutor charges the man with the crime of voluntary manslaughter on grounds of the sexual condition of the victim.

Court Ruling:
The Court dismisses the possibility that the homicide may have been committed in self-defense or in the heat of passion, as the defense proposed; however, it decides to condemn the accused to 14 years of imprisonment for the crime of negligent homicide aggravated by the use of a firearm, considering that, having been impossible to prove that the resentment or rage experienced by the accused with regard to the victim have its origin in the victim's sexual orientation, he could not be charged with voluntary manslaughter.

8.3.1.6 Matters for Debate[49]

This case might become paradigmatic of the way in which violent acts against women perceived as lesbians are treated in most of the countries of Latin America. It is

---

[48] Colombian Constitutional Court, Judgment T-153 of 1998 (emphasis added).

[49] The arguments for this analysis come from my personal communication with Natalia Milisenda, the plaintiff's lawyer, and from Cronicas Marcianas, a report by Andrea Lacombe for CLAM in http://www.clam.org.br/publique/cgi/cgilua.exe/sys/start.htm?from_info_index=51&infoid=8504&sid=21

characterized by insistence on the absence of conclusive evidence to prove an existing cause and effect relationship between the crime and the victim's sexuality. What is not included in the ruling are the arguments of Natalia Milisenda, the plaintiff's (the victim's family) lawyer and her witnesses that render such relationship evident.

The ruling presents some progress in relation to the majority of these cases, since the notion of self-defense, and above all, the very problematic argument of the crime of passion or committed in the heat of passion were dismissed. Yet, the judges did not "see" nor were they capable of opening up the juridical horizon to the evidence of violence based on "lesbophobia" that Milisenda forged in her arguments. In her arguments, three elements stand out:

1. Social resistances and its lack of consideration in the present legal context of alternative gender expressions, in particular, female masculinity.
   The victim deployed gender as a masculinity associated to a woman's body. The defense used this characteristic as an expression of Gaitán's (the victim) alleged aggressiveness, an argument that the plaintiff's lawyer dismounted by presenting witnesses and revealing the fear that non-hegemonic masculinities arouse in many strata of society. The defense counsel expressed: "I found in Torres a person who was frightened and overwhelmed by the situation. The truth is that Pepa [the victim's nickname, which in Córdoba may refer to a man or a woman] was a robust person who practiced boxing and Street Fighting. Pepa Gaitán was a person who induced fear." Milisenda took care of putting into context this causality relationship that the defense argued, reiterating that: "Pepa did not die merely because she was a lesbian, but because she was a masculine lesbian, because of an '*illegal bearing of masculinity*'." She recalled how Gaitán had been the object of persecution and exclusion throughout her life, detained by the police, harassed, excluded from access to work and education, and had limited circulation in the city by the application of the Petty Offense Code. Counsel ended her argument saying:

   > That same violence is repeated once again in this trial when instead of being the victim she has been suspected and demonized once and again, projecting on Pepa the blame for her own death, which many media have echoed. The worst thing about these descriptions is that they contribute to perpetuate and reproduce the social disciplining that imposes the lesbophobia which makes the phrase: Don't be like Pepa, or you'll end up just like her, resonate in the ears of each woman, each teenager and each girl in Córdoba.

   What female masculinity does in a context of hegemonic masculinity is to recall the contingency of the latter, and consequently, it generates the need to affirm it, in this case, through the institutional ignorance or denial of the existence of alternative masculinities. The prosecutor of the case himself is compromised in such invisibility when he stated that lesbophobia is a "...word I had never used. I prefer to speak of discrimination based on sexual preference,... lesbophobia is too rigid a label." In his opinion, it was "an incident associated to violence based on gender. If discrimination existed, it was because she was a woman and not because she was a lesbian..."
2. The victim's alleged promiscuity as argument for the defense
   Pepa's mother declared, with the aim of stressing the fact that her daughter had a successful love life, that she "was a highly coveted woman.... Women fought over

her, they competed for her, they gave her clothes, sneakers, even a motorcycle once, knowing that they were her passion; she had some impressive women and I did not go about investigating my children's hearts, they are grown-ups now…" Karen, the victim's previous partner, also a witness for the prosecution, stated that "*with la Pepa I always had a very good relationship, even after we separated, because she was an excellent person who only chose to be with someone else.*" The defense tried to use these testimonies to transform Pepa's affective success into promiscuity, an argument frequently wielded to stigmatize non-hegemonic sexualities and justify before the judges the use of verbal and physical violence as a mechanism for sexual control.

3. <u>The family weft</u>

   In cases of discriminatory attacks or practices against women perceived as lesbians, the presence of family tensions is usually significant and constitutes an element that differs from what generally occurs in the cases of violence against men perceived as gay, in which the protagonists and settings appear to be unfamiliar. In the case of lesbians, several elements intersect to generate a highly complex family and affective scenario. In some initial version it was argued, among other things, that Silvia, the mother of Dayana, Pepa's girlfriend, was in love with the victim and that this was the reason why she had caused the crisis with Torres. Silvia denied the version and recounted how she went to consult a psychologist in the Province (Córdoba), concerned with the situation, and because she wanted her daughter to be "normal," that she frequent men. She also argued that the age difference between Dayana, who was 17, and Pepa, who was 27, had also caused her great concern. The prosecutor called the psychologist as a witness, and she declared:

> Silvia Sánchez came to see me because she was worried about her daughter; first she manifested her anxiety because she lived with an older [woman]…but then she explained that what worried her was her sexual orientation. She asked me to help her make her daughter change, that she could be normal again; I referred her to another specialist who would help her accept her daughter's sexual choice.

Thus, it is recorded that the concern was about her daughter's sexual orientation and not about her age. Still, in the psychologist's testimony, the question of the age difference is mentioned as the mother's initial preoccupation. Dayana was a minor, when she lived with the victim, and although in Argentina the age of consent to have sexual relations is 16, the prosecutor himself, in his final arguments, remarked that he understood the mother's concern and her right to the exercise parental authority. Milisenda dismissed this argument and argued in turn:

> When the prosecutor brings up the matter of the right granted by parental authority, he forgets that as of [that] change of paradigm [Law 26.061 of 2006] all the rights of adults must also be respected and guaranteed with regard to children and adolescents, for which reason I do not consider it viable that in the name of the parental authority a mother may tyrannize her daughter in what concerns her right to live and express her sexual orientation. Sexual orientation is not acquired through coming of age but is rather a personal and constant construction that develops over the course of a person's life.

On the other hand, Liliana Suárez, Silvia's sister and Dayana's aunt, declared that Dayana and Pepa had a love relationship and that Dayana was healthy and stable after abandoning her home as a result of the harassment Torres, her step father, and Silvia, her mother, subjected her to, when they saw she was in this relationship with Pepa.

The previous arguments reconstruct evidence of the family's prejudice with regard to the relationship between Dayana and Pepa for being in a lesbian relationship, and show the mother and step-father's issues concerning this matter and the infringement upon Dayana's rights. They also trace the defense's efforts to de-legitimize and stigmatize the victim, "to render her responsible for her own death" and they also present the way in which the plaintiff's counsel, with her arguments and witnesses, managed to prove the prejudiced nature of the attack and of the arguments of the defense. However, none of this sufficed for the judges to admit the existence of a causal connection between the attack and the victim's sexual orientation.

8.3.2 Heat of Passion and Ire and Intense Pain as Extenuating Factor

This sub-section will call attention on the existence of a potential tension around the juridical-penal remedies for violence based on prejudice: the majority of the laws that directly or indirectly punish homophobic-based violence provide an increase in penalties. As mentioned earlier, creating these kinds of laws occupies a large part of the efforts of LGBTQ organizations in the region. However, many of the homicides involving characteristics of homophobic-based violence, whether acknowledged or not, either entail lighter sentences because the authors benefit from plea bargaining or the crimes are classified as incidents committed in the heat of passion or prompted by ire or intense pain, or are classified as "passion crimes" and therefore receive the benefit of extenuating circumstances.

At first sight, these aspects reveal a tension, centered on the criminal system, between increasing penalties or reducing them. We see this tension in two aspects: on the one hand, the attacks motivated by sexual orientation or gender identity, being historically embedded in the socio-cultural prejudice (homophobia, transphobia) deserve special protection and incrementing the penalties constitutes an exemplary punishment to show the State's non-tolerance in their regard. On the other hand, when the incident involves the sexual orientation or the gender identity of the actors, especially the victims, police reports and the courts tend to concentrate their efforts on "identifying/recognizing" the following: that the offender in an incident deserves the benefits of the extenuating circumstances of heat of passion or ire and intense pain, i.e., the reduction or suppression of the penalty when it is considered that his/her conduct has been provoked by a grave and unjust act committed by the victim, who is then partially responsible for the aggression, or when the same occurs in the case of a crime of passion between couples/persons who share a bond of affection and whose conflicts generated the perpetrator's state of uncontrollable emotion. In both cases, what is worth examining is the cultural framework that backs the juridical interpretation and the reproduction of certain social "values," in our case, those that make it possible to articulate the aggression in a state of violent and uncontrollable emotion with the homosexual condition/provocation.

The extenuating factor of violent emotion or ire and intense pain involves subjective aspects that compromise the perpetrator's free will at the moment of committing the violent act, and therefore entails a reduction of the sentence. The legal doctrine points out that an extenuating circumstance is not, in principle, a mechanism to eliminate responsibility but rather, a tool to reduce the penalty. Extenuating circumstances are sought in sentencing when it is possible to prove that the aggressor was unable to control him/herself in the presence of the provocation, generated by a serious and unjust offense on the part of the victim. Therefore, its possible applicability presupposes that without this extreme provocation, the author of the crime is an ordinary person, known to be hardly or not at all dangerous, that the act/action is exceptional and of improbable recurrence and deserves, for this reason, a reduction in the penalty.

Supreme Court of Justice of Colombia
Criminal Chamber of the Court of Cassation
Lawsuit No 23093.
Bogota, February 9, 2005

Main Legal Issue:
Is the application of the extenuating circumstances of ire and intense pain valid in cases of violence based on sexual prejudice?

Facts:
Faced with the possibility that J.A.G. should show L.F.C.'s wife the content of a video-cassette in which they had filmed the homosexual relations they had engaged in, the latter killed the former. The ruling of the Court of First Instance determined that since the crime had been committed in a "state of ire and intense pain, caused by another person's serious and unjustified offense," he would serve a short sentence. The Courts of Second and Third Instance sustained the decision.

Court Ruling:
The final sentence carried 22 months and 23 days of imprisonment, a reduced sentence insofar as the act was carried out in a "state of ire and intense pain, caused by another person's grave and unjustified offense." The defense requested a suspended sentence and the appeal was denied by the different courts. The Criminal Chamber of the Court of Cassation upheld the judgment of the lower courts.

8.3.2.1 Matters for Debate

The challenge implied in criminal law is that of weighting the demands of individual psychology—the subjective elements of the conduct—in the application of extenuating circumstances, without this entailing the reproduction of socially constructed prejudices, in this particular case, of sexual prejudice. The particular conditions in which extenuating circumstances are guaranteed, have, in addition to the individual benefits of the convict, a symbolic value, i.e., they express State recognition of the fact that certain practices and conducts induce, in a justifiable manner, altered emotional states which may lead to violent conducts. The question focuses on the character of these practices and conducts, and on the conditions in which the State participates and institutionalizes in the law a kind of "support" to those who react violently against them. On the one hand, the effort to generate less onerous sentences in systems that resist constructing criminal subjectivities based on dangerousness and the merely retributive nature of the penalty is commendable. On the other hand, considering certain violent reactions justified demands reexamining the context of such justification.

The prior ruling contains no clarifications regarding the circumstances in which the homicide occurred, nor the reasons for justifying the extenuating circumstances of ire and intense pain. What is explained is the pronouncement of a minimum sentence (between 119 and 150 months imprisonment), since although the seriousness of the act is recognized, "there are no circumstances carrying a greater penalty and there exists for C.B. one that is conducive to a lesser penalty, which is the absence of a criminal record."

In the Court of Second Instance,[50] the reconstruction of the facts is drawn entirely from the testimonies of those implicated: that is to say, the state of ire generated by the threat to make public the intimate relations that the accused maintained with the victim. In the initial ruling,[51] it was asserted that there was premeditation, at least as regards the construction of a setting for the recovery of the video. Although little is said in this respect in the rulings of the lower instance courts, it is possible that the accused took the victim to an isolated place with the aim of recovering the video. Such premeditation seems incompatible with the version that prevailed on the commission of the act in a state of violent emotion (of both persons involved in the crime?), which is contrary to premeditation. It would therefore be interesting to know what was argued on one side and the other. Why does the defense's version prevail?

The argument the defendant's counsel used to defend the conduct of the accused was prejudiced and even paradoxical. First, it is adduced that for the accused, "death was justified to avoid a great injustice." Such injustice consisted in making public, to his wife, his own acts: the intimate relationship he maintained with the victim. There is no commentary whatsoever on the use of force or coercion to have maintained such relations, which makes it possible to assume that the encounters were consensual. According to the defense, the gravity of the offense resides, therefore, in "the dreadful vision" of the facts, the "drama caused by extortion" and the nature of the video, "its brutality … aberrations and morbidity." There is no direct allusion

[50] *See* Superior Court of the Judicial District, Criminal Section, Pereira, August, 2004.

[51] Fourth Circuit Penal Court, Dosquebradas, Risaralda. June 7, 2004.

to the homosexual nature of the relationship, but the adjectives used to describe the content of the video together with the fact that there are no signs of coercion in its filming, seem aimed at imposing a prejudicial appraisal partially achieved because extenuating circumstances were granted in the courts at lower instances. What is brutal, aberrant and morbid? The images? Or that the images portray two same-sex persons having sexual intercourse? Intimate practices between two adults, if they are consensual and do not violate other rights are constitutionally protected, through the right to privacy and right to sexual freedom. Infidelity—it seems pertinent to point out—generates conflicts and, on occasions, moral and social sanctions, but it is not illegal. As a matter of fact, the Latin American idiosyncrasy positively values an unfaithful man, his peers and even women exalt his virility and "success" of the seducers or the seduced. That is to say, on many occasions, being unfaithful when one is a man is a source of prestige. It is obviously not the case with the evidence of engaging in sexual practices with same-sex persons. Such practices reveal a displacement and a threat for the symbolic and instrumental privileges of compulsory heterosexuality, such as socio-political and economic belonging and classification into well defined and productive binaries. Homophobia is fear of losing "the masculine credentials"[52] that constitute a defense against the symbolic and material sanctions of dissent. Somehow, homophobia or sexual prejudice consists in the stubborn and on occasions, violent resistance to accept the variations of the heterosexual norm.

In the cases we address the granting of extenuating circumstances were successful and expressed the homophobic overtone of the juridical system, because it accepted that fear in view of the possibility of being spotted in sexual practices with same-sex persons, especially if they are men, and the violent reaction that accompanies it, are justified. In cases involving heterosexual relationships, extenuating circumstances are usually granted to violent conducts based on jealousy, which grants to the irrational possession of the body and the emotional life of the 'other.'

There is no explicit argument in this case, but the triumph of the defense through the application of extenuating circumstances allows the following interpretation: homosexuality is considered aberrant; the accused is a decent person and represents no social danger whatsoever; "he works, he lives with a woman and he has a son," and, it seems to suggest, he did not have one but two episodes of violent emotion. In the first one, he consented in engaging in sexual practices with someone of his same sex, and in the second one, he reacted violently, and in a justified manner when the "aberrant nature of the same," the "dreadful vision of the facts," was revealed to him and the fear that all this became public made him lose control to the point of justifying the death of the person who threatened him. Prejudice filters into the language that describes the content of the video and in making it the crux of the matter.

The defense's arguments are not alone paradoxical; the very conduct of the accused too, is paradoxical. As pointed out before, the violent homophobic act is paradoxical because it confirms, by making public that which he tried to eliminate,

[52] The expression is taken from Gail Mason, "Not Our Kind of Crime", *op.cit.*

the homosexual character of the practices and, consequently, of those implicated in them. The conflict that appears to prevail is derived from the clash between sexual practices and identities. Neither juridical discourses nor social imaginaries establish differences between them, and, in any case, the status of non(hetero) sexual practices—and of (hetero)sexual identities—are held in contempt by a society of compulsory heterosexuality.

An element that introduces itself in the ruling of the Supreme Court, in addition to the reiteration of the already mentioned ones, is the allusion to a crime of passion, its deep psychological roots, and its link with the "ipso jure" conditional suspension of the execution of the penalty. The legal term, "crime of passion," operates as a smokescreen in the identification, definition, and development of the processes that concern violence against non-normative sexualities. A crime of passion is usually understood as a crime committed by an individual, linked to another, by bonds of affection of a sexual/amorous nature and who, in a fit of violent and uncontrollable emotion, generated by jealousy, abandonment, or another threat to the relationship, makes his love/sexual object or what he perceives as a threat, an attack target. Classifying crimes based on sexual prejudice or misogyny as crimes of passion does not only contribute to reduce the penalties but it also diverts attention from the institutionalization of power structures that reproduce misogynous and homophobic practices, and concentrates the responsibility for the offense on the victim. If this were not so, why should the State need to justify, to "understand" the individual psychology of the misogynist and the homophobic? Is it not because it considers it reasonable? May it not be that this reasonability originates precisely in accepting, supporting and reproducing social prejudices and, consequently, justifying them in individual behaviors? Might it not be that classifying a homicide based on sexual prejudice as a crime of passion, places the responsibility for the aggression on the victim, is tolerant with the individual aggressor, and expiates the social and juridical responsibility in the reproduction of the prejudice?

But let us look at some particularities of what is usually erroneously classified as crime of passion in the case of crimes involving persons of the same sex, in particular, gay men. A first element is that the victim does not know the perpetrator. According to the cited accounts of the murders of gay men in Bogota, it may be that the victims usually fall into traps. For example, by making out in a public place and then inviting that person home, getting trapped in a fatal situation. A stranger irrupts with or without violence but he kills with cruelty and sends a terror message. Conversely, in the cases classified as crimes of passion involving heterosexual persons, the condition of the same is the familiarity between the victim and the aggressor. In both cases, however, the blame is shifted to the victim in the first case under the moral accusation of promiscuity and, in the second, for example, under the accusation of infidelity. It would be interesting to make a diagnostic of the differences between the men who kill their female partners in a state of violent emotion, and the women who kill their abusive partners in self-defense.

A second element of violence based on sexual prejudice is derived from the aggressors' intolerance vis-à-vis a real or perceived approach seen as a homosexual provocation. This is the violent reaction and the subsequent attack in the presence of any gesture perceived by the aggressor as an advance of a homo(sexual) nature on the part of the victim. Needless to say that in the compulsory heterosexual order, the advances or insinuations of a sexual type are usually called flirting and they are configured as models of naturalized behavior. In the judicial acceptance of violent emotion in the face of an advance of a (homo)sexual type, there should be no confusion between the notion of provocation via grave and unjust offenses, and the notion of non-violent homosexual advances. The distinction is fundamental to disassociate the pertinence of the extenuating circumstance from the reproduction of prejudice.

A third element of analysis may arise from the differences that have been established with regard to hierarchical and exclusionary uses of violence.[53] In hierarchical violence the aim is to situate the other in his place of subordination, while in exclusionary violence, it is a question of eliminating the other who has become a threat. In both cases the violent gesture may produce death, but the meaning of the gesture is different. I would dare state that gender-based violence tends to express hierarchical aspects, while violence against non-normative sexualities tends to be exclusionary. We have already seen, however, the paradox of such exclusion. The perpetrator wishes to eliminate any allusion to his potential connection with non-normative sexual interests, desires or practices, but by exercising the violent act, he confirms his connection with them instead of making them disappear.

Another harmful use of the legal term, "crime of passion," has become palpable in the reports of *Amnesty International* on violence against women and non-normative sexualities in the Colombian armed conflict. The report points out that "…often, crimes based on political motives and crimes based on sexual violence are not even reflected in the official numbers, excluded to encompass them within the so-called crimes of passion," and recommends,

> Maintain reliable and updated statistics on the incidence of the reports on sexual violence, whether related or not with the armed conflict. Guarantee that the data records reflect the abuses aimed at concrete groups, and that *any category that may distort statistics, such as that of "crimes of passion," be eliminated.*[54]

I consider, in general, that the legal term "crime of passion," should be eliminated from the criminal legal system. Its unfortunate value is derived from its camouflaging misogynous and homophobic power relations and cultural patterns in the private ambit of "uncontrollable" emotions, generated, according to the perpetrators and with the acquiescence of the criminal system, as acts of defense of the sacredness of spaces of privacy, family, and honor.

What we are trying to argue here is, namely, that homophobia or prejudice have social and cultural roots, and that any gesture of violence of this kind is "successful"—that is, expresses its hatred/prejudice—because it occurs in a public context that allows it to signify.

---

[53] *See* Maria Mercedes Gomez, "Los usos jerarquicos y excluyentes de la violencia", *op.cit.*

[54] Amnesty International, "Scarred bodies, hidden crimes", AMR 23/040/2004 (emphasis added).

8.3.3 *The Public Space*

The following presents some tensions manifest in issues dealing with violence based on sexual prejudice and the use of public spaces. On the one hand, related to the right to association and to circulate freely, and to public expressions of affection between same-sex persons linked to the right of free development of the personality. On the other, the private enjoyment of non-normative sexual practices by individuals who define themselves as heterosexuals and the simultaneous need to deny these practices, in some cases recurring to violence if there is a possibility that these will become public, or when these are made public.

Constitutional Court of Colombia
Ruling T-301of 2004

Main Legal Issue:
Does preventing the meeting and the public expressions of affection of sexual minorities constitute discriminatory treatments?

Facts:
JPNV filed a writ for protection of constitutional rights against the Police Commander of the Department of Magdalena, denied in first and second instance. The claimant recounts that, for months, police agents and auxiliaries from the city of Santa Marta informed him and his friends that homosexual persons could not remain on the strip near the bay. A police captain had once told him that homosexuals gathered gave a bad image to the sector and that there was a "central banishment order."

Court Ruling:
The Constitutional Court overturned the ruling of the First Penal Court of the Santa Marta Circuit and granted JPNV "the protection of the rights to equality, to integrity, to the free development of the personality, to honor, to a good name and to free circulation." Likewise, the Court ordered the Commander of the Police Department in Magdalena to impart to his personnel the "necessary and sufficient instructions" in order that harassment may cease immediately.

Extracts:
[…]
[T]hat in the case of reference, it is necessary to apply a strict proportionality test since (a) the basis for the discriminatory treatment is a suspicious concept—sexual condition –, and (b) the aim pursued by the administrative measure is the safeguard of public morals (an extremely vague concept). From the application of this appraisal, it may be easily deduced that the homosexual preferences of some citizens are part of their right to privacy and self-determination, which the State can only exceptionally restrict. In this sense, it is not possible to discern how the constitutionally protected right—social morals—is safeguarded through the almost absolute circulation imposed on a group of citizens and through the administrative detentions to which they are subjected. It is necessary to reiterate that having certain sexual preference (which does not infringe upon the rights of third parties) is part of the right to determine the plans for one's own life and deploy in consequence a

relational life, without this being limited by the personal prejudices of the officials with police faculties.

Secondly, the Court deems that the measure restraining the free circulation of citizens in the national territory is not necessary or adequate to guarantee a constitutional value. [...]

Lastly, it is evident that the measures adopted by the Magdalena police are disproportionate and they sacrifice constitutional values, without there being sufficient cause. The pretension to create databases including information on HIV carriers presented by the Police Commander as one of the motives to administratively detain the actor, infringes upon his rights to free circulation, to human dignity, and to privacy, among others. [...]

8.3.3.1 Matters for Debate

Although the above referenced case is not associated to explicit physical violence, it does evidence, the production of homophobic contexts in which physical violence finds a favorable environment. Violence based on prejudice is, by definition, expressive, and issues a message of terror which expands to those persons other than the particular victim who identify themselves with the real or perceived characteristics that generated the attack. The spreading of terror motivated by prejudice is only possible if the context in which it is disseminated contains the conditions required by the violent gesture to signify and fulfill its end. For this reason, creating a homophobic social context leads to violent action finding a favorable space to produce and reproduce its message of terror. In this case, the police commander's arguments conveyed in the name of public morals, and the dismissal of the first writ filed for the protection of constitutional rights, have the power to stigmatize persons with non-normative sexualities as threatening, dangerous and potentially deserving violent exclusion. This is a matter which the ruling of the Constitutional Court pretends to repair.

The public expressions of affection or the recurrent circulation of persons with non-normative sexualities generally constitute a source of great social anxiety. Professor Kenji Yoshino identifies three discrimination aspects around such publicity, not only of the displays of affection but of the expression of non-normative sexualities in general: conversion, passing, and covering. In the conversion, people are expected to abandon an "alteration" (non-normative sexual) of an alleged essence (hetero/norm), which under favorable conditions may resurge. In passing, the person is allowed to exercise his/her sexuality, but without displaying it in public, and in covering, the person is allowed to exercise sexuality and make it public, but not to flaunt it.[55] An example of covering may be found in what would be expected from the group of friends in question: is it tolerated or does one simulate ignorance, about what they do in private, they can even talk about, but they cannot do—with their

[55] Kenji Yoshino, "Covering" *op.cit.*

bodies and in their bodies—anything that permits to discern in public their non-normative sexual and cultural practices. If they express their non-heterosexuality, they are *a priori* considered dangerous, lethal, and suspected of altering public order and morals. What seems to prevail is the appraisal of non-normative sexualities as dangerous in the context of a compulsory heterosexuality that is on a level with the very vague notion of public morals and local "customs." Let us recall that the police commander of the region points out that in the coastal communities of Colombia, and unlike what happens in other countries, it is considered that the practices of "the persons who are homosexuals diverge from healthy habits and public morals."

As pointed out by a large part of Colombian Constitutional Court's jurisprudence, there is no interpretation of public morals which places it above the duties and rights enshrined in the Constitution and equally guaranteed to all citizens. Persons with non-normative sexualities can in no way be punished for having public behaviors which are allowed and protected in the case of heterosexual persons. In any case, in the presence of a potential restriction on freedom and of the vagueness of the notion of public morality, a strict proportionality test must be applied. It would be worth analyzing if in these procedures compulsory heterosexuality does not continue to prevail as the regime against which all digressions and all rights are measured.

Another aspect of interest for the debate is the inquiry into the methods and criteria employed to determine who "the homosexuals are." The Police Commander of Magdalena says that due to the complaints of the community, "different raids have been organized with the aim of verifying and establishing which were the homosexuals who had been disturbing the security and the tranquility of the sector," to which end, persons who circulated in the area were detained "without distinguishing their sexual condition … in order to identify them and verify if they had a criminal record." In the same way, people suspected of being HIV carriers had to identify themselves.

The sexual option of citizens is an essential component of their self-determination and, therefore, an inalienable right, and it is unconstitutional to compile data on HIV carriers. Besides, it is untrue that the homosexual community is more vulnerable to HIV than the heterosexual community. This said, wanting to identify and preventively arrest these "potential public dangers" is curious, to say the least, among other things, because neither "homosexuals" nor "HIV carriers" are visually identifiable.

The suspicion criterion indicated is, therefore, absurd, in addition to its being unconstitutional since it marks the entire population as potentially "dangerous" and, consequently, susceptible of preventive detention. As the Court points out, "preventive detention of an administrative nature only proceeds, as a general rule, in the face of eminent infringements on fundamental rights having criminal relevance. An arrest which must be based on serious incriminating evidence and not on suspicions."

In concluding, it is worth calling attention to the tensions that exist when non-normative sexual practices, even those exercised by individuals who do not identify themselves as "homosexuals," are "made public."

In an effort to account for homophobia, Elisabeth Young-Bruehl[56] integrates theories of individual and social prejudice and she identifies three types, which correspond to the sociological paradigm of prejudice. Anti-Semitism exemplifies the obsessive character; racism and classicism, the hysterical type; and sexism, the narcissistic type.[57] Young-Bruehl affirms that homophobia appears in any of the three forms of prejudices and the homosexuals may be their victims for all purposes. Here we are interested, above all, in the hysterical prejudice and its relationship with homophobia. In this type of prejudice, people must be *kept in subordination* because they serve the purposes of the group or of prejudiced individuals.[58]

For persons with hysterical prejudices, homosexuals serve as objects of sexual fantasies or as subjects of prohibited but desired acts. These persons, says Young Bruehl, "do not want to eliminate homosexuals; they want to exploit them…[they] may enjoy, in an indirect way, the love between same–sex persons, watch [alternative sexualities in] pornographic movies, imagine [them] as their lovers, perhaps even be briefly with them or experiment with them and then… [forget that they have done so]."[59]

Hysterical prejudice, as Young-Bruehl formulates it, focuses on the instrumentality of the homosexual as incarnation of a *secret* pleasure that requires a contradictory form of externalization: the homosexual must "be there," available as an object of sexual fantasies and as an *inferior* being—a scapegoat, perhaps—that must be punished—with his subordination—for that same reason of his "being there"—on the side of transgression.

We can see an example of this form of homophobia in a story narrated by the psychoanalyst Donald Moss[60]: He recounts the case of a 30-year-old man who began therapy to work on his latent homosexuality. The man affirmed that all his relationships had been with women, and that they had always been brief. But, after 2 years of analysis, he reported that a telephone call made by an unknown man who knew his name had woken him up in the middle of the night. The call was openly sexual; both of them became excited, both of them masturbated and he had an orgasm. The next morning the patient said, "never in his life had he felt so close to another person." He reported that, at first, he was concerned about the "homosexual" nature of his experience, but that he soon relaxed and felt sorry for that good man who needed to "resort to homosexuality and to telephone sex." "In the morning," Moss adds, "the patient's feelings of manliness, masculinity, and potency had been restored."[61]

But what happens if the *secret* becomes *public*? What would have been the reaction of the man in the example? We have already examined a similar case that cul-

[56]Elizabeth Young-Bruehl, The Anatomy of Prejudices, Cambridge: Harvard University Press, 1996. *op.cit*, p. 158.

[57]*Id.* pp. 157–158.

[58]*Id.* p. 34.

[59]*Id.* p. 158.

[60]Donald Moss, *Hating in the First Person Plural. Psychoanalytic Essays on Racism, Homophia, Misogyny, and Terror*, New York: Other Press, 2003 Moss, *op.cit*, p. 285.

[61]*Id.* pp. 285–286.

minated in homicide. That is why it is possible to assume that the separation between the secret and the public, always on the verge of disappearing, is repeated in the blurry frontiers between prejudice and violence, that is, in the imperious need to *mark* the difference once the porosity of sexual practices and identifications becomes explicit. In these examples, the fact of maintaining the homosexual available but inferior is instrumental to the realization of the secret wishes of the homophobic person. But, once the secret becomes public, the danger must be eliminated—the non-normative sexual body—with the aim of marking the difference and recovering a "coherent heterosexual identity."[62]

In a similar way, but in cases that illustrate fatal attacks on transgender persons, the tensions between the sexual practices and their public recognition can be discerned. Two murder cases in the United States evidence the dilemmas of "making public" the "truth" of the gender identity and establishing its relationship with the motives of the crime. The first case is the murder of the transgender teenager Gwen Araujo on October 3, 2002.

Gwen, who lived as a woman, was murdered by four men, and it is said that she had sexual relations at least with two of them. Forced to submit to an examination to confirm her biological sexuality, she was beaten to death when they found out that she had masculine genitalia. The murderers were tried in California, a state which has laws that increment the penalties in cases of crimes committed by reason of the victim's gender identity. However, the sentence handed down in the case of three of the defendants was for manslaughter and not for homicide. The fourth, was condemned for involuntary homicide. The jury considered that the murder took place because the situation went out of control and not that it was based on the victim's sexual orientation/gender identity; for this reason, the decision did not include an increment in the penalty; the incident was not recognized as a hate crime.[63]

Another similar case was presented by Arthur Dong in his excellent documentary film, "*Licensed to Kill.*"[64] David Feikema met Larry Venzant on December 19, 1993, and he invited him to his house with sexual intentions. Feikema confesses that he thought that Venzant was biologically a woman and they engaged in a discussion on the type of sexual relations they wanted to have. The discussion ended in the fight that led Feikema to stab Venzant, causing his death. After realizing that Venzant was a man, Feikema cut off his penis and inserted it in his mouth. He was condemned to 21 years of imprisonment, although he was declared mentally insane and confined to a psychiatric institution, with a possibility of probation as of May 2004. In the course of the interview, Feikema assures that by cutting off his penis, "he was giving Venzant what he wanted, that is, to be a woman," and he emphasized that the opinion regarding his insanity at the moment of the crime was not unanimous. Most of his interlocutors, he assures, when listening to the details of his case, generally say that he "did the right thing," what anyone in his situation would have done.

---

[62] *See* Mason, *op.cit.*

[63] *See* http://www.transgenderlawcenter.org/gwen/index.html; http://www.sfgate.com

[64] *See* Arthur Dong, "Licensed to Kill". Deep Focus Film, 1997. Dong, *op.cit.*

MIX
Papier aus verantwortungsvollen Quellen
Paper from responsible sources
FSC® C105338

If you have any concerns about our products,
you can contact us on
ProductSafety@springernature.com

In case Publisher is established outside the EU,
the EU authorized representative is:
Springer Nature Customer Service Center GmbH
Europaplatz 3, 69115 Heidelberg, Germany

Printed by Libri Plureos GmbH
in Hamburg, Germany